Mobilizing Islam

Mobilizing Islam

Religion, Activism, and Political Change in Egypt

Carrie Rosefsky Wickham

COLUMBIA UNIVERSITY PRESS   NEW YORK

COLUMBIA UNIVERSITY PRESS
Publishers Since 1893
New York, Chichester, West Sussex
Copyright © 2002 Columbia University Press
All rights Reserved

Library of Congress Cataloging-in-Publication Data

Wickham, Carrie Rosefsky,
    Mobilizing Islam : religion, activism, and political change in Egypt /
Carrie Rosefsky Wickham.
        p. cm.
    Based on the author's dissertation.
    Includes bibliographical references (p.) and index.
    ISBN 0–231-12572-0 (alk. paper) — ISBN 0–231-12573-9 (pbk. : alk. paper)
    1. Egypt — Politics and government — 1952–. 2. Islam and politics — Egypt.
    3. Political participation — Egypt. 4. Jam°'yat al-Ikhwân al-Muslimân (Egypt).
    I. Title.

DT107.827 .W53 2003
962.05 — dc21

                                                                          2002067450

c 10 9 8 7 6 5 4 3 2 1
p 10 9 8 7 6 5 4 3 2 1

To Yousevia

Contents

Preface

The events of September 11, 2001, pierced the American consciousness like an arrow through the heart. The terrorist attacks of that day in New York and Washington, D.C. culminated in the mass murder of thousands of innocent civilians, leaving the survivors to a world indelibly changed. The millions who bore witness to the devastation, whether in person or through televised broadcasts shown again and again, were drawn together in a collective state of outrage and grief. As Americans mourned for the victims and their families, many also responded with a desire to understand the mind-set of the young men who perpetrated the attacks, as well as to learn more about the religious tradition they invoked — however perversely — to justify them. The awakening of this nationwide pursuit of knowledge — evidenced by the dramatic surge of interest in Osama bin Laden, the Taliban, Islam, and the Middle East — is one of the most admirable aspects of the American response to the acts of terror and, to the extent that insight yields power, a step toward preventing their recurrence.

As Americans educate themselves about this little-known region and culture, they are discovering that many people in the Arab world harbor deep grievances against the West in general and the United States in particular. Such grievances are in part a response to American policy in the Middle East, which is widely perceived as systematically biased against Arab and Muslim interests. Anti-Western sentiment also has surfaced as a defensive reaction to the global spread of Western values and ways of life, a trend that some Muslims see as a threat to their own religion and culture. Finally, at a time when dissatisfaction with several aspects of their own societies runs high, it is often more palatable — and less dangerous — for people in the Arab world to deflect responsibility for the region's problems onto external actors than to acknowledge the causes that are rooted in their own politics and culture.

This obsession with external foes is most pronounced in the ideology of Osama bin Laden and his followers. Despite their claims that they are acting in defense of Islam, bin Laden and other members of the al-Qaʿida network reject that part of their Islamic heritage that emphasizes tolerance and respect for human dignity and instead give primacy to the tradition of *jihad*, or holy war. Moreover, they flout the rules that historically have constrained the exercise of *jihad*, including the injunction against harming civilians. In so doing, they have stripped their religion of all its humane elements and reduced it to an ideology of hate in which all people who do not share their views — fellow Muslims included — are defined as "enemies of Islam" and hence legitimate targets of violence.

The fanaticism of those responsible for September 11 is hardly representative of the Islamic movement as a whole. Across the Muslim world, many people are convinced that the only effective way to remedy the ills of contemporary society is to initiate comprehensive Islamic reform. Those who promote Islamic change tend to be highly critical of U.S. policy in the Middle East, and at times this criticism is laced with disturbing prejudices and misconceptions. Nevertheless, for most Islamists the main priority is not to confront the West but to stimulate a moral, social, and political renewal of the Muslim community itself. Furthermore, unlike bin Laden and other Islamic militants, the majority of citizens in the Islamic movement reject the use of violence and are committed to a strategy of incremental reform through legal channels.

No one disputes the need for greater intelligence about the global network of Islamic terrorist cells plotting to strike at Western interests. But Americans also need to learn more about the goals and strategies of the Islamic movement's nonviolent mainstream, for they enjoy far broader support in the Arab world today. What kinds of social changes do these mainstream Islamic groups desire; how are they pursuing them; and why does their message resonate so powerfully for many of the region's educated youth? This book addresses these questions, focusing on Islamic groups in Egypt. It demonstrates that the rise of the Islamic movement was in part a response to local conditions of political and economic exclusion. The book also shows that the movement is not simply *against* the status quo but also *for* a better alternative. Though couched in religious terms, this vision of a better society embodies many of the same hopes and aspirations — for freedom from dictatorship and for social justice and public accountability — that have inspired secular movements for democracy elsewhere around the globe.

The leaders of Egypt's moderate Islamic groups have yet to reconcile their call for Islamic law with a full commitment to democracy and political pluralism. Indeed, whether and to what extent the movement should move in this direction is a matter of debate among the Islamists themselves. The key point is that such groups should be understood on their own terms and not grouped together with the militants of al-Jihad or al-Qa'ida with whom they share little other than a common reference to Islam. In sharp contrast to the ideology of bin Laden, the project of moral and social renewal advanced by such groups is a constructive and life-affirming one, and the hope it offers of a better future is the main source of its appeal.

In sum, Egypt's moderate Islamic groups represent a compelling alternative to the ideology of destruction advanced by those who attacked the United States on September 11. Who such moderate Islamists are, what they stand for, and how they have captured the hearts and minds of many of Egypt's educated youth are explored in this book.

Acknowledgments

This book has been a work in progress for many years. As a result, I have incurred many debts, some of which I would like to acknowledge here. First, I would like to thank the members of my dissertation committee in the politics department at Princeton University: John Waterbury, Atul Kohli, and Nancy Bermeo. Without ever imposing their own vision on my project, each of them pushed me to increase its analytic clarity and rigor. I thank them for their wisdom and support. I also am grateful to several institutions for supporting my Arabic-language study and dissertation research in Egypt. A Rotary Foundation Ambassadorial Scholarship enabled me to undertake a year of advanced Arabic-language training at the Center for Arabic Studies Abroad (CASA) at the American University of Cairo from 1986 to 1987. The American Research Center in Egypt (ARCE) funded my dissertation research from January to June 1990, and the Fulbright Commission supported an additional twelve months of research from June 1990 to June 1991. Special thanks to Dr. Ann Radwan, director of the Fulbright Commission in Cairo, and to Ghada Howeidy, program officer, for helping me obtain the multiple security clearances I needed to conduct my fieldwork.

During my dissertation research, I was fortunate to receive support from a number of senior Egyptian scholars. I would like to express my gratitude to Dr. 'Ali ed-Din Hilal Dessouki, then director of Cairo University's Center for Political Research and Studies, for serving as my adviser and helping me adjust my research plans to unanticipated logistical and political constraints. In addition, I would like to thank Sa'd ed-Din Ibrahim, director of the Ibn

Khaldun Center for Development Studies, for sharing his encyclopedic knowledge of Islamic groups and helping me establish contact with leaders in the professional associations. Several other Egyptian scholars were also generous enough to share their insights with me. More than anything else, my long conversations with Ahmad 'Abdalla helped me frame the questions that animate this study. I thank him for continually challenging me to rethink my assumptions and inspiring me with the example of his own life's work as a scholar and social activist.

Although I cannot mention all the Egyptian scholars who assisted me here, I would like to thank the following individuals for enriching my understanding of Egyptian politics and society: Nabil 'Abd al-Fattah, Galal Amin, Gihad 'Awda, Tahsin Bashir, Nadir Fergany, Milad Hanna, Osama al-Ghazzali Harb, Ashraf Hussein, Hisham Mubarak, Sayyid Naggar, Salim Nasr, Amani Qandil, Diya' Rashwan, Mustafa Kamal al-Sayyid, Muhammad Sayyid Sa'id, Zaynab Taha, Ahmad Thabit, Abbas al-Tonsi, and Farid Zahran.

I also would like to acknowledge my debt to a number of leaders in the Islamic movement who were ready to set aside their preconceived stereotypes and engage in extended dialogue with an American researcher. My heartfelt thanks to Abu-l-'Ila Madi Abu-l-'Ila, 'Abd al-Mun'im Abu-l-Futuh, 'Isam al-'Iryan, 'Isam Sultan, Salah 'Abd al-Karim, Hilmi Gazzar, and Badr Muhammad Badr for sharing their candid reflections about their entry into the Islamic movement; the evolution of their goals and strategies; their experiences as elected association officials; and their relationships with the Muslim Brotherhood, the secular opposition, and the regime. As I emphasized repeatedly during our interviews, my purpose was to understand the Islamist project of reform and present it fairly and accurately to a Western readership. In this I hope I have been successful.

I also wish to thank Sharif Qasim for sharing lessons learned during his years as an elected official of the Commercial Employees' Association. Finally, I want to express my appreciation to Zuhra Murabit of the North-South Consultants' Exchange (NSCE) and the Ford Foundation for permitting me to participate in their study of unemployed graduates in the governorate of Beni Suef.

I am indebted to several American institutions for supporting me as I wrote my dissertation and converted it into a book. A two-year predoctoral fellowship with the Harvard Academy for International and Area Studies from 1992 to 1994 freed me from teaching responsibilities, provided me with an office at Harvard's Center for International Affairs, and allowed me to begin this project in the company of a lively group of area scholars. I am grateful to Ira Kukin, the academy's founding benefactor; Dean Henry Rosovsky, the academy's chairman; and Chester Haskell, its executive director, for granting me this unparalleled opportunity for writing and reflection at an early stage of my career. My thanks also to Professors Samuel Huntington and Roy Mottahedeh for valuable feedback on my work and to Professor Emeritus Barrington Moore, who became an unexpected mentor and friend.

I also am grateful to several colleagues in the field of Middle East politics for reading and commenting on my work at various stages of the project. My thanks to Raymond Baker, Eva Bellin, Lou Cantori, John Entelis, Roxanne Euben, David Mednicoff, Joel Migdal, Augustus Richard Norton, Marsha Pripstein Posusney, Diane Singerman, Denis Sullivan, and Sami Zubaida for engaging with — and ultimately enriching — my work.

I also wish to thank the Department of Political Science at Emory University for supporting the completion of my dissertation and its conversion into a book. Department funds, supplemented by grants from Emory's University Research Committee (URC) and Institute for Comparative and International Studies (ICIS), provided me with part-time research assistance and covered the cost of research trips to Egypt in 1997 and 2000. I owe a special thanks to Professor Richard Doner, a colleague in my department, for commenting on successive drafts of the book's introduction and for sound advice concerning the revision of the chapters. I also would like to thank Devin Stewart, professor of Middle East Studies at Emory University, for reviewing the Arabic transliterations in my book. I am indebted as well to Charles Kurzman of the Department of Sociology at the University of North Carolina at Chapel Hill for enriching my understanding of social movement theory and encouraging me to relate the core propositions of my book to ongoing debates in the social movement field.

Finally, I would like to thank Columbia University Press for bringing this book to print. My thanks to Kate Wittenberg, the press's former editor in chief, for her early and enthusiastic support for the project and to Peter Dimock, senior executive editor, for bringing it to completion. Many thanks also to Margaret B. Yamashita, my copy editor, for her excellent work.

While many people contributed to the making of this book, the responsibility for any errors and omissions is entirely my own.

I would like to extend my thanks as well to several people outside the academic world. First, to the families of Cairo's sha'bi neighborhoods who welcomed me into their homes and hearts, I extend my deepest gratitude. Thanks to all those who answered my endless questions, patiently explained local norms, showered me with food and affection, attempted to remedy my unmarried status, and insisted on calling me "duktura" long before I earned my Ph.D. It is to these Egyptians, who faced life's difficulties with such dignity and generosity of spirit, that this book is dedicated. If any good comes from its publication, I hope that it accrues directly to them.

Finally, I would like to thank my family and friends for supporting me through this long journey. Above all, I am indebted to my husband, Joe, for believing in this project since its inception. In recent years he has filled in for me so often that this book has become as much as part of his life as of my own. I thank him for the love and support that helped me bring it to fruition.

I extend a last word of appreciation to my five-year-old daughter, Anna May, for her straightforward assumption that "mamas write books" and for tolerating the frequent separations that writing this one required. She is *nur 'ayni*, the light of my eye.

Mobilizing Islam

1 Introduction

Over the last quarter century, authoritarian regimes the world over have found it harder than ever to coerce their citizens into silence. In Latin America, Eastern Europe, Asia, Africa, and the Middle East, ordinary men and women have managed to overcome their fear and do what once seemed unthinkable: confront their own leaders with demands for sweeping reform. Recent challenges to authoritarian rule embody different hopes and dreams. In places as diverse as Prague, Santiago, Johannesburg, Manila, and Beijing, protesters have raised the banner of liberal democracy, invoking the example of earlier democratic struggles in the West. In the Muslim world, however, the most insistent calls for reform have come not from movements favoring secular democracy but from those seeking to establish a political system based on Islam. Indeed, Islam has eclipsed secular ideologies as the primary source of political activism in much of the Muslim world. Although the goals and strategies of Islamists differ, they are united in their conviction that the most vexing problems facing contemporary Muslim societies can be resolved through an individual and collective return to religion. The Islamic movement is not confined to a single geographic region, but the idea that *al-Islam huwa al-hall* — Islam is the Solution — resonates with particular force in Arab politics. In the Arab world today, the best organized, most popular, and most effective opposition movements call for an Islamic reform of society and state. Moreover, the prototypical Islamic activist is not an illiterate peasant or laborer but a young, upwardly mobile university student or professional, often with a scientific or technical degree. Far from embodying the defensive protest of traditional social classes on the decline, the Islamic movement is strongly associated with the most "modern" citizens in Arab societies.

Although Islamic groups are at the forefront of opposition politics in many Arab states, their support among students and professionals runs especially deep in Egypt. The latest wave of Islamic activism in Egypt has its roots in the universities, where independent Islamic student associations began recruiting students in the early 1970s. By the end of the decade, Islamist student leaders controlled the student unions in most faculties at Cairo University and other institutions of higher learning, and graduates with Islamic orientations were reaching out to a wider circle of youth in the residential neighborhoods of large cities and provincial towns. Then in the mid-1980s, the Muslim Brotherhood — the largest organization of the Islamic movement's reformist wing — submitted its own list of candidates in the elections for leadership of the country's national professional associations. Through a series of stunning electoral victories, the Brotherhood gained a controlling majority on the boards of several associations, including those of the country's engineers, doctors, pharmacists, scientists, and lawyers. Indeed, by the early 1990s, Egypt's professional associations — which Sami Zubaida aptly described at the time as "the most advanced sectors of public life in Egypt, enjoying high status and speaking with an autonomous and respected voice"[1] — had become major sites of Islamic political experimentation, giving rise to new models of political leadership and community that stood in sharp contrast to the policies and practices of state elites.

There is a special irony in the fact that the largest opposition movement in Egypt derives the bulk of its support from educated youth. After the "revolution" of 1952, the Nasser regime abolished all school fees up to and including the university level, thereby enabling Egyptian youth from nonelite backgrounds to obtain a coveted *shahada*, or university degree. In an even more stunning act of generosity, the regime promised every university and high-school graduate a government job. Not surprisingly, the graduates on the receiving end of such entitlements were, as Malcolm Kerr observed, "among the most reliable enthusiasts" of the new regime, quick to embrace its twin projects of Arab national self-assertion abroad and socialist revolution at home.[2]

Why, then, did the sons and daughters of the revolution turn against it? And why did so many of them join an opposition movement calling for a return to Islam? This book explains how Islamist groups captured the hearts and minds of educated youth — the high achievers at the apex of Egypt's educational pyramid — during the first twelve years of Hosni Mubarak's presidency, from 1981 to 1993. This period represents a critical phase in the evolution of Islamic activism in post-1952 Egypt, when participation in the movement reached its height. After that, beginning in the mid-1990s, a new wave of repression brought the movement's self-confident expansion to an abrupt end. After more than a decade of toleration, the government launched a major counteroffensive against the Muslim Brotherhood, arresting many of its most dynamic leaders and hammering away at its reputation by condemning it as an "illegal organization with ties to extremist groups." Yet despite the government's best efforts, it has been unable to significantly erode the movement's mass support.

One clear indication of the Brotherhood's continued popularity was its surprisingly strong performance in the parliamentary elections of November 2000. Despite the government's intensive media campaign against the Brotherhood, the arrest of several prominent Brotherhood leaders before the elections, and attacks on Brotherhood candidates and their supporters by security police during the election period itself,[3] Brotherhood candidates won seventeen seats, the same number as those won by all of the country's legal opposition parties combined.[4] In an ironic twist, the banned Muslim Brotherhood now controls the largest opposition bloc in the Egyptian parliament. The Brotherhood's recent comeback, together with the persistent weakness of the country's secular opposition parties, suggests that the Islamic movement is likely to remain Egypt's largest opposition force for years to come. The success of Islamic outreach in the 1980s and early 1990s thus remains profoundly relevant to the analysis of Egyptian politics today.

Western media reporting on Egypt's Islamist movement has often focused on the acts of terror committed by members of its underground militant cells. This trend intensified after the events of September 11, 2001, when it was revealed that the alleged leader of the hijackers, Muhammad Atta, was an Egyptian national and that two of Osama bin Laden's most senior commanders, Ayman al-Zawahiri and Muhammad 'Atef, were leaders in the Egyptian group al-Jihad.[5] Despite the high profile of Egypt's Islamic militants, it should be recalled that (1) they represent only a tiny fraction of those Egyptians active in the Islamic movement as a whole and that (2) their use of violence is repudiated not only by the general Egyptian public but also by the majority of people in the Islamic movement itself.[6] Rather than dwelling on the Islamic movement's militant fringe, therefore, this book explains why thousands of Egyptian graduates have chosen to participate in the nonviolent, reformist groups of the movement's mainstream. Hence it concentrates on the dominant (but not the only) form of Islamic activism in Egypt since 1952.

The rise of a popular Islamic reform movement in Egypt not only has transformed the character of opposition politics in the world's largest Arab state but also has affected political trends beyond Egypt's borders. For example, the Muslim Brotherhood, an organization founded in Egypt in 1928, currently has branches in several other Arab states, and Egyptians have directly influenced their evolution through the dissemination of ideas, resources, and personnel. (In fact, over the past century a conspicuous number of the Islamic movement's leading ideologues have been Egyptian nationals).[7] Looking ahead, Egypt's stature as a leader in the Arab world is such that an Islamist victory — at the polls or in the streets — could significantly alter regional alliances, as well as offer a model and source of inspiration for Islamist parties in neighboring states. Finally, the Mubarak regime's status as an American ally and strategic partner in the Arab-Israeli peace process has given to a broader set of international actors a stake in Egypt's political stability. Egypt's cultural and political centrality in the Arab world and its strategic role in preserving the current regional balance of power have thus raised the profile of the Islamic trend in Egypt, regardless of whether its progression is met with enthusiasm or alarm.

An Islamic Social Movement?

The rise of Islamic activism in Egypt is important because of its immediate political impact and also because it raises some broader questions about how opposition movements reach out to potential recruits and why their appeals succeed or fail. Such questions occupy a central position in social movement research, an interdisciplinary field encompassing works in sociology, psychology, history, and political science. Until recently, the study of Islamic activism in the Arab world was detached from theoretical developments in the social movement field.[8] But over the past few years, a small but growing number of scholars have come to appreciate the potential analytic payoff to be gained from applying social movement theories and concepts to the study of Islamic groups.[9] My work is part of this emerging trend. In particular, I contend that our understanding of the rise of Islamic activism in Egypt — and, by extension, elsewhere — can be enriched by attention to social movement research, which illuminates how mobilizing agents, structures, and ideas mediate the progression from individual grievances to collective action.

If scholars of Islamic activism have only recently begun to harness the analytic power of social movement theory, social movement scholars have yet to devote systematic attention to Islamic groups. Contemporary social movement theory derives almost exclusively from research on movements in the democratic polities of Western Europe and the United States. Acknowledging this point in 1996, several leading movement scholars called for an enlargement of the field to include studies of contentious politics in non-Western, nondemocratic settings.[10] Since that time, the number of studies in this genre has grown, and they have been cited more frequently in mainstream theoretical texts.[11] Yet compared with the vast literature on American and European movements, the study of movements outside the West remains at an early stage and has yet to be extended to movements in the Arab-Islamic world.[12]

The study of Islamic activism in Egypt raises some interesting theoretical issues that have not been fully explored. First, such a study can help illuminate whether and in what ways the conditions, dynamics, and outcomes of mobilization are different in authoritarian settings than they are in democratic ones. While benefiting from theory building in the social movement field, the study of Islamic activism in Egypt can also contribute to it by helping clarify how and why citizens become active in opposition politics under conditions of authoritarian rule. Second, the Egyptian case enables us to explore the role of religion — and "culture" more generally — in the generation of opportunities, resources, and motivations for collective challenges to powerful institutions and elites. In so doing, it allows us to address a puzzle largely neglected by "rational-actor" models of collective action, namely, what motivates citizens to participate in opposition politics when self-interest should propel them toward political abstention.

To integrate the study of Islamic activism into the social movement field, I have treated Islamic activism in Egypt as a case of social movement activism, subject to the same methods of analysis used to study movement activism elsewhere. As a point of departure, I adopt Sidney Tarrow's definition of social movements as "collective challenges, based on common purposes and social solidarities, in sustained interaction with elites, opponents and authorities."[13] The instances of movement activism that concern us actually form a subset of this broader category. First, I look at popular participation in a particular *type* of social movement, that is, those seeking a fundamental change in existing social and political institutions and elites, as opposed to "issue-oriented" movements promoting (or resisting) more discrete changes in public policy or behavior. I refer to the participation of citizens in movements oriented toward systemic change as "opposition activism."[14] Second,

I explain the rise of opposition activism in a particular setting, that is, in authoritarian political systems in which freedoms of speech and association are circumscribed and, as a consequence, independent political activity is, to varying degrees, restricted.

A primary contention of this book is that the rise of Islamic activism in Egypt — and, by extension, of other instances of opposition activism in other authoritarian settings — was not a natural result of accumulated grievances but hinged on the mobilizing efforts of opposition elites. In Egypt, Islamists marshaled resources and created opportunities for opposition activism outside the formal political channels controlled by the authoritarian state. Moreover, through a massive project of ideological outreach to educated youth, they created new motivations for activism that transcended the logic of self-preservation underlying dominant patterns of political abstention. Before I discuss what strategies of mobilization the Islamists employed and why they were successful, let me clarify why prevailing explanations of Islamic activism are incomplete.

Challenging Grievance-Based Explanations of Islamic Activism

Scholarly interest in the resurgence of Islam as a force for social and political change has grown in the wake of such dramatic events as the Islamic revolution in Iran and the assassination of Egyptian President Anwar Sadat, and over the past two decades a sizable literature has developed on what has been alternatively described as the "Islamic revival," the "rise of Islamic fundamentalism," or the "rise of political Islam." This literature includes some excellent studies of the ideology, organizational structure, and membership of Islamic groups, as well as their relationship with incumbent political elites.[15] While such studies provide valuable insight into many aspects of the Islamic resurgence, they do not offer a persuasive theoretical account of citizens' participation in Islamic groups. What has motivated thousands of students and professionals across the Muslim world to join the Islamic movement, despite the personal risks that such participation often entails?

Many studies of Islamic activism draw implicitly or explicitly on one of two major explanatory models, which we might call the "cultural identity" and "political economy" models, respectively. Although they differ in focus, both locate the origins of Islamic activism in the grievances of potential recruits. According to the "cultural identity" viewpoint, the rise of Islamic activism is a reaction to the domination of Muslim societies by the West.

Beginning with the European colonial expansion and continuing, albeit in more subtle forms, to the present day, Western influence has insinuated itself into not just the economic and political domains of Muslim societies but also, and more fundamentally, into their cultural domain. From this viewpoint, the Islamic resurgence is a collective protest against decades of Western cultural domination, in which Muslims have reclaimed their Islamic heritage as a positive and "authentic" source of identity and values.[16]

Other studies attribute the rise of Islamic activism to the absence of economic prosperity and political freedom in the new states of the Middle East and North Africa. From what we might call the "political economy" viewpoint, the secular authoritarian regimes that have dominated the region since the era of decolonization have failed to provide economic growth, social equity, and political rights for their citizens. Political mismanagement and corruption also have contributed to chronic housing shortages and rising unemployment, particularly among ambitious, educated, lower-middle-class youth whom the modern sector of the economy cannot absorb. Such youth express their "real-world grievances" through the idiom of political Islam. Hence from this perspective, Islamic activism is more a vote "against" the status quo than a vote "for" a specific (in this case, Islamic) alternative.[17]

Whether defined in terms of cultural alienation or political and economic deprivation, the rise of Islamic activism is typically portrayed as a collective protest against the abject conditions prevailing in much of the contemporary Muslim world. That this protest has assumed an Islamic form is either incidental, following the logic of the political economy viewpoint, or natural, from the cultural identity viewpoint, given the salience of conservative Islamic beliefs and values in contemporary Muslim culture.

Grievance-based explanations of Islamic activism are not wrong, but they are incomplete. Even under the most extreme conditions of human misery and exploitation, the emergence of collective protest is not assured. As social movement theorists have observed, individuals may not view their circumstances as amenable to change, and even when they do recognize the possibility for change, they often lack the motivations, resources, and opportunities to achieve it through collective action.[18] The progression from environmental conditions to grievance to collective action is thus far more contingent than mainstream explanations of Islamic activism care to admit.

Contemporary social movement theory suggests that "contentious" collective action is not a direct outcome of accumulated grievances but hinges on the success of movement efforts at mobilization. To mobilize citizens into politics, it is not sufficient for movement leaders to tap into preexisting discontents; they must also generate motivations, resources, and opportunities for collective action. If such efforts fail, then even the most aggrieved citizens are unlikely to participate in collective protest. By demonstrating that citizens' participation in movements depends on successful mobilization, recent work in the social movement field has exposed the deficiencies of grievance-based explanations of Islamic activism and highlighted the need for a closer investigation of the processes of mobilization that translate grievances into collective action.

Islamic Activism as an Outcome of Mobilization

The principal contention of this book is that the rise of Islamic activism in Egypt — and, by implication, in other settings — was contingent on a deliberate process of mobilization initiated and sustained by Islamic counterelites. By granting center stage to the question of how opposition leaders mobilize support, this book introduces an element of agency that is missing from — or at least underdeveloped in — most accounts of Islamic activism in Egypt and beyond.

Understanding Islamic activism as an outcome of mobilization raises a set of questions that neither the literature on the Islamic resurgence nor the literature on Western social movements have fully explored. Under what conditions does mobilization by opposition groups become possible in authoritarian settings? Why did Islamist groups have more success overcoming authoritarian constraints than their secular rivals did, and why did their message resonate more powerfully with potential recruits? Finally, how can mobilization contribute to broader and more enduring forms of political change?

Obviously, mobilization does not occur in a vacuum but in a specific political, social, and cultural environment. As contemporary social movement theory suggests, environmental factors constrain the options available to movement organizers and affect whether their mobilizing efforts succeed or fail.[19] Most of what we know about environmental constraints derives from the study of social movements in Western Europe and the United States. A close study of the Egyptian case thus addresses existing gaps in the social movement literature by helping identify the barriers that restrict mobilization by opposition groups in authoritarian settings, as well as the ways in which such barriers can be overcome. Toward this end, I develop five general analytic propositions from the specifics of the Egyptian case.

Proposition 1: More than democratic regimes do, authoritarian regimes directly and routinely intervene to block opposition groups' outreach to the mass public.

Opposition groups trying to mobilize support in authoritarian settings confront a set of formidable challenges. The first is that in any political system, movements seeking a radical change in the established social and political order arouse the suspicion and hostility of powerful government, business, and civic elites who, out of self-interest and/or conviction, have a stake in preserving it. Hence even in a liberal democracy like that of the United States, groups that are — justly or unjustly — perceived as trying to subvert the public order (for example, the Communists, neo-Nazis, or Black Panthers) are likely to encounter more resistance from powerful interests than, say, an energy-conservation group would.

If radical groups are likely to generate intense opposition in democracies, the obstacles they confront are even greater in authoritarian settings, where they are subject to the full coercive powers of the state. Authoritarian governments assume a variety of forms, including single-party regimes, military regimes, and personal dictatorships. While they differ in structure and policy, authoritarian regimes have two basic features that distinguish them from democracies: (1) their leaders possess administrative, legislative, and coercive powers typically unavailable to leaders in democratic systems, and (2) they use such powers to retain control of the state apparatus regardless of how much support they have in the electorate. That is, authoritarian regimes are both better equipped and more determined than their democratic counterparts are to harass opposition groups and limit their outreach to the mass public.

In a democratic political system, a movement's adversaries — whether government officials, politicians, or members of rival movements — can attempt to undermine it in various ways.[20] Even so, their options are sharply constrained by the constitutionally guaranteed freedoms of expression and assembly available to the movement's leaders and adherents. However much they might like to, a movement's opponents cannot typically block it from disseminating its message.[21] By contrast, in authoritarian regimes, political power tends to be concentrated in the hands of the decision-making elite at the apex of the authoritarian state, and their power is far less constrained by formal guarantees of citizens' rights. When authoritarian leaders believe that a group or movement is directly threatening their own values and/or interests, they have a wide array of administrative, legislative, and coercive levers to deploy against it. In particular, they can use such levers to control the *agents*, *sites*, and *targets* of mobilization.

The first and most direct way for a regime to preempt the rise of opposition activism is to disable potential *agents* of mobilization. That is, authoritarian leaders may ban a group they consider offensive and harass, arrest,
imprison, exile, torture, or even execute its members. But the forcible sup-
pression of an opposition group can be logistically difficult and politically
costly. The second strategy available to authoritarian leaders is to control
potential *sites* of mobilization. That is, they may tolerate the existence of an
opposition group but systematically limit its access to the mass public. For
example, they may deny the group access to public spaces, censor its publications, and/or prohibit it from raising funds and providing services, thereby
limiting its political visibility and influence. The third strategy available to
authoritarian leaders is to co-opt the *targets* of mobilization and "inoculate"
them against the opposition group's appeals. For example, authoritarian leaders may utilize state-controlled media, schools, and religious institutions to
cultivate support for official policy while simultaneously discrediting their
rivals. Furthermore, they can "buy" the loyalty of strategic groups by distributing scarce goods (for example, education, housing, jobs) in exchange for
political support.

The virtual disappearance of opposition activism in Egypt from 1954 to
1967 during the reign of President Gamal 'Abdel Nasser was a direct outcome of his regime's intervention. Chapter 2 explains how the Nasser regime
preempted the rise of opposition activism by (1) subjecting would-be agents,
sites, and targets of mobilization to state control and (2) cultivating support
for the regime's own "revolutionary" agenda. In 1954, Nasser banned the
Muslim Brotherhood — by far the largest political movement in prerevolu-
tionary Egypt — imprisoning many of its leaders and forcing the remainder
underground. Then, by subjecting all major public institutions to state control, the regime deprived the Brotherhood of its main sites of outreach to
the mass public. At the same time, through intensive political indoctrination
and strategic rewards, Nasser cultivated the loyalty of the very stratum of
educated youth that had furnished the bulk of the Brotherhood's support
before 1952.

For a time, Nasser managed to preempt the rise of opposition activism,
but it resurfaced toward the end of his rule and escalated under his successors. In the early 1970s independent Islamic groups took root on university
campuses, and over the next decade the Islamic trend coalesced into a well-
organized, well-financed opposition movement with broad support among
students and professionals. The resurgence of Islamic activism after the lull
of the Nasser era begs an explanation. Under what conditions are authori-

tarian regimes unwilling or unable to preempt mobilization by opposition groups? That is, why did Nasser's successors tolerate — and/or were unable to prevent — the Islamic mobilization of educated youth?

Proposition 2: The co-option of strategic constituencies is difficult for authoritarian regimes to sustain under conditions of underdevelopment and scarce resources.

In the 1970s and 1980s, the leaders of centralized, authoritarian states in Eastern Europe, Africa, Asia, and the Middle East faced mounting evidence of poor economic, political, and military performance. In response, many of them cautiously experimented with political and economic reform. State controls over the economy were relaxed to stimulate private initiative, and political systems were expanded to include "safety-valve" channels of dissent. However, when shifting from "closed" to "semi-open" systems, authoritarian leaders faced a common dilemma, as the reforms intended to bolster the authoritarian system often had the unintended effect of increasing the resources and opportunities available for organized challenges from below.

In Egypt, as in many other new states throughout the developing world, the achievement of political independence was accompanied or soon followed by the rise of authoritarian regimes promising to deliver the masses from a long history of exploitation by foreign and local elites. These regimes set up one-party political systems and launched ambitious programs of state-led development, attempting to simultaneously generate rapid economic growth, improved living standards, and high levels of political and ideological conformity. Such ambitious state projects ultimately ran out of steam, and authoritarian elites faced growing pressures for political and economic reform.

The collapse of Nasser's statist model of political and economic organization has been analyzed elsewhere.[22] Suffice it to note here that the regime's ambitions eventually outpaced its institutional resources and capacities. Chapter 3 explains how its efforts to co-opt strategic urban youth by providing them with free higher education and guaranteed jobs eventually confronted hard resource constraints it could not overcome. In an attempt to meet the ever growing demand for such entitlements, the regime expanded the circle of beneficiaries beyond its means, leading to fiscal crisis and growing pressures for reform. The regime's retreat from the entitlement program stirred intense resentment among would-be recipients who had come to regard state benefits as their "right." Chapter 3 explains how the regime deliberately fostered graduates' dependence on the state but — under conditions of resource scarcity and underdevelopment — ultimately failed to deliver on its promises. It also shows that the exhaustion of the statist model and the regime's moves toward reform contributed to the rise of a frustrated stratum of educated, underemployed youth "available" for mobilization by opposition groups.

In addition to reducing the state's role in the economy, Nasser's successors experimented with limited political reform. Contemporary social movement theory links the rise of movements to the opening of formal political institutions and/or the realignment of political elites to the advantage of challenging groups. In this respect the Egyptian case represents something of an anomaly, for the Islamic movement mobilized widespread support at the same time that its participation in the formal political order was sharply restricted. Chapter 4 observes that even after some opposition parties were legalized in 1976, contestation for power within Egypt's formal political system was still controlled from above. For example, the Muslim Brotherhood remained banned and was prohibited from running its own list of candidates for parliament; members of the Brotherhood who ran as independents or as affiliates of legal parties were routinely intimidated and harassed; and under the country's emergency laws, it was illegal for Brotherhood members to disseminate their literature or assemble in public without a permit.

In order to account for Islamic mobilization under these conditions, we need to broaden our understanding of "political opportunities" to include resources and institutional spaces on the periphery of the formal political system that are further removed from state control.

Proposition 3: Even when an opposition group's access to formal political institutions is restricted, it may seize opportunities for organization and outreach in ostensibly "nonpolitical" settings beyond the state's control.

The social movement literature on political opportunities focuses on environmental changes that "render the established order more vulnerable or receptive to challenge."[23] As summarized by Sidney Tarrow, these expanding political opportunities include (1) the extension of participation to new actors, (2) changes in political alignments, (3) emerging divisions among elites, (4) the appearance of influential allies, and (5) a decline in the state's capacity or will to repress dissent.[24] But when we look at Egypt's formal political system at the time of the Islamic movement's resurgence, we find as much continuity as change. Authoritarian elites remained unified; the vast internal security apparatus of the state remained intact; and while a few opposition parties were legalized, the ban on the Muslim Brotherhood remained in place. In sum, we find a coherent authoritarian elite with both the desire and the institutional arsenal to block Islamic opponents from challenging their grip on power.

The picture changes significantly, however, when we extend our conception of "opportunity structures" beyond the realm of formal political institutions and elites. As I elaborate in chapter 5, while the core of the Egyptian political system remained closed, new opportunities for Islamic organization and outreach began to emerge on the periphery. ("Core" refers to a country's national representative institutions; here it refers to the Egyptian parliament and the legally constituted political parties that participate in parliamentary elections. "Periphery" refers to social, cultural and economic groups, institutions, and networks that enable citizens to participate in public life but that do not compete for political power.)[25] Chapter 5 traces the development of a vast, decentralized network of Islamic institutions in Egypt in the 1970s and 1980s and explains how such institutions furnished the infrastructure, resources, and cadres for the Islamist mobilization of educated youth. While social movement theory has tended to portray strong, centralized organization as a definite advantage for movements, in Egypt it was precisely the dispersed, informal, and local character of Islamic institutions that enabled them to evade the watchful eye of authoritarian elites and hence to serve as "safe" sites of contact with potential recruits.

Together, chapters 4 and 5 reveal that even when opposition groups are excluded from the formal political order, they may be able to exploit new opportunities for organization and outreach in "nonpolitical" settings removed from state control. They also show that in authoritarian settings, a process of uneven political liberalization designed to safeguard incumbent elites can have the unintended effect of privileging opposition activity outside the formal party system, shifting the locus of political dynamism from the center to the periphery "by default."

By the mid-1980s when the Muslim Brotherhood entered the elections for leadership of Egypt's professional associations, the institutional groundwork for Islamist mobilization was already in place. Yet the emergence of structural opportunities for mobilization does not explain its occurrence. We still need to investigate *how* Islamists mobilized the support of Egyptian students and professionals and *why* their outreach efforts were successful. To answer these questions, we need to shift our focus from macrochanges in the institutional landscape to the microdynamics of Islamic outreach.

Proposition 4: To explain the rise of opposition activism in high-risk settings, we must (1) acknowledge that ideas — as much as interests — can motivate action and (2) specify how and why certain ideas acquire mobilizing power for certain citizens in a given place and time.

In recent years, "rational-actor" models of human behavior have come to occupy a privileged position in the American disciplines of political science and sociology. Informed by such models, much of the American social movement literature defines movement participation as a form of goal-seeking behavior by self-interested individuals.[26] Nonetheless, a theory that links behavior to "rational" calculations of self-interest would be hard pressed to explain the participation of thousands of students and professionals in Egypt's Islamic movement. In authoritarian settings, in which the risks associated with participating in an opposition movement are high and the prospects of effecting change are, at best, uncertain, the "rational" response of the self-interested actor would appear to be a retreat into self-preserving silence. Indeed, when we examine the political behavior of lower-middle-class graduates in Egypt, we find that most of them — including those with the greatest grievances — refrain from any kind of political involvement whatsoever. If the "rational-actor" model accounts for the response of the passive majority, then what explains the altogether different response of the activist minority?

Those who insist on a strictly interest-based explanation of Islamic activism might argue that Islamists mobilized recruits through the provision of "selective incentives," that is, by attaching material, social, and psychological benefits to participation in the movement (or, conversely, attaching costs and risks to nonparticipation).[27] In fact, Islamic groups did use a range of "selective incentives" to attract potential recruits and ease their entry into the movement. Interest-based appeals thus help account for initial, lower-risk forms of Islamic activism. But they cannot explain graduates' eventual transition from lower-risk to higher-risk and more overtly political forms of activism.[28] Once the risks of participation extend to a potential loss of livelihood, psychological intimidation, arrest, imprisonment, torture, and death, an explanation grounded in the logic of narrow self-interest appears strained. Moreover, a focus on individual cost-benefit calculations fails to capture the ways in which movement participation is subjectively experienced, as graduates involved in the movement repeatedly stressed the normative basis for their actions, explaining that — self-interest aside — they were obligated to participate in the task of Islamic reform.

Even under conditions of authoritarian rule, in which the desire for self-preservation drives most citizens toward political abstention, citizens may participate in opposition politics on the basis of deeply held values, commitments, and beliefs. Rational-actor models of movement participation fail to account for situations in which ideas — as much as if not more than interests — motivate political action. "Thick" versions of rationality linking all political behavior to considerations of self-interest cannot explain why citizens are sometimes willing to jeopardize their own well-being in pursuit of some higher goal. Even "thin" versions of rationality — that is, those acknowledging the infinite variety of individual objectives (or preferences) and focusing instead on the rational choice of means to pursue them — fall short. By accepting individual preferences as given, such models fail to explain where the beliefs and values that motivate high-risk activism come from.

A full account of Islamic activism — and, by extension, of high-risk activism in other settings — requires attention to how rival socializing agents and institutions compete to influence the priorities of private citizens. Individuals establish their priorities (or "rank-order their preferences") in a particular social and cultural environment and are influenced by prevailing values and norms. Indeed, such ostensibly private rank-orderings are routinely the target of intensive ideological contestation, as government leaders, parents, religious clergy, movement organizers, and others compete for the "hearts and minds" of their constituents. This leads to a key point: movement leaders not only tap into existing preferences but also may try to alter the preference-orderings of individuals through deliberate efforts at persuasion.

In recent years, some American social movement scholars have begun to shift away from strict "rationalist" accounts of movement participation toward new synthetic models that acknowledge the causal role of culture and ideas.[29] Building on the pioneering work of David Snow and Robert Benford, movement scholars have begun to investigate the ideological "frames" that movements employ to diagnose social problems, prescribe solutions, and motivate participation.[30] Despite growing interest in the connections between ideas and action, research in this field has only recently progressed beyond describing frames to systematically investigating movement-framing processes and dynamics.[31]

Chapters 6 and 7 analyze these Islamist framing processes, pointing out that movement organizers in Egypt utilized a respected social convention known as the *da'wa* (the "call" to God) to promote a radically new, activist interpretation of the Islamic faith. Rather than simply — or even primarily — appealing to the self-interests of potential recruits, the Islamists promoted a new ethic of civic obligation demanding that every Muslim participate in the Islamic reform of society and state, regardless of the benefits and costs incurred by those involved. Chapter 6 explores the content of Islamist ideology and discusses the media used by Islamist leaders to transmit their message to educated youth. Chapter 7 shifts from the description of Islamist strategies of outreach to an explanation of their success. Why were so many lower-middle-class graduates in Egypt ready to embrace — and act upon —

an ideology that stressed the primacy of the public good over the pursuit of narrow self-interest?

One of the greatest analytic challenges confronting movement scholars is explaining how a particular set of ideas acquire mobilizing power in a given place and time. Islamists typically claim that it is "natural" for Muslims to support a political agenda based on Islam. Yet frame theory suggests that no message is inherently persuasive; rather, its appeal depends on specific attributes of the movement's organizers and its target audience, as well as on the social relationships in which they are embedded. Chapter 7 explains why the Islamist *da'wa* was positively received by lower-middle-class Egyptian youth. It contends that movement organizers successfully arrogated the authority to interpret sacred Islamic texts and developed ideological frames that "resonated" with the life experience and broader belief system of potential recruits. Finally, it proposes a strong causal link between intensive small-group solidarity and value change, suggesting that the integration of new recruits into the close-knit nuclei of movement networks reinforced their new Islamist commitments and weakened the hold of competing loyalties. Islamist networks thus constituted the structural mechanism for the development of a new activist Islamist subculture and the creation of venues in which new commitments could be translated into practice.

So far we have considered the *conditions* and *dynamics* of mobilization in authoritarian settings. The third and final analytic issue to be addressed is that of *outcomes*. When and how does mobilization contribute to broader and more enduring forms of social and political change?

Proposition 5: In authoritarian settings the type of organization that enables opposition groups to mobilize support conflicts with the type of organization that they need to convert that support to tangible political gains.

Islamist outreach to educated youth took place in local mosques, community associations, informal study groups, and peer networks, the building blocks of a vast, decentralized Islamic sector with substantial autonomy from state control. The dispersion, informality, and small size of such myriad Islamic groups and associations enabled the Islamists to reach out to potential recruits beneath the radar of the authoritarian state.[32] The very structures that facilitated mobilization were, however, ill equipped to convert the movement's growing support into tangible political gains. Rather, as chapter 8 shows, it was the Muslim Brotherhood — a nationally based, formal "quasi-party" organization — that succeeded in aggregating support mobilized on the periphery and converting it into electoral victories closer to the political center.

The political reforms introduced by Sadat and Mubarak in the 1970s and 1980s transformed Egypt from a "closed" to a "semi-open" authoritarian system in which genuine political contestation was blocked in some arenas but tolerated in others. While electoral competition for seats in parliament remained tightly controlled from above, the regime tolerated relatively free contests for leadership positions in the interest-group associations of Egypt's new middle class. Though barred from running as a bloc in parliamentary elections, from the mid-1980s to the mid-1990s the Muslim Brotherhood ran its own list of candidates for the governing boards of many of the country's student unions, faculty clubs, and national professional associations. Chapter 8 explains how the Muslim Brotherhood tapped into support mobilized by Islamist groups on the periphery to achieve sweeping electoral victories in several of the country's largest and most prestigious professional associations. Under the Brotherhood's control, these associations became important sites of Islamic political experimentation and outreach near the center of national politics. Chapter 8 thus demonstrates how a process of Islamic mobilization that was gradual and largely invisible to the regime ultimately paved the way for the stunning defeat of government-backed elites.

The same high-profile electoral victories that enabled the Muslim Brotherhood to win control of Egypt's national professional associations alarmed the regime's leaders and, in so doing, made the Brotherhood more vulnerable to attack. As just noted, the progression of the Islamic movement from mobilization on the periphery to political change at the center was contingent on (1) the regime's tolerance for unrestricted electoral competition in at least some arenas of the polity and (2) the presence of a national "quasi-party" organization with the leadership, infrastructure, and resources to channel the movement's support into electoral gains. As the ultimate arbiters of power in the authoritarian system, President Mubarak and his security officers retained the capacity to alter both of these conditions, and beginning in the mid-1990s, they did.

This leads us to consideration of a final issue — the failure of the Egyptian Islamist movement to sustain its political ascent over time. As Sidney Tarrow has observed, a movement's very success can lead to instances of counter-mobilization by its opponents, changing the environment in which the movement had initially thrived.[33] In its progression from unobtrusive activities on the periphery to a series of bold electoral challenges close to the political center, the Islamic movement ultimately reached the limits of the regime's tolerance. According to chapter 9, in Egypt — as in several other

Arab states — Islamist gains provoked a massive counterattack by government authorities. Beginning in the mid-1990s, the Mubarak regime closed off opportunities for electoral competition within Egypt's interest-group organizations and targeted the Brotherhood's most dynamic leaders in a new wave of repression. The Brotherhood's vulnerability to the regime's assault was exacerbated by both its failure to generate support beyond its core constituency and the "stickiness" of the nonviolent repertoires of contention for which its constituency had been trained. Without support from broader sectors of the mass public and without the desire or capacity to attempt a revolutionary challenge, the Brotherhood was temporarily paralyzed by the regime's crackdown. The first eight chapters of the book thus show how Egypt's Islamists gained the power to challenge incumbent authoritarian elites, while the concluding chapter highlights the limits of that power. In sum, with the pillars of the authoritarian state intact, the Islamists' ascent remained contingent on the regime's forbearance, and the more visible, influential, and outspoken the Islamists became, the more likely it was that this forbearance would be revoked. Chapter 9 concludes with a brief discussion of the larger theoretical implications of the Egyptian case, suggesting how the study of Islamic activism in Egypt can contribute to the explanation of "high-risk" activism in other cultural and political settings.

Research Methodology

I conducted the research for this book in Egypt during the eighteen months from January 1990 through June 1991. In addition, I made follow-up visits to Cairo in 1993, 1997, and 2000. Before beginning the research for this book, I worked to become proficient in the Arabic language. After completing first- and second-year Arabic in the United States, I spent eighteen months (January 1986–June 1987) as a full-time student of Arabic at the American University in Cairo, first in the Arabic Language Unit (ALU) and later in the year-long advanced program offered by the Center for Arabic Studies Abroad (CASA). This period of intensive language study (of both modern standard Arabic and the Egyptian dialect) provided a crucial foundation for my research, as it enabled me to utilize Arabic-language print media, government documents, and scholarly sources, as well as to converse, without the aid of an interpreter, with Egyptians from different socioeconomic and educational backgrounds.

During my fieldwork, I used a variety of research methods. To assess change in graduate education, employment, and earning prospects over time, I collected data from several Egyptian government agencies, including the Ministry of Higher Education, the Ministry of Manpower and Training, the Central Agency for Organization and Administration (CAOA), the Central Agency for Public Mobilization and Statistics (CAPMAS), and the Cabinet Information Support Center, as well as from international organizations and Egyptian and Western scholarly sources. In addition, I conducted a series of in-depth interviews with senior government officials and participated in an NGO-sponsored survey of 1,000 unemployed university graduates in the governorate of Beni Suef. To trace the electoral ascent of the Muslim Brotherhood in Egypt's professional associations, I gathered membership and electoral data; interviewed association officials as well as Islamist, leftist, and pro-regime candidates for elected office; and conducted an exit poll of 100 voters at the headquarters of the Engineers' Association in February 1991.

Given the absence of reliable public opinion survey data and the overwhelming political and logistical barriers to launching my own large-scale survey,[34] my investigation of Islamist mobilization strategies necessarily relied on qualitative research methods. To investigate the institutional mechanisms of Islamist outreach at the grassroots level, I conducted fieldwork in three lower-middle-class residential neighborhoods of Greater Cairo known for their moderate to high levels of Islamic activism. Between January 1990 and June 1991, I conducted open-ended interviews with recent graduates in each neighborhood (more than fifty graduates in total).[35] Each sample included graduates with no political affiliations, who can be seen as representing the pool of "potential recruits" to whom Islamic outreach was targeted. In addition, each sample included a number of graduates who identified themselves as Islamists with varying levels of commitment and activity, from movement organizers to participants.[36] My research on Islamist outreach also entailed the collection and content analysis of a sample of Islamic da'wa materials, including recorded sermons, pamphlets, and books. In addition, I engaged in participant observation during prayer services and religious lessons at small independent mosques and witnessed numerous conversations and interactions in private homes.[37]

Besides my research in three neighborhoods of Greater Cairo, I conducted interviews with individual Islamists in other settings, including Islamic bookstores, the headquarters of the Islamist newspaper al-Sha'b, the offices of Islamist-controlled professional associations, the campus of Cairo University, and several other residential neighborhoods. The Islamists I interviewed do not constitute a representative sample in any scientific sense.

However, the inclusion of several independent clusters of individuals re-
duces the likelihood that my sample was systematically biased or skewed. As
a supplement to my own field research, I conducted a series of "elite interviews" with Egyptian political activists, journalists, and intellectuals with
expert knowledge of the subject of Islamist mobilization. In addition, I gathered relevant information from Arabic-language books, articles, and scholarly conference papers, including articles in the official and opposition press.

At a time when the social sciences have become increasingly dominated
by large-n studies involving the statistical analysis of quantitative data, this
book seeks to affirm the theoretical value of qualitative, case-specific research. Arguably the main advantage of in-depth case studies is that they
facilitate "causal process tracing," that is, allow us to specify the nature of
the linkages between initial conditions and outcomes with greater precision
than is possible in large-n, quantitative studies.[38] Employing such qualitative
methods as open-ended interviewing and participant observation, I was able
to explore the microdynamics of Islamic mobilization in settings on the
periphery of the formal political system and hence to clarify the mechanisms
through which individual grievances are converted into collective action. In
sum, qualitative research strategies enabled me to address a question largely
unexplored by contemporary social movement theory: how and why citizens
join opposition movements under conditions of authoritarian rule.

2 Nasser and the Silencing of Protest

I said — the graduates will come out of university without work!
And they replied: "We don't care if they sell *ta'miyya* [felafel
sandwiches] on the street; they want the degree for its own sake!"

— Kamal ed-Din Hussein, then minister of education, recalling the
opposition of members of the National Assembly to his proposal in 1957
for reducing university admissions

On July 23, 1952, a group of young army officers overthrew
Egypt's constitutional monarchy in a military coup. After a brief leadership
struggle in 1954, Gamal Abdel Nasser gained control of the new regime and
remained its leading force until his death in 1970. For our purposes, the
most striking feature of the era from 1954 to the June 1967 War was the
virtual disappearance of opposition activism among modern-educated,
lower-middle-class youth. This lull is conspicuous because such youth figured prominently in the opposition movements before 1952 and formed the
main base of the reconstituted Islamic movement after Nasser's death. What
explains the silence of educated youth in Nasser's Egypt?

This chapter contends that Nasser preempted the rise of opposition activism by subordinating potential agents, sites, and targets of mobilization to
state control. He banned all opposition groups and imposed state control
over sites where they had formerly reached out to the mass public. At the
same time, the regime robbed such groups of a key constituency through
the co-optation of educated, lower-middle-class youth. A close examination
of the Nasser era reveals that through a preemptive strategy combining repression, redistribution, and resocialization, authoritarian leaders can diminish the prospects for mobilization to the point that it hardly occurs at
all. As chapters 3 through 5 show, it was only after the effectiveness of this
strategy declined — and was subsequently abandoned — that Islamic activism
resurfaced among the students and professionals of Egypt's cities and provincial towns.

What kind of regime did Nasser establish, and how did it tame one of
the most politically volatile sectors of Egyptian society?

"Authoritarian-Populism": Repression, Redistribution, and Resocialization

It is useful to examine Egypt under Nasser as an example of a broader phenomenon that Raymond A. Hinnebusch Jr. described as "authoritarian-populism," a regime type that emerged during the era of decolonization in many states of the Middle East and Africa:

> It is typically the product of nationalist reaction against imperialism; that is, of struggles for independence or against extroverted, dependent development; it is also chiefly a phenomenon of the early middle stages of development, the product of a challenge by a rising salaried middle class to traditional upper middle class dominance, prior to a large-scale mobilization of the masses. It may grow out of a nationalist movement, occasionally a revolution, frequently a military coup by middle-class officers. Formation of a strong independent state, free of imperialist control, is its first priority. In addition, state power is put in the service of economic modernization and a reformist redistribution of wealth and opportunity to the middle and lower classes.[1]

Reformist in nature, such regimes "stop short of the great transformations of communist societies." Rather than promote radical change with organized mass support, they attempt to reconcile competing interests through populist ideology and massive redistribution. But as Waterbury observed for Egypt, the regime's capacity to simultaneously finance economic growth and distribution eventually becomes strained, and it must either compromise its agenda or seek additional funding from external sources.[2] While Waterbury emphasized the contradictions inherent in the regime's development model, Hinnebusch attributed its decline to the growing influence of the private bourgeoisie and the resurgence of "patrimonialism," that is, the appropriation of public office for private ends by actors in the state itself. Such forces sapped the populist-authoritarian regime of its reformist potential, leading ultimately to social stabilization and economic liberalization.[3]

Nasser's "populist-authoritarian" regime eventually succumbed to profound external and internal pressures for reform. For a time, however, it was extraordinarily successful in securing the political acquiescence — if not outright support — of strategic sectors of the mass public. This absence of overt protest was in part an outcome of repression. After consolidating his own power base, Nasser launched a frontal assault on all organized opposition. By the mid-1950s, all of the country's independent political groups were banned, and those that survived were forced underground. Nasser never managed to eliminate all his opponents, though, as indicated by the underground Islamist cells that were uncovered at various points during his rule. Yet by subjecting to state control all the country's major public institutions — including its universities, schools, media, and mosques — the regime was able to close off former sites of outreach, limiting the opposition groups' access to the mass public.

Repression was one bulwark of the Nasser regime. But the disappearance of opposition activism between 1954 and 1967 was not a product of coercion alone. First, it is unlikely that the regime ever achieved the technical capacity to maintain effective surveillance of society at large, and second, it appears to have enjoyed the genuine support of some sectors of society, including a large share of the country's educated youth. In part, this support was a response to Nasser's tremendous personal charisma, yet neither Nasser nor his advisers were prepared to stake the regime's stability on charm alone. Rather, Nasser preempted opposition activism by granting strategic groups a material and symbolic stake in the "revolutionary" order.

Although Nasser claimed to represent the oppressed *sha'b*, or people, as a whole, a disproportionate share of state resources was channeled to urban, educated, lower-middle- and middle-class youth. The priority accorded them derived less from an assessment of their objective needs than from their perceived strategic importance. That is, Nasser singled out educated, lower-middle-class youth for extra entitlements — as well as for extra indoctrination — in order to defuse their capacity to threaten the regime's survival. Yet rather than following a well-thought-out plan, the regime's efforts at cooptation had an ad hoc quality, in which policy decisions intended to address a specific problem or emanating from a brief period of social experimentation acquired a life of their own. Costly to maintain, the entitlements granted to educated youth proved even more difficult to retract.

The Social Contract

Nasser's policy of state distribution is often referred to as the "social contract," according to which the regime provided goods and services to the public in exchange for their political support.[4] To some extent the term is misleading, as the arrangement was never a bargain entered into voluntarily by equal partners but was a strategy of co-optation initiated by the regime for its own purposes. Moreover, the term presumes that economic distribution, rather than such factors as charismatic leadership or indoctrination, was the basis of the regime's popularity, a claim that is open to debate. Despite such shortcomings, the term is a useful shorthand for regime policies of distribution targeted at non-elite sectors of Egyptian society.

The Nasserist "social contract" raised popular living standards in several ways. It offered employment in the expanding state sector and provided subsidized food, energy, health, and housing to lower- and middle-class groups. Because state employment, benefits, and services were concentrated in the cities, urban residents (including recent migrants from the countryside) profited disproportionately from them.

Among the most coveted benefits of the "social contract" was expanded access to free higher education and, from 1964, the promise to every university graduate of a government job. Free higher education and guaranteed state employment opened new avenues of social mobility to the children of lower- and middle-class Egyptian families and, in so doing, indebted them to the patron-state.

The Expansion of Higher Education

The army officers who seized power in 1952 did not start out with an educational plan that emphasized higher education. On the contrary, under such banners as "every day — a new primary school," priority was given to universalizing primary education and eradicating illiteracy. By contrast, the regime neglected higher education, cutting budgets and limiting the number of new students. The regime's initial emphasis on primary education may have stemmed from the Free Officers' commitment to egalitarianism or their provisional assessment of the country's manpower needs; it most certainly also reflected their reluctance to expand those institutions that had long figured as major sites of political dissent. Soon after consolidating power, Nasser reorganized the universities, banning independent student unions, purging faculty and administration, and posting security police units on campus. After that, he launched a series of reforms increasing popular access to higher education. In 1954, university tuition fees were lowered; eligibility for university scholarships was expanded; and the education budget was reordered at the expense of primary education.[5] Over the next eight years, the budget of the universities almost quadrupled while the Ministry of Education's budget little more than doubled, raising the allocation for higher education from 14 percent to 22 percent of the general education budget.[6] Over the Nasser period as whole, the number of students enrolled in primary education per thousand of population increased by 234 percent, and the number of students enrolled in higher education rose by 325 percent.[7] Annual university enrollments climbed from 51,681 in 1952/53 to 161,517 in 1969/70.[8]

The regime's emphasis on higher education after 1954 stemmed in part from the country's growing need for educated manpower, particularly for graduates trained in such fields as engineering, agriculture, and veterinary medicine, to implement plans for rapid state-led growth. In keeping with the recommendations of various government manpower-planning committees, Egypt's output of engineers and other technical specialists increased markedly in the Nasser era. Nonetheless, the expansion of higher education during this period was not solely, or even primarily, driven by labor considerations, for the university system soon began to overproduce engineers while acute shortages remained for vocationally trained technicians. Against manpower needs estimated at between 1,100 and 2,650 engineers per year, by the early 1970s more than 5,000 engineers were graduating each year.[9]

Two factors propelled educational expansion beyond the country's labor needs. The first was Nasser's ideological commitment to equalizing social and economic opportunities. As he explained in a speech on October 16, 1961: "I want a society in which class distinctions are dissolved through the equality of opportunities to all citizens. I want a society in which the free individual can determine his own position by himself, on the basis of his efficiency, capacity and character."[10] Hence in addition to filling the manpower needs of the expanding public sector, Egypt's system of higher education was intended to soften, if not completely eliminate, class privilege by providing new opportunities for meritocratic advancement. By reducing fees and expanding the number of secondary students admitted to university, Nasser put his rhetorical commitments into practice. As Ibrahim Hilmi 'Abd al-Rahman, who served briefly as minister of planning under Nasser, explained, "Hundreds of technical studies were done, so many efforts at numerical coordination, but it was all nonsense. The goal was to effect social change through education, not economic change."[11]

Educational expansion was also a means of winning popular support. Since the reign of Muhammad 'Ali (1805–1848) and certainly since the days of Cromer and Dunlop, higher education has been closely associated in Egypt with access to prestigious civil service employment. Historically, the domination of the private banking and commerce sectors by Westerners and local minorities had limited native Egyptians' opportunities for entrepreneurship. In this context, the pursuit of higher education, rather than private enterprise, became the favored channel of advancement. By 1952, about one-third of all Egyptians with a primary school certificate or above were employed by the government. Moreover, according to a system known as the "pricing of certificates," from the turn of the century, civil service salaries were determined in accordance with formal academic qualifications. Both the rank at which a graduate entered the civil service and his subsequent opportunities for career advancement hinged on his educational degree.[12]

As 'Abd al-Rahman observed, by the time the Free Officers seized power, education was valued not only as a means of economic advancement but also as an end in itself: "Having an educated son became an achievement, regardless of his employment prospects." Similarly, Mahmud 'Abdel-Fadl wrote, "There is a heavy demand for higher education relative to available places because of the high social status usually associated with such a type of education. Middle-class values rather than 'pure money income' prospects may explain much about the job expectations of university graduates in Egypt."[13]

By fulfilling the aspirations of lower- and middle-class youth for access to higher education, Nasser hoped to secure their political support.[14] During the "Socialist Years" from 1960 to 1966, Nasser opened up the university system to youth from non-elite backgrounds. Having reduced tuition fees in 1956 and 1961, the government abolished all but nominal fees in 1962, making university education virtually free. Moreover, according to one estimate, nearly 75 percent of dormitory residents were exempted from paying any room charges, and students were given special privileges, including inexpensive transport, entertainment, and, most important, an exemption from military service.[15] Surely we should not exaggerate the impact of these policies on Egyptian society. Data from UNESCO indicate that gross enrollment ratios at the university level (the ratio of enrolled students to the total age cohort) never exceeded 8 percent in the Nasser era.[16] But while educational expansion failed to eliminate completely the class biases of the educational system, it did create new avenues of mobility for urban lower-middle- and middle-class youth who scored sufficiently high on the national baccalaureate exam to gain admission to university. As elaborated in later chapters, possession of the coveted *shahada* (university degree) not only raised their social status; it also guaranteed them a permanent, white-collar job in the state.

Nasser's Graduate Appointment Policy

In addition to offering university education free of charge, the Nasser regime instituted a policy guaranteeing every university graduate a government job. Codified in decree 185 of 1964, the *siyasat al-ta'yin*, or graduate appointment policy, coincided with a dramatic expansion of the public sector in the 1960s.[17] Public employment grew by about 70 percent from 1962 to 1970, at a time when growth in national employment as a whole did not exceed 20 percent.[18] Government officials formulating the graduate appointment policy contend that it stemmed less from a sober assessment of the state's manpower needs than from the regime's anxiety about the potential political risks of graduate unemployment. Though instituted on a temporary basis, it quickly became institutionalized and proved difficult to retract.

As Kamal ed-Din Hussein, the best-known minister of education under Nasser, recalled:

> In 1962 and 1963, the government saw there were graduates who couldn't find work. I proposed a temporary solution because Nasser wanted a solution. At the time, I led the Executive Council, which included the president and the ministers. I proposed that the government hire those graduates who had not found employment elsewhere. It was never meant to be a permanent solution. At the time, there were certain ministries with a shortage of manpower, which needed educated people; for example, there weren't enough teachers for all the schools. So we decided to take the graduates and employ them. We did this in 1962 and/or 1963, with the majority of them going to the Ministry of Education. It made sense at the time, as it helped us fill existing gaps.
>
> But it was meant as a temporary measure, not a permanent one. Then after I left, it became routine . . . it became anyone who graduates from university will be employed. We only took the university graduates. We were afraid if we didn't, they would be sitting out on the street. Nasser looked at it as why not employ everyone: if a factory can absorb one, it can absorb two.
>
> So in 1964, it became a permanent solution. First the appointment

policy involved only university graduates, then later was expanded to include two-year technical institute graduates, and then secondary school graduates. It was part of the socialist thinking. If you have enough bread for 100, feed 150; everyone will lose a little, but so what, at least you won't have unemployment, and you'll be able to absorb more people.[19]

Ibrahim Hilmi 'Abd al-Rahman agreed that the graduate appointment policy scheme was motivated by short-term political considerations:

In its early history, the *ta'yin* policy was a political measure. The number of graduates was small at the time. The decision involved no one except those at the apex of the government. It was a decision made by the inner circle, because it was regarded as politically sensitive.

The *ta'yin* policy was motivated by a fear of political agitation. At the time we were very afraid of graduate unemployment. Nasser was conscious of this potential problem and considered it very serious, because he understood it as a potential source of political instability.

After a while, the *ta'yin* policy lost its initial rationale. But once you offer it, it is hard to take back. It becomes a fact.[20]

By 1969 the state employed 450,000 graduates with a secondary-school degree or above, including more than 153,300 university degree holders, or roughly 60 percent of the entire pool of university graduates that the country had produced. This included virtually all the country's engineers, scientists, and agronomists, more than 87 percent of its physicians, and two-thirds of its lawyers.[21] The combination of free higher education and guaranteed jobs enabled graduates from non-elite backgrounds to join the ranks of Egypt's "new middle class." Such entitlements, however, placed an enormous ongoing financial burden on the state. Furthermore, by diverting scarce resources away from productive investment, they arguably hindered the country's overall economic development. As Robert Mabro noted, the government's appointment policy transferred income to the educated at the cost of future economic growth, ultimately eroding the state's resource base for future distribution.[22] The strategic distribution of resources to educated youth was supplemented during the Nasser era by propaganda efforts to reinforce their loyalty to the regime and to "inoculate" them against appeals from opposition groups.

The Resocialization of Educated Youth

The military officers who seized power in Egypt in 1952 declared that the achievement of full national sovereignty, economic growth, and social justice required political unity and consensus. Claiming that party conflict in the liberal era had divided the nation and weakened it from within, the Free Officers dissolved all political parties in 1953.[23] The Muslim Brotherhood was initially exempted from this ban, ostensibly on the grounds that it was not a party but a "nonpolitical" religious association. But this exemption was more likely a result of the Free Officers' reluctance to risk a direct confrontation with the country's largest political organization. Relations between the regime and the Brotherhood quickly soured when it became clear that the latter would not acquiesce quietly to military rule. An attempt on Nasser's life in 1954 by a Brotherhood member gave Nasser the pretext he needed to ban the organization and imprison its leaders, thereby bringing to heel the nation's strongest potential agents of antiregime mobilization.

After dismantling Egypt's liberal parliamentary regime, Nasser established a corporatist political system in which interest groups were organized along functional lines and subsumed within the framework of a single official representative body, known as the Liberation Rally from 1953 to 1958, the National Union from 1958 to 1961, and the Arab Socialist Union from 1962 forward. As part of this transition, all standing professional association boards were dissolved, and beginning in 1958, board members were required to belong to the ruling party. While Egypt's professional associations increased in number and expanded in size as a result of the steady influx of new graduates, they ceased to function as sites of independent political expression.[24]

Beginning in the mid-1950s, Egypt's universities also were placed under state control. Independent student unions were banned, and the youth section of the government-sponsored party became the only sanctioned channel for student political activity. At the same time, professors deemed politically suspect were fired or demoted. Then in the early 1960s, the regime further tightened its grip on the universities. A new Ministry of Higher Education was established to coordinate university affairs; military officers and ex-officers were assigned to senior positions in the university administration; the so-called University Guard, consisting of police troops under control of the Interior Ministry, was stationed in each faculty; and both university staff and students were placed under surveillance by security agents.[25]

Having converted the country's independent public institutions to appendages of the authoritarian state, Nasser enlisted them to disseminate the regime's propaganda. The most intensive indoctrination efforts were focused on students, who, together with the armed forces, were viewed as the most likely targets of opposition appeals. Although the Nasser regime never developed an elaborate ideology, it appropriated many of the themes and concerns of the opposition movements of the liberal era. Intrinsic to Nasser's social vision was the promise of a meritocratic system of advancement, based on the principle of *takaful al-furas* (equality of opportunity). As articulated in numerous speeches and articles, Nasser's state project constituted an assault on the privileged position of foreigners, Egyptianized minorities, and large landowners, an assault consonant with the sensibilities of the middle and lower echelons of Egypt's native intelligentsia.

The regime launched a program of resocialization, or *ta'wiya*, in the public schools. As Egyptian political scientist Mahmud Faksh recalled:

In the primary and preparatory schools strong efforts are directed toward developing a strong loyalty to the regime. Here the students are repeatedly taught the various patriotic themes of Islam, nationalism, Arabism and socialism. Textbooks are full of stories about the glory of medieval Islamic heroes and the great Arab nationalist struggle against colonialism and other political and socio-economic injustices that culminated in the 1952 revolution. . . .

Based on my own experience with this kind of socialization I underwent in my primary, preparatory, and secondary school years, it would be safe to assume that such ceaseless efforts to bring about an identification with the regime have been somewhat successful. My classmates and I developed a strong sense of identification and pride with Arabism, anticolonialism, and nationalist leaders of Nasser's caliber. On different occasions, as the government deemed it necessary, we were able to express these feelings and attitudes by demonstrating in support of regime causes and against anti-regime causes, domestic or foreign.[26]

Resocialization continued at the university level, where new courses like "Arab Society," "The July 23 Revolution," and "Socialism" were required of all students. In addition, the regime attempted to create a vanguard of youth activists committed to regime goals. To this end, it established several new organizations for university students and graduates, the most significant of which was the Socialist Youth Organization (SYO), set up in 1965 after the regime discovered that members of the Muslim Brotherhood, now underground, were again attempting to recruit on campus. Erlich estimates that at its peak, the SYO counted 200,000 members between the ages of sixteen and thirty-three.[27]

From 1954 to 1967, Egypt's educated strata ceased to function as the country's leading source of opposition activism. Denied an independent voice in the new political order, students and graduates acquiesced to the regime's initiatives, dutifully affirming its achievements at official youth meetings, rallies, and demonstrations. As Malcolm Kerr stated in the mid-1960s:

> Student political activity is now a tame affair organized in support of the regime through various officially inspired channels such as the Arab Socialist Union, which is the sole and official party. Indeed, students and the younger intelligentsia as a whole are now perhaps among the most reliable enthusiasts of the regime.[28]

The political loyalty of educated youth ultimately proved contingent on the regime's performance. The regime's stunning military defeat by Israel in the 1967 War opened a Pandora's box of accumulated frustrations and disappointments. For the first time since the early years of the revolution, students and graduates took to the streets to hold the regime responsible for failing to deliver on its revolutionary promises.

The Resurgence of Opposition Activism: The Student Movement Protests of 1967–1973

Beginning in 1965/66, the Egyptian economy entered a period of retrenchment (or *inkimash*, shrinkage). While Egypt's national income had risen by an average of more than 6 percent per year from 1960 to 1965, this rate dropped to an average of roughly 1 percent from 1966 to 1970, due in large part to the huge cost of the Arab-Israel and Yemen wars.[29] In a period of economic contraction, the earning power of graduates positioned at the base of the bureaucratic pyramid declined. While university graduates continued to enter the civil service at a higher grade than did less educated groups, many of them, and especially those who lacked technical expertise, swelled the ranks of the "lumpen salariat," the army of white-collar workers struggling to maintain the appearance, if not the reality, of a middle-class lifestyle. In 1965, Malcolm Kerr described the plight of these strata in particularly vivid terms:

> [Such] graduates ... constitute a large and rapidly growing group whose skills are largely substandard and unwanted, and whose native talents are mediocre, but whose sights have been trained since childhood on the attainment of a dignified job carrying economic rewards and social prestige. The disappointments are naturally sharp as these thousands of not-so-bright young men in their soiled collars and cheap suits eke out a shabby and insecure but desperately respectable existence on ten pounds a month as minor clerks, bookkeepers, school teachers, and journalists. They are assured from time to time in the press and in the president's speeches that as educated men they are the "vanguard" of the nation's progress, but they are impotent to fashion even their own progress, and they can only listen anxiously to the officially propagated theme of equal and widening opportunities under the new socialist economic development plan which ambitiously pledges to double the national income in ten years.[30]

Costly to maintain and politically difficult to retract, the "social contract" began to deliver less and less as an instrument of political control. At the same time, Nasser's heavy-handed tactics in dealing with any form of political opposition generated resentment. By the mid-1960s, graduates began to exhibit the signs of a "politics of withdrawal," a retreat into passivity and noninvolvement in public affairs. Observers of the period note the preoccupation of university students with sports, especially football; others stressed the visible signs of "negativism" (al-salbiyya), frustration, and despair.[31]

This silent undercurrent of frustration did not translate into overt protest before 1967. Although a small number of alienated youth became active in underground Marxist or Islamist cells, the majority simply abstained from any form of political involvement. This pattern was not disrupted until the regime's crushing military defeat by Israel in the 1967 War. The defeat sparked sporadic waves of popular strikes, sit-ins, and demonstrations, culminating in the massive student uprising of 1972/73.

The first major uprising against the regime occurred in February 1968, beginning with a spontaneous demonstration by industrial workers in the Cairo suburb of Helwan protesting the light sentences received by senior military officers held responsible for Egypt's defeat in the 1967 War. Students soon joined the uprising, marching out of the gates of the universities into the streets of Cairo and Alexandria for the first time since 1954.[32] The reappearance of opposition activism thus occurred during a serious political crisis, in which not only the officers but, in a sense, the regime itself was on trial. What permitted such opposition activism to continue beyond the immediate aftermath of the war was the reconstitution of an independent student movement on Egyptian university campuses. Although it was industrial workers who initiated the collective protests in 1968, it was university students who sustained the wave of protest over the next few years. At the time, student activists were self-conscious about their position as the country's only vocal opponents of the regime's policy. As Ahmad 'Abdalla wrote, "The students' sense of their own power after 1967 was influenced by the fact that they were virtually alone in challenging the existing authorities."[33]

How did the universities reemerge as an important site of opposition activism? After the February 1968 uprising, Nasser made a series of critical concessions to students which broadened the space for independent political expression on university campuses. The authority of the University Guard was reduced; a new student newspaper was approved; and a more permissive legal framework for student activities was established by presidential decree. Such reforms created new "structures of opportunity" for protest on university campuses at a time when other institutional arenas remained tightly controlled from above.[34]

The prominent role of students in the protests of the 1968–1973 period was also a function of their high level of political consciousness, paradoxically a result of the regime's own ideological outreach. It was the students who had been most thoroughly socialized in the goals of Nasser's revolution and who were therefore the most disillusioned when its leaders appeared unable or unwilling to achieve them. By indoctrinating a generation of educated youth in the ideas of anti-imperialism and socialism, the Nasser regime had created the very cadres that would ultimately turn against it.

Three aspects of the 1968–1972 wave of collective protest distinguish it from later patterns of Islamic activism. First, this protest occurred against a backdrop of enormous disruptions at the highest levels of the authoritarian state, including military defeat, the death of Nasser in 1970, and the assumption of power by the lesser-known Anwar Sadat. As Theda Skocpol argued in her seminal work on revolution, military defeat and crisis at the highest echelons of the state apparatus can create new space for political protest in authoritarian situations by temporarily paralyzing the regime's capacity for repression.[35] One could argue that it also creates space by triggering a "perceptual breakthrough" in which the legitimacy of the regime suddenly is open to doubt.

A second defining characteristic of the opposition activism of this period was the leading role of the left. Leftists of various ideological strands (Marxist, Nasserist, Communist, and "independent") were at the forefront of organized protest during this period and constituted the most active and energetic political force on university campuses more generally. In part, this reflects the ideological hegemony of secular nationalism, socialism, and anti-imperialism in this period, not only in Egypt but also in other Arab states and in the Third World at large. Moreover, the ideological proximity of leftist groups to the regime itself positioned them to exploit most fully the "new structures of opportunity" that emerged after the war both inside and outside official party and youth organizations.

A third characteristic of this wave of collective protest was its domination by supranational issues. Although the student protesters had a long list of demands, including calls for greater freedom of expression and a renewed commitment to social justice, their foremost demand was for a military confrontation to end Israel's occupation of Egyptian and other Arab territory. The primacy of supranational issues is suggested by the fact that the resumption of hostilities with Israel in the war of October 1973 was followed by a period of relative calm.

Beginning in the mid-1970s and accelerating in the 1980s and early 1990s, a sea change took place in the political orientations and behavior of educated Egyptian youth. First and most striking was the replacement of the left by the reformist wing of the Islamist movement as the country's leading opposition force. Although calls for political freedom, social justice, and confrontation with Zionism and imperialism could still be heard, they were henceforward cast in an Islamic idiom. Furthermore, the popular organizations of the left atrophied at the same time that Islamic groups and associations expanded their scope and influence. A second major transformation was the spillover of opposition activism from the universities into wider arenas of public life, in which Islamists established independent religious, cultural, and service organizations; acquired their own independent press and publishing houses; and gained control of the country's leading professional associations.

Finally, the forms of opposition activism changed as well. Rather than being expressed in a series of high-profile demonstrations directed against a regime in crisis, Islamic activism assumed the form of gradual institution building and persuasion. While less visible and dramatic than the wave of collective protest from 1968 to 1972, Islamic outreach since the mid-1970s facilitated the entry of citizens into opposition politics after the authoritarian state's power had reconsolidated. How the Islamists managed to mobilize educated youth within the framework of a stable authoritarian state is explored in the next chapters.

Conclusion

Some observers, including many Islamists, explain the absence of opposition activism under Nasser as an outcome of repression. Without denying that both the exercise and threat of state violence played a role, I contend that the country's educated youth also were silenced by their economic, political, and ideological incorporation by the Nasser regime. That is, the regime not only suppressed potential *agents* and *sites* of mobilization but also used the state apparatus to inoculate potential *targets* of mobilization against opposition groups' appeals.

While successful in the short run, the regime's co-optation of educated youth proved unsustainable in the long run. At the end of the Nasser era, in a context of economic recession, military defeat, and political crisis, the silenced sectors of society again found their voice. The collective protest that erupted in the aftermath of military defeat was not a popular rejection of Nasserism so much as a reaction against the regime's failure to deliver, underscoring the risks associated with linking the regime's legitimacy so closely to its performance. Beginning in the mid-1970s, Nasser's successors attempted to devise a new formula of legitimacy, one in which limited rights to participation were offered as a substitute for material and symbolic gains. The regime-led political and economic liberalization, however, served less to forge new ties between the state and educated youth than to deepen their mutual disengagement, thus paving the way for the latter's mobilization by Islamic groups.

3 Educated and Underemployed

The Rise of the Lumpen Intelligentsia

Spring, 1991. In a bare one-room apartment without running water on the outskirts of Cairo, an American visitor inquired about a framed document hung on the wall. The young, unemployed father of four took down the frame and wiped off the dust with a corner of his torn *gallabiyya*. "This," he said, "is my university diploma."

Nasser's system of free higher education and guaranteed state employment not only survived under his successors but even expanded to cover a growing circle of beneficiaries. By the early 1980s, however, the country's output of university graduates exceeded the state sector's capacity to absorb them, forcing an increasing number of graduates to accept jobs they considered beneath their station or to join the ranks of the unemployed. Paradoxically, a system of populist entitlements designed to reinforce the political loyalty of educated youth ultimately increased their expectations beyond the regime's capacity to deliver. It thus inadvertently produced an enormous reservoir of discontent that, in the more permissive political environment of the 1980s and early 1990s, could be exploited by the regime's opponents.

The Educated Middle Strata: Class or Status Group?

Before tracing the erosion of graduates' employment and earning prospects, let us clarify the nature of the group in question. Translating directly from the Arabic, *al-muta 'allimin* or *al-muthaqqafin* (the "educated" or "cultured" ones) are technically not a class but a status group, defined not by occupation, income, or relation to the means of production but by possession of a *shahada*, or formal educational degree. The possession of higher degrees in Egypt was historically associated with white-collar employment and, given the small size of the Egyptian private sector, primarily with technical, professional, and administrative positions in the state. Indeed, at the height of the Nasser era, the absorption of nearly all graduates into the state apparatus made the association between higher education and state employment virtually complete. Hence scholars referred to the educated strata as the "new middle class," a stratum characterized by modern, white-collar employment and a corresponding middle-class income and lifestyle.[1]

Beginning in the mid-1970s, however, the tight link between higher education and public employment in Egypt began to loosen. No longer able to absorb all eligible youth immediately, the government gradually lengthened the time between graduation and appointment until it approached ten years. As the prospects of immediate state employment waned, more and more graduates resorted to manual work in the informal sector (for example, as mechanics, carpet installers, housepainters, plumbers, and taxi drivers) or remained unemployed. Hence within a decade, a status group that had once corresponded to a distinct social class had come to assume a pyramidal structure, with older, established professionals at its apex and a large pool of young, economically marginalized graduates at its base. As later chapters show, it was the young, déclassé members of this status group — the "lumpen intelligentsia" or, simply, the "lumpen elite" — who became the Islamist movement's main base of support.

This chapter recounts how the overexpansion and subsequent exhaustion of the Egyptian state system of populist entitlements helped create an aggrieved constituency "available" for mobilization by Islamic groups. To begin, let us trace the overexpansion of the system during the "resource boom" of the late 1970s and early 1980s.

The Overextension of the Egyptian Patron-State, 1974–1983

In economic terms, the decade following the October War of 1973 in Egypt is best characterized as the era of the resource boom, with growth fueled by "windfall" revenues from sources outside the domestic economy's productive sectors. This resource boom was made possible by the *infitah*, Egypt's open-door economic policy. Initiated by President Sadat in the mid-1970s, the *infitah* entailed a series of legislative measures to attract foreign investment, stimulate the Egyptian private sector, and liberalize foreign trade.[2] The partial relaxation of state control over transnational flows of labor, capital, and goods facilitated the economy's growing extroversion. The Egyptian economy grew at an impressive average rate of 9.1 percent per year,

with the main contribution coming from four exogenous sources: oil revenues, workers' remittances, Suez Canal receipts, and tourism.[3]

Despite the rhetoric emanating from high circles about improving government productivity, efficiency, and discipline, both Sadat and Mubarak
channeled a large share of these "windfall" profits into the system of populist
entitlements they inherited from Nasser. Even during the boom times of the
infitah era, state spending grew at a faster rate than revenues, generating
chronic budget deficits that were financed through foreign debt.[4] First, public employment continued to expand. Between 1977 and 1981, at the height
of the country's purported economic liberalization, employment in the state
sector grew by an average of 6.3 percent per year, while the labor force grew
by an average of 2.8 percent per year.[5] Moreover, the state sector — that is,
government administration and the public-industry sector combined — remained the country's largest source of new jobs. Ragui Assaad estimates that
between 1977 and 1984, the state generated 55.3 percent of all new employment for Egyptians (including jobs abroad), or 70.7 percent of all new
employment inside the country.[6] According to the CAPMAS Population Census of 1986, the Egyptian state employed 3.78 million people, representing
nearly one-third of total employment and more than half of all employment
outside agriculture (see table 3.1).

The resource boom also helped finance a dramatic expansion of Egypt's
system of higher education. In a bid for popular support, Sadat opened the
country's national universities to an unprecedented number of students and
extended the system into the provinces. Between 1974 and 1978, seven new
provincial universities (Tanta, Mansoura, Zagazig, Helwan, Minya, Menu-
fiya, and the Suez Canal) were added to the existing four (Cairo, Alexandria,
Ein Shams, and Asyut, plus al-Azhar), as well as several new four-year higher
technical institutes and regional branches of established faculties. In addition to expanding the system's infrastructure, Sadat increased the proportion
of students admitted to university from roughly 40 percent of those who took
the baccalaureate exam in the early 1970s to more than 60 percent in the
late 1970s and early 1980s. This expansion broadened access and fueled
aspirations to higher education among students further down the social ladder, including thousands of students from the lower-class neighborhoods of
Egypt's provincial cities and towns. In just a decade, the country's annual
output of university graduates nearly tripled, rising from 41,916 in 1975 to
115,744 in 1985 (see table 3.2).

The rapid expansion of Egypt's graduate pool placed a heavy burden on
the government's guaranteed-employment scheme. By the 1970s the scheme

TABLE 3.1 Growth in State Employment, 1976–1986

A. *Employment Growth by Sector (%, 1976–1986)*

Government	43.7
Public enterprise	24.5
Private enterprise (10+)	7.8
Private agriculture	−6.4
Private nonagriculture	35.9

B. *State Employment (1976–1986)*	1976	1986
State employment (government and public-sector enterprise), in millions	2.75	3.78
As share of total employment (%)	27.20	32.20
As share of total nonagricultural employment (%)	52.65	2.40

Note: Employment figures are for domestic employment only; they do not include the unemployed or those working abroad.
Sources: Sectoral employment growth rates for 1976 to 1986 are from World Bank, *Egypt: Alleviating Poverty During Structural Adjustment* (Washington, D.C.: World Bank, 1991), graph 3.5, p. 45. State employment between 1976 and 1986 is calculated from Ragui Assaad, "Structural Adjustment and Labour Market Reform" (unpublished manuscript, May 1993), table 2. Both sources draw on the CAPMAS Population Censuses of 1976 and 1986.

covered all graduates with secondary school (intermediate), two-year technical institute (advanced-intermediate), and four-year university (higher) degrees. Available data indicate that in the late 1970s, slightly fewer than half of all university graduates and more than half of all intermediate degree holders sought public employment.[7] Graduates covered by the guaranteed-employment scheme received priority over other prospective employees in the state's hiring decisions. Indeed, by one estimate, they obtained roughly half of all new jobs created by the state from 1977 to 1981, even though in 1976 they constituted just 14.2 percent of the employed labor force.[8]

Maintenance of the guaranteed-employment policy was predictably expensive. First there was the literal cost, as indicated by the swelling government-wage bill, which in nominal terms doubled every 3.6 years, thus growing at an annual compound rate of 22.8 percent.[9] Second was the less tangible but no less real cost to bureaucratic performance posed by severe overstaffing. Already by the late 1970s, hidden unemployment in the state sector was

TABLE 3.2 Annual Number of University Graduates in Egypt, 1964/65–1984/85

Year	No. of Graduates	Growth Since 1964/65
1964/65	16,268	100 (baseline)
1969/70	23,016	141.5
1974/75	41,916	257.6
1979/80	76,125	467.9
1984/85	115,744	711.5

Population Growth, 1976–1986 (6 years +)

Average annual compound growth rate: 2.55%

Growth in No. of University Graduates (1974/75–1984/85)

Average annual compound growth rate: 10.69%

Sources: CAPMAS data from Muna al-Tahawi, "Tahlil zahirat al-bitala bayn al-muta'allimin fi Misr" [Analysis of the Phenomenon of Educated Unemployment in Egypt], in *Al-Bitala fi Misr: Al-Mu'tamar al-awwal li-qism al-iqtisad, 1989* [*Unemployment in Egypt: The First Conference of the Faculty of Economics, 1989*] (Cairo: Faculty of Economics and Political Science, Cairo University, 1989).

estimated to be between 15 and 50 percent. Moreover, as indicated by the average three-year time period between graduation and appointment, there was a substantial backlog of graduates awaiting government jobs even before the onset of fiscal crisis in the early 1980s.[10]

Perhaps most ominously, the steady growth in new graduate appointments reduced public salaries, at a time when wages in other sectors of the economy were rising. From 1974 to 1984, average annual GDP growth rates of 9 percent permitted per capita incomes to double, from $334 to $700.[11] New earning opportunities opened up in the highly lucrative fields of petroleum, banking, construction, and trade. At the same time, the construction boom increased the demand for various categories of skilled and unskilled labor, both within Egypt and in the oil-rich states of the Persian Gulf. The massive outflow of unskilled rural laborers into the construction sector created labor shortages in the countryside, leading to the tripling of real wages in agriculture between 1973 and 1984.[12] As wages rose throughout the private economy, between 1974 and 1984 in the public sector the real wages of white-

collar workers dropped by 8 percent, and those in government administration fell by 23 percent.[13]

The era of the resource boom coincided with a decline in the incomes
of degree holders relative to those of other groups in Egyptian society, as
well as with the emergence of new lines of stratification within the educated
middle class itself. The grievances of degree holders only intensified in the
1980s when, in the midst of a fiscal crisis, the Egyptian state attempted to
scale back the system of entitlements that had ballooned so large over the
preceding decade.

The Exhaustion of the Egyptian Patron-State, 1983–1991

Beginning around 1982, the collapse of world oil prices led to a prolonged
economic recession in Egypt and other oil-exporting states. With exogenous
revenues accounting for three-quarters of the Egyptian state's current-
account receipts and more than 40 percent of GDP,[14] the Egyptian economy
was particularly vulnerable to external shocks. Annual growth in GDP fell
from an average of 9 percent in the decade between 1974 and 1984 to
roughly 2.6 percent from 1986 to 1988, and beginning in 1986, per capita
consumption growth turned negative.[15] To address the "twin gaps" between
investment and savings and between imports and exports, the Mubarak regime increased its borrowing abroad. By 1988, aggregate debt exceeded 115
percent of GDP, with debt service amounting to more than 60 percent of
exports. In addition, the regime accelerated its use of deficit financing, contributing to inflation, which was conservatively estimated at 15 to 25 percent
per year.[16] Facing mounting pressure from external donors to reduce the
government's budget deficit, the regime cut back public spending from 63.5
percent of GDP in 1982 to 41.4 percent of GDP in 1989.[17]

Despite the growing budgetary constraints, the Mubarak regime continued to channel a large share of available funds into the "social contract."
Fearing a repeat of the 1977 "bread riots," the regime kept consumer subsidies at a high level (roughly 20 percent of GDP if implicit subsidies are
included) through the 1980s.[18] After the informal sector, the state was also
the largest source of new domestic employment. In his 1989 May Day
speech, President Mubarak claimed that the number of jobs created by the
state since 1982 had reached 1.2 million, or 170,000 jobs each year. He
explained: "This is because the private sector alone cannot provide enough
jobs for all the people who enter the labor market every year."[19] Despite

pressures for budgetary reform, state employment continued to expand, rising from 3.78 million in 1986 to 4.62 million in 1991.[20]

Graduates covered by the guaranteed-employment scheme took most of the new state jobs. Indeed, according to one estimate, in the early 1980s they received more than 90 percent of new jobs in the state sector.[21] The diversion of public resources from growth and services to the government's mushrooming wage bill indicates the priority the Mubarak regime placed on the absorption of new graduates. Above all, this priority reflected the regime's concern about the political risks of massive educated unemployment.

The Phenomenon of Educated Unemployment

Owing to the rapid expansion of Egypt's education system, a growing share of the roughly 400,000 to 500,000 workers entering the Egyptian labor market had intermediate and university degrees. Egypt's labor force grew by about 2.2 percent per year from 1976 to 1986, whereas the supply of graduates grew by 7.4 percent per year.[22] Hence just as the Egyptian economy was entering a period of recession, there was an enormous influx of new graduates seeking work. Classified reports circulating in various government ministries revealed some alarming trends. In 1987, an internal study by the Ministry of Labor warned that only 29.8 percent of new university and intermediate-level graduates were being directly absorbed by the domestic labor market. A parallel study by the Cabinet Information and Decision Support Center in 1991 indicated that the domestic labor market was employing only 25 percent of new university and intermediate-level graduates but that it was hiring 90 percent of those who were illiterate or in the next-to-last educational category of "can read and write."[23]

Open unemployment among graduates was reflected in the lengthening queue for government jobs. Unwilling to abandon the guaranteed-employment scheme yet unable to hire graduates right away, the government simply extended the waiting period between graduation and appointment. For university graduates, the waiting period between graduation and appointment increased from three years for the class of 1979 to nine to ten years for the class of 1985, with the waiting period for intermediate graduates an average of one year longer than that of university graduates.[24]

Simultaneous with the slowdown in graduate appointments, the "safety valve" provided by outmigration came under strain. Through the early 1980s, the economies of the oil-rich Gulf states were an important outlet for

Egyptian labor. According to the government's Egyptian Emigration Survey (EES), 1.2 million Egyptians were working abroad in the mid-1980s. Although 56 percent of Egyptian migrant workers had little education (primary degrees or lower), 13 percent had university degrees.[25] Moreover, a study presented in 1990 at a CAPMAS-sponsored conference on Egyptian migration reported that a quarter of university graduates were working abroad in 1986. Then, falling oil prices led to an economic slowdown in the Gulf, depressing the demand for Egyptian workers.[26] Finally, political disturbances in the late 1980s and early 1990s triggered a massive wave of return migration from the Gulf, including an estimated 390,000 workers from Iraq and Kuwait as a result of the Gulf War.[27]

The introduction of an unprecedented number of graduates into the Egyptian labor market during a period of regional economic contraction led to a sharp rise in educated unemployment. Official census figures indicate that the rate of unemployment in Egypt rose from 2.2 percent in 1969 to 7.7 percent in 1976 to 12 percent (or 1.65 million people) in 1986. They also reveal that open unemployment was primarily among those with intermediate and university degrees entering the labor market for the first time. According to the population census of 1986, more than three-quarters (76.4 percent) of the unemployed were new entrants to the labor force, and within this group, 91 percent had at least an intermediate-level degree. Thus even though degree holders (intermediate-level and above) accounted for only about one-third (32.0 percent) of the total labor force in 1985, they made up three-quarters (74 percent) of the unemployed. According to the 1986 census, the unemployment rate for intermediate-degree holders was 28.8 percent and for university graduates was 25.5 percent.

Educated unemployment remained a serious problem into the 1990s. According to the 1991 CAPMAS Labor Force Sample Survey (LFSS), 1.46 million Egyptians were unemployed, of whom 78 percent held at least an intermediate degree.[28] It is possible that the official figures grossly underestimated real unemployment. In 1991, U.S. embassy officials estimated total unemployment in Egypt to be between 2.5 million and 3 million, nearly double the official government estimate.[29]

The Problem of Educated Unemployment in Public Debate

Beginning around 1988, the problem of unemployment, and educated unemployment in particular, became the subject of intense public debate. For the first time, the once-sacrosanct legacy of free higher education and guaranteed employment came under attack, not only by academics and opposition figures, but, most strikingly, also by leaders in the state itself.

It is difficult to determine who first brought the issue of educated unemployment to the public eye, but officials of the Engineers' Association claim that distinction: "We at the Engineers' Association were the first to utter the word 'unemployment,' in 1988. At that time the government was still trying to hide the information, as it was afraid."[30] In late December of that year, the association, then under Islamist leadership, sponsored a public forum, "Unemployment Among Engineers." Association officials claimed that the fifteen research papers presented at the forum represented the first "objective study" of unemployment among professionals.[31] Most often cited was the finding that about 30,000 engineers were currently unemployed, most of whom were under the age of thirty-five.

Another candid discussion of educated unemployment appeared in an *al-Ahram al-iqtisadi* (*Economic al-Ahram*) editorial in October 1988. In a poignant appeal, the editor in chief, Essam Refat, departed from the technical economic commentary for which the journal is known:

> As the problems accumulate, I receive dozens of letters from university graduates asking me to help them get a job. In fact, although I try to welcome whatever I receive by way of letters, and care greatly about what is written in them, I now stand helpless in the face of this phenomenon. And I suffer, as I cannot help anyone.[32]

It was not until 1989, however, that the problem of educated unemployment — and, by implication, the broader system of state entitlements to which it was linked — became a major focal point of public debate. In addition to several academic conferences on the subject,[33] the issue of unemployment was raised in parliament, in the annual conference of the ruling National Democratic Party (NDP), and President Mubarak's annual May Day speech. It was also the focus of numerous articles in both the official and the opposition press.[34]

Once the issue of educated unemployment became a subject of public debate, the Mubarak regime attempted to use the discussion for its own purposes, seeking ways to extricate itself from populist commitments inherited from the Nasserist past. At conferences, on television, and in the press, regime spokesmen warned graduates and their families that they must shed unrealistic expectations and learn to accept manual and vocational work. As the minister of planning, Kamal al-Ganzuri, stressed at the annual NDP conference in 1989, in the coming period, "the issue [of unemployment] will be an issue of the people as a whole, and its solution will be in their hands and not in the hands of the government alone."

This viewpoint was the dominant, but by no means the only, message contained in the state's rhetoric. Some government officials also wanted to defend the "revolutionary gains" of the Nasser era. This perspective was most closely associated with socialist-leaning politicians in the state establishment, the most visible being Rif'at al-Mahgub, speaker of the People's Assembly, although its sympathizers included influential senior bureaucrats and, to some degree, the president himself. Their warning cautioned against a retreat from populist entitlements, partly on ideological grounds and partly on the grounds that such a move was likely to provoke a massive protest. At the annual NDP conference in July 1989, Rif'at al-Mahgub confirmed that in the future, the private sector must help create jobs, but, he insisted, reform of the current system could take place only on condition that it did not violate the right of the citizen to work. He concluded with the promise that the "employment of graduates and free education and the subsidy system will remain despite all the difficulties."[35]

Perhaps most revealing of the conflicting forces shaping the regime's policy was the tentative position staked out by President Mubarak himself. He repeatedly expressed his commitment to an economic reform program which, he admitted, would bring hardship in the short term.[36] At the same time, however, the president portrayed himself as standing up to the International Monetary Fund (IMF) in order to protect the Egyptian people. For example, in his 1990 May Day speech, Mubarak referred to the IMF as the "Fund of Misery" and asserted that "the country's economy can only be reformed gradually." In a televised speech at Alexandria University in July 1992, the president again challenged both the pace and content of proposed reforms:

When we started the five-year plan in 1982, many economists told me during our meetings: Mr. President, the situation requires a courageous step. What sort of courageous step? They said: Cancel subsidies, cancel free education, lay off 25% of the government's employees. Oh no!

Reduce the Army, they said. The Egyptian Army supports every citizen; it backs the Egyptian people. . . . Who makes up the Army but our own sons? If you were to reduce the Army, what would you really be doing? You would be dismissing your own sons. People have sons and brothers in the Army. These sons would have nothing to do outside the Army and would become unemployed. What would you do then?[37]

In sum, the president tried to have it both ways, taking credit for undertaking urgently needed economic reforms, on the one hand, while claiming to defend the Egyptian people against such reforms, on the other.

By the mid-1980s there was a growing awareness — both inside and outside the Egyptian government — that a large pool of graduates had emerged that the modern sector of the economy could not absorb. That the government allowed the problem of educated unemployment to gain such visibility and, indeed, acknowledged it so starkly reveals the urgency of its search for a solution.

Graduate Entitlements in a Period of State Retrenchment and Reform

Beginning in the early 1980s, the state's shrinking revenues forced the Mubarak regime to scale back the guaranteed-employment scheme. Yet rather than abandon it wholesale, the regime retreated by stealth: extending the time between graduation and appointment; allowing the wages for standard, entry-level jobs to lag behind inflation; and devising alternatives to civil service employment for new graduates.[38]

The financial burden posed by the guaranteed-employment scheme remained enormous, even though the benefits it provided were far less generous in the 1980s than they had been in the past. Under simultaneous pressure to increase employment and reduce the budget deficit, the Mubarak regime allowed the prime burden of adjustment to fall on state salaries. According to the World Bank,

> As the government struggled to maintain a full employment economy, it did so by dividing the wage bill among an expanding workforce. Real wages plummeted as inflation surged. The real wages of workers in the public sector failed to keep pace with those in the private sector. Government workers suffered the largest reductions in real wages.[39]

While average wages in the private sector remained constant and public enterprise wages fell only slightly, by 1987 the salaries of government employees had fallen to slightly more than half (55 percent) their level in

1973,[40] forcing employees to hold second or even third jobs to make ends meet. Despite spending ever larger shares of the state budget to finance graduate employment, the government was still unable to guarantee its employees a decent wage. Meanwhile, the burden of maintaining such a large workforce had left government services in a debilitated state. As the World Bank observed,

> The social ministries are faced with the paradox of spending most of their budget on salaries at the expense of indispensable supplies and other non-wage expenditures while, at the same time, being unable to offer a level of remuneration sufficient to motivate their teaching force and health personnel.[41]

The growing time lag between graduation and appointment and the decline in real wages associated with guaranteed jobs encouraged significant attrition from the "waiting list." Through the mid-1980s, about half of all university graduates applied for government jobs, but in the late 1980s, that proportion had dropped to slightly more than one-third.[42]

Unfortunately, there are no systematic data on the social profile of graduates on the "waiting list." However, anecdotal evidence gathered by me, Egyptian government officials, and other researchers suggests that the applicant pool has become increasingly rural, female, and/or lower-middle class, reflecting these groups' more limited alternatives.[43]

At the other end of the spectrum, urban upper- and upper-middle-class graduates expressed no interest in the guaranteed-employment scheme. Consider, for example, the results of my informal survey in the spring of 1991 of thirty university students in an upper-division political science course at the American University of Cairo, a private college attended by children from elite families. When asked if they planned to apply for a government job through the Ministry of Manpower and Training (MMT), twenty-eight said no, and the two who said yes specified that they sought jobs in the Ministry of Foreign Affairs (an elite state agency that does not accept graduates from the MMT but has its own highly competitive selection process). When asked why they did not want guaranteed government jobs, respondents cited the poor quality of the jobs ("boring," "not stimulating"), low pay ("they won't make a living"), limited promotion opportunities ("no future"), and long time lag before appointment. In addition, one respondent frankly admitted that if she took a guaranteed government job, she "wouldn't be working with people of my same class or social standard."

Beyond such explanations, many of those surveyed treated the idea of a guaranteed government job with derision — "It's a joke," "It's useless," or, as one respondent wryly put it, "They won't miss me."

Despite the growing awareness of the urgent need for reform, the regime's withdrawal from the guaranteed-employment scheme was slow. Reform was hindered by the scarcity of funds for other options and by the persistence of countervailing impulses in the state establishment, including populist impulses, bureaucratic self-interest, and, above all, the fear of political repercussions. Even the most senior architects of reform acknowledged that more drastic reforms were not politically feasible. Although the IMF categorically denies that it placed any conditions on Egypt concerning graduate employment,[44] several government officials alluded to such pressure. As 'Atif 'Ibed, minister of cabinet affairs and a leading proponent of reform, observed:

> The IMF tells us we have to reduce the government labor force. Suppose I could muster the political will and let go 50 percent of them — where are they going to go? If you let them go, you will end up with social instability; some will become drug dealers or criminals. We would be taking a huge political risk. The best way is to give graduates the opportunity to take the decision for themselves on a voluntary basis: lift the restriction on taking leaves, offer retraining in areas where jobs are available in the private sector, and keep the government pay scale as low as possible, to discourage them from entering the system.[45]

Similarly, when asked whether the government would ever fire any of the surplus civil servants, a senior administrator at the Cabinet Information and Decision Support Center replied:

> Absolutely not. That could not happen. Ultimately what determines decisions here is a political, not an economic, logic. We accept the IMF's point that we need to streamline the civil service, but we will find the means of doing that which are appropriate to Egypt. Firing people is not one of them. So we are trying to come up with alternatives — like providing incentives for early retirement, and so on. Sure, these schemes are expensive, but we can fund them with external donor support. The president, in his last Labor Day speech, compared the size of our civil service with those of other countries, implying ours was too big. Sometimes just openly admitting these things has a po-

litical meaning. But he is not going to do anything too drastic or too quick.

Perhaps most revealing of the popular pressures constraining the regime's latitude for reform were the comments by a senior official in the Central Agency for Organization and Administration (CAOA):

> The system of guaranteed employment helps the poor graduates find jobs. It helps those without influence, patrons, and money. If you do away with the system, you will hurt the poor most. And he — [here, he pointed above his head to the portrait of President Mubarak] knows it. He knows that when the poor graduate can't find a job, he will get mad, grow a beard [*yirabbi da'nu*, to become religiously committed], and curse the government, holding it responsible for his problems. . . .
>
> The IMF puts all this pressure on us, but they don't understand. If I let go all these extra civil servants, where will they all go? They'll take him [that is, the president] out of his seat. And naturally he wants to stay in power.[46]

The Reform of Higher Education Policy

The tension between "rational" technocratic and political considerations also complicated the regime's efforts to reform the country's system of higher education. Beginning in the late 1980s, government officials sought to link educational policy more closely to the demands of the labor market. In practice, this meant shifting students from the universities to postsecondary vocational institutes. The regime's efforts to restrict university enrollments, however, aroused opposition in both government circles and the public at large, to whom the idea that all citizens have the "right" to a free university education remained strong.

As noted earlier, during the era of the resource boom, the Egyptian government launched a major expansion of the Egyptian university system. University admissions increased from 68,127 in 1977 to a peak of 93,486 in 1983. Reform of the system followed the onset of a fiscal crisis in the early 1980s. After 1983, admissions began to fall, slowly at first and then more rapidly by the end of the decade. In 1990/91, Fathi Surur announced that 65,579 students would be admitted to the university, representing a return to the "preboom" levels of the mid-1970s (see table 3.3).

TABLE 3.3 Change in University Admissions, Enrollments, and Graduates, 1977/78–1989/90

Year	No. Admissions	No. Enrolled	No. Graduates
1977/78	68,127	433,199	64,966
1978/79	71,422	443,696	71,071
1979/80	79,050	458,809	74,143
1980/81	89,026	[479,080] (563,150)	77,579 (81,863)
1981/82	91,048	508,438 (611,452)	82,227 (86,841)
1982/83	93,409	530,756 (659,635)	85,973 (93,660)
1983/84	93,486	552,512 (681,704)	96,333 (106,622)
1984/85	86,440	553,313 (682,348)	101,043 (115,744)
1985/86	84,280	527,433 (661,347)	105,073 (119,216)
1986/87	82,897	507,772 (629,723)	98,972 (115,106)
1987/88	82,299	502,532 (604,846)	97,081 (112,615)
1988/89	75,375	482,972 (587,033)	96,335 (103,641)
1989/90	66,990	467,611	89,548
1990/91	65,579		

Sources: *Supreme Council of Universities Handbook*, March 1993; CAPMAS *Statistical Yearbooks* of 1987 and 1990. Numbers in parentheses are from the CAPMAS *Statistical Yearbooks* of 1987 and 1990 and include graduates of al-Azhar. The number of enrolled students in 1980/81 (in brackets) is approximate, as it was misprinted in the *Supreme Council Handbook*. The data for 1990/91 are from press reports quoting Fathi Surur, minister of education, in *al-Wafd*, June 30, 1990, and the *Middle East Times*, August 28–September 3, 1990.

To reduce enrollments, the Supreme Council of Universities (the quasi-independent body that oversees university admissions and higher education planning more generally),[47] reduced the percentage of college-entrance exam takers admitted to the university, from more than 60 percent in the early 1980s to slightly more than 45 percent in the early 1990s. In addition, in 1991 the Supreme Council of Universities announced that beginning the next year, the university entrance exam would include two advanced subjects in addition to the regular exam. Those students who passed the regular exam but not the advanced subjects would be admitted to a vocational higher institute rather than a university.[48]

The government's efforts to push students into secondary and post-secondary vocational programs ran up against the popular obsession with university degrees. As one senior CAOA official wryly observed:

The government pays for students' education. And parents want their children to have the degree for social status, so they can say "my son has a university degree"; that way he's better than the son of the next-door neighbor. That is the most important thing. It's the greatest reason people seek university degrees. It doesn't matter how much the educated son earns. Some boys work in a car repair shop or a bakery and earn a decent living. But I want my son to sit around waiting for his government job, at which he'll earn 50 pounds a month after waiting for seven years. That's how it is: we are society of degrees.[49]

Another CAOA official noted that popular resistance to reform percolated up to senior decision makers by way of the ruling party:

The NDP party officials in the villages and districts, they sit with the people and hear them out. Then, when the NDP holds its national convention, they tell the NDP leaders: "Our people are complaining"; they want their children to get into university or to get jobs. In this way their voice reaches the top.[50]

In the areas of both guaranteed employment and higher education, the regime opted for a middle path, seeking to reform the system of entitlements without provoking social unrest. A total overhaul of the system was mandated on rational-technical grounds, but according to senior government officials, this was not an option. Reforms were blocked by bureaucrats with an ideological or institutional stake in the entitlement system as well as by popular expectations of continued state largesse. In regard to the latter, what is most striking is that even though Egypt's authoritarian leaders were formally insulated from popular demands, they believed they could not openly defy them without jeopardizing the regime's survival.

Despite the implementation of cautious reforms, the core pillars of the entitlement system — free higher education and guaranteed employment — remained intact. Hence it was the dilution of the gains offered by the system, rather than any decisive retreat from it, that most seriously undermined the regime's ability to co-opt educated groups. During the 1980s and early 1990s, the benefits offered by the patron-state were dwarfed by those available through the market. Access to lucrative positions in private and joint-venture firms, however, required specific skills, such as fluency in a foreign language or computer training, that many graduates lacked. As the market came to play a greater role in determining graduates' job prospects, Egypt's "new

middle class" splintered into different tiers. Among recent graduates, stratification followed class lines, with the prospects of lower-middle-class graduates limited to low-paid government jobs, entry sales positions, and manual
work in the informal sector, whereas the offspring of the country's socioeconomic elite were eligible for high-paid professional, technical, and administrative jobs in the private sector.

The Stratification of Egypt's Graduate Pool: Some Preliminary Evidence

The sketchy wage data prohibit a systematic comparison of entry-level
graduate salaries across and within the private, joint-venture, and state sectors
of the economy. Nevertheless, by culling information from a variety of
sources, I was able to derive some rough estimates of the monthly earnings
associated with entry-level positions in different sectors (shown in table 3.4).

TABLE 3.4 Estimated Typical Monthly Compensation for Entry-Level Positions
in the Early 1990s (in Egyptian pounds)

Regular government administration (Ministries of Health, Education, Local Administration)	70 (including base pay and allowances)
Elite government administration (Ministries of Justice, Finance, Petroleum)	150–250 (plus bonus and incentive pay)
Sales position, private Egyptian firm	120–150 (or up to 200 with bonus and incentive pay)
Accounting, computer, and secretarial positions in multinational corporation	400–600 (including bonus and incentive pay)
Geologist or petroleum engineer, multinational corporation	700–800 (including bonus and incentive pay)

Note: In April 1991, 2.61 Egyptian pounds equaled 1 U.S. dollar.
Sources: Staff of the Office of Graduate Administration, Ministry of Manpower and Training;
"Needs Assessment Survey," American Chamber of Commerce, 1991, survey of 61 joint ventures and foreign-owned firms; in-house survey of total compensation packages in six multinational petroleum firms, 1991; interviews with job recruiters and printed job listings at the
employment fair at the American University in Cairo, December 8, 1990.

The lowest-paid graduates work in local branches of state government, that is, in the village, district, and governorate branches of the Ministries of Health, Education, and Local Administration. In the early 1990s, the starting salary for such graduates was about 70 pounds per month (about $30) including base pay and allowances. Hence, Ministry of Manpower and Training officials emphasized, they were truly among the poor (al-ghalaba). Jobs in joint ventures and foreign firms stood at the opposite extreme. Such jobs represented only 2.5 percent of total wage labor in urban areas but were in high demand because, particularly in the areas of finance and petroleum, they offered generous salaries and benefits.[51] For example, a survey of private firms (most of which were joint ventures or foreign-owned firms based in Cairo) conducted by the American Chamber of Commerce in Egypt in 1990 and 1991 indicated that they paid new recruits between 400 and 600 pounds per month.[52] Furthermore, according to an in-house compensation survey of six foreign petroleum firms operating in Egypt, salaries for an entry-level engineer or geologist at Conoco in 1989 ranged between 450 and 750 pounds per month. Together with bonuses and allowances,[53] total compensation ranged between 7,500 and 11,000 pounds per year, or an average of 770 pounds per month. The same survey found that comparable positions at ARCO-Suez offered total earnings of about 10,000 pounds per year. Graduates in joint ventures and foreign firms thus stood to earn roughly twelve times as much as their counterparts in local government administration did.

The differentiation in salaries corresponded directly to differences in graduate qualifications and, indirectly, to differences in class background. This is because lower-middle-class graduates of Egypt's public universities typically lacked the qualifications sought by private firms. The jobs posted at the employment fair at the American University in Cairo offer a case in point. Every year, the private, fee-based, American University in Cairo hosts an employment fair, a free-of-charge service linking prospective employers with its alumni and graduating seniors.[54] Seventy-seven companies participated in the fair in 1990, including multinational engineering, chemical and construction firms, international hotel chains, and international financial and consulting firms. Most of the posted job listings sought graduates with degrees in engineering, computer science, or business administration; other qualifications were cited as necessary or desired. Most common was fluency in the English language. Several jobs also required specific computer skills. Finally, some listings sought specific personality traits, such as graduates who were "ambitious," "self-motivated," "aggressive," or "resourceful," with "excellent communication skills" and strong "analytical and intuitive abilities." Other listings stressed that graduate applicants must be "presentable," have a "pleasant personality," or "own a car."[55]

Several recruiters noted that American University of Cairo graduates were more likely to fill such requirements than were graduates of Egypt's national universities. According to one recruiter quoted in the university newspaper *Caravan*, its graduates were in demand "because of the quality of their education and the style and pattern of their thinking."[56] Employers also saw American University graduates as possessing superior social skills by virtue of their upper-class backgrounds. Such skills were deemed especially important in the areas of sales and tourism. When pressed on the subject, the representative of a leading foreign-owned hotel chain I interviewed admitted that a lower-middle-class female graduate wearing a *higab*, or Islamist head scarf, would not meet their requirements, explaining that "employees must be able to relate to customers and know how to handle their needs."[57] The recruiter for a large American consumer chain concurred. The company targets American University graduates, he noted, "because they are well educated and because they are well groomed and come from good family backgrounds." By selecting graduates whose families "can pay a fortune for education," the company is "guaranteed graduates of a certain social level."

Beyond the walls of the American University in Cairo, thousands of graduates entered the labor market each year in search of jobs offering middle-class status and incomes. But in a context of state retrenchment and slow private-sector job growth, the search for a "respectable" white-collar job often proved elusive. Graduates unable to find permanent white-collar employment joined the growing ranks of the "lumpen intelligentsia," not unemployed so much as forced to accept jobs they perceived as beneath the dignity of someone with a university degree.

Mechanics with a University Degree: Egypt's "Lumpen Intelligentsia"

What fate awaited lower-middle-class graduates in a period of state retrenchment and reform? To gain a clearer sense of their options, I conducted open-ended interviews with a sample of twenty-seven recent graduates. All the respondents were from "typical" lower-middle-class backgrounds, with family incomes averaging about 250 pounds per month.[58] Nearly all were male (26 of 27) and lived in *sha'bi* (popular, lower-middle-class) neighborhoods in Greater Cairo (25 of 27). Although some of the respondents were unemployed at the time of the interview, nearly all had earned money during the previous year from odd jobs, a temporary job, or a permanent position. Their responses are summarized here in narrative form.

After leaving university and completing their military service, the graduates began their search for work. A few managed to secure a job in the Gulf, working abroad for a few years and returning with enough savings to buy an apartment, get married, and, in some cases, establish a small business. Most graduates, however, lacked the connections and resources needed to acquire work abroad, and so they concentrated their search on the local job market.

Most graduates aspired to white-collar jobs in their academic field of specialization. The respondents stressed that such jobs were few in number and required *wasta* (personal connections). Furthermore, they often required special qualifications or previous work experience, which they lacked. Several graduates recounted the experience of applying for a desirable job listed in the newspaper, only to discover that hundreds of other graduates were competing for the same job. In some instances, they paid an application fee, sat for an exam, were interviewed, but were not chosen for the position.[59]

The crucial role of personal and family connections in obtaining work in a "clean" establishment (for example, a bank or insurance company) was emphasized by nearly all the graduates I interviewed. When asked, "What are the most important factors in obtaining a good job?" most cited connections first. As one graduate put it, "If a bank opens up ten jobs and hundreds apply, the ten chosen will each have *wasta* of some kind." Even more telling was the fact that nearly all the graduates who had succeeded in obtaining work in public and private-owned firms had relied on help from friends or relatives. In some cases, they had been informed of an internal job search in a firm or had been recommended for a position; in other cases, the graduate or his benefactor (for example, a father, cousin, or friend) knew the personnel manager or office director personally.

Most graduates employed in the formal sector had jobs in sales, advertising, or services. Typically, graduates were employed as sales representatives (*mandubin*), with part or all of their earnings coming from commissions. After passing a three-month "testing period," they were hired on a one-year, renewable contract. Total earnings for typical entry-level sales jobs ranged from 120 to 150 pounds a month, occasionally rising to 200 pounds with bonuses and incentive pay. Although few graduates objected to this level of compensation, many complained about the long hours and physically exhausting nature of the work, as well as the lack of job security. One graduate noted that he worked from 11 A.M. to 11 P.M. each day. "The private sector gives you one *'irsh* [cent] but requires effort equal to ten *'irsh*," he noted. "You can be let go at any time," another explained, "depending on the ups and downs of the market."

Other graduates found work in the informal sector of petty manufacturing and services. One graduate worked in a small industrial workshop; others worked as plumbers, carpenters, housepainters, or electricians. Some graduates had learned a trade during their student years and had returned to it during summer vacations for extra income. In a few cases, they ended up working in a family-run workshop or small business. Most of these graduates described their resort to manual work as temporary. However, noting that some of their peers had yet to find paying jobs of any kind, many said they were grateful to have a vocational trade to fall back on.

In the early 1990s, the plight of university graduates seeking work received extensive coverage in the opposition press. For example, in March 1990, *al-Wafd* ran a series entitled "Diary of an Unemployed University Graduate," in which an investigative reporter took a leave of absence and recounted his own "long days of suffering" on the job market.[60] Other articles exposed private companies that made a profit charging graduates a fee to apply for illusory jobs; hiring graduates as sales representatives on a provisional basis and releasing them after they had worked for several weeks or months without pay; or listing jobs for "secretaries" or "house managers" as a means to lure young women into prostitution.[61] One article in *al-Wafd* featured a photograph of a coffeehouse filled with idle youth and quoted the unemployed graduates sitting at the tables. When asked about his search for a job, one law graduate replied,

Where are all these jobs? They are for the favored sons [*awlad al-mahasib*], not for me. As for the poor people like us, there is no work. I graduated from the Faculty of Law in 1987 and till now I am still looking for a job. A lawyer needs some income to live on during the period of apprenticeship with a big lawyer who teaches you the practice. And even though most of the work falls on the shoulders of us young lawyers, the wages we get are extremely low, and sometimes there is no wage at all. So how am I supposed to learn to practice law without any resources to live on, for rent or food or drink or other expenses? And anyway, I'm not from Cairo, and I don't have any relative to stay with.

So I left law and went to work in advertising for one of the monthly journals, but that work requires a thief and not someone with a conscience ... so I didn't stay in that work long. ... Then I read an advertisement looking for a supervisor in a private school, and of course I failed because I am not fluent in a foreign language or, to be more precise, because I didn't have the necessary connections. So then I went to one of the publishing houses that needed a sales representative to market its publications, and I passed all the tests and interviews, and the director promised me a position and asked for my papers (my diploma, military service card, birth certificate), so I brought them at the appointed time, only to find out that the position I had been promised had been filled by someone else, a person I had never seen before, who had not been there during the testing period. So what am I supposed to do now? Should I resort to crime? And God knows, it is only my fear of God that has stopped me from doing so. Should I look for a job abroad? I don't have anywhere near the amount I would need to travel. ... The only thing I do now is go to the coffeehouse, and may God forgive those in power in our country.[62]

Minister of Manpower and Training Asem abd al-Haq and other state officials repeatedly called on educated youth and their families to "give up their degree complex and accept the idea of manual labor."[63] Although the graduates I interviewed strongly preferred a white-collar desk job, under economic pressure some had become more resigned to manual work, particularly as a temporary substitute for a "real" (that is, white-collar salaried) job. As one graduate explained:

I am ready to do any kind of work, work in the street, anything, I won't say that's 'eb [shame]; I've gotten used to it. Others feel — "Because I have a baccalaureate, I won't do work that's below me." That's when he gets the idea to go abroad. Here he can't accept a lowly job, he says, "my dignity won't allow it, won't let me wash dishes in a restaurant," says that would be impossible. So he sits at home and becomes a burden on his family. That's if his father can provide for him. If he can't, then he's forced in spite of himself to work.

The graduate earned about 400 pounds a month working a taxi in the afternoons. Then, a month before our interview, he received a letter offering him a guaranteed government job. He planned to accept the appointment and continue his work as a taxi driver in the afternoons. Like many other graduates, he aimed to combine the social status of a white-collar job with the earning power of a trade. In explaining why he would accept the government job offered him, he noted,

> I'm just buying a name [that is, social status]. I'm trying to get both, status and money; when you want to marry, you need both. If you tell the family of a girl you're interested in marrying that you have a government job but you're only earning 70 pounds a month, they tell you to finish your tea and go home. And if you're just a plain taxi driver and the girl is educated, they also might not agree.

As other graduates explained, holding an office job offers a graduate "prestige," "safeguards his social standing," and "looks good." In addition, despite their low starting salaries, government jobs offered graduates opportunities for promotion and a pension upon retirement.

Even when resigned to vocational work, many graduates continued to regard it as "beneath their station" (*mish min mustawaya*). Many graduates considered work in the service sector demeaning, whether it was selling products, waiting tables, or answering phones. As an official of the Commercial Employees' Association told me, a history of weak private-sector development in Egypt had reinforced negative attitudes toward commercial activities. In particular, the act of trying to persuade someone to buy something was perceived as humiliating, and the notion of selling was associated with offering and receiving bribes. Just as male graduates looked disdainfully at sales work, female graduates viewed secretarial positions as shameful, that is, as implying some sort of subservience to or improper relationship with the boss. "Everyone wants to be a manager or a supervisor," one association official complained.

> The graduates want a job where they can sit at a desk, with a pen and a telephone. They don't want to be out on the streets. The salaries aren't that important. What counts is the prestige, thinking he's not less than the next guy. It's a psychological complex. He wants to be a human being who can look you in the eye and say "good morning" [that is, maintain his self-respect].[64]

The poignant image of a university graduate forced to accept a job beneath the dignity of a degree holder was routinely exploited in the Egyptian press. Articles included interviews with graduates who had accepted menial positions in the modern sector, for example, working as maids, launderers, waiters, dishwashers, or porters in the tourist sector. Others emphasized their having to work in the informal sector. For example, one article focused on university graduates who hawked fruit, shoes, cosmetics, and underwear at the Ataba open-air market in Cairo. One underwear vendor declared, "I only employ graduates! And only if they come with connections!" The same article quoted a graduate who was employed as a tea server in a coffeehouse. After a fruitless search for an office job, he had settled on waiting tables and had made his peace with it:

> I am happy with this work . . . it's better than extending my hand to beg or resorting to crime! It's gotten so that I'm not embarrassed by it anymore; I don't concern myself with the fact that I'm a university graduate. Everyone is equal these days, the world is that way. . . . Everyone here knows I'm a lawyer and I'm serving tea. They call me, "Ya muhami, wahid shay min fadlak!" [Hey attorney, one tea please!], and I rush over to them with the tray in my hand.

A second article focused on graduates selling books, incense, and tooth-picks in front of mosques, and a third profiled a university graduate who had resorted to reciting the Qur'an in the cemetery in exchange for a few piasters. In each case, graduates insisted that no work is shameful as long as the means of earning a living was *halal* (religiously permitted).[65] Although some graduates had a positive outlook on their job prospects, others were bitter. For example, one law graduate interviewed worked as a housepainter, earning 300 to 400 pounds per month. Despite making what he acknowledged was a good income, he was angry because he was forced to breathe in toxic paint fumes that might shorten his life; if he fell off his ladder and got hurt, he would receive no disability pay or insurance; and the demand for his services was uneven, depriving him of a steady income. Moreover, as more graduates learned a trade, his high earnings were likely to diminish. What was needed was a "total overhaul" of the present system, with a change of leadership at the top. He concluded, "The government keeps us quiet by leaving us no choice but to run around in circles in search of a piece of bread."

For other graduates, the single greatest source of anxiety was the problem of *al-madda*, or inadequate financial resources. In the early 1990s, numerous articles and cartoons highlighted the gap between the monthly earnings and expenses of young government employees. For example, one article focused on the plight of the "destitute civil servant" in a context of rising prices. The report claimed that even though salaries had risen by 75 percent (presumably in the 1980s), prices had increased by 231 percent. As a result, employees had replaced the old slogan "a job for every employee" with the new slogan "two jobs for every employee," noting that the only choice for the civil servant today was to take an additional job or take bribes and engage in other illicit activities.[66]

Although graduates working in private firms enjoyed somewhat higher earnings, they too found it difficult to accumulate enough savings to get married. According to prevailing social customs, the costs related to marriage and setting up an apartment represented the greatest financial challenge a male graduate would face in his lifetime.[67] A young male graduate and his family, either independently or together with the bride and her family, needed to save money for the engagement gift (shabka, usually a gold ring and several gold bracelets); the wedding celebration; the "key money" (khil-iww) to reserve a rented apartment or, rarely, the far greater sum needed to purchase one; and furniture for each room of the new apartment. According to the youth director of a community center in one sha'bi neighborhood of Cairo, a young man needed a minimum of 6,000 pounds to get married. Some graduates cited higher estimates of 10,000 to 15,000 pounds.

The graduates I interviewed noted that the surest way to accumulate the funds necessary for marriage was to work in the Gulf for a couple of years. But now that there were fewer such opportunities, they had to rely more heavily on help from their families or postpone their marriage. As a twenty-seven-year-old graduate explained:

> When I entered university, I knew there were no decent jobs in Egypt, but I thought I'd have the chance to work abroad, save some money, get married, establish a home, and live like anyone else. But there weren't any opportunities to work abroad. Now there's no way I can get married for quite a while because I don't have the money. If I had the money, I'd get married today; I'd stop talking to you and get married this afternoon. But it will take at least five years until I can even think about marriage.

To ease the heavy financial burden of marriage, some couples lowered their expectations, agreeing to a one-room apartment or even a room in their parents' home. In addition, it became more common for couples to split the start-up costs more equally, rather than placing the main financial burden on the man. Nevertheless, graduates stressed that the parents of many girls refused to accept a marriage proposal unless an apartment and major appliances were purchased in advance, according to the logic that once postponed, they might never be bought at all.

The huge start-up costs turned marriage into a virtual "mission impossible." As one graduate admitted, "Marriage is considered impossible because the costs are very high and our incomes are very low." In the socially conservative milieu of *sha'bi* neighborhoods, where dating was not an option, the high costs of marriage forced many lower-middle-class Egyptian men and women to delay an adult sexual life well into their thirties. To the disappointment of failing to obtain a job commensurate with their educational degree thus was added another source of frustration.

Conclusion

A central legacy of the Nasser era was a system of free higher education and guaranteed employment that promised graduates entry into the country's "new middle class." While the system conferred real benefits, it also reinforced the dependency of lower-class graduates on the state, generating expectations that could be met only through ever increasing intervention by the state. It was not an abandonment of the system so much as its overexpansion and dilution that diminished the system's incorporating power. Extended to a wider circle of beneficiaries, the quality of higher education deteriorated, civil service wages fell, and the time lag between graduation and appointment lengthened. While the value of state entitlements decreased, the rewards of the market increased both in Egypt and abroad. As Fu'ad Hashim of the Arab Investment Bank explained, "The position of the civil servant has declined since the start of the *infitah*. It's not so much that his situation has worsened but that more attractive, better-paid alternatives were created. The government horse continued at the same speed. But the new horse started to gallop."[68] For graduates with marketable skills and social connections, the liberalized economy offered new opportunities for economic advancement. Yet for graduates without such advantages, the gold ring represented by the rewards of the new economy remained beyond reach.

By the late 1980s, the phenomenon of educated unemployment had become a major focus of public attention, but it was only one facet of a broader predicament. While many graduates described themselves as unemployed, few could afford to "sit home waiting for a government job." Instead, to earn an income, they were forced to accept menial jobs outside their field of specialization. Hence the greater problem was the gap between graduates' career aspirations and their actual employment and earning opportunities. Given their status as degree holders, lower-middle-class graduates blocked from permanent white-collar employment experienced a blow to their *karama*, or dignity. As one graduate noted,

> The educated get shocked faster. They are in school for eight or nine years, and in the end, after all that patience and sacrifice, they may have to sweep streets, or clean anything, something they consider not of their station, and in the end, they get appointed to a job that pays a base amount of 60 pounds per month. With all that, it's not surprising that many of them look at things from a view of despair.

The decline in the economic prospects of university graduates was all the more vexing because of the simultaneous ascent of less-educated strata able to tap into the new job opportunities available through the market. An editorial in *al-Watan* alerted readers to recent advertisements placed by foreigners and wealthy Egyptians, including one for a housekeeper offering 500 pounds a month and one for a nanny offering 800 dollars per month. Brimming with indignation, the editorial observed:

> Believe it or not, these and similar advertisements appear in the daily papers in the classified section. The salary of a maid has reached three times that of a public-sector manager, or two and a half times that of a general director, and ten times the salary of a university graduate, even of graduates of the Faculties of Medicine![69]

In sum, it was the growing perception that worldly success depended more on connections and luck than on merit and sacrifice that generated the greatest grievances among Egyptian university graduates. How Islamist groups converted such grievances to their own political advantage is discussed next.

4 Parties Without Participation

No one can do anything. If I saw a mass demonstration going on, of course I'd join it. But as long as I don't see any demonstration, what am I supposed to do? Stand on the street with a sign that says "Down with Mubarak"? If I did, it would take the security forces only a few minutes to throw me in the back of a van and put me in prison. And what purpose would that serve?

—An Egyptian graduate's response to the question of why young people don't get involved in politics, spring 1991

By the mid-1980s, a large number of Egyptian graduates found themselves blocked from the upward mobility they had come to associate with possession of a university degree. But their frustrated ambition did not automatically give rise to Islamic activism. No matter how great their grievances, citizens may lack the motivations, resources, and opportunities to participate in opposition politics. Hence collective grievance is as likely to generate political alienation and abstention as political protest.

To explain the rise of Islamic activism in Egypt, we therefore need to look beyond the frustrations of educated youth and examine how and why Islamist groups succeeded in mobilizing them into politics. As noted earlier, authoritarian leaders typically use the administrative, legislative, and coercive powers at their disposal to limit opposition groups' access to the mass public. This begs the question: under what conditions is mobilization by opposition groups even possible in authoritarian settings?

Put simply, the prospects for mobilization are better in "semi-open" authoritarian regimes than in fully closed ones. Authoritarian regimes differ in their *propensity* and *capacity* to use the state as an instrument of control. Historically, the state's penetration of society reached a peak in the "totalitarian" regimes of Nazi Germany and Stalinist Russia. In the Third World, the self-declared revolutionary regimes that seized power in the era of decolonization (see chapter 2) also utilized the state to penetrate society, but their aspirations for control largely exceeded their capacity to achieve it.[1] More generally, authoritarian regimes are sometimes willing to accommodate or are unable to prevent the existence of public institutions with a substantial degree of autonomy. The classic example, as described by Juan Linz, was the Franco regime in Spain after World War II.[2]

How deeply an authoritarian state penetrates society not only varies across regimes but also is subject to change within a single regime over time. As state control over society is — deliberately or inadvertently — relaxed, the space for autonomous mobilization expands. In the Middle East and elsewhere in the Third World, authoritarian elites have cautiously experimented with political reform, permitting the resurgence of independent political activity in some arenas while continuing to suppress it in others. In Egypt, political liberalization began under Sadat in the mid-1970s and continued under Mubarak through the early 1990s. During this period, the regime's revolutionary impulse waned and was replaced by a more narrow concern with self-maintenance. The single party atrophied as an instrument of popular mobilization, and the dissemination of propaganda through the state-run media and schools was scaled back. In addition, the government legalized several opposition parties and allowed them to compete for seats in parliament, as well as to publish their own newspapers and journals.

But political reform in Egypt was partial and uneven. As this chapter explains, authoritarian leaders closely regulated the activities of the country's legal opposition parties, preventing them from developing into effective vehicles of political representation. At the same time (as described in chapter 5), on the margins of the formal political order, there emerged a large and decentralized network of Islamic institutions with a substantial degree of autonomy. Partial and uneven liberalization thus created a political system with a hollow core and a dynamic periphery, in which Islamists barred from contesting power within the formal party system diverted their activity to institutional outlets outside the regime's control.

This chapter highlights a central paradox: political reform did not bolster — but, ironically, undermined — the legitimacy of Egypt's formal political institutions and elites. The shift from one-party rule to an ersatz form of democracy led to widespread alienation among the country's educated youth, regardless of their partisan affiliation (or lack thereof). And as chapters 6 and 7 show, the Islamists drew on this "culture of alienation" to make a powerful case for Islamic reform.

Between Accommodation and Control: The Contradictions of Regime-Led Liberalization

In the mid-1970s, President Anwar Sadat initiated a controlled retreat from the Nasserist system of single-party rule. This political opening began in 1975 with Sadat's recognition of alternative platforms (*manabir*) — right, left, and center — within the Arab Socialist Union and their participation in elections for the People's Assembly in 1976. Encouraged by the overwhelming victory of the center, Sadat permitted the conversion of these platforms to legal political parties. From the beginning, however, admission to the party system was restricted to only a few actors. For example, the Political Parties Law (law 40 of 1977) excluded parties based on class, religion, or regional affiliation.[3] The practical result (and, most likely, the unstated intention) was to bar the two groups with the greatest capacity for popular mobilization — the Nasserists and the Muslim Brotherhood — from forming their own parties.[4] By restricting participatory rights in this way, the regime created a new category of political actors, those groups and movements whose existence was tolerated but that were denied formal legal status (*mahgub 'an al-shar'iyya*).[5]

Sadat not only confined participation to a small and rather artificial set of parties but also restricted their right to political expression. For example, criticism of the regime was to be "constructive" and was not to attack Sadat's major reorientation of Egyptian foreign and economic policy. As Hinnebusch notes, when they crossed these boundaries in 1978, both the leftist National Progressive Unionist Party (NPUP) and the liberal-right New Wafd Party were effectively banned from open political activity. In the years just before Sadat's assassination in 1981, there were only three legal parties: the ruling National Democratic Party and two "loyal" opposition parties (center right and center left) headed by politicians close to the regime and lacking ties to a mass base.[6] Just as important, parliament failed to develop into a site of independent power. As president, Sadat retained control over the direction of state policy. Furthermore, since the ruling party controlled an overwhelming majority of seats in parliament, the latter served more as an instrument of regime prerogative than a constraint upon it.[7]

How should we judge Sadat's experiment in political reform? On the one hand, he can be credited with launching Egypt's transition to a multiparty political system, strengthening the civilian judiciary, and reducing the role of the secret police.[8] On the other hand, Sadat curtailed the representative character of the new system from the outset and progressively undermined it with increasingly heavy-handed tactics, culminating in a massive crackdown on all opposition forces in June 1981.

Suspended just before Sadat's assassination in October 1981, controlled liberalization resumed under Hosni Mubarak. First, Mubarak affirmed his commitment to growing freedom of the press,[9] and indeed by the mid-1980s the print media included a number of opposition newspapers that were openly critical of the regime. Also under Mubarak the judiciary displayed a substantial measure of assertiveness and independence, as in a series of high-profile decisions challenging the constitutionality of legislation introduced by the regime.[10] Mubarak's willingness to accommodate public institutions with a significant degree of autonomy reflected the modesty of his own political agenda. As Hinnebusch observed, "Having no 'mission' comparable to Sadat, Mubarak can afford to be more tolerant of opposition, and since his legitimacy rests squarely on legality, he has a greater interest in respecting it."[11]

Finally, the multiparty system was further institutionalized during Mubarak's first decade. Parliamentary elections were held in 1984, 1987, and 1990, and the number of legal parties was expanded to thirteen.[12] (Several new parties gained legal status in the administrative courts, where they successfully challenged their exclusion by the government's Committee for Political Party Affairs.)[13] Mubarak's approach to the nonviolent Islamist opposition during this period stood midway between accommodation and exclusion. The Muslim Brotherhood maintained its own national and regional offices; issued public statements; and published its own journal, but it was barred from forming its own party. Although it technically remained an illegal organization, the Brotherhood was allowed to participate in the 1984 and 1987 elections as a junior partner of the Wafd and Labor Parties, respectively, and in 1987, Brotherhood candidates also ran as independents. In the 1980s and early 1990s, the Brotherhood ran its own candidates in elections for the governing boards of many of the country's student unions, university faculty clubs, and professional associations (see chapter 8).

Optimistic observers initially heralded Egypt's experiment in political liberalization as the country's first steps toward democracy. For example, Michael Hudson wrote in 1991 that "there have been some remarkable rumblings of political liberalism and even democratization in the past several years. . . . Egypt under President Hosni Mubarak is perhaps the 'trail-blazing' case."[14] Yet rather than propel Egypt toward democracy, controlled liberalization produced a new variant of authoritarian rule, one that is best described as "limited" or "restricted" pluralism.[15] This was in fact the outcome intended, for neither Sadat nor Mubarak ever favored a full democratic transition in Egypt. Above all, neither leader was willing to relinquish his hold on power, although both also articulated a broader rationale for the slow pace of political reform. For example, President Mubarak argued that the country's highest priority was to achieve economic reform, which would require national unity rather than debate and dissension. In his May Day speech of 1989, President Mubarak called on

> all democratic parties and groups to put aside, even momentarily, their differences over public work so that all patriotic efforts could be focused on positive cooperation to achieve the undisputable national goals, over which people should not differ.
> . . . Brothers and sisters, political action is patriotic work. There is little room for controversy, campaigns, and exchanges of accusations; the toiling masses will not tolerate them.[16]

The president also claimed that neither the Egyptian masses nor the opposition parties themselves were mature enough to function in an open democracy. As he observed in a speech at Alexandria University in July 1992,

> We are suffering from irresponsible political party activity. I understand that political party activity must be for the homeland's and the citizens' benefit. The party that does not act for the good of the citizens and to improve their living standards — to tell you the truth — does not deserve to live. In our democracy, we exploit the citizens' simplicity. We have a high rate of uneducated people. Because of this simplicity and the high rate of uneducated people, we can infuse very dangerous ideas into the people's minds. Democracy can be soundly established when you have educated people, people who can read and write. Are you asking me to open the door wide with the illiteracy rate I have here? If this will work, please tell us.[17]

Egypt's experiment in political reform was self-limiting from the outset, designed not to transform the authoritarian regime but to preserve it.[18] The transition to a multiparty system was arguably intended to strengthen the authoritarian system by enhancing its capacity to contain and moderate dissent. During Mubarak's first decade of rule, several opposition groups, including nonviolent Islamists, gained representation in the People's Assembly.

Opposition members drafted bills, submitted questions and interpellations, and raised issues for debate. But given the weakness of parliament and the NDP's dominant position in it, the role of the opposition was limited to that of "parties of opinion" with no real influence over state policy.

Finally, Egypt's opposition parties failed to develop into effective vehicles of interest aggregation and representation. Most important to our purposes, they failed to give the country's growing "lumpen intelligentsia" a stake in the process of political reform.

Parties Without Participation

Throughout the 1980s, Egypt's legal opposition parties were roundly criticized for failing to develop effective linkages with the broader constituencies they claimed to represent. As the *Arab Strategic Report* of 1988 observed,

> There is no doubt that the lack of a popular base is a problem characterizing all the Egyptian parties, both those with and without power. It is one that has characterized these parties since their inception, and what is cause for alarm is that over time it has tended to grow rather than diminish in intensity.[19]

Criticism of the parties' distance from the mass public reached a fevered pitch in the early 1990s in a context of escalating conflict between government security forces and militant Islamic groups. In particular, critics alleged that the parties' failure to mobilize disaffected youth created a vacuum in which militant Islamic groups thrived. For example, in a 1990 editorial on the violence in the Upper Egyptian village of Abu Kourkas, 'Ali ed-Din Hilal Dessouki wrote:

> It was not strange for what took place to occur or for it to be repeated in other places because of the general atmosphere present in the country. There is an almost total absence of all the political parties from the field of public work among the citizens except the Islamic political groups. . . .
>
> We should blame for this not these groups but other parties and other official institutions responsible for youth, which have chosen the easy way and held back their presence in the real effort among the masses, preferring, or considering it sufficient, to fire off articles in

the newspaper or to hold showy media activities or to show unjustified interest in sports issues, imagining that these ways will keep the youth busy, away from other issues, and ignoring the real interests of youth.[20]

Party officials candidly acknowledged their isolation from the mass public. As Rif'at Sa'id, a senior leader in the left-wing NPUP, pointed out,

All the political parties are isolated from the people. We are like boats floating on a river. Some of us trail longer anchors than others, but we all are floating on the surface, even the Islamic associations. The overwhelming majority of the citizens are simply not politicized.[21]

How large was the popular base of Egypt's legal opposition parties? An attempt to capture the size and composition of opposition party cadres and the manner in which they are recruited is hindered by the weakness of available data. Among the few sources of published information on party membership is the *Arab Strategic Report* (*Al-Taqrir al-istratiji al-'arabi*), published annually by al-Ahram's Center for Political and Strategic Studies, though its coverage of the topic varies from year to year.[22] In addition to tapping what information was available in print, my inquiry included several interviews with senior party activists in three major opposition parties — the liberal-right Wafd, the Islamist-oriented Labor Party, and the leftist National Progressive Unionist Party (the NPUP).[23] By piecing together and comparing evidence from different sources, we can draw some tentative conclusions about the size and profiles of opposition party cadres in the 1980s and early 1990s.

Although led by elder statesmen with a long history of political struggle, all of Egypt's main opposition parties relied on a committed core of young activists. Many of the latter obtained their political experience in student groups on university campuses and continued their political activity after graduation. As Mahmud Abaza, youth secretary for the Wafd Party explained, "The *shabab* [youth] who graduate, begin a family, and remain politicized — those in their thirties and forties are the backbone of all the parties except the governing National Democratic Party, which is built on the notables."[24] The size of each party's activist core was actually quite small. My own observations at three parties' headquarters in Cairo suggest that in the early 1990s each party had at most one or two dozen full-time party activists (either paid or volunteer), most of whom produced the party newspaper rather than doing outreach at the grassroots level.

How many people were involved in party activities? Given the absence of reliable data, we must depend on firsthand reports. Opposition party officials claimed that they could gather a few thousand supporters to attend rallies or demonstrations in exceptional circumstances (such as at the height of the Gulf War). However, they acknowledged that the number of people who regularly attended party events was much smaller, ranging from several hundred to a few dozen.

More broadly, none of the country's legal opposition parties constituted a national, mass-based organization with a strong presence at the grassroots level. The Wafd Party was heir to a long history of popular agitation before 1952 and maintained a strong presence in several provinces in the Delta, but its presence was based more on ties of kinship and notability than on organization and ideology. Wafd leaders admitted that their party organization was weak in large urban areas, with popular outreach confined to the publication of *al-Wafd*, the country's only daily opposition newspaper. Both the Labor Party and the NPUP aspired to mass party status, but in practice their activities were, for the most part, limited to publishing a weekly newspaper, issuing public statements, and holding seminars and conferences at party headquarters. Both parties also had official youth organizations, but the scope of their membership and activities appeared to be small.[25]

Despite the small size of their activist core, all three opposition parties claimed to enjoy much greater levels of support in Egyptian society at large, although it is impossible to obtain an accurate count of opposition party members. In authoritarian settings, opposition parties have compelling reasons to conceal the identity of their members. The leftist NPUP, for example, decided to burn all membership applications in 1977 for security reasons.[26] Apart from security concerns, Egyptian opposition parties generally lacked a centralized system for tracking membership. Since membership lists were not regularly updated, they often included the names of individuals who had permanently emigrated or died.[27] At the same time, party officials stressed that some of their supporters were not officially registered as party members.

It is thus not surprising that estimates of opposition party membership vary wildly. The *Arab Strategic Report* of 1988 noted that firm data on party membership do not exist and that self-reported figures often appeared to be grossly exaggerated.[28] The NPUP is a case in point. According to the *Report*, the NPUP claimed 250,000 members, but in 1994 an Egyptian scholar reported that after undergoing a reregistration process, the NPUP had published a membership figure of between 17,000 and 18,000.[29] This wide discrepancy suggests that at the very least, different definitions of membership were being applied. More generally, it calls into question the accuracy of self-reported data on party membership.

However large a base the opposition parties claimed, few of their alleged supporters actually participated in party activities. Leaders in all three opposition parties claimed tens of thousands (if not hundreds of thousands) of supporters, and although we would not expect all of them to attend a party seminar or rally, the enormous gap between alleged members and actual participants is nevertheless striking. Citizens' noninvolvement in opposition politics reflects the legal, political, and psychological barriers to political participation erected by the authoritarian state. Such barriers are elaborated on next.

Structural Barriers to Participation

Opposition parties' outreach to the Egyptian public occurs under the watchful eye of the authoritarian state. Egypt has been ruled under a state of emergency nearly without interruption since June 1967.[30] Emergency laws augment the state's authority to monitor, arrest, and detain those suspected of activities deemed threatening to national security. They also restrict the exercise of the freedoms of speech and assembly guaranteed by the Egyptian constitution in ways that hinder party efforts to recruit support.

The state of emergency, together with other authoritarian laws and procedures carried over from the Nasser era, has limited the formation of party cadres in two ways, (1) by hampering outreach by legal opposition parties and (2) by altering the cost-benefit calculations of potential recruits.

The primary channel of contact between Egypt's legal opposition parties and the mass public is the party newspaper. Indeed, the primacy of the opposition press has led critics to speak derisively of "newspapers padded by political parties."[31] Reliance on the party newspaper is clearest in the case of the Wafd Party, whose daily newspaper *al-Wafd* had an estimated circulation in 1991 of between 150,000 and 180,000.[32] Mahmud Abaza of the Wafd confirmed the importance of the party newspaper: "The newspaper takes all our energy; it is our spoiled child. Without it, the party would fall. It is our only permitted connection with the masses."[33] Reliance on the written word reflects the Wafd Party's emphasis on persuasion rather than mobilization at the grassroots level. As Mahmud Abaza explained, the party "depends on consensus, not organization."

Both the NPUP and the Labor Party published weekly newspapers. The circulation of the NPUP's paper, *al-Ahali*, was reported at about 150,000 in the mid-1980s but appears to have declined precipitously since then.[34] The Labor Party (SLP) published the Islamist-oriented weekly *al-Sha'b*, edited from 1985 to 1993 by the well-known Marxist-turned-Islamist 'Adil Hussein.[35] Circulation figures for *al-Sh'ab* vary widely, from 50,000 to 130,000 weekly.[36] According to Magdi Hussein of the SLP, the party does not have exact figures, but before the Gulf War it published about 100,000 copies per week. During and immediately after the Gulf War, however, its circulation increased to 250,000. "It was very popular during the war," he noted. "People would buy twenty copies and distribute them to friends. If someone couldn't find it, they'd borrow it from someone else. One newspaper would be read by twenty people."[37]

The opposition media faced a number of structural limitations. First, they confronted supply-side constraints, such as the lesser quality of the newsprint available to them and their reliance on advertising revenues (rather than state subsidies) to cover printing costs.[38] In addition, there were pressures to engage in self-censoring and instances of harassment and detainment of newspaper staff by state security agents.

Although the opposition parties were allowed to express their views in print, various laws restricted their access to "the street." Holding an outdoor party rally or conference was illegal without a permit; indeed, under the emergency law, any meeting of six or more individuals "for political purposes" was technically illegal.[39] As Magdi Hussein of the Labor Party explained, "There are restrictions on our activities due to limits on freedom of assembly. We are allowed to hold activities in places where only a few hundred can fit. For example, seminars are allowed only inside our headquarters. The place itself limits the extent of participation."[40]

The Ministry of Interior also prohibited the distribution of opposition party literature in public places, thus limiting citizens' familiarity with them. As the *Arab Strategic Report* noted, "Parties need to attract citizens not only to their ideas but also to their headquarters in order to make those ideas known."[41] As a result, participation in party seminars and gatherings was limited to members and others already sympathetic to the party's goals.

On special occasions, the parties could shift their activities into the public domain. For example, most parties held a national conference at least once every several years. In addition, parties were allowed to campaign for support before parliamentary elections, by holding open-air rallies or distributing campaign literature. Yet party organizers knew that state security agents were

ever present. For example, at an open-air rally for NPUP candidate Fathi
Mahmud in the popular neighborhood of Ezbekiyya, held shortly before the
1990 elections, the lead speaker criticized the ruling-party candidates for
"forgetting the people who are smaller than they are," noting that "those
who sit in luxury and eat pineapple don't know the poor person's problems
or even care." Then he addressed his remarks directly to the security officers
presumably on site:

> I know what I'm saying is being recorded and that the security forces
> are paying attention, and I want them to listen well. You fear political
> instability? The common people are calmer and more peaceful than
> anyone. In the end, the police, the military, and the security forces
> are the people. Politics depends on the treatment of the people.[42]

Some party officials stressed that their commitment to operating within
the bounds of the law limited their contact with the public. As Mahmud
Abaza explained, "Ever since the Wafd became a majority party [that is,
before 1952], it has depended on elected representatives, not on militant
organization." The Wafd, he claimed, placed greater emphasis on legality
than did its leftist and Islamist counterparts, which hindered its ability to
conduct political outreach at the grassroots level: "The laws constrain us.
For example, we can't do political work in the universities. That is against
the law; it is criminal activity and can be punished legally. This doesn't affect
the Islamists and the Communists as much because they operate underground." Similarly, he noted, the Wafd does not hold public demonstrations,
because "legitimate forces must act in legitimate ways." Confining their work
to legal channels was not simply an expression of principle; it also protected
Wafd Party members from the repressive arm of the state. As Abaza reasoned,
"It would be virtually impossible to hide anything from the security forces
anyway; hence it is better to have nothing to hide."

Magdi Hussein of the Labor Party likewise observed that self-imposed
limits eroded the party's effectiveness: "The government wants a superficial
opposition. It confines parties to expressing acceptable differences of opinion. The parties are expected to limit themselves to this role, and this makes
them weak."

In addition to restricting opposition parties' outreach to the mass public,
the overwhelming presence of the authoritarian state altered the cost-benefit
calculations of potential recruits. Given the powerlessness of Egypt's opposition parties and of parliament in general, citizens were apt to discount

the utility of political involvement. As Magdi Hussein pointed out, "There isn't much activism because democracy is absent. The citizen feels getting involved in the public sphere is a waste of time, that it will have no benefit. There is no sense of the importance of public work."

In addition, the authoritarian state threatened to punish citizens who did participate in opposition politics. For citizens not sufficiently constrained by daily economic struggles, the risk of harassment, imprisonment, or worse served as a powerful deterrent. As Magdi Hussein noted:

> Citizens feel the presence of the state. . . . Some people are not willing to sacrifice their lives; they don't want to go to prison. In addition, there are the difficulties of daily life: to get married, you need to struggle to earn enough income, and this takes up all one's energy and time.[43]

In addition to the risk of arrest or imprisonment, politically active citizens confronted more subtle forms of pressure. Rif'at al-Sa'id recalled an instance when the families of NPUP members were denied permits to visit Port Said's duty-free shopping zone; in another instance, the police took down the names of party members in a town on the Red Sea and submitted them to the joint-venture company they worked for, which subsequently threatened to fire them. In both cases, al-Sa'id noted, the party asked the members to resign for their own protection. Such tactics also undermined the NPUP's ability to provide health and education services in urban neighborhoods. As al-Sa'id explained:

> How does the government combat us? Let's say we open a small health clinic or a literacy class. The police find out who is coming to it, and they go to the father of the person involved and tell him: "Your son is going to that place of the communists; you better tell him to watch his step." They deprive us of possibilities by pressuring people.

Such pressures weighed not only on the potential beneficiaries of party services but also on those who were prepared to offer the party their resources and time. According to al-Sa'id, a party cannot legally accept more than 500 pounds from a single individual without disclosing his name. Some supporters were willing to give the NPUP far more than that but refrained from doing so because they were afraid their names would be reported to state security. Al-Sa'id cited the example of a prominent doctor with leftist sympathies who was willing to treat party members free of charge. When al-Sa'id asked if he could mention the offer in print in order to reach a larger client base, the doctor said no, because he was afraid. Under these circumstances, al-Sa'id maintained, "you've got to be a hero" to get involved in politics.[44]

Al-Ightirab: Political Alienation Among Lower-Middle-Class Educated Youth

The shift to a multiparty system might have been expected to offer aggrieved sectors of the mass public greater representation in the formal political system. In particular, we might have expected it to encourage higher levels of participation — for example, increased electoral turnout and party membership — among lower-middle-class educated youth.

But rather than create new incentives for participation, Egypt's experiment in controlled liberalization only served to deepen graduates' alienation from formal political institutions and elites. Borrowing from Schwartz, I define political alienation as "attitudes of estrangement from or lack of identification with the political system."[45] In the tradition of the nineteenth-century French social theorist Emile Durkheim, Western scholars once viewed political alienation as an outcome of the disruptive transition from agrarian to modern industrial society.[46] For example, Kornhauser argued that industrialization, urbanization, and related trends led to the breakdown of integrative social structures and the rise of a "mass society" characterized by "anomie," or normlessness. The political consequences of modernization were grim, as the atomized individuals of mass society became alienated from the established political order and susceptible to manipulation by antidemocratic elites.[47]

The problem with such broad formulations is that the complex social conditions associated with "modernity" have in fact generated a wide range of political responses, ranging from system-threatening alienation to system-enhancing attitudes of civic efficacy and trust. Those aspects of modern society that may contribute to political alienation therefore require further specification. My contention is that political alienation is better viewed as a response to particular aspects of a country's dominant political institutions than as a product of "modernity" writ large.[48]

What causes political alienation? We might conceive of it as a response to authoritarian rule, but the causal links between regime type and alienation are actually more complex. Some authoritarian regimes enjoy genuine popular support because of the personal charisma of their leader, the appeal of their programmatic agenda, and/or their performance, for instance, in restoring law and order or distributing goods and services. "Authoritarian-populist" regimes cultivated support in these ways, as was the case under Nasser, Vargas, and Perón. At the same time, political alienation can surface in democratic settings. Rather than conceptualizing political alienation as a function of regime type, I contend that it is rooted in perceptions of political exclusion. Moreover, I propose that whether citizens feel excluded depends on their perception of the following three aspects of the formal political system:

1. Whether existing leaders and institutions represent them (they share and promote their values, interests, and objectives).
2. Whether the system is efficacious (it has the capacity to translate their values, interests, or objectives into desired outcomes).
3. Whether the system is open to change (those in power are accountable to the electorate and can be replaced through peaceful means).

In sum, citizens' orientation to the formal political order depends on whether, and to what degree, they perceive it as *representative, efficacious,* and *accountable*.[49] Of course, the relative importance of each factor varies for different groups and individuals. Nevertheless, we can hypothesize that alienation is greatest when citizens perceive their political system as deficient in all three categories.

How does an authoritarian regime's movement toward political liberalization affect aggregate levels of political alienation? To the extent that a shift to multipartyism strengthens citizens' perceptions of the country's political elites and institutions as representative, efficacious, and accountable, we would expect it to reduce political alienation. But the formal shift to a multiparty system does not necessarily engender such changes. If the parties of the new system are viewed as unwilling and/or unable to represent the interests and values of societal groups, levels of alienation may not decline. Similarly, if political contestation remains circumscribed, the shift to a multiparty system may not enhance the perceived accountability of the country's most senior power holders. Indeed, it is possible that the shift to a multiparty system could actually deepen political alienation if the new order were viewed as less efficacious (and scarcely more representative or accountable) than the one it replaced.

Given the absence of public opinion survey data, we cannot compare levels of alienation among different social groups in Egypt or determine whether and how they have changed over time. Nevertheless, there is considerable impressionistic evidence of two trends: first, that levels of political alienation are particularly high among urban educated youth and, second, that their alienation may have increased since the onset of political reform.

The Culture of Political Alienation

Pointing to the low voter turnout in parliamentary elections, the widespread cynicism toward politicians, and the lack of popular affiliation with established parties, Egyptian commentators have argued that Egyptian political culture is increasingly characterized by alienation (*al-ightirab*), defeatism (*al-salbiyya*), and indifference (*al-la-mubalah*). Furthermore, although it is not confined to one segment of society, this "culture of alienation" appears to be most pronounced among the educated youth of Egypt's cities and provincial towns.

When exactly the problem of alienation surfaced, how widespread it is, and whether it has increased over time are matters of debate. Egyptian scholars and journalists have been writing about the phenomenon since at least the early 1980s. After the assassination of President Sadat in 1981, a series of articles on the "crisis of youth" appeared in the Egyptian and wider Arab press; several books on the subject were published; and the "massive alienation of the younger generation" became a focus of public discussion.[50] Public debate on the causes and consequences of alienation escalated in the early 1990s, in a context of growing concern about the flow of educated youth into militant Islamic groups.

Despite widespread acknowledgment of the "crisis of belonging" affecting Egyptian youth, its precise boundaries are difficult to define. There are no nationwide opinion surveys on the subject. While several smaller-scale surveys in the mid-1980s indicated that most university students did not participate in any kind of political activity whatsoever, they did not systematically explore the reasons for this abstention.[51]

The following discussion is based on a series of in-depth, open-ended interviews with twenty-seven recent university graduates. All the graduates were residents of lower-middle-class or "popular" (*sha'bi*) neighborhoods in Cairo, and nearly all were male. In order to find out the graduates' political attitudes before their mobilization by opposition groups, my sample excluded any graduate who identified himself or herself, or was identified by others, as affiliated with a specific political group or trend.[52] Although the graduates I interviewed were not "representative" in any statistical sense, there is no reason to believe they were atypical. Although I cannot be certain that the frequency with which the views expressed by those in the sample accurately reflect those in the broader graduate pool, it is probable that the spectrum of views represented indicates the range of opinion held by the graduate pool at large.

My interviews with a sample of recent graduates found a general pattern of estrangement from formal political institutions and elites. At the same time, they revealed a pervasive skepticism concerning the possibility of systemic change and the utility of personal effort to promote it.[53]

Most of the graduates I interviewed were preoccupied with the struggle to earn a livelihood. Compared with earlier generations, they explained, their situation was far worse: the white-collar jobs for which they had been educated were scarce; the available jobs did not pay well; and the opportunities for temporary work in the Gulf had dried up (see chapter 3). A large majority of respondents believed that neither the government nor any opposition party offered a solution to graduates in economic distress. When asked whether government leaders were aware of their problems, most respondents said yes. When asked to explain the government's inaction, however, their responses varied. According to one strand of opinion, the problems facing Egypt were so great that no government, no matter how well intentioned, could resolve them. "Our country's been exhausted by four wars," one graduate noted. Or as another observed: "The government is doing the most that it can." Is there anything more it could do? "No, there isn't. As long as the country is in debt, there is no solution." Similarly, another graduate asserted: "No matter who took power, he wouldn't be able to solve the problems." By contrast, other respondents claimed the real problem was one of political will. According to this view, government leaders had failed to confront the problems of educated youth because their priorities lay elsewhere. As one graduate put it, "Everyone works for his own interest only; no one cares about youth."

Most graduates also viewed the country's legal opposition parties as either unwilling or unable to represent them. A majority of respondents said they felt no connection with political parties, had little information about party platforms and candidates, and doubted the utility of political participation. The comments of Samir,[54] a recent economics graduate, are typical: "Parties are just names in our country; I don't belong to a party, nor do any of my friends. Most young people aren't very interested in politics. Politics isn't for youth; it's for older people."

In addition, some graduates claimed that people joined parties only in pursuit of private ends. As Akram, an engineering graduate, explained, "I don't have any affiliation. I feel people join parties for personal reasons, to benefit somehow. Belief in ideology was important before, like when the British were here and people felt patriotic."

The graduates claimed that opposition party leaders were not seriously committed to solving the problems of youth. As one graduate maintained: "Words are nice, but there is no implementation. They need to collect votes, so they claim to be concerned about the problems of youth, but when they're in power, they don't do anything."

Or as another graduate observed: "The people in the parties are too busy fighting one another; as to a solution to youth's problems, there isn't one [mafish]."

A few graduates noted that even if the parties did come up with solutions, they lacked the means to implement them. As Shihab, a literature graduate, said: "The parties don't have the power to do anything. They don't care; they don't try to find solutions. But even if they did have an idea, they would be unable to carry it out. The NDP controls parliament and doesn't allow the other parties to carry out their plans."

According to many graduates, the greatest obstacle to positive change was the nature of "the system" [al-nizam] itself. Some blamed the nature of the state apparatus, particularly the bureaucratic red tape and inertia that undermined governmental performance. As one graduate noted:

> The government tries; it plans, but the plans don't get implemented. The main problem is certain individuals in the bureaucracy. They follow the routine, there's no flexibility; it's also a problem of coordination. The land reclamation schemes are a good example: the graduates go out there in the desert and find out there isn't any water or electricity. The government promises to provide them, but it doesn't happen.

Hence, many graduates stressed, the state apparatus (gihaz ad-dawla) needed to be reformed before their problems could be addressed. In addition to the suffocating weight of bureaucratic routine, respondents claimed that individuals inside and outside the state hampered the implementation of solutions out of self-interest or indifference. Politicians and bureaucrats were more "worried about keeping their seats" than about assuming responsibility for bold new initiatives, and rich Egyptians were unwilling to invest their money in Egypt. As one graduate explained:

The new cities are a good idea. But those who should be investing in them are parasites, who focus on trade in imports and exports. They don't want a risk, they want a fast return and an assured profit. Most capitalists will not launch projects for youth because that opposes their own interests. They act not in the national interest but in their own selfish interest.

Even when graduates could identify dedicated and energetic public officials, they insisted that the "system" muted their impact. As one graduate noted:

Isma'il Sabri 'Abdalla, for example, he is very smart. He looks out for the people, not the government. But unfortunately the decisions are made up above. The ministers know only how to criticize. The result is to stifle any new initiatives.

Or as another graduate exclaimed,

Even if I had some good ideas, some solutions to the problems, and I told a minister or something, he wouldn't be convinced. And even if he was, he wouldn't implement it, because it comes from someone underneath. It's a type of backwardness we have here. . . . There's always talk that Egypt is progressing. Who are we advancing beyond? Only those who are even more backward, like those in the Gulf.

In regard to the three components of regime legitimacy noted earlier, the graduates' critique of the political system extended beyond complaints about the government's performance (or efficacy) to encompass deficiencies in the system's representativeness and accountability. In response to open-ended questions about the country's political life, several graduates lamented the enormous gulf separating those at the apex of the political pyramid from those at its base. As one graduate asserted: "There shouldn't be such a large distance between those in power and the youth. Our views don't reach the leaders. We want to say, 'Come a little closer.' You should give us more importance; you shouldn't neglect us."

When asked what advice he would offer to the government, another graduate replied:

I would do as 'Umar ibn al-Khattab [the second caliph in seventh-century Arabia] did. I'd see what problems people had. I wouldn't go to Zamalek [an affluent neighborhood in Cairo]; I'd go to the *furn* [bread oven located in popular neighborhoods] and see what they were selling. I'd go on a surprise visit. I'd go down to the streets and live an ordinary life and see what the problems were and find whoever was doing something wrong and take him to account and throw him out.

The most pervasive theme in the graduates' critique of the political order was the lack of accountability in all spheres of Egyptian life. The rich get richer from illicit means and no one stops them; public figures exploit their positions for private gain; judges and policemen take bribes; and individuals get ahead through connections rather than through merit or hard work. The graduates repeatedly stressed that the system encouraged the rich and the powerful to behave with impunity, alleging that "there are no principles," "there's no conscience," or "there's a crisis of morals." In this vein, they distinguished between "dirty" (corrupt) and "clean" (honest, upright) behavior. When asked how society's problems could be solved, one graduate replied, "The way people think has to be cleaned up."

Further insight into this perceived "crisis of morals" can be gleaned from the graduates' commentary on someone many regarded as a striking exception to the rule — Ahmad Rushdi. The outpouring of graduate affection and respect for a former minister of the interior is puzzling to say the least. How did an official who once headed the ministry responsible for internal security become the object of such veneration?

Ahmad Rushdi was the minister of interior for two years, from 1984 to 1986. Robert Springborg described his tenure:

> Although personally severe, Rushdi was a keen reformer who preferred dialogue with rather than intimidation of the opposition. Mubarak's only Minister of Interior not to be implicated by prisoners testifying in the "torture case" of 1986, Rushdi vigorously directed his ministry's efforts to such mundane but important tasks as improving the traffic flow in Cairo, as well as to the important and politically sensitive matter of rounding up drug dealers. For these efforts he earned the grudging admiration of the opposition and the enmity of various powerful forces and personages, not the least of them being his successor, Zaki Badr.[55]

Rushdi was forced to resign after the Central Security Forces riots of 1986. Nonetheless, through the early 1990s he remained widely admired for both his personal qualities and his achievements in office. Indeed, graduates who had just finished excoriating all politicians, past and present, changed their tone when asked about Rushdi. Intrigued by this distinction, I began asking all graduates, as well as Egyptians more generally (including, as it turned out, many taxi drivers),[56] their opinion of Rushdi. The responses were overwhelmingly favorable and emphasized certain themes. Rushdi was a devout Muslim and was honest, efficient, and "clean." Moreover, he was tough on crime and fair in applying the law. As one taxi driver put it: "During his period, there was real order in the country — if you did something wrong, you paid a fine or got punished; it didn't matter if you were big or small, even the ministers would be punished."

In his effort to relieve the traffic situation in Cairo, Rushdi chose to go into the streets to assess the problems firsthand, rather than sitting comfortably behind a desk in his office. When asked what he thought of Rushdi, another taxi driver replied:

> A great man. [Why?] When he ran the Interior Ministry, things went right. You didn't get arrested without just cause, and if you were doing something wrong, you paid for it. He would go into the streets, check on things, make sure things were going OK. Now the young police officers, they sit in the station with their feet up, drinking tea. Ahmad Rushdi was different. He'd go down to the neighborhood police stations dressed in a *gallabiyya* and check to see if people were doing their jobs. Dressed in a *gallabiyya*, just like a peasant from the countryside!

The graduates surveyed emphasized the same attributes: Rushdi's efforts to improve the system in tangible ways, as well as his fairness, courage, and personal integrity. They also commended his willingness to mix with the people, to "go into the streets," just as some had described the revered second caliph, 'Umar ibn al-Khattab. Finally, a few graduates mentioned Rushdi's respect for freedom of expression, praising him for dealing with the opposition through discussion rather than repression.

Those graduates who admired Ahmad Rushdi viewed his removal in 1986 as an inevitable consequence of his efforts to reform the system; *itshal* (he was thrown out), or *shaluh* (they threw him out), because he threatened the interests of senior-ranking officials. Some graduates even suggested that the government had fabricated the Central Security Forces riots to embarrass him. As one concluded, "It doesn't pay to be good; you have to be a criminal (*harami*) to maintain your seat."

Although many graduates traced the problems of contemporary political life to a "lack of principles," they did not necessarily believe the Islamic movement offered a better alternative. Most graduates identified themselves as observant Muslims, and some who did not claimed they intended to become more observant in the future. When asked who their role models were, aside from their parents the most frequent answer was the prophet Muhammad and the *sahaba* (the companions of the Prophet) or the *salihin* (the "upright ones," that is, the exemplary leaders of the first Muslim community in seventh-century Arabia). Several graduates stressed that a return to religion would help resolve society's problems by encouraging a shift from self-interested behavior toward greater concern for the public good. As one graduate noted, "In Islam, people would look out for one another; now everyone looks out for himself."

But when asked specifically what they thought of the Muslim Brotherhood or the Islamic trend in general, many graduates reacted with the same skepticism they directed toward other opposition groups. Some noted that the Islamists faced the same structural constraints as did other opposition groups and thus, like them, could achieve only limited results; others claimed that the Islamists "have not presented any clear solutions" or that the application of Islamic law "would solve many problems but create other problems, like a more closed society with little room for opposition." Some graduates mentioned recent scandals involving the Islamic investment companies of al-Rayyan and al-Sa'd as evidence that the Islamists exploited religion for personal gain. More generally, one graduate said: "The application of Islam would be good, but it must be far from private ends. Many people use Islam as a curtain behind which to achieve their own goals."

In addition, many graduates were unfamiliar with the services provided by Islamists. When asked whether the Islamists helped young people find jobs and housing, some graduates expressed disbelief. As one replied, "Who told you that? They don't help youth. If they did, all the youth would be pouring into the Islamic associations. You wouldn't find any of them on the street."

A minority of graduates were openly contemptuous of the Islamic trend. As one graduate noted, "'Islam is the solution.' The words are nice, but the way they want to apply it is wrong. They use brainwashing and they say if you vote for us, we'll provide you with services." Or as another declared, "The Islamic leaders can't provide a solution — what they offer is an escape to the past."

In sum, the graduates I surveyed all believed that Egyptian society lacked a moral order in which principles of right and wrong regulated individual behavior. Interestingly, this is close to Durkheim's image of modern society as pervaded by "anomie" (normlessness, from the Greek *anomia*, lawlessness).[57] As ironic as this first appears, graduates regarded public life under authoritarian rule as characterized not by too much order but by too little, with the caveat, of course, that what was missing was an order based on public morality and law rather than coercion.

The graduates' perception that Egyptian society was afflicted by moral chaos heightened their receptivity to the Islamist message. Indeed, as later chapters show, it was the Islamists' promise to enforce public accountability through the application of religious law — rather than, say, a more straightforward emphasis on jobs and other material benefits — that resonated most powerfully in their outreach to educated youth.

Alienation from the political order did not automatically lead to opposition activism. On the contrary, the dominant response of the graduates surveyed was not political protest but political abstention. Yet abstention did not indicate apathy. Most of the graduates I interviewed expressed a great deal of interest in social and political affairs, although nearly all of them believed there was little hope of change. As one graduate put it:

> We can talk about what is the most appropriate form of government for Egypt, and we can say that Western-style democracy would be nice. But the problem is that none of these options is realistic. None will bring a result because of the crisis of morals; anyone who reaches power will exploit it to the fullest extent.

Most graduates thus saw little reason to participate in politics. Some stressed that the electoral process was artificial, both because election results were subject to falsification and because real power lay not with the parliament but with a president who was not directly chosen by the electorate.[58] When asked if he or other people he knew voted in elections, one graduate laughed and replied, "No. Definitely not. They are just for show. They are a way for people to forget their own problems for a while, to take some time off from their own worries. As for the MP from our area, I've never seen him."

Political participation was viewed not just as ineffectual but also as dangerous. As one graduate noted, "Here we have emergency laws. If I make a commotion, I could affect my future; I could find myself in prison. I stay away from problems."

Given the risks — and the dubious payoff — of political participation, most graduates saw themselves confined to the role of bystander. One graduate stated this view with particular poignancy:

> There's no solution. The government's projects are only words. Even if God gave me true insight and vision, the ability to see things clearly and speak clearly, no one would listen, and even if they did, no one would implement anything. There are lots of nice words, but as for implementation, there's nothing. The parties have good ideas some-times, but they can't do anything about them; they don't have the authority. I sometimes read the opposition newspapers. We read the papers and we enjoy it. Sometimes I find they're saying things I felt inside and wanted to say; other times they make me laugh. But then I close the paper and return to the same miserable life, and that's it.

For most graduates, this sense of impotence was accompanied less by rage than resignation. As one graduate concluded, "Forget us, and the next gen-eration. There is nothing that can be done for us. Think about the little ones."

A major indicator of political participation in a multiparty system is the rate of voter turnout in parliamentary elections. As further evidence of the dominant pattern of abstention, let us examine the voter turnout rates during the first decade of Mubarak's rule.

From Alienation to Abstention: Voter Turnout in Parliamentary Elections

Political reform was intended to accommodate opposition voices in Egypt's formal political arena without threatening the regime's grip on power. Under Mubarak, Egypt's multiparty system did include several legal opposition parties, but they functioned primarily as "parties of opinion" with minimal influence over state policy and weak ties to the mass public. Thus rather than nurture a more participatory political culture, controlled liber-alization fostered widespread cynicism about the efficacy of participation in the formal political sphere.

If we take voting as a rough but reasonable proxy of political participation, we find that during Mubarak's first decade, political abstention was especially pronounced in the large urban areas where the educated sectors of the popu-lation were concentrated. Although no survey data disaggregate voting behavior by class or education level, certain trends can be inferred from aggregate voter turnout rates and electoral results.

Elections for Egypt's parliament, the People's Assembly (Majlis al-sha'b), have been held five times under Mubarak's tenure, in 1984, 1987, 1990, 1995, and, most recently, in the fall of 2000. Given this book's attention to the political environment in Egypt before the "authoritarian reversal" of 1992, my analysis focuses on the first three elections. Despite the considerable volume of reporting on Egypt's parliamentary elections,[59] information on voter turnout is sketchy. Official estimates of participation in parliamentary elections since 1976 range between 40 and 50 percent. For example, Hussein cites official turnout rates of 40 percent in 1976, 40 percent in 1979, 43.4 percent in 1984, and 50.4 percent in 1987.[60] Similarly, voter turnout has been estimated at 45 percent in 1990 and 50 percent in 1995.[61] Yet we cannot take these percentages at face value, because they indicate the proportion of adult citizens registered to vote who actually did vote. When we consider that roughly half the adult population over age eighteen was not even registered,[62] the actual participation rate drops to roughly 20 to 25 percent of the adult population.

Thus, during Mubarak's first decade, roughly one-quarter of Egyptians eligible to vote participated in parliamentary elections. When we disaggregate voters by place of residence, we find marked differences in participation, with turnouts significantly higher in rural areas than in urban ones. As Hussein observed, in 1984 voter turnout exceeded 50 percent in the three most rural governorates (al-Sharqiyya, al-Manufiyya, and al-Minya), while in the four most urban governorates (Cairo, Alexandria, Port Said, and Suez), the rates were 23.9 percent, 27.8 percent, 35.6 percent, and 20.6 percent, respectively.[63] Given that these are percentages of registered rather than eligible voters, the actual rates would be slightly more than 25 percent in rural areas and between 10 and 18 percent in urban areas.

A field study conducted by Salwa Gom'a in 1987 further clarifies the urban voting rates. Gom'a compared voting behavior in two electoral districts, East Cairo and the governorate of Suez. East Cairo, the country's largest electoral district, included a total of 4 million people, of whom about 226,000 had voting cards; 40,946 individuals, or 18.1 percent of registered voters, voted in the 1987 elections. Although Gom'a did not specify the exact number of adults in the district *eligible* to vote, if one assumes that consistent with national trends, it was roughly double the number of those registered, the actual voting rate would be closer to 9 percent.[64] Similarly, in Suez, of the 85,375 registered voters, 19,068 took part in the elections, yielding a turnout rate of 22.3 percent, or an effective rate of about 11 percent. Regarding voter turnout rates, Gom'a commented, "We may note that despite the fact that both districts are distinguished by a high level of awareness and education, their participation rates are extremely low and are not in keeping with the educational level of the district's sons."[65]

Another study of voter turnout in the Cairo area confirmed these trends, indicating that voter turnout in 1987 did not exceed 16 percent in North Cairo, 11.4 percent in South Cairo, 14.8 percent in East Cairo, and 19.8 percent in the fourth Cairo district, Sayyida Zeinab. Because these rates were calculated against the total of registered voters, the effective participation rates were probably somewhere between 6 and 10 percent.[66]

We can conclude from these data that in the metropolis of Greater Cairo, only about one in thirteen adults voted in the parliamentary elections in the 1980s and that twelve of thirteen abstained. Even President Mubarak felt compelled to comment on the low turnout rates in Egypt's large cities. He mentioned it in his May Day speech on May 2, 1987, as well as in an interview with Makram Muhammad Ahmad, editor of *al-Musawwar*, published in June of that year. In the interview, Mubarak mentioned:

> What most hurt me in the last elections was the decline in the attendance rate in the cities to unreasonable levels, in Cairo 1,200,000 people are registered to vote and only 200,000 went to the polls, and Cairo is the capital of the cultured and the educated. . . . Your problem as *muthaqqafin* [cultured ones] is that you do a lot of talking, but as to going out and putting it into practice, that's something else. I'd even go so far as to say that the only ones who go [vote] are the ideologues of every type. As to the rest, they don't go because each one of you has the wrong idea in his head: "Why should I go if they're going to win anyway."[67]

In the absence of public opinion data, low voter turnout in urban areas may be the "hardest" evidence available for the existence of a culture of political alienation among urban, educated sectors of Egyptian society. Moreover, when we look more closely at voting behavior, we find that most citizens who chose to vote did so as a means to secure access to government services. Hence rather than frame a contest among genuine programmatic alternatives, the electoral process chiefly served as a mechanism for renewing patron-client ties between citizens and the government's National Democratic Party.

Voting for the Patron-State: Explaining the NDP's Control of Parliament

When we examine the broad sweep of electoral history in Egypt since 1976, what is most striking is the overwhelming dominance of the government party, now known as the National Democratic Party (NDP), in its share of both votes and seats in parliament. In regard to seats, the ruling party won 82 percent in 1976, 92 percent in 1979, 87 percent in 1984, 69 percent in 1987, 58 percent in 1990, and 71.4 percent of all seats in 1995.[68] Yet such figures are misleading, for they exclude NDP supporters who ran as independents and joined the NDP majority in parliament after the elections. In 1990, more than two-thirds of the 177 "independent" candidates who won seats eventually joined the NDP majority in parliament. When we include NDP-affiliated independents, the NDP's share of seats increases to 79 percent in 1987, 86 percent in 1990, and 94 percent in 1995.[69]

Such huge NDP majorities exceeded the party's share of the popular vote. Electoral laws effective during the 1984 and 1987 elections required parties to receive at least 8 percent of the popular vote in order to obtain a seat in parliament, and the votes of any party that did not meet this minimum were automatically transferred to the largest party.[70] In addition, certain seats in parliament were reserved for women and members of the Coptic Christian minority, to be appointed directly by the president.[71] Finally, as noted earlier, many independents, whether or not they were NDP members, often joined the NDP majority after the elections. Such considerations aside, there is no doubt that the NDP has captured a majority of votes in every election in Egypt since 1976. For example, the NDP won 72.9 percent of the popular vote in 1984 and 69.6 percent of the vote in 1987. Do such outcomes reflect broad support for the NDP's platform? A closer look suggests otherwise.

Critics attribute the NDP's strong showing in some elections to outright fraud. For example, after the 1987 elections, rumors circulated about the "correction" of electoral returns by a computer located in the Ministry of Interior.[72] In addition to charges of blatant falsification, the opposition newspapers reported numerous cases of harassment of opposition candidates and supporters by police and security agents, the "sale" of voting boxes to the highest bidder, and votes cast by individuals who were outside the country or deceased. Opposition party activists echoed such claims in personal interviews. Such incidents were reportedly more common outside Egypt's large cities, where fewer mechanisms were in place to deter government intervention in the election process.[73]

Despite the repeated allegations of government intervention in the electoral process, few would contend that it was sufficient to explain the NDP's huge electoral gains. To make sense of these gains, therefore, we must take into account the basis on which most citizens vote. Egyptians typically vote for the NDP not out of support for its platform but as a means to secure access to government resources. As an appendage of the state apparatus, the NDP is an important vehicle for the distribution of patronage. As Springborg explained:

> The list of rewards and punishments is almost endless. It includes various forms of distribution of governmental largesse, including salary and pension increases, bonuses, relaxation of mandatory crop deliveries required of producers, appointments to public bodies, the discretionary granting of licenses and permits, and various other inducements offered in the weeks and days prior to elections.[74]

Within opposition circles, the NDP's exchange of goods for votes is legendary. For example, Rif'at al-Sa'id recalled how the government challenged the leftist NPUP in a rural district in the Delta where, through ties of kinship and notability, the party had acquired a strong electoral base. According to al-Sa'id, the government dug the ditches and installed the poles for electricity in the area in the weeks before an election, but villagers were notified that the poles would not be wired unless they voted for the government party.[75] Whether this incident actually occurred or is better seen as apocryphal, it reveals the enormous advantage the NDP enjoys by dint of its access to state resources.

The NDP's electoral dominance in the countryside was also a result of its manipulating ties of notability and kinship. As Springborg confirmed, "The large and powerful families that dominate electoral politics in rural constituencies are the primary conduits through which patronage is delivered."[76] The NDP's mobilization of voters along clan and tribal lines helps explain both the comparatively high turnout and the NDP's strong showing in rural areas.

Recent voter surveys indicate that party choice was linked to patronage in urban areas as well. For example, Gom'a's survey of 550 voters in East Cairo revealed that the most important factor in choosing a candidate was the ability to provide services (mentioned by 44 percent of the sample) or a personal acquaintance with the candidate (29 percent of the sample); far fewer mentioned "issues" (14 percent) or "party belonging" (12 percent) (see table 4.1). Pro-NDP respondents typically explained their support for the party

TABLE 4.1 Factor Identified by Voters as "Most Important" in Choosing a
Candidate, People's Assembly Elections, 1987 (%)

District	Party Belonging	Issues	Candidate Personality	Ability to Provide Services	Kinship Ties
East Cairo	12	14	29	44	1
Suez	15	9	23	51	2

Source: Salwa Sha'rawi Gom'a, "An Explanation of Voting Behavior: A Comparative Study of
the District of East Cairo and the Governorate of Suez," *The People's Assembly Elections: 1987*
(Cairo: Al-Ahram Center for Political and Strategic Studies, 1988), table 8, p. 50.

as support for the government, as in this representative quotation: "I belong
to the NDP because it is the government and my interest is with the
government."[77]

Another important finding of Gom'a's survey was that a majority of voters
who supported opposition candidates "sympathized with political trends not
represented legally on the political map." This was a reference to the support
received by the Muslim Brotherhood in the 1984 and 1987 elections, when
it was permitted to run candidates under the umbrella of a legal party.[78] In
both elections, the coalition encompassing the Brotherhood received more
votes than any other opposition party. In 1984, the Muslim Brotherhood–
Wafd alliance gained 15.1 percent of the vote, while none of the other
opposition parties managed to exceed the 8 percent minimum. In 1987, the
Brotherhood switched partners, and the alliance it forged with the Labor
Party and the tiny Liberal Party gained 17.1 percent of the vote, while the
Wafd gained 10.9 percent and the NPUP only 2.2 percent. Hence in both
elections, the party bloc encompassing the Brotherhood received more votes
than all other opposition parties combined (see table 4.2).

The support for opposition parties was particularly high in Egypt's large
cities. For example, in 1984 the opposition won roughly 27 percent of the
total vote nationally but captured 38.4 percent of the votes in Cairo, 32.7
percent in Alexandria, 36 percent in Suez, and more than 50 percent in Port
Said.[79]

From these election data, we can derive three general conclusions about
Egypt's multiparty system during the first decade of Mubarak's rule. First,
the system was characterized by low levels of political participation. As noted
earlier, approximately twelve of thirteen adult citizens did not vote. More-

TABLE 4.2 Party Share of the Opposition Vote, 1984 and 1987

Opposition Party	Percentage of Votes	
	1984	1987
Wafd Party	**56.0**	36.2
Labor Party	26.2	**56.5**
Liberal Party	2.4	— *
National Democratic Progressive Party (NPUP)	15.4	7.3
Total	100.0	100.0

Note: The total opposition vote in 1984 was 1,390,206, out of a total of 5,146,565. The total opposition vote in 1987 was 2,060,119, out of a total of 6,811,877.
* The Liberal Party allied with the Labor Party and the Muslim Brotherhood in 1987. Percentages in boldface indicate the percentage of the opposition vote received by the party bloc containing the Muslim Brotherhood.
Source: Fauzi Najjar, "Elections and Democracy in Egypt," *American-Arab Affairs* 29 (1989): 96–113.

over, voter turnout was lowest in the cities, where the better educated and more politically aware citizens were concentrated. Second, parliamentary elections did not involve meaningful competition among different programmatic alternatives. Most voters supported the ruling party on pragmatic rather than ideological grounds, reflecting their dependence on services offered by the patron-state and on the continued salience of ties of kinship and notability.[80] As an arm of the state, the NDP was far better equipped than any of the opposition parties were to reward loyal constituents. Yet the NDP was not the only party that gained votes through patronage and notability. Support for the Wafd and the NPUP in the Delta home provinces of their old-guard leaders had less to do with party ideology than with clan loyalties. At the same time, many independent candidates had no ideological platform at all but rather were businessmen who made good during the *infitah* and sought to "purchase" a parliamentary seat. As leftist critic Amina al-Naqqash commented following the 1990 elections: "It was natural, in the absence of real political issues, to have wealthy businessmen, investors, merchants, and the like enter the elections on an unprecedented scale. They spend lavishly on the campaigns to 'buy' the votes." Al-Naqqash estimated that more than 50 million Egyptian pounds were spent by parliamentary candidates in the 1990 election campaign.[81]

A third conclusion is that despite not having legal status, the Muslim

Brotherhood was the opposition group with the greatest ability to mobilize the popular vote. As noted, in 1984 and again in 1987 the opposition bloc containing the Brotherhood received more votes than any other opposition party or alliance. Just as important as the number of votes the Brotherhood received was the character of its appeal. The Islamists' provision of services in urban neighborhoods (see chapter 5) certainly contributed to the Brotherhood's electoral success. But more than any other opposition force, the Brotherhood offered a programmatic alternative to the incumbent regime. Furthermore, it had a much more tangible presence on the street. For example, during the 1987 elections, Brotherhood members distributed campaign literature, hung up banners declaring "Islam is the solution" and "Give your vote to Allah, give it to the Muslim Brotherhood," and organized political meetings and rallies in urban neighborhoods. In sum, by the mid-1980s the Brotherhood had emerged as the only opposition movement in Egypt capable of mobilizing substantial popular support for an ideological program distinct from that of the Mubarak regime.

Conclusion

The multiparty system created by Nasser's successors could not offer effective representation of the country's educated youth. The ruling party no longer tried to absorb them, and the country's legal opposition parties did not provide an outlet for their discontent. Given the perceived risks — and dubious benefits — of political participation, most graduates did not become involved in public affairs.

There was a conspicuous exception to this rule, however. In sharp contrast to the dominant pattern of political abstention, a substantial minority of graduates became active in the reformist wing of the Islamic movement. The electoral campaigns of the Muslim Brotherhood in 1984 and 1987 hinted at the movement's impressive capacity for mobilization. As Ashraf Hussein observed, they revealed that the Islamists had somehow managed to "circumvent the restrictions that prevent the other opposition forces from connecting with the masses."[82] How did the Islamic movement overcome the barriers to mobilization erected by the authoritarian state?

To answer this question, chapter 5 traces the rise of a vast and decentralized network of Islamic institutions on the periphery of the formal political system and explains how it provided new "structures of opportunity" for Islamist outreach to educated youth.

5   The Parallel Islamic Sector

Uneven political liberalization under Sadat and Mubarak created a political system with a hollow core and a dynamic periphery. Although contestation for power in Egypt's formal political system remained tightly controlled from above, outside the sphere of party politics, there emerged a vast network of Islamic institutions with de facto autonomy from state control. During the 1980s and early 1990s, these ostensibly "nonpolitical" institutions became important sites of Islamist outreach to educated youth. This political opening thus inadvertently gave rise to new kinds of political participation detached from — and opposed to — the country's formal political institutions and elites.

Whether, when, and how an opposition movement comes to life depends on the opportunities and constraints that face would-be movement organizers and supporters in the general political environment. In recent years, scholars seeking to determine how broad environmental conditions shape a movement's trajectory have developed the concept of "political opportunity structures."[1] Although different definitions have been proposed, Doug McAdam observed that the concept tends to highlight four dimensions of the political environment:

1. The relative openness or closure of the institutionalized political system.
2. The stability or instability of the broad set of elite alignments typically undergirding a polity.

3. The presence or absence of elite allies.
4. The state's capacity and propensity for repression.[2]

The "political process model," an influential model of social movement formation in the United States, portrays expanding political opportunity structures as the ultimate trigger for the formation of movements.[3] Based primarily on the study of movements in the democratic polities of western Europe and the United States, this model focuses on expanding political opportunity structures *within* the formal political order. Yet in authoritarian settings, in which opposition groups' access to formal political institutions and elites is typically restricted, we must also consider the space available to opposition actors in ostensibly "nonpolitical" arenas less subject to state control. Toward this end, it is useful to distinguish among the "center," defined as the national parliamentary arena in which legal political parties compete for power; the "semiperiphery," comprising the major occupational or professional interest groups (for example, labor unions, student unions, professional associations); and the "periphery," encompassing all other potential arenas for collective action, including religious institutions, local community and youth centers, schools, and even private households.

As Garreton argued in the case of Chile under Pinochet, when regular party channels are blocked, other institutional arenas can become important sites of political contestation "by default."[4] The Egyptian case indicates that these "substitute" sites can also permit formally excluded opposition groups to reach out to the mass public. Indeed, an important finding is that even when opposition groups are denied access to the formal political order, ruling elites are unified, and the state's capacity for repression is high, an authoritarian regime may permit — or be unable to prevent — the emergence of "autonomous zones" in which mobilization is possible.

This chapter explains how political and economic reform facilitated Islamic institution building on the periphery and how the "parallel Islamic sector" that ensued created new space for Islamist outreach to urban, educated youth. While institutional growth on the periphery created a structural opening for mobilization, to understand its occurrence we must address the question of agency. As I explain next, it was the conjuncture of expanding "structures of opportunity" on the periphery with the rise of a leadership cadre able to exploit them that paved the way for the Islamic mobilization of educated youth in Egypt in the 1980s and early 1990s.

The Parallel Islamic Sector

The Phenomenon

By the time Hosni Mubarak assumed power, a broad network of Islamic institutions had begun to coalesce in the interstices of Egypt's authoritarian state. These institutions had different functions, served different constituencies, and varied in geographic reach. Yet despite their diversity, they can be thought of as forming a loose network, given the ties of family and friendship, resource flows, and ideological commitments that bound them together. This network is referred to here as the "parallel Islamic sector," that is, a sector largely independent of — and competitive with — the cultural, religious, and service-oriented arms of the Egyptian state.

To understand how the parallel Islamic sector emerged, we must return to the 1970s, when Islamic institution building in Egypt was aided by two crucial developments: the accession to power of a leader who sought to bolster his own Islamic legitimacy, and a regional oil boom that generated resources for community projects beyond state control. Because both these developments have been analyzed elsewhere, it should suffice to describe them only briefly here.

The Origins

All of Egypt's leaders since 1952 have been Muslims and have claimed to rule in a manner compatible with Islam. But while Nasser portrayed his goals as consistent with Islamic precepts (a convergence readily affirmed by clerics on the government payroll), Islam did not figure prominently in either the formation or the justification of his agenda. Instead, in keeping with the ideological themes in vogue throughout the Third World at that time, Nasser's rhetoric was secular, nationalist, and revolutionary in tone, emphasizing the struggle against "Zionism and imperialism" abroad and against "capitalist exploitation" at home.

By contrast, Islam was central to Anwar Sadat's self-image and claim to political authority. Styling himself the "Believer-President," Sadat made a public show of his personal piety; promoted Islamic programming in the media, schools, and universities; expanded the government's support of of-

ficial Islamic institutions; and used religious themes to justify the regime's
policies, including the decision to go to war with Israel in 1973.[5]

As both a personal example and a patron of the Islamic establishment,
Sadat encouraged the trend toward higher levels of religious observance in
Egyptian society at large. In addition, he rehabilitated the Muslim Brotherhood, which had suffered years of repression under Nasser. Brotherhood
leaders were released from prison shortly after Sadat took office, and others
were allowed to return to Egypt from exile. Though still technically illegal,
the Brotherhood was permitted in 1976 to publish its own newspaper, al-
Da'wa, which enjoyed an estimated circulation of 100,000 before it was shut
down in 1981.[6]

Sadat also encouraged the development of Islamic student associations,
or gama'at, on university campuses, in the hope of developing an effective
counterweight to the leftist groups that dominated student politics at the
time.[7] This tactical maneuver had unforeseen consequences, however, as
the gama'at quickly evolved into vocal critics of infitah and Sadat's rapprochement with the West. As the Islamists' relationship with the regime
grew more confrontational, Sadat shifted from accommodation to repression, but he ultimately failed to contain the forces he had unleashed. On
October 6, 1981, not long after ordering more arrests, Sadat himself was
gunned down by Islamic militants.

While the Brotherhood was reconstituting itself as a national political
organization and Islamic groups were gaining ground on university campuses, a new wave of Islamic institution building began to reshape the landscape of Egyptian cities and towns. Economic liberalization facilitated this
trend by expanding the private wealth available for investment in communal
projects. Fueled by the regional oil boom, Egypt's GDP grew by an average
of 9 percent per year in the decade between 1974 and 1984, more than
doubling the per capita income from $334 to $700 by 1984.[8] A major new
source of capital was the remittances of Egyptian migrants working in Libya
and the Gulf, who increased in number from about 10,000 in 1968 to 1.2
million in 1985.[9] Much of this remittance income, officially valued at more
than $3 billion annually in the early 1980s,[10] found outlets beyond state
control. Some of it was captured by the Islamic banks and investment companies that were established under the new investment laws of infitah.
Springborg, for example, estimates that between 1974 and 1984, about 1
million Egyptians invested in the Islamic investment companies.[11] Another
share of the remittance income was invested in business ventures inside
Egypt, including those headed by Egyptian businessmen with Islamist sym-

pathies. In *Who Owns Egypt?* Samya Sa'id Imam reported that as of the late 1980s, Egypt's private economy was effectively controlled by eighteen families and their close associates; Brotherhood members accounted for eight. The study also calculated that Brotherhood interests might control more than 40 percent of all economic ventures, many of them centered on real estate and currency speculation.[12]

Under Mubarak, the parallel Islamic sector continued to grow in absolute size and complexity, although its exact parameters are difficult to pin down. For example, there are no systematic data on the number of Islamic institutions in Mubarak's Egypt, let alone how they are disaggregated by size, function, or geographic location. Similarly, only sketchy information is available on the social background and orientations of their personnel and the mechanisms through which they are financed. Finally, only anecdotal information exists about how these institutions relate to the state and to each other. Despite such limitations, however, it is possible to discern some general trends.

The Parallel Islamic Sector in Mubarak's Egypt

For purposes of analysis, the institutions of the "parallel Islamic sector" can be divided into three general categories: (1) private mosques; (2) Islamic voluntary associations, including welfare societies, cultural organizations, health clinics, and schools; and (3) Islamic for-profit commercial and business enterprises, such as Islamic banks, investment companies, manufacturing firms, and publishing houses. These institutions are subject to different regulatory arrangements: mosques officially fall under the jurisdiction of the Ministry of Religious Endowments (Awqaf); private voluntary associations are subject to law 32 of 1964 and are administered by the Ministry of Social Affairs; and for-profit Islamic organizations are regulated by commercial and business legislation. Yet as will be noted, the factors determining which laws apply to a particular type of Islamic institution in practice are even more complex.

Egypt's Private Mosques

Among the most striking institutional developments in Egypt in the 1970s and 1980s was an unprecedented wave of private mosque building. Unlike government (*hukumi*) mosques, which were maintained by state funds and staffed by government-appointed imams, private (*ahli*) mosques were self-constituted organizations, financed through private donations and staffed by imams selected by members of the local community. According to one estimate, the number of *ahli* mosques increased from 20,000 in 1970 to more than 46,000 in 1981. Of those 46,000, only 6,000 were directly administered by the Ministry of Religious Endowments.[13]

A major source of financing for the new private mosques was the voluntary donations of private Egyptians collected through the system of *zakat* (the Islamic religious tithe); private mosques also received financial support from institutional and individual patrons in the Gulf. The proliferation of new mosques was encouraged by legislation making any building containing a mosque a religious site and therefore tax exempt. With a domestic construction boom under way, builders had a clear incentive to establish new "mosques," which often consisted of little more than a tiny prayer room (*zawiya*) located on the ground floor or in the basement.

Private mosque building continued under Mubarak. According to the minister of religious endowments, Dr. Muhammad 'Ali Mahgub, there were 91,000 mosques in Egypt in 1991, including 45,000 private mosques and 10,000 *zawiyas*.[14] In December 1992, the Egyptian journal *Akhir sa'a* set the number of private mosques at 60,000.[15] Other estimates were even higher. For example, the international human rights organization *Middle East Watch* estimated that as of 1993 there were 170,000 mosques in Egypt, of which only 30,000 were operated by the government.[16]

In addition to hosting daily and Friday noon prayers, private mosques often provided a wide variety of religious and community services. Some mosques sponsored religious lessons (*durus diniyya*) for both sexes, after school and day-care programs for young children, and competitions for reading the Qur'an and hadith in celebration of Islamic holy days. Others served as the nuclei for a network of satellite institutions, which might include a health clinic, kindergarten, charity distribution center, and a bookstore or lending library for Islamic books and cassette tapes. Particularly in low-income neighborhoods on the periphery of Cairo, where government services were scarce and networks of communal self-help were undeveloped, the local mosque and its satellite institutions often became the focal points of community social life. Not only did they loom large as service providers, but they also were one of the few socially sanctioned arenas where young men and women could congregate outside the home.

Islamic Voluntary Associations

In addition to private mosques, the parallel Islamic sector included thou-sands of quasi-independent Islamic voluntary associations, or *gam'iyyat*. The growth in the number of Islamic voluntary organizations can be seen as part of the broader proliferation of nongovernmental organizations (NGOs) in Egypt during the Mubarak era.[17] The term "NGO" is misleading, however, because in Egypt such organizations are subject to state control. According to law 32 of 1964 — a holdover from the Nasser era — all private and civic associations in Egypt are administered by the Ministry of Social Affairs (MSA). Law 32 stipulates that all prospective associations must apply to the MSA for a license, which it has the authority to grant or withhold. In addition, the MSA can intervene in the functioning of existing associations. For example, it can appoint members of an association's board, demand written reports on its activities, and supervise the collection of funds and their uses. More-over, it has the right to dissolve the association and seize its assets on rather elastic grounds, for instance, if its activities defy "the general order and proper behavior" (*al-nizam al-'amm wa'l-adab*).[18]

The total number of private voluntary organizations (PVOs) in Egypt in the early 1990s is most often estimated at about 14,000 to 15,000, although some estimates reach as high as 30,000.[19] Writing in 1992, Sarah Ben-Nefissa Paris claimed that these numbers were exaggerated; adding up the total of registered associations, she arrived at a total of 11,360, 27.6 percent of which were Islamic in character.[20] According to Ben-Nefissa Paris, there were slightly more than 3,000 Islamic private voluntary associations in Egypt in the early 1990s. Yet this figure may actually understate the phenomenon, for in 1994 Saad ad-Din Ibrahim claimed that 8,000 of a total 14,000 Egyp-tian private voluntary organizations were Islamic in character.[21]

Whatever their numbers, by the 1980s Islamic voluntary associations had gained a central role in Egyptian public life. Some Islamic PVOs retained a traditional religious focus, such as those promoting memorization of the Qur'an, helping Muslims perform the pilgrimage (*hajj*), providing charity (*zakat*) to needy families, and aiding in the renovation and beautification of local mosques. Others provided social services. Service-oriented PVOs in-cluded Islamic health clinics, day-care centers, schools, and job-training centers. In some instances, the PVOs' activities were limited to a single neigh-borhood or local area. Other PVOs were well-financed national organizations with branches in many cities and towns. Among the most prominent of the national Islamic organizations was al-Gam'iyya al-shar'iyya, with branches in all twenty-six governorates and 123 branches in Cairo alone.[22]

Although the information about financial flows in the Islamic sector remains largely anecdotal, certain trends are evident. Many Islamic voluntary associations operated under the aegis of a mosque or religious foundation (*waqf*), giving them access to charitable donations collected and distributed through networks away from government supervision. Access to such donations enabled Islamic PVOs to circumvent provisions of law 32 restricting the independent collection of funds, giving them an enormous advantage over their non-Islamic counterparts.[23]

Some Islamic associations also received support from wealthy patrons in the Gulf. For example, the modern hospital attached to the Mustafa Mahmud Society in Cairo was allegedly built with funds that came from a benefactor in the Gulf with close ties to the society's founder.[24] Similarly, an Egyptian scholar who was studying financial flows to Islamic PVOs mentioned a private mosque in Zaytoun, whose sheikh visited Saudi Arabia every year shortly before the pilgrimage season. He made the rounds of wealthy Saudi families, giving lectures and asking for donations, and returned to Egypt with millions of pounds to build a modern hospital attached to the mosque.[25]

Islamic associations also received financial support from Islamic investment companies and banks,[26] as well as from parastatal banks that helped collect and distribute *zakat*. For example, Ben-Nefissa Paris noted that with the aid of 4,500 committees to collect *zakat*, the Nasser Social-Service Bank collected and distributed nearly 21 million pounds in 1991 to Islamic service organizations, including day-care centers and health clinics. In addition to cultivating a reputation for philanthropic activity, the bank had all funds directed toward *zakat* deducted from its tax base.[27]

Islamic associations were also funded by their own profit-making activities. This was the case for many of the country's Islamic health clinics and hospitals, which — in contrast to government clinics — were generally clean, well-run operations with up-to-date medical equipment. Subsidized by monetary gifts and donated materials, the clinics also charged a modest fee for their services.[28] In some instances, the fees generated enough profit to subsidize other religious activities and services.[29]

The parallel Islamic sector also included profit-making enterprises in banking, construction, manufacturing, and trade. The Islamic financial sector included Islamic banks (which, according to Islamic law, do not charge interest) and Islamic investment companies. According to one estimate, in the mid-1980s, the total assets of the latter were 16 billion Egyptian pounds.[30] Likewise, the sector included large Islamic manufacturing conglomerates like al-Rayyan and al-Sa'd with investments in such strategic areas as food production and housing construction, and with close ties to government officials. Such firms were well placed to provide financial and logistical support to Islamic service associations in daily contact with the mass public.

Islamic firms also became active in cultural production. Islamic publishing houses and bookstores flourished in the 1980s and early 1990s. Concentrated in Egypt's large cities, such Islamic publishing houses as al-Dar al-islami li'l-Tawzi' wa'l-Nashr, Dar al-Shuruq, Dar al-Wafa', and Dar al-I'tisam published a wide variety of Islamic literature, including commentaries on the Qur'an and hadith, volumes on particular aspects of Islamic belief and practice, histories of the Islamic movement in Egypt and abroad, the speeches and essays of prominent Islamic thinkers, and small books and pamphlets on the da'wa, or call to Islam. In Cairo, these works were available for purchase in large central bookstores owned by the publishers, in smaller Islamic bookstores located in lower-middle-class neighborhoods, and in newspaper kiosks on the street.

Several independent Islamic periodicals emerged in the 1980s as well. Foremost among them was al-Sha'b, the weekly newspaper of the Labor Party, which became increasingly Islamist in tone under the editorial leadership of 'Adil Hussein. In addition, three independent Islamic monthly journals were in circulation — Liwa' al-islam, al-Mukhtar al-islami, and al-I'tisam, as well as a number of smaller-run journals on specialized topics, such as Islamic economics.

How many Islamic books and journals were published, how many were sold, and what their profits were is hard to determine. Editors of al-Sha'b, as well as most of the Islamic bookstore vendors I interviewed either claimed they lacked such data or were unwilling to share it. I did, however, learn something about these issues from 'Abd al-Mun'im Salim, editor-in-chief of Liwa' al-islam. Salim's journal was often described as the successor to al-Da'wa, the popular Brotherhood journal published from 1976 to 1981. According to Salim, the circulation of Liwa' al-islam grew from 35,000 when it was first published in 1987 to about 95,000 in 1991, with just over half of all issues (50,000 to 55,000) sold in Egypt. "Many people can't buy it because they can't afford it," he explained, "so it is often xeroxed and distributed to much larger numbers."[31]

The regular purchase of books or journals was indeed beyond the financial means of many lower-middle- and middle-class Egyptians. Relative to the price of other books, however, the price of Islamic publications was conspicuously low. Some Islamic bookstores were able to sell their materials cheaply because they received a subsidy from patrons; others earned a profit from their sales. For example, *Liwa' al-islam* earned a profit from its sales outside Egypt. Some Islamic bookstores also succeeded commercially. For example, in 1993 the publishing house Dar al-i'tisam sold a poster containing an aerial photograph of a forest in Bavaria in which the trees appeared to spell out a passage from the Qur'an in Arabic script. At one pound apiece, sales of the poster demonstrating this "miracle of nature" were reported to have run into the millions.[32] Critics claimed that Islamic bookstores' profit margins were widened by the discounts they received from certain printers, suggesting the presence of a network of Islamic suppliers and distributors in the industry.[33]

The institutions of the Islamic parallel sector were not "political" in the narrow sense of the term. That is, they did not advocate a particular political agenda or take part in the competition for political power. Moreover, in personal interviews, Egyptians involved in running Islamic welfare societies, kindergartens, and religious classes typically claimed that they had nothing to do with politics (*malish fi-s-siyasa khalis*). Instead, they saw themselves as educating fellow Muslims of their rights and obligations in Islam and forging new kinds of communal solidarity based on Islamic principles of charity and self-help.

Nevertheless, in the 1980s and early 1990s the institutions of the parallel Islamic sector directly contributed to Islamic mobilization in two ways. First, they provided financial and logistical support to Islamic groups with political objectives, including the Islamic student associations (*gama'at*), the Muslim Brotherhood, and underground militant Islamic groups. Second, they provided the space for a diffuse process of ideological outreach and network building by small clusters of independent activists, expanding the base of reformist and militant Islamic political groups alike.

In the early 1990s, a spate of attacks on government officials, tourists, and civilians by Islamic militants raised new alarm over the conversion of Islamic institutions into sites of political outreach. As an article published in the semiofficial journal *Akhir sa'a* noted,

> The deviations of the extremists are many and varied, but at the same time they indicate a new phenomenon, that the extremists are entrenching themselves in the private mosques scattered across the entire country of Egypt.

From inside the private mosques, the light of religious extremism beams forth . . . after the militant groups dominate the mosques, they plan inside them to assassinate prominent people and publish propaganda, execute terrorist activities, and store weapons![34]

The editors of *Akhir sa'a* stressed that they were not calling for a halt to the building of new mosques but, rather, for "a change in what is going on inside them, especially now that some of them have become laboratories for the incubation of extremism."

Growing anxiety over Islamist outreach on the periphery begs the question: why did the regime tolerate the emergence of the parallel Islamic sector in the first place? It is to this question that we now turn.

Mubarak's Policy of "Selective Accommodation"

Although it was Sadat who initially encouraged the revival of Islamic groups in Egypt, it was under Mubarak that the quasi-independent institutions of the parallel Islamic sector reached their fullest development. To understand this outcome, we must take into account the Mubarak regime's objectives as well as its capacity to realize them through the agency of the authoritarian state.

Mubarak's toleration of the parallel Islamic sector was part of a broader strategy to consolidate his regime. In an apparent attempt to learn from the mistakes of his predecessor, whose policy toward the Islamist opposition vacillated between outright encouragement and naked repression, Mubarak adopted a more consistent approach toward the Islamists in the first decade of his rule. In what Robert Bianchi termed a policy of "selective accommodation and selective repression," the regime authorized its security forces to deal harshly with militant Islamic groups while permitting nonviolent Islamic groups and associations to expand their presence in Egyptian public life.[35] By distinguishing between militants and reformists, Bianchi contends, the Mubarak government accomplished several goals. Not only did it isolate the militant fringe of the movement, but it further enhanced its own image among mainstream Islamic groups and their law-abiding followers. Indeed, given the strength of the Islamic movement in the early 1980s, Bianchi argued, the regime had little choice but to seek some form of accommodation, as it "would be flirting with suicide if it repeated Sadat's blunder of attacking the Islamic movement as a whole."[36]

In sum, Mubarak chose to accommodate the nonviolent mainstream of the Islamic movement as a means of defusing tensions and consolidating his own position. It is likely that several other factors informed the regime's policy toward the Islamic sector. First, Mubarak and his close advisers probably did not regard the establishment of Islamic welfare societies, schools, and health clinics as particularly threatening. Indeed, they may actually have viewed such institutions as contributing to social stability in poor urban areas where state-run services were absent or deficient. Beyond this, Egypt's authoritarian leaders have tended to evaluate Islamic groups and institutions according to how much they directly threatened the regime's security. By this yardstick, societies promoting memorization of the Qur'an or providing charity to needy families were likely to be deemed politically irrelevant.

The Mubarak regime initially tolerated the expansion of the parallel Islamic sector because it suited its own objectives. But when those objectives changed, the regime found it difficult to reclaim the space it had ceded to Islamist groups. As the following shows, the regime's efforts to reassert state control over the periphery in the early 1990s were hampered by (1) the decentralized structure of the parallel Islamic sector, (2) the alliances Islamists had forged with members of the state administration, and (3) the structural deficiencies of the state apparatus itself.

Parallel Islamic Institutions and the Limits of Regime Control

In Egypt, as in other authoritarian political systems, the institutions of "civil society" do not enjoy an effective legal guarantee of autonomy from state control. As noted earlier, all civic associations in Egypt must be licensed by and are subject to regulation by the Ministry of Social Affairs. While formally subject to state control, the institutions of the parallel Islamic sector nevertheless enjoyed a substantial degree of de facto autonomy during Mubarak's first decade. In part, this was a by-product of their religious character. As noted earlier, too, the right to dispose of voluntary donations collected by mosques gave Islamic institutions a way around law 32's restrictions on the right to raise funds. Further, Islamic institutions, and especially mosques, were surrounded by an aura of religious sanctity. Government efforts to restrict activities inside a mosque could be construed as interfering with the right to worship, thus raising the specter of a public backlash against the regime for offending Islam or even offending God. Hence, the prevailing cultural climate afforded Islamist institutions a measure of immunity un-available to their secular counterparts.

In addition to the religious character of the Islamic sector, we must con-sider its organizational structure. With thousands of independent mosques, business firms, welfare societies, health clinics, and schools scattered across the country, the Islamic sector was extremely decentralized, complicating the regime's efforts at regulation and control. As one observer commented, independent mosques "have been set up everywhere, in every nook and cranny in urban neighborhoods, markets, and villages across the country."[37] In addition to their geographic dispersion, the physical manifestations of parallel Islamic institutions were often inconspicuous, in some instances no more than an unmarked door leading to a basement mosque. Furthermore, their funding was difficult to track, as was the exact nature of their activities, which were largely publicized by word of mouth. Finally, although we do not know how many there were, some Islamic associations simply chose not to register with the government at all, preferring the risk of operating without a permit to the risk of intervention by state authorities.[38]

Mobility also enhanced institutional autonomy, as Islamists active in a given institution were often able to relocate their activities when their au-tonomy was threatened. For instance, when the government became aware of an activist mosque and took measures to incorporate it or shut it down, its cadres could evade the state by moving to another site. As *Akhir sa'a* observed: "In many cases, if you take their mosques, they proceed to the *zawiyas* [small prayer rooms] in the basement of buildings and meet there. . . . Hence we ask every building owner to take the necessary measures, such as to appoint a qualified *khatib* [preacher] from the Ministry of Religious Endowments."[39] Alternatively, Islamists affiliated with an activist mosque could challenge its closure or incorporation in court.[40]

The flexibility and decentralization of the parallel Islamic sector were not coincidental; rather, they reflect the Islamists' efforts to evade government control. Such findings suggest that an authoritarian regime's monopoly over the means of coercion is not enough for it to control the day-to-day activities of opposition activists dispersed across broad reaches of society. The mech-anisms necessary to achieve such control, from the use of high-technology surveillance techniques to maintenance of an extensive network of party cells, reached their fullest development in totalitarian regimes like Nazi Germany. In the Middle East, they are best approximated by the quasi-totalitarian regime of Saddam Hussein in Iraq. By contrast, Egypt's author-itarian leadership had neither the political will nor the capacity to achieve such dramatic levels of centralized state control. On the contrary, in the mid-1990s when the Mubarak regime sought to contain oppositional activity within the parallel Islamic sector, its efforts were hampered by institutional deficiencies of the state apparatus itself.

The Authoritarian State in Developing Contexts

Like its counterparts in other developing countries, the Mubarak regime must stretch the government's limited resources to meet conflicting goals. Sustaining an authoritarian regime is expensive; in addition to the resources needed to finance growth and distribution, regime leaders must channel substantial funds to the large coercive apparatus on which its power ultimately rests.

As the ultimate guarantors of regime survival, the military and internal security units are generally accorded a high priority in budgetary decisions. But faced with a serious fiscal crisis in the 1980s, the Mubarak regime appears to have allocated far fewer resources for the more mundane forms of control exercised by the "second-tier" arms of the state such as the Ministry of Social Affairs and the Ministry of Religious Endowments. Let us consider some of the anecdotal evidence for this finding, as well as its wider implications.

In December 1992, the regime announced a plan to tighten its control over private mosques and to eventually fold them into the mosque network administered by the Ministry of Religious Endowments. Law 175 of 1960 granted the ministry the authority to incorporate such mosques, but in practice, its ability to do so was hampered by a shortage of manpower and funds. In 1992, the general director of the Ministry of Religious Endowments declared that the government wanted to incorporate 10,000 private mosques per year. However, he explained, the "incorporation of mosques is very expensive," with each mosque requiring 6,000 pounds per year to maintain. Facing acute budgetary constraints in the 1980s, the ministry had enough money to incorporate only 400 mosques per year, increasing to 1,000 in 1991.

Assertion of government control over the country's private mosques was also hindered by a serious "imam shortage." In 1992, the ministry needed 40,000 new imams (prayer leaders). To begin filling the vacant positions, it hired every one of the 5,000 graduates trained in religious studies at al-Azhar, but only 3,000 showed up for work.[41]

As of the mid-1990s, the majority of private mosques in Egypt remained subject to little or no government oversight. Dr. Muhammad 'Ali Mahgub, the minister of religious endowments, claimed that of the 45,000 private mosques and 10,000 *zawiyas* in Egypt in 1991, about 25,000 (45 percent) of them had been brought under government control by 1994. But as noted earlier, Middle East Watch estimated the number of independent mosques in Egypt in the early 1990s at around 140,000. If the latter estimate is correct, then even after the incorporation of 25,000 mosques, more than four-fifths of all private mosques were still outside the state's control.

According to Mahgub's figures, in the early 1990s, around 30,000 mosques were outside the government's control. Of these, he admitted, 1,750 mosques, concentrated in the triangle area of Asyut, Minya, and Sohag in Upper Egypt, were known to be controlled by "extremists," and the government's first priority was to incorporate them as well as the mosques "that are not run by anyone." According to Mahgub, the annexation project would cost the state a total of 300 million pounds. Part of this substantial sum was needed to hire thousands of new imams. In order to avoid adding them to the state payroll, the ministry began to offer some imams a cash payment for every sermon they delivered. Because of the high demand, by the early 1990s the going rate per sermon had risen from 3 to 5 pounds to 15 to 20 pounds. To reduce the shortage, Mahgub noted, the government was training about 15,000 candidates to become imams in a two-year night program offered by preachers' preparation centers in the governorates.[42]

Lacking sufficient manpower and funds to complete its annexation plan, the government continued to rely on independent Islamist associations to staff, finance, and operate thousands of mosques in Egypt. In an interview published in *al-Musawwar*, Mahgub claimed that such mosques posed no immediate threat to the regime's security because the associations running them "were committed to the state's plan in terms of the content of the Friday sermon, technical supervision, and field inspection of preachers by the ministry's inspectors."[43] Mahgub's assurances notwithstanding, we can safely assume that degrees of compliance varied. The level of supervision to which private mosques were subject was undoubtedly uneven and in most instances was unlikely to have included day-to-day administrative control over such crucial matters as hiring decisions, sermon content, the collection and distribution of *zakat*, and mosque sponsorship of adjunct organizations or activities. Moreover, the article containing Mahgub's interview alleged that each week, around twenty preachers were found guilty of infringements and violations. Beyond the shortages of manpower and funds, the regime's ability to use the state as an instrument of control was impeded by the porous and fragmented nature of the state itself.

The Fragmentation (and Islamist Penetration?) of the Egyptian State

In regard to employment levels, geographic scope, and range of activities, the Egyptian state is enormous, approaching that of the socialist states of Eastern Europe before 1989. Employing an estimated 5 million people in the early 1990s, the Egyptian state had branches in nearly every district, town, and village; exerted direct or indirect control over much of the economy; administered private and civic organizations; and provided health and educational services to millions of citizens.

Although the Egyptian state apparatus was enormous in size and function, it remained an inefficient tool for implementing the regime's goals. Efforts to streamline the bureaucracy and impose strict performance criteria competed with the regime's long-standing dependence on the state as a source of domestic employment. Fearing the political consequences of high unemployment, particularly among educated youth, the regime lowered the barriers to entry to the civil service in the 1960s and subsequently added millions of employees to the state payroll (see chapter 2).

In most cases, the regime made little effort to screen applicants or, once they were appointed to government jobs, to inculcate them with a distinctive bureaucratic ethos.[44] In addition, as noted in chapter 2, in the 1980s and early 1990s most state employees were poorly paid, relative to both their private-sector counterparts and state employees in the past. Furthermore, the sheer size and geographic dispersion of the state's labor force — along with chronic budgetary constraints, scarcity of information, and limited technology — hampered the regime's efforts to monitor compliance with its objectives.[45] Finally, laws dating back to the Nasser era restricted the conditions under which a civil servant could be fired, making it more difficult to penalize noncompliance by termination. In sum, as a result of low barriers to entry, minimal socialization, and low pay, state employees were likely to retain and act on private interests and orientations. At the same time, its weak internal monitoring and enforcement mechanisms limited the regime's ability to identify and sanction such behavior.

As Islamic institutions and ideas grew in status and visibility outside the state, they began to influence the orientations of those positioned inside the

state as well.[46] At the same time, numerous opportunities emerged for the
rise of linkages between state employees and Islamists based on prior ties of
kinship or acquaintance, mutual economic interest, or shared ideological
commitments. At this point, evidence of the linkages between Islamists and
state employees, and of penetration of the state by Islamists, remains largely
anecdotal. Neither Islamists nor state officials have an incentive to acknowledge such relationships; on the contrary, both have reasons to conceal them.

Although the evidence is fragmented, it appears that some Islamists have
secured the tacit cooperation of state authorities, including the staffs of the
very ministries intended to control them. For example, Ministry of Social
Affairs (MSA) officials reportedly enjoy close ties with some of the Islamic
societies under their jurisdiction. In addition, MSA officials are included on
the executive boards of some Islamic associations, for which they are paid a
salary. These officials are said to favor Islamic associations over their non-
Islamic counterparts. As evidence, critics point out that a disproportionate
number of the associations that the ministry has categorized as in the "general" or "public" interest — a category that grants the association special privileges, including protection from having their funds confiscated — have an
Islamic reference.[47] In addition, MSA officials are alleged to favor Islamists
when distributing licenses to form new associations and granting permits to
raise funds.[48]

Islamic activists have also developed ties with the members of municipal
councils, even though these bodies are usually dominated by the government's National Democratic Party (NDP). For example, *Akhir sa'a* reported
that some Islamists have responded to government annexation efforts by
shifting their activities to smaller, less visible outlets, such as basement *zawiyas*, obtaining licenses from local town councils without informing the
Ministry of Religious Endowments.[49]

In addition, private Islamic groups and associations have gained support
from senior religious authorities. Egypt's official religious establishment is
headed by two major figures, the grand mufti and the sheikh of al-Azhar
University. It encompasses thousands of formally trained clergy ('*ulama*')
serving as teachers, preachers, judges, scholars, and administrators in the
religious system supervised by the Ministry of Religious Endowments. As
functionaries on the state payroll, the official '*ulama*' have historically been
subservient to the regime. In recent years, however, some of them have
become outspoken in their demands for the further Islamic regulation of
Egyptian public life. In the early 1990s, the sheikh of al-Azhar, Gad al-Haqq
'Ali Gad al-Haqq, pressured the government to ban books that he regarded

as offensive to Islam, condemned the government's decision to sponsor an international population conference in Cairo, and sharply criticized the actions of individual ministers, most notably the ministers of education and culture. While the linkages between the *'ulama'* and the personnel of private Islamic associations remain poorly understood, it is clear that they share many of the same views and that whatever informal relationships they have established offer the latter a measure of protection.

Finally, both senior religious authorities and other types of government officials have developed ties with Islamists based on economic self-interest. As Springborg notes, several al-Azhar sheikhs have headed *"shari'a* committees" for Islamic banks and investment companies, for which they have received generous compensation. Islamic investment companies also have gained support from local government officials; formed partnerships with "popular development" companies attached to the NDP; and, in some instances, retained influential politicians as consultants, as al-Rayyan did when it hired former Minister of Interior Nabawi Isma'il.[50]

The linkages between state officials and Islamists are one symptom of bureaucratic fragmentation in Egypt. Another is the Islamists' direct appropriation of public offices and resources to advance their own agenda. Anecdotal evidence suggests that many of the doctors, teachers, and administrators being appointed to jobs in the state-run system of health, education, and local government are sympathetic to and, in some cases, active proponents of Islamic reform. In contrast to the graduates assigned to centralized, elite arms of the state such as the Ministry of Finance or the Ministry of Foreign Affairs, the graduates appointed to service posts in the governorates receive less specialized training, work for less pay, and are subject to less oversight. They also have greater access to the mass public, and in some instances, state employees with Islamist orientations have used their positions to advance an agenda directly opposed to the regime's goals.

Perhaps the most striking evidence of the growing use of public office for Islamic outreach emerged as a result of the controversy that broke out in the Ministry of Education in 1994. In that year the Egyptian minister of education, Hussein Kamal Baha' ad-Din, publicly complained that numerous government schools were staffed by Islamist teachers who used their positions to indoctrinate Egyptian youth. "The terrorists have been targeting schools for years," the minister alleged. "We have found schools where students are told not to salute the flag, sing the national anthem or talk or study with Christian students."[51] In the summer and fall of 1994, the government removed or punitively transferred more than 2,000 teachers suspected of

Islamist affiliations and began to screen the applicants to teachers' colleges.[52] Hampered by shortages of manpower and funds, however, it was unlikely that the ministry could keep the 25,000 government schools under constant surveillance.

Although Islamists have penetrated the state to some degree, they clearly have not prevented the Mubarak regime from using the state to dominate the private lives of citizens and distribute resources in exchange for political support. What the Islamist penetration of the state does suggest, however, is the possibility of *incoherent domination*, that is, of a considerable gap between the regime's goals and the actual purposes to which the state's offices and resources are directed.

In sum, when faced with the question, who is the state? we discover that by the early 1990s the Egyptian state contained individuals with orientations and interests that motivated them to sabotage the regime's goals. The fragmentary character of the Egyptian state — its size, porousness, and responsiveness to outside pressures and inducements — goes far toward explaining how the parallel Islamic sector was able to be established and illuminating the obstacles that have stymied the regime's efforts to control it.

Anecdotal evidence of the Islamists' penetration of the state alerts us to forms of political contestation we might otherwise overlook. Much of the literature on resistance to authoritarian rule focuses on struggles between regimes and political opposition groups. Such studies view the state apparatus as an extension of the regime in power, that is, as a weapon wielded by one (and only one) of the adversarial parties. The Mubarak regime's harsh treatment of suspected Islamic militants, its detention in the mid-1990s of an estimated 50,000 political prisoners,[53] and its assault on the Muslim Brotherhood after 1992 all demonstrate that the state is still an effective, if blunt, instrument of coercion. Yet at the same time that some agencies of the state function as *parties to* contestation, others may simultaneously become *objects of* contestation. In Egypt we find Islamists competing with the regime over those arms of the state that are in direct contact with the mass public — in particular, those responsible for delivering services, education, and local government. Although the scope of such competition may be marginal at present, it is not difficult to envision a long-term scenario in which Egypt's authoritarian regime retains control of the security apparatus but gradually loses control of its social and ideological levers of domination.

So far we have traced the emergence of new "structures of opportunity" for mobilization in parallel Islamic institutions on the periphery. Uneven political opening in Egypt thus triggered an expansion in "group-specific opportunities" for mobilization, a process that Tarrow and others have described elsewhere.[54] But even if the emergence of new space on the periphery created the *possibility* of mobilization, it does not explain its occurrence. It is not structures, but actors, who mobilize citizens into politics. Before broader social strata can be incorporated into an opposition movement, an opposition leadership must emerge with sufficient vision and organizational skills to mobilize them effectively.

The Islamic mobilization of educated youth in Mubarak's Egypt was largely the work of a specific age cohort of Islamic activists. Younger than the veteran leaders of the Muslim Brotherhood but older and more politically experienced than the graduates of the 1980s and early 1990s, this "middle generation" of Islamic activists propelled the expansion of the Islamist movement out of the universities into the larger arenas of Egyptian public life. First, they spearheaded ground-level efforts at ideological outreach on the periphery; second, as Brotherhood candidates in professional association elections, they aggregated the movement's growing support and channeled it into electoral contests closer to the political center. The dynamics of mobilization and aggregation are explored in later chapters. First, we must consider where the mobilizers fit into the Islamic movement as a whole. Only then can we determine who exactly was engaged in mobilization, in what ways, and toward what ends.

Islamic Political Opposition Groups in Mubarak's Egypt

The Islamic movement in Egypt in the 1980s and early 1990s encompassed a multitude of groups and organizations working in different ways to promote Islamic change. No single agenda united them, as their understandings of how Islam should be applied to contemporary social and political life and how Islamic change could best be achieved varied widely. Moreover, many of those in the Islamic movement did not openly identify with an Islamic *political* group or organization.[55] Of course, when asked, even those who did identify with such a group might deny it, given that the country's main Islamic political organizations — including the reform-oriented Muslim Brotherhood — were technically illegal. Despite such barriers, however, some Islamists did claim membership in (or affiliation with) a particular political opposition group and portrayed their own activism as directed toward its goals.

Islamic political opposition groups in Egypt can be divided into two categories — reformists and militants — based on differences in goals and tactics. The largest organization in the nonviolent mainstream of the Islamic movement was the Muslim Brotherhood (formally, the Society of Muslim Brothers, or Gam'iyyat al-ikhwan al-muslimin), founded by Hasan al-Banna in 1928. At the time of the Free Officers' coup in 1952, the Brotherhood was the largest movement in the country, with an estimated half a million members nationwide.[56] Bitterly opposed to the British occupation, the Brotherhood called for an end to the foreign domination of Egyptian politics, economy, and culture and the creation of an Islamic order (al-nizam al-islami) in which the shari'a, or Islamic law, would play a central role.[57] While the Brotherhood's primary activities were in the areas of community service and education, its "secret apparatus" engaged in violent attacks on both political rivals and British and minority targets.[58]

Although the Brotherhood initially welcomed the "revolution" of 1952, it ended up as one of its main victims. Once his own grip on power was secure, Nasser moved to eliminate the movement as a political rival. Then, after an attempt on his life by a Brotherhood member in 1954, Nasser banned the organization and interned thousands of its members in prisons and concentration camps. In 1970, Nasser's death and his replacement by Anwar Sadat paved the way for the Brotherhood's return to public life. Under the leadership of its supreme guide, 'Umar al-Tilimsani, the mainstream faction of the Brotherhood renounced violence and redirected itself to the promotion of above-board, incremental change. As Raymond Baker observed, the Brotherhood's grudging reconciliation with the Sadat regime and its promise to work within legal channels laid the groundwork for the subsequent expansion of its activities in the Mubarak era.[59]

Although it remained technically illegal, by the start of the Mubarak era the Brotherhood had reconstituted itself as a formal political organization. At its apex was the supreme guide (al-murshid al-'amm), a position occupied in the late 1980s and early 1990s by Hamid Abu al-Nasr, an octogenarian veteran of the pre-1952 organization. Directly beneath the supreme guide was the Brotherhood's executive board, or Guidance Bureau, which operated out of an office headquarters in Cairo. In addition, the Brotherhood allegedly had branches in the governorates, organized at the neighborhood, city, and district level.[60] According to its members, the Brotherhood aimed to reform Egyptian society in preparation for the ultimate establishment of an Islamic state based on popular consent.

During the 1980s and early 1990s, the Islamic movement also included several groups wanting to overthrow the Mubarak regime and establish an

Islamic state by force. The fragmentation of the Islamist movement into separate reformist and militant strands dates back to the mid-1970s. At this time, some younger activists opposed to the Brotherhood's rapprochement with Sadat formed a number of underground cells committed to jihad, which they defined as the struggle to overthrow the *kafir* (apostate) regime and establish a virtuous Islamic state. One of these militant cells — Jihad (al-Gihad) — was responsible for the assassination of Anwar Sadat. During Mubarak's first decade, the militant wing of the movement contained several independent groups, the largest of which were Jihad (al-Gihad) and the Islamic Group (al-Gama'a al-Islamiyya).[61]

Both reformists and militants in the Islamic movement sought to establish an Islamic state, but neither group articulated a clear vision of how such a state would function in practice. Both factions stressed that the defining characteristic of such a state was the application of *shari'a*, or Islamic law. And both pointed to the period of rule by the prophet Muhammad and the "rightly guided caliphs" — the Prophet's first four successors — in Medina in seventh-century Arabia as a model of righteous Islamic government. But neither faction developed a coherent set of guidelines for translating Islamic principles into modern political institutions. To some degree, this reflects the fact that both types of groups placed a greater priority on organization and outreach than on intellectual output. As one sympathetic observer noted, "Their primary goal is to build a new majority, not articulate a new program."[62] In recent years, several prominent Islamist scholars loosely affiliated with the reformist wing of the movement have used *ijtihad* (the reinterpretation of sacred texts) to arrive at a more detailed, more comprehensive, and — significantly, more liberal — vision of Islamic government. These scholars have not yet arrived at a consensus on major issues, however, and as of the early 1990s, their formulations had not had a major impact on the Brotherhood's political agenda.[63]

The paucity of specifics in the political platforms of reformists and militants alike makes it difficult to compare their objectives, but their differences are most apparent in their strategies. While the Brotherhood's approach to change is gradualist and long term, seeking the Islamization of society from the bottom up, Islamic militants advocate the use of violence to achieve power and impose Islamization from the top down.

How much popular support did the reformist and militant Islamic opposition groups in Egypt enjoy during the first decade of Mubarak's rule? In the absence of public opinion data, the levels of support for different types of Islamic groups in Egypt are impossible to gauge precisely. However, it is widely acknowledged — both inside and outside the movement — that most Egyptians who identified with a particular Islamic political organization in the 1980s and early 1990s supported the reformist Muslim Brotherhood, albeit with important regional and class variations. Judging from the results of student elections, patterns of violent incidents and arrests, and the impressions of informed observers, the Brotherhood was the dominant political force in Cairo, Alexandria, and the towns of the Delta, and the more militant Islamic groups had the upper hand in the towns and villages of Upper Egypt, particularly in the governorates of Asyut, Minya, and Sohag.[64] Moreover, data gathered by the Ibn Khaldun Center for Development Studies indicate that by the early 1990s, militant groups had begun to recruit further down the social scale, with the result that those individuals arrested and charged for Islamic violence were younger, poorer, more rural, and less educated than were militants in the 1970s and 1980s.[65]

Support for the Brotherhood in the 1980s and early 1990s was concentrated among the lower-middle- and middle-class students, graduates, and professionals of Egypt's cities and provincial towns. This support was the result of mobilization but, interestingly, not by its senior leadership. The Brotherhood was formally headed by veteran leaders in their sixties and seventies. Having spent much of the Nasser era in prison, such leaders were rehabilitated by Sadat; under Mubarak, they served as the Brotherhood's official spokesmen and represented it in formal interactions with other opposition parties and the regime.[66] But it was not the old guard who attracted educated youth to the movement in the Mubarak era. Rather, such mobilization was the work of skilled and energetic Islamic activists in their thirties and forties. It was these "middle-generation" activists who launched a massive project of ideological outreach on the periphery, and — with one foot in the country's decentralized, grassroots Islamic networks and the other foot in the Brotherhood's national political organization — channeled support mobilized on the periphery into electoral contests closer to the political center. Given the vital role of this "middle generation" in the reproduction of Islamic cadres, let us take a closer look at how they developed into a "counter-elite" with aspirations for social and political power.

The "Middle Generation" of Islamist Activists

The most dynamic motors of the Islamic movement in the 1970s were the *gama'at*, or independent Islamic student associations on Egypt's university campuses. These associations provided a wide array of services to Egyptian students, as is well known.[67] At the same time, the gama'at prepared a new generation of Islamic leaders who, a decade later, spearheaded the movement's expansion out of the universities into broader arenas of public life.

Before examining how Islamic activism spread beyond the universities under Mubarak, it is important to understand how his predecessors helped foster a strong and independent Islamic student movement. Following Egypt's defeat in the June 1967 War, Nasser made a crucial concession to student demands by permitting the formation of independent student groups on university campuses. Through decree 1533 in 1968, he established the nationwide General Union of Egyptian Students, which, compared with student bodies earlier in the Nasser era, gained some real autonomy. In 1976, the union's independence was enhanced when Sadat approved a new and more lenient student charter.

In addition to establishing a more permissive framework for students' political activity, Sadat covertly encouraged the formation of Islamic student groups to serve as a counterweight to the left. Sadat's liaison with the Islamic student groups in this period was Muhammad 'Uthman Isma'il, the organization secretary of the Arab Socialist Union. Isma'il fostered the growth of the gama'at in Cairo as early as 1971 and in Upper Egypt beginning in 1973, when he was appointed governor of Asyut.[68] Initially dependent on the regime's encouragement, the gama'at soon developed their own momentum. Beginning in 1973, the gama'at at Cairo University sponsored summer camps for religious instruction, which, Kepel notes, "served as schools for the cadres and future cadres of the Islamicist movement."[69] At the same time, the gama'at established cells in the General Union of Egyptian Students, which included elected branches in every university faculty as well as universitywide and nationwide executive boards and committees. In 1975, the Islamists gained control of the General Union's national information and publishing committee, enabling them to use the organization's funds to publish and distribute low-cost Islamist pamphlets.[70] During the 1976/77 academic year, they won other important leadership positions, including the presidencies of the universities' student unions in Cairo and Minya. The Islamists continued to gain strength from that point forward, winning a landslide victory in elections for the General Union's national board in 1978/79.[71] The Islamists' electoral takeover of the student movement — which occurred at the faculty, university, and national levels — was especially striking in such faculties as Cairo University's faculty of engineering, which had long been regarded as a fortress of the left.

Within the framework of a liberal student charter, Islamist student associations flourished in the mid-1970s.[72] Student activists held religious conferences and seminars; disseminated Islamic books and pamphlets on designated "Islamic Days"; offered classes on the Qur'an, the Sunna,[73] and Islamic jurisprudence (fiqh); and organized religious camps during summer vacations. In addition, they initiated a wide range of services, such as copying academic books at low rates, selling inexpensive "Islamic" clothes, and providing, for women, separate bus transportation to campus.

As elected leaders of the General Union's national board, Islamist student leaders served as official spokesmen for student concerns with the university administration and even with the Sadat regime itself. For example, in February 1977, 'Abd al-Mun'im Abu-l-Futuh, a charismatic Islamist medical student and national student union representative, participated in a discussion with the president in a live broadcast in which, in a heated verbal exchange, he exposed the gap between the president's democratic rhetoric and his authoritarian practice.[74]

In sum, the Islamic student associations of the mid-1970s served as an important training ground for a new generation of Islamic leaders, who gained experience providing services, disseminating Islamic ideology, countering alternative groups on campus, and negotiating with the regime. Such experience left an indelible mark, as the young Islamic leaders gained both self-confidence and political skill and sophistication.

Confronted by an Islamic-led student movement increasingly critical of his foreign and economic policies, Sadat tried to reassert government control over the universities. In 1979, the lenient student charter of 1976 was replaced with a more restrictive version that eliminated the nationwide and universitywide student organizations and limited union activities to the faculty level. In addition, the faculty unions were placed under the supervision of a joint committee of students, teachers, and administrators. Most conspicuous was the return to Egyptian campuses of the security force known as the University Guard, eight years after its withdrawal.

Such measures reduced the opportunities for Islamist outreach on university campuses. Even so, during the 1980s and early 1990s, the Islamists strengthened their domination of student union politics, with a particularly strong presence in the elite technical faculties. For example, at Cairo University in 1990/91, the Islamists won 47 of 48 seats on the student union's board in the science faculty, all 72 seats in the medical faculty, and all 60 seats in the engineering faculty. These Islamist victories were due as much to the decline of the left in these faculties as to their own mobilizing success. In those faculties in which leftist and liberal groups retained a presence, such as Cairo University's faculty of economics and political science, the Islamists won only 13 of 48 contested seats.[75]

The Islamist trend remained the dominant force in student politics during Mubarak's first decade, even though its political activities on campus were subject to more and more government intervention.[76] First, security controls — including physical searches of students at the entry to university campuses and random checks of dorm rooms — increased. Second, the practice of requiring student groups to obtain security permission before sponsoring a public event became more widespread. Third, the distribution of group literature was prohibited on some campuses. Fourth, it became routine for university administrators, working closely with state security officials, to eliminate the names of Islamic candidates from the lists in student elections. While such practices were not new, government intervention in student life was more forceful and frequent in the 1980s than in the mid-late 1970s and became even more pronounced in the early 1990s.[77] For instance, when student demonstrations were held at the height of the Gulf War in early 1991, they were met by security forces armed with tear gas and live ammunition.

At the same time that the space for Islamist outreach was shrinking on university campuses, new space became available in the parallel Islamic sector, providing an important outlet for the political energies of the country's young and dynamic Islamic counter-elite. While their leftist counterparts dispersed among various splinter groups or exited from politics altogether, the Islamist student leaders of the 1970s sustained their activism in the 1980s and early 1990s in the parallel Islamic sector, in which they converted neighborhood mosques, Islamic community and service organizations, and even private homes into sites of outreach to educated youth.[78] And after graduation, some of the most prominent Islamist student leaders made a momentous decision: they decided to join the Muslim Brotherhood. Although they were forced to relinquish some of their autonomy, they gained access to the centralized resources and organization of a "quasi party," ultimately enabling them to channel support mobilized on the periphery for electoral contests near the center of national politics.

How did middle-generation Islamist leaders mobilize educated youth into politics in the 1980s and early 1990s? What outreach strategies did they employ, and why were they successful? It is to these questions that we now turn.

6 "The Call to God"

The Islamist Project of Ideological Outreach

The frustrations of Egypt's educated youth are not sufficient to explain the rise of Islamic activism. It is now widely acknowledged that even the most aggrieved citizens may end up avoiding any kind of political involvement. The reasons are, first, that as social movement scholars have emphasized, participation entails costs.[1] Not only does participation in an opposition movement impose on a citizen's time, energy, and resources but, in some instances, may expose him or her to serious risks. In authoritarian settings, such risks can extend to job loss, arrest, imprisonment, or physical harm. Second, citizens may doubt the efficacy of political participation as a means to achieve desired change. Particularly in authoritarian settings, in which regime survival is not based on the support of the governed, citizens may view any kind of protest as an exercise in futility.

Authoritarian regimes generate powerful *disincentives* for political participation that would-be mobilizers must somehow overcome. According to "rational-actor" models of movement participation, opposition leaders mobilize citizens into politics by appealing to their self-interests. In particular, they offer potential recruits a range of material and/or psychological benefits that are contingent on participation. A central contention here is that interest-based appeals are insufficient to explain the participation of thousands of graduates in Egypt's Islamic movement. When the risks of opposition activism are high and the prospects of positive change are, at best, remote, the most "rational" response of the individual is a retreat into self-preserving silence. Under these circumstances, participation in an opposition movement is likely to be motivated less by self-interest than by deeply held values and beliefs.

The proposition that ideas as much as, if not more than, interests are likely to motivate high-risk activism is only our point of departure, for a central question has yet to be addressed. Where do the ideas driving high-risk activism come from? At times, I believe, they come from the opposition movements themselves. Movement organizers do not simply tap into the preexisting grievances of potential recruits. Rather, as Alison Brysk contends, mobilization is a form of persuasion, in which movement leaders deliberately and self-consciously promote new values, identities, and commitments as a basis for political action.[2] Such efforts at persuasion are crucial in authoritarian settings, in which opposition movements must create motivations for activism that transcend powerful impulses toward self-preservation.

Islamist mobilizers in Egypt did not simply exploit the frustrations of unemployed and underemployed youth. Rather, they engaged in a massive ideological project to capture the hearts and minds of potential recruits. Through the medium of the *da'wa*, or "call to God," they promoted a new, activist conception of Islam, claiming that it was a *fard 'ayn*, a duty incumbent on every Muslim, to participate in the Islamic reform of society and state. In sum, the Islamists challenged dominant patterns of political alienation and abstention by promoting a new ethic of civic obligation that mandated participation in the public sphere, regardless of its benefits and costs.

Contemporary social movement theory depicts the creation of motives for movement participation as an act of "framing." As defined by David Snow, framing is "conscious strategic efforts by groups of people to fashion shared understandings of the world and of themselves that legitimate and motivate collective action."[3] Rather than simply attending to the logistics of collective action, movement organizers act partly as "signifying agents," articulating and transmitting ideas that can serve as a basis for action.[4] While movement scholars now widely acknowledge the role of ideas in motivating participation, research into how frames are socially constructed and how and why they acquire mobilizing power is still at an early stage.[5]

This chapter analyzes Islamist framing processes and dynamics, beginning with a description of the sociocultural environment in which Islamist mobilization occurred. It then looks closely at the Islamist project of ideological outreach — the *da'wa*, or call to God, describing the content of the Islamist message, the audience to which it was directed, and the agents and mechanisms of its transmission. As I show, it was by presenting activism as a religious obligation that Islamists mobilized graduates into politics in the 1980s and early 1990s.

Islamist outreach to educated youth did not occur in a vacuum but took place in a particular sociocultural milieu, in which the Islamists were only one of several competing influences on the beliefs and behavior of educated youth. Hence let us begin by taking a closer look at the *sha'bi* (popular, that is, urban, lower-middle-class) neighborhoods where Islamist outreach efforts were concentrated.

Egypt's *Sha'bi* Neighborhoods: The Social Context of Islamist Outreach

A major site of Islamist outreach to educated youth were the *sha'bi* neighborhoods of Egypt's cities and provincial towns. In contrast to the broad tree-lined avenues, neocolonial mansions, and modern concrete and glass apartment buildings of neighborhoods housing the country's upper-class Westernized elite, Cairo's *sha'bi* neighborhoods contain tenement-style apartment buildings crowded together along narrow, often unpaved, alleyways. As of the early 1990s, some of these neighborhoods still had no indoor plumbing and running water. Characterized by extreme overcrowding (with large families confined to a two-room, or even a one-room, apartment) and dilapidated housing stock, such neighborhoods would strike the Western observer as poor. But in fact, both within and across *sha'bi* neighborhoods, residents varied considerably by education, income, and degree of urbanization. Several factors contributed to this heterogeneity: the push by illiterate and semiliterate parents to provide their children with higher education; the growing wage and income differentials resulting from increased migration to the Gulf as well from new business opportunities created by the *infitah*; and the pressures of an acute housing shortage, which forced highly educated, urbanized newlyweds into neighborhoods on the periphery of Greater Cairo formerly occupied almost exclusively by recent migrants from the countryside. As a result of these trends, many of which date back to the mid-1970s, the same neighborhood — and even the same apartment building — might house illiterate residents side by side with those who had advanced degrees in medicine or law. Likewise, one might find some families barely scraping by on a single civil service salary, while others, in which a father or son had found work in Saudi Arabia or Kuwait, had sufficient income to launch a small business, purchase expensive consumer durables, and finance elaborate weddings.

Despite such differences in private circumstances, the residents of Cairo's *sha'bi* neighborhoods shared a number of social and cultural traits that distinguished them from the country's upper-class elites. For example, in *sha'bi* culture, extended family ties and ties between neighbors and peers served a wide range of functions, including the distribution of goods and services and the maintenance of social control.[6] In addition, demonstrations of Islamic faith, knowledge, and ritual performance were accorded high esteem, despite considerable variation in the residents' actual observance. Egyptian migration to the Gulf in the 1970s and 1980s had the effect of reinforcing the influence of Islam in *sha'bi* communal life. As noted in the previous chapter, the regional oil boom dramatically increased private wealth, some of which was channeled — by either Egyptians or Gulf Arab patrons — into the development of private mosques and Islamic service associations in *sha'bi* neighborhoods. At the same time, the intensive exposure of Egyptian citizens to the social mores of Saudi Arabia and other Gulf countries where Islamic law was strictly applied pushed their own religious beliefs and practice in a more conservative direction upon their return home. Indeed, by the early 1990s, critics had begun to openly lament that the influence of "Wahhabi" Islam (the ultraconservative strand of Islam dominant in Saudi Arabia) had begun to erode the more flexible and permissive form of popular Islam that had evolved in Egypt.[7]

In which of Cairo's *sha'bi* neighborhoods was Islamic outreach activity concentrated? They can be divided into three distinctive subtypes: (1) traditional urban quarters located in the city's oldest sections, some of which have been continuously inhabited since the medieval era; (2) Nasser-era neighborhoods dominated by clusters of uniform concrete apartment houses (*bulukat*) initially built for the families of public-sector workers and employees; and (3) newer neighborhoods located in former agricultural zones on the periphery of Greater Cairo. Such distinctions are relevant to us, because the available evidence suggests that Islamic activism was most extensive in the third type of neighborhood.[8]

Why has Islamic activism been concentrated in newer neighborhoods on the urban periphery? According to the conventional wisdom, such areas are fertile zones for Islamic activism because they are populated by rural migrants. The argument is that young adults born to migrants from the countryside are more prone to join Islamic groups because of their deeply conservative religious values as well as their physical and cultural marginalization. As Kepel wrote,

The milieu that is the most fertile source of Islamicist militants is the 20–25 age-group in the sprawling neighborhoods on the outskirts of the big cities. These people are marginal in every sense of the word, to begin with in their physical location in a middle ground that is no longer the countryside from which they came but not yet the city, whose heartland they do not penetrate. Their cultural complexion, too, is marginal: the traditional village structures no longer work for them, and can no longer provide them with the resources of material life or with any real social integration. They are the children of the rural exodus, and they arrive in the suburbs with outdated customs. Contrary to their expectations, however, education (even higher education) fails to provide them with the keys to modernity.[9]

In sum, the geographic distribution of Islamic activism is often explained in terms of the social characteristics of the movement's potential recruits. Although such explanations are not wrong, they are incomplete. Islamic activism was most extensive in neighborhoods on the periphery not only because their residents were predisposed to embrace the Islamist message but also because Islamic activists concentrated their efforts at institution building and outreach in these neighborhoods. There are two reasons why Islamic activism was concentrated on the urban periphery. First, such neighborhoods lacked the well-established institutions of communal self-help that flourished in the older quarters of the city's interior. The latter were arguably less prone to Islamist penetration because local needs were already being met by preexisting community associations and informal networks. Likewise, neighborhoods with a strong tradition of grassroots leftist activism, including the working-class *bulukat* neighborhoods in Shubra, Helwan, and Ein al-Sira, were less opportune sites for Islamic activism. As a former leftist community activist in one *bulukat* neighborhood explained with regard to Islamist attempts at mobilization in the 1970s and early 1980s, "They couldn't confront the left in our neighborhood because they couldn't match our ability to address the real-life problems of the community."[10] By contrast, in the new neighborhoods of Greater Cairo, the poor state of state-run services and the virtual absence of secular community organizations created an institutional void that independent mosques and Islamic service organizations established since the mid-1970s were able to fill.

There is another reason for the concentration of Islamic activism on the periphery. Given the shortage of apartments in older, more centrally located *sha'bi* neighborhoods, young married couples in the 1980s and early 1990s were often forced into more distant, peripheral neighborhoods where affordable housing was still available. In sharp contrast to the image of the semiliterate rural migrant, such young couples included university-educated professionals, some of whom had prior experience in the Islamic student movement. After settling into their new neighborhood, such graduates used the skills they had honed as Islamic student organizers to help establish and maintain a dynamic network of independent mosques, day-care centers, health clinics, and other community services. The forced exodus of former Islamic student leaders into peripheral neighborhoods, I would argue, explains the vitality of local Islamic institutions at least as much as does the marginalization of potential recruits.

Islamic Outreach on the Urban Periphery

In order to investigate Islamic strategies of outreach, I conducted fieldwork in three sha'bi neighborhoods in Greater Cairo known for their moderate to high levels of Islamic activism. According to the division of sha'bi neighborhoods discussed earlier, one neighborhood fell into the second category, and the other two neighborhoods fell into the third.[11] In all three neighborhoods, I conducted in-depth, open-ended interviews with approximately two dozen graduates affiliated with the Islamic movement, including graduates who helped organize and lead Islamic activities as well as those who simply participated in them. In addition, I visited several independent Islamic service organizations, attended a religious class for women at a private mosque, and observed an Islamic study circle for young women that was held in a private household.

The typical Islamic activist at the neighborhood level was a university graduate who had developed his or her Islamist affiliations as a secondary school or college student. During the 1980s and early 1990s, many of these graduates turned to the parallel Islamic institutions of sha'bi neighborhoods as an outlet through which to continue their activism after graduation. While some graduates secured full-time employment in the Islamic sector, more commonly they took their main job elsewhere and worked in the Islamic sector part time. Thus young lawyers and engineers doubled as imams in private mosques, delivering the sermon at Friday noon prayers, offering religious lessons, and organizing special activities on Islamic holy days. For their services, they might receive a small monthly stipend or a fixed fee per sermon or lesson, or they might volunteer their services. Similarly, graduates worked or volunteered in Islamic health clinics, day-care centers, kindergartens, and after-school programs. In some instances, working in the Islamic parallel sector could be quite lucrative. For example, many young doctors employed in the state-run public health system supplemented their incomes by working in the Islamic health clinics, in some instances earning more in their "second job" than in their primary one.[12]

Scattered across a large, decentralized network of institutions, those graduates active in the parallel Islamic sector could not be said to work for a single organization or to support a single platform. Some of them openly identified with the Muslim Brotherhood, whereas others claimed to be affiliated with one of the "nonpolitical" Islamic community associations (*gam'iyyat*) that sought to deepen public religious faith and observance, such as al-Gam'iyya al-Shar'iyya, al-Salafiyya, al-Shabab al-Muhammadiyya, and Gam'iyyat al-Tabligh. Other Islamists deliberately avoided identifying with any particular group or organization. As one female activist explained, "When someone asks me, do you belong to the Salafiyya or the Shabab Muhammadiyya, etc., I respond, "I am all of those."

Despite their different affiliations, graduates involved in the parallel Islamic sector shared an activist conception of Islam that informed their relations with one another as well as with the "ordinary Muslims" whose beliefs and conduct they sought to change. Through the medium of the *da'wa*, such activists tried to educate their uninformed peers about their duties in Islam, duties that, they claimed, included the obligation to personally assist in the Islamic reform of society and state.

The *Da'wa*: The Islamist Project of Ideological Outreach

Graduates active in the parallel Islamic sector explained that a central obligation of the committed Muslim was to elevate the religious consciousness of those around him (or her, for the obligation fell equally on men and women). That is, the committed Muslim was required to engage in the *da'wa ila llah*, literally, the "call" or "invitation" to God. One who calls, the *da'i*, is thus one who spreads the message of Islam. Perhaps the closest equivalent in English is "missionary," although it is difficult to dissociate this term from its roots in Christian theology and practice. Alternatively, one might refer to the *da'i* as a propagandist, but this term has pejorative connotations. To most observant Muslims, the *da'wa* has the positive meaning of spreading moral and spiritual enlightenment.

The *da'wa* is not a new phenomenon in either its conception or practice but dates back to the prophet Muhammad's efforts to convert the polytheists (*al-mushrikin*) of seventh-century Mecca. Historically, the content, mecha-

nisms, and target audience of the *da'wa* have varied, as has its political significance. In regard to ideological content, there is no single *da'wa*, as Islamists
across the ideological spectrum promote different and, at times, conflicting
interpretations of Islam. Indeed, the varying content of the *da'wa*-as-message
reflects important differences in the training and orientation of the individuals
who promote it. Currently, the term *da'i* refers to both a specific religious
occupation and, as more Muslims have assumed the responsibility for the call,
a role embraced by Muslims without formal religious training.

Religious scholars assume the formal title of *du'at* (the plural of *da'i*) after
completing the appropriate course of study at al-Azhar University (the "Islamic
da'wa" is one of several possible areas of concentration at al-Azhar); they are
then appointed to a position in the official religious establishment, usually in
a government-run mosque.[13] Since the mid-1970s, those engaged in the *da'wa*
have included graduates who obtained their religious knowledge through self-
education or through lessons and study groups offered by Islamist student
groups or independent mosques. Despite their lack of formal religious status
and credentials, such graduates nevertheless claim to have the authority to
interpret Islam to the general public. As Dale Eickelmann and James Piscatori
have pointed out, these new claims constitute part of the "fragmentation of
sacred authority" in Muslim societies, as new, self-confident Islamic activists
have begun to compete with established *'ulama'* and the state.[14]

Islamist mobilizers drew on the respected cultural tradition of the *da'wa*
but adapted it to new purposes. First, they shifted the target of outreach from
the non-Muslim to the "ordinary Muslim," that is, to self-identified Muslims
whose understanding and observance of religion were viewed as faulty or
incomplete. Second, they introduced new content into the message of the
da'wa. Rejecting the confinement of religion to matters of private faith and
ritual, they emphasized that Islam was both *din wa-dawla*: both a system of
individual faith and conduct and a comprehensive guide for the organization
of society and state. In addition to enlarging the domain of Islamic regulation, the Islamists propagated a new, activist, interpretation of proper Muslim
conduct. Before turning to the question of how their message was received,
let us first consider how the Islamists themselves understood their mission.

Islamist Conceptions of the Da'wa

According to those Islamists engaged in outreach in Cairo's *sha'bi* neighborhoods, the Islamic reform of society begins with reform of the individ-

ual.[15] This reform begins by awakening the faith (*iman*) of the individual, which in turn prompts change in his or her private conduct. Quoting Hassan al-Banna, the founder of the Muslim Brotherhood, the Islamists explained that reform would ultimately expand outward in concentric circles to encompass every wider sectors of society. As one put it, "We begin with the individual, then the family, then the local neighborhood or community, and then the society at large." And what about the state? "When society itself has become truly Islamic," he answered, "it will be only a matter of time before Islam is extended to the sphere of the state." The idea that change must proceed from the bottom up was echoed by others. As one female activist noted: "I won't go to the government now and say, this is wrong and this is right. I will go to those around me and build them up, teach them. When we are 90 percent of society, then those who I have brought up will go to the government, not me."

The prototypical target of Islamic outreach was the "ordinary Muslim" (*al-muslim al-'adi*), who was born into the faith, was more or less observant, but did not realize all the rights and obligations that a full commitment to Islam entailed. By contrast, the "committed Muslim" (*al-muslim al-multazim*) understood the norms of Islamic conduct and applied them in practice. From the activist's viewpoint, then, the goal of outreach was to propel ordinary Muslims toward a greater commitment (*iltizam*) to Islam. From a more critical standpoint, one might say the Islamists' purpose was to indoctrinate their targets with a particular interpretation of Islam that stood apart from — and challenged the validity of — mainstream forms of religious faith and practice.

The institutions of the parallel Islamic sector and, above all, the independent mosques, became important sites of Islamic outreach. In a group interview with several young activists, I asked about the ways in which a student committed to Islamic reform might sustain his or her activism after college. One graduate replied:

> After graduation the mosque is the first place. You have to understand that when someone gets involved in Islamic activities on campus, it is not in isolation from the rest of his life. He may also have a group of friends in his neighborhood with whom he can continue his activities after graduation.

Another explained that most graduates preferred to continue their activism in "nonpolitical" associations in order to limit their vulnerability to interrogation or arrest by the security police. One popular choice was al-Gam'iyya al-Shar'iyya, a national Islamic religious and service organization with local branches across the country: "Most people don't want to subject themselves to torture, arrest, and repression. So they choose the Gam'iyya Shar'iyya. It stays far away from politics. It focuses on spreading the reading of the Qur'an, religious commentaries, religious culture, and promoting a religious consciousness."

Respondents emphasized that the committed Muslim (*al-muslim al-multazim*) had an obligation to monitor and — if possible — correct the behavior of those around him. How was this to be accomplished? The answer was through persuasion (*al-iqna'*). One female Islamist was active in the movement as a university student in the 1970s and then moved to a *sha'bi* neighborhood on the urban periphery after marrying a fellow Islamist who wrote for several Islamic newspapers and journals. She explained that she identified with the goals of the Muslim Brotherhood as elaborated by its founder Hasan al-Banna: "Our goal in life is to promote the *da'wa*. I want to add a brick to the edifice of Islam in my society and in the world." To this end, she added, "I will raise my children in the correct way and, through my work, try to ensure that the people around me come closer to Islam." After settling in the neighborhood, she helped establish an Islamic kindergarten in order to raise "a new generation." "When mothers come to the mosque, I encourage them to send their children to our school; I tell them not to worry about the money." She stressed that the earlier a child was imbued with the principles of Islam, the better. "The new generation is in our hands," she declared. "It is much harder to affect the older generation, because they have grown up with a mistaken understanding of Islam." For example, they attended public schools run by the Ministry of Education where religious instruction was distorted. "The textbooks rely on religious sources which are not right . . . for example, important hadiths were taken out."

As proof that the committed Muslim was required to modify the behavior of those around him, the Islamists frequently mentioned certain phrases from the Qur'an or hadith. Cited most often was — *al-amr bi'l-ma'ruf wa'l-nahy 'an al-munkar* — the injunction to command what is good and to prohibit what is evil. Yet respondents claimed that reformists and militants in the movement had different understandings of how this was to be accomplished. To highlight these differences, several respondents cited another Qur'anic verse: "There is a Qur'anic saying that if you can't achieve an Islamic society by the hand [*bi'l-yad*], then try to achieve it by the tongue [*bi'l-lisan*]. If that is not possible, then try to achieve it by the heart [*bi'l-qalb*]."[16]

The problem, according to reformists, was that the "jihadis" misinterpreted this command. As one reformist explained:

They see it as a command to try first to achieve their goals by the hand [*bi'l-yad*], that is, by force. In our view, you should use only the authority that is in your rightful possession. If you are a father and your son does something wrong, then you discipline him; but if you are the son, do you discipline your father? Obviously that wouldn't be right.

When then asked what *al-amr bi'l-ma 'ruf* [to command the good] entails, he replied,

It means you should give advice. Islam is not in power. If it were, then the state would have a role to play in ensuring adherence to the rules. But as a regular citizen, it is not my right to mete out punishments. The authority is not in my hands.

Such views were echoed by other respondents. For example, the female Islamist mentioned earlier cited the same saying about the hand, the tongue, and the heart and explained:

What this means is that Islam can be promoted in three ways. The first, by heart, means that you observe something that is wrong and choose not to participate. The second, by tongue, involves persuading others to change their ways. The third, by hand, involves imposing change by force.

The Brotherhood, she added, viewed the use of compulsion as the exclusive right of a legitimate government, not of an individual. However, in exceptional situations, the use of force was justified. For example, if a young man saw a rape in progress and thought that by intervening he could stop it, he should do so. Similarly, he should act to stop a robbery, as long as by doing so he did not endanger his own life. As a general rule, however, an individual does not have the authority to change others' behavior by force. The problem with members of Jihad, she noted, "is that they are in a rush. They have their eyes on the ends, but they don't attempt to find the proper means. While they are prepared to use force, we stress the means of upbringing and persuasion [*al-tarbiya wa-l-iqna'*]."

If the Islamist's primary responsibility is to enlighten fellow Muslims about their responsibilities in Islam, how is this to be done? Having just examined the Islamists' conception of the *da'wa*, let us now turn to the mechanisms through which they translated their commitments into practice.

The *Da'wa Fardiyya*: Person-to-Person Forms of Outreach

Books and pamphlets on the *da'wa* emphasize that the most effective form of outreach is through direct personal contact, and the Islamists I interviewed agreed. Having applied Islamic principles to his own life, the committed Muslim is ready to engage in the *da'wa fardiyya*, the person-to-person dissemination of the call to God. When I asked a group of Islamists whether it was possible for them to distribute pamphlets outside private mosques at the conclusion of Friday prayers, several in the group noted that of course the government would not allow it. But as one of them commented,

> Anyway, handing out pamphlets is the least effective way to reach people. I hand out a pamphlet, a guy or girl reads it, then throws it away and forgets about it. What is needed is a change of heart; it goes much deeper than distributing leaflets. For example, a group of my committed friends and I will think of getting two or three other guys from our neighborhoods more involved. So we invite them to play soccer, but of course it's not only soccer; we also talk to them about right and wrong. They see that we play fair, that we don't cheat, that we set a good example, and gradually, gently, over time, we try to show them the right path.[17]

Rather than approach a stranger, such activists explained, one begins by propagating the *da'wa* among relatives, neighbors, and peers. Tapping into prior relationships enables the *da'i* to build on a foundation of familiarity and trust, raising the prospects that his or her message will be well received. Graduates involved in the Islamic movement typically mentioned that they were introduced to the movement by a brother, cousin, neighbor, or friend. As Salma[18] recounted:

> I used to be an actress, involved in plays in my high school. In my junior year, I was asked to play a big role. Then Nihad [a classmate]

began talking to me about the *khimar* [according to the movement's prevailing interpretation, the "Islamically correct" veil, which covers the hair, neck, and torso], and she suggested that I come talk to Siyam, who is *munaqqaba* [who wears the *niqab*, the veil covering a woman's entire body and face]. I talked to her, and she explained that acting was forbidden in Islam. At her suggestion, I began reading certain passages in the Qur'an. I cried and asked them, how can I leave acting? And they said, what's more important, to please God or to be an actress? I told them, I will start wearing the *khimar* on the first day of Ramadan. So two weeks later, at the start of Ramadan, they brought me the *khimar*. The girls all helped with the cost; that's how they do it, they bring it to you as a gift.

One of the young women who introduced Salma to the movement explained that she and others in her Islamist circle had identified Salma as someone who would be receptive to the idea of veiling, given that she was serious and well meaning. "We saw in her the desire to be a good person and to obey God." In sum, Islamist recruitment built on preexisting social ties while at the same time fostering a new kind of solidarity based on shared values and commitments.

The *Da'wa 'Amma*: Institutional Forms of Outreach

Person-to-person Islamic outreach, or the *da'wa fardiyya*, was supported by various institutional forms of outreach known collectively as the *da'wa 'amma* (the general, or public, *da'wa*). Parallel Islamic institutions propagated the Islamist frames through "lectures, lessons, the media, books, newspapers, magazines and tapes."[19] By far the most important institutional vehicle of outreach was the independent mosque. As one activist put it, the mosque occupies the leading role. In the independent mosques, the Islamist *da'wa* was transmitted via the sermons of independent preachers (imams), particularly during Friday prayers, when turnout was highest. In Cairo's *sha'bi* neighborhoods, some mosques were known for their charismatic and persuasive imams. Their views, backed by the authority attached to their formal status as prayer leaders, often had a profound impact on their congregants. A journalist at the Islamist newspaper *al-Sha'b*, who had just completed a survey on the "religious acculturation" (*al-tathqif al-dini*) of university students, found that their most important source of religious knowledge was mosque sermons, followed by Islamic radio programs, with family and religious books tied for third place.[20]

Interviews and participant observation in three *sha'bi* neighborhoods confirmed the crucial role of local imams as agents of Islamic outreach. The imams involved in propagating the Islamic *da'wa* were typically affiliated with independent mosques, particularly with those referred to by residents as "Sunni mosques." The overwhelming majority of Egyptians belong to the majority "Sunni" sect of Islam, but as used here the term *sunni* does not refer to the sectarian schism between Sunni and Shi'i Muslims. Rather, it refers to mosques controlled by Muslims who were said to have patterned their lives on the Sunna (path, way) of the Prophet and his companions — that is, who were exceptionally devout and observant. Amin, a graduate from one of the neighborhoods where I conducted my fieldwork, mentioned that in 1988 a sheikh from a nearby mosque affiliated with the Sunna[21]:

> convinced a group of us to start coming to the dawn prayer. . . . He organized a seminar that we attended. We focused on religion, talked about religion; we read the *mushaf* [text of the Qur'an] and religious books together. I would watch only a little TV, and I stopped playing chess and dominoes. I grew a beard [*lihya*], and prayed five times a day.

Amin remembers that period in his life, which lasted for just over a year, as one in which he felt very connected to God and had a sense of inner peace. But after a long time without work, he said, "I shaved my beard to get a job," explaining that many employers were reluctant to hire graduates with Islamic-style untrimmed beards. Once he started a new job with *al-Ahram*, the government-run newspaper, he had less time for intensive religious study: "I still pray, but not the dawn prayer."

In another neighborhood, several young women in their late teens and early twenties who wore the *niqab*, or face veil, cited the sermons of a young charismatic imam as a major factor in their decision to adopt Islamic dress. The imam preached at a small, independent Sunni mosque within walking distance of their homes. Not only did he succeed in convincing many young women to adopt Islamic dress, but he also chastised parents who objected to it. As one young woman told us, "He has rebuked parents who oppose their daughters wearing the *niqab*. He says, 'What's wrong with it? Isn't it proper, following in the path of the Prophet?' At first my mother was skeptical about the *niqab*, but after hearing the sheikh, she began to appreciate its virtues."

In addition to presenting sermons, local imams and other Islamic instructors held weekly religious classes (*durus diniyya*) for members of both sexes. In choosing a time to meet for our interviews, I was told by these veiled young women that they were not free to meet on Thursdays, Fridays, or Saturdays, because on those days they attended lessons at the mosque. During our group discussions, they also referred to an "Islamic council" (*majlis islami*) that provided Islamic instruction, with teachers circulating from one mosque to another so that "lessons of some kind are offered somewhere in the neighborhood every day."

What did these religious lessons cover? The young women said that either a woman gives a *tafsir* (commentary or analysis) to other women, or a man offers the *tafsir* to the women from behind a screen. One of the young women I interviewed, Mona, offered lessons in Islamic jurisprudence (*fiqh*) to young women on Saturdays. When asked what these lessons focused on, she answered, "They concern how to be a good Muslim. They discuss Islamic rulings, for example, those relating to marriage."

I had the opportunity to attend religious lessons for women at a small independent mosque in another *sha'bi* neighborhood.[22] The mosque was located in the basement of a tenement apartment building; no external markers identified it to passersby outside. Once a week, a thirty-year-old imam, known simply as Sheikh Ahmad, offered religious lessons to women, from whom he was separated by a green curtain. On the day I visited, about fifty, mostly young, women were in attendance, many accompanied by babies or young children. About two-thirds of the women wore the *niqab* (made of a heavy black or dark blue cloth), but upon entering the all-women area, they took off the segment of the veil that covered their faces. The remaining one-third wore the *khimar*, the veil covering the hair, neck, and torso.

The religious lessons offered by Sheikh Ahmad followed a question-and-answer format. Reflecting the assumption that a woman's voice is *'awra* (a physical adornment or attraction capable of arousing male desire), the women did not ask their questions outright but wrote them down on a small piece of paper and passed them under the curtain to the sheikh, who read them out loud and then answered them by way of an extended commentary, in which he cited Qur'anic verses and hadith. Several women took notes in small notebooks as he spoke.

Most of the questions the women asked dealt with specific aspects of marital relations (for example, what to do if my husband doesn't pray). In his answers the imam told the women that their role was "to be a door to your husband's happiness." He emphasized that women were more cherished (*mu'azzaza, mukarrama*) in Islam than in other religions. He also stressed women's important role in creating the "Muslim home," which is the "foundation of Islamic society." Women's behavior was a barometer of society: "If she is corrupt, then society is corrupt." Women were hence advised to confine their social interactions to those with a religious purpose — "Encourage your friends to come to the mosque. Don't go out of the house just for the sake of going out, but to learn your duties as a Muslim."

The young woman who had invited me to the lessons mentioned that the imam was a university graduate who was known to have an extensive knowledge of Islam. In previous lessons, she recalled, he had emphasized that a woman's voice is *'awra*. Therefore a woman should avoid talking to men and, if she must, should deepen and roughen her voice. "I find some of his views rather extreme," she went on, "but most of the girls, especially those who aren't very educated, take what he says and don't question it."[23]

"Print Islam": Cultural Production in the Parallel Islamic Sector

Islamic ideological outreach was typically a personal, even intimate process, rooted in face-to-face human relationships. But such relationships were reinforced by the wide range of Islamic books, pamphlets, and cassette tapes produced in the parallel Islamic sector. Such materials were often distributed directly in local neighborhoods. For example, one private mosque frequented by several of the graduates I interviewed had a lending library from which Islamic books and cassette tapes could be borrowed for a nominal fee.[24] In addition, cassette tapes with recorded sermons of such well-known *du'at* as Sheikh Kishk, Sheikh Mahallawi, Wagdi Ghunem, and Ahmad al-Qattan were sold outside neighborhood mosques on Friday after noon prayers.[25] The dissemination of the Islamist *da'wa* through print and audio technologies at the microlevel was intricately related to institutional developments at the macrolevel. Beginning in the mid-1970s and accelerating in the 1980s, independent Islamic publishing houses and bookstores launched new forms of cultural production and created channels through which their output could be distributed to a mass market. Citing Benedict Anderson's *Imagined Communities*, Dale Eickelman and James Piscatori have argued that in the contemporary Muslim world, as much as in premodern Europe, "Print and other technologies create new forms of community."[26] Such technologies permit the transmission of a common set of beliefs or ideas to a much larger public than would be possible through face-to-face individual contact alone. If such technologies have assisted in the formation of broad national or communal identities, they have served equally well to disseminate more specific ideological frames, including, in this case, a new, activist conception of Muslim faith and observance.

Independent Islamic publishing houses and bookstores have proliferated in Egypt since the mid-1970s, and by the 1980s they were printing and distributing a wide range of Islamic journals, magazines, newspapers, books, and pamphlets. In addition to the Islamic texts published by the government press, the output of such Islamic institutions constituted part of the cultural reservoir that informed the graduates' own understanding of Islam.[27]

In the early 1990s, Islamic newspapers and journals available on the Egyptian market spanned a wide ideological spectrum, from the government-produced newspaper *al-Liwa' al-islami*, to the Brotherhood journals *Liwa' al-islam* and *al-I'tisam*, to the eclectic *al-Sha'b*, the mouthpiece of the Islamist-oriented Labor Party. Despite their different orientations vis-à-vis the regime (which ranged from supportive to sharply critical), it is both my own assessment and that of other informed observers that regardless of its source, the printed media tended to promote a socially conservative version of Islam, in part as an outcome of Saudi influence.

The political affiliations of independent Islamic book publishers are harder to pin down. A large share of the output of such publishers is not overtly political. In addition to publishing works of traditional Islamic jurisprudence, as well as exegesis and commentary on the Qur'an and hadith, the Islamic publishing houses print and distribute books on the lives of the Prophet and his companions, on the early history of the Islamic community, and on such spiritual matters as the soul and the afterlife. Interviews with staff members at several independent Islamic bookstores in Greater Cairo suggest that books on traditional religious topics sell better than those on political or social matters. In particular, books on the Qur'an and hadith, on the Prophet and his companions ("anything on the wives of the Prophet is popular"), and on such matters as the Day of Judgment and the hereafter generate the most sales. A minority of graduates coming to the bookstores (perhaps one-third, a staff person at one bookstore estimated), ask for books about the Islamic revival, the application of Islamic law, or the *da'wa*. According to another staff person,

> A few young people, but not many, are interested in social and political affairs; most people are interested in Islamic jurisprudence [*fiqh*] and

explanations of the Qur'an. They aren't that interested in books on politics or the reform of society, or at least, that's not what most people come here to buy.[28]

What this suggests is that a much broader segment of Egyptian society have been touched by the revival of private faith and observance than are committed to an Islamic project of transformative social and political change. Nevertheless, a substantial minority of graduates (those from the *gama'at*, one staff person noted) wanted to participate in the Islamic reform of society and requested books and pamphlets on the *da'wa*.

A close reading of a sample of *da'wa* materials available on the Egyptian market reveals the predominance of a Brotherhood or "reformist" perspective. This is a result of both the Brotherhood's emphasis on the printed word and the absence of comparable output by its rivals. As of the early 1990s, the Egyptian government had not yet begun a full-scale production of its own printed *da'wa* materials to counter the Brotherhood's propaganda. Instead, the regime relied primarily on the religious curriculum of state-run schools, the sermons of state-appointed clerics, and the religious broadcasts of government-controlled radio and television to transmit official interpretations of Islam to the public. In addition, the Ministry of Religious Endowments and his staff periodically conducted religious caravans (*qawafil diniyya*) through the rural provinces to "correct" popular misconceptions of Islam.

Islamic militants recognized the importance of the printed word as much as their reformist peers did. According to several informants, members of underground militant cells regularly circulated books and pamphlets among their supporters. One young militant explained that his group routinely transferred xeroxed leaflets from one safe house to another to avoid confiscation by the police. But the militants' limited access to legal publishing firms, as well as their close surveillance by the security police, made a wider circulation of these materials difficult if not impossible.

Da'wa pamphlets and short books were produced by Islamic publishing houses and sold at low cost at Islamic bookstores and general-purpose kiosks, where they were displayed alongside newspapers and sports magazines.[29] Although secondary in their impact compared with that of other forms of Islamic ideological outreach, such as peer contact and sermons, these publications are extremely valuable to the researcher whose access to private conversations and prayers services in small independent mosques is necessarily more limited. Of course, we cannot automatically assume that the ideas contained in a given set of pamphlets are "representative" of the Islamist project of ideological outreach as a whole. Nevertheless, the views presented in the pamphlets I read closely resemble those expressed by my Islamist informants. Indeed, the convergence was so great that the pamphlets may be seen as a reasonably accurate summary of views widely shared by activists within the movement's reformist mainstream.

The Da'wa in Pamphlet Form

Sold as paperbacks about thirty to sixty pages in length, da'wa pamphlets are generally long enough to present a sustained argument yet short enough to be read in one sitting. In contrast to the sophisticated analysis of such prominent Islamic thinkers as Sheikh Muhammad al-Ghazzali, Yusuf al-Qarada'i, and Sayyid Qutb, the pamphlets present Islamist themes in formulaic or excerpted form. And in contrast to the detached style of more scholarly Islamic works, such pamphlets read more like a sermon or lecture, and in fact, several of them consist of the written text of Islamist speeches from various eras and settings. In keeping with this format, the pamphlets alternately praise, warn, reassure, advise, and cajole the reader to action, in language ranging from the stern and lofty, to the emotionally charged, to the intimate and conversational. References to the Qur'an and hadith, stories of the Prophet's companions, and the advice of medieval 'ulama' lend authority to the arguments presented and offer historical figures to be emulated. At the same time, the authors occasionally draw on their own experience, sharing lessons based on their own trials in the real world.

A brief review of the titles of some of these publications highlights their concerns. One series, entitled Toward a Muslim Generation, is published by the Islamic Publishing and Distribution House in Cairo and contains such titles as The Call to God: The Individual Da'wa, Faith and Its Requirements, and False Accusations Regarding the Application of Islamic Law. A second series, The Da'wa's Selection, published by the Da'wa Publishing House in Alexandria, includes two pamphlets by Hasan al-Banna, the Martyred Imam (al-Imam al-Shahid) and the founder of the Muslim Brotherhood: To Students and To Youth and Especially to Students. A third series, Toward an Islamic Consciousness, published by the Foundation of the Message in Beirut, includes the pamphlets Youth and Change and How We Call to Islam.

Other titles include The Duties of the Muslim Youth, Islam and Sex, The

Prohibition on Seclusion with Foreign Women and Unrestrained Mixing of the Sexes, and several pamphlets focusing on women's issues, such as *The Muslim Woman, Why the Veil, My Son?* (which addresses the issue from the viewpoint of a mother whose son is selecting a bride), *Islam and Its Exalted View of Women*, and *Islamic Laws Concerning the Muslim Woman*. Although many of the books and pamphlets are targeted at youth (*al-shabab*) without reference to gender, a subset of them deal specifically with the status and obligations of women in Islam. Also, as their titles indicate, some pamphlets directly address the misconceptions and misconduct that pervade contemporary Arab society, including the "false allegations" spread by Islam's enemies and the moral decline resulting from blind imitation of the West, particularly in regard to sexual relations.

The following analysis of six pamphlets and books focuses on one strand of this larger corpus of *da'wa* literature, those publications concerned with the special destiny or mission of educated youth.[30]

1. *The Duties of the Young Muslim*, by Dr. Magdi al-Hilali (Abu Hazim)
2. *Youth and Change*, by Fathi Yakan
3. *How We Call to Islam*, by Fathi Yakan
4. *The Call to God: The Individual Da'wa*, by Mustafa Mashhur
5. *To Students*, by Hasan al-Banna
6. *To Youth and Especially to Students*, by Hasan al-Banna

At least three of these six pamphlets blatantly represent the ideological handiwork of the Muslim Brotherhood: two are reprints of speeches delivered to university students in the 1940s by Hasan al-Banna, the Brotherhood's founder, and a third was written by a senior Brotherhood leader, Mustafa Mashhur. Two others in the sample were written by the prominent Lebanese *da'i* Fathi Yakan, whose views tend to parallel those of reformists in Egypt. *Youth and Change* is the text of a lecture that Yakan delivered to Muslim students in Perugia, Italy, in 1979. The sixth work, *Duties of the Muslim Youth*, was written by Magdi al-Hilali, an author whose background I was not able to determine, who offers a cogent presentation of many of the same themes voiced by other writers in the sample. Although these texts were originally composed in different eras, they all were published or republished in the 1980s. When comparing the text of al-Banna's speeches from the 1940s with texts written thirty or forty years later, what is most remarkable is how little the movement's emphases and priorities have changed.

Obligations of the Muslim Youth: A Content Analysis of Da'wa *Pamphlets and Books*

Da'wa pamphlets explain how a full commitment to Islam translates into practice. According to the pamphlets surveyed,[31] this commitment flows from *'aqida*, belief in God and his revelation as transmitted by the Prophet Muhammad in the Holy Qur'an. The most basic obligations of Muslim youth who have embraced the *'aqida* are possessing a steadfast faith in God (*iman*) and adhering to the five pillars of worship (*al-'ibada*): the profession of faith (*al-shahada*), ritual prayer (*salat*), fasting (*sawm*), the giving of charity (*zakat*), and the pilgrimage to Mecca (*hajj*).[32] Intimately related to faith in God is the injunction to love God and fear his wrath (*al-taqwa ila'llah*) and to believe in the Day of Judgment when God will hold each individual to account for his or her conduct.

Faith, worship, and acts of kindness constitute the foundation (*al-qa'ida*) of the Islamic personality, but they are not enough. Islam is more than a set of codes applicable to private conduct; it is complete and comprehensive (*kamil wa-shamil*), with a program (*manhaj*) for organizing society at large. So long as the social and political affairs of the community of believers (*umma*) are not based on Islamic precepts, it is incumbent on every Muslim to help hasten the establishment of Islamic rule. As Hasan al-Banna explained, "The Muslim is required, by virtue of his Islam, to concern himself with the affairs of his community. . . . I can declare quite frankly that the Muslim can express his Islam fully only if he is political, takes into his regard the affairs of his *umma*, is preoccupied with it, and guards it zealously.[33]

Or as Mustafa Mashhur states in *The Call to God*:

According to our religion, it is not enough that we are Muslims in ourselves as individuals, observing the required forms of worship and endowed with good morals and not harming anyone and that's it. Rather, our Islam is a collective religion; it is a system of life and government and legislation and state and struggle and *umma* in one. And this correct understanding of Islam fills us with public responsibilities and obligations that we must perform according to the command of God in order to ensure that society is established according to Islamic principles in all spheres, political and economic and legal and social, and so on, and we also know it is our duty toward our religion to establish it on earth and propagate it among all people.[34]

Islam thus requires individuals to assume responsibility for the conditions of the *umma* in which they live and to ensure that Islamic principles are applied in all spheres. Yet the full application of Islam is possible only through the establishment of an Islamic state. According to Yakan,

> If submission to the authority of God's Law [*shari'at allah*] is a divine ordinance, and if fulfillment of this ordinance depends on the existence of a state, then the effort to establish the Islamic state — and among the most important means is the call to God — is a religious duty incumbent on every Muslim until the existence of this state is realized.[35]

Under present conditions, Yakan explains, such change can best be effected from the bottom up, through both the collective struggle of the Islamic movement and the efforts of the individual *da'i*, whose outreach to the noncommitted is needed to expand the movement's activist core. Yakan thus presents the *da'wa* as a *fard 'ayn* — a religious obligation incumbent on every Muslim — as distinct from a *fard kifaya*, or a duty of the Islamic community as a whole.[36]

While all Muslims are obligated to help advance the cause of Islam, the leading role in the struggle is to be performed by youth (*al-shabab*). Several of the pamphlets explain why youth are particularly well qualified to lead the movement for Islamic transformation. For example, in *Youth and Change*, Fathi Yakan states that according to the logic of Islam, every person has a role, and the duty to effect social change weighs most heavily on youth. Youth is when humanity is at the height of its strength and ability, after which both begin to decline. From this stems the need "to benefit from youth in fulfilling the difficult tasks and surmounting the obstacles and confronting the challenges imposed by the logic of civilizational change." Unfortunately, however, most Muslim youth today are "lost, helpless, and confused"; they have "lost their own personality and imitate others like an ape"; they have "lost their morals, have lost their manhood, or have been mobilized by the powers of evil and oppression and joined the ranks of the nonbelievers and the devil." Hence in order to perform the role required of them, the present generation of youth itself must be transformed into a "generation characterized by a sense of Islamic belonging and adherence to its principles."[37]

The need for youth to assume their role as the vanguard of Islamic change is particularly urgent given the deplorable state of the Muslim community today. *Duties of the Muslim Youth* describes in vivid terms the depths to which the *umma* has sunk:

> The frank observer of our situation sees the exile of Islam from its dwelling place. . . . All the powers have allied against us, such as the Crusaders [that is, Christians], the Communists, the Zionists, and the idolaters; we have become the lowest people on earth. They have seized our land and our wealth and our blood, to the point that the blood of the Muslim has become, in their view, the cheapest blood. . . . It is enough for any one of us to put a finger blindfolded on any place on the map of the world, and he will land on a red line from which drops the blood of Muslims. . . . How many youth have died on the gallows . . . how many women . . . how many nursing children . . . and all the while, the Muslims have been sleeping! That is our situation in many countries . . . and in those countries where it is alleged that Islam is applied, the conditions are no better; the sinfulness and debauchery speak for themselves in these countries night and day . . . sinfulness and perversion and nudity have become "moderation" while religiosity is extremism and backwardness. . . . This bitter reality with which Muslims live everywhere imposes on each one an individual duty [*fard 'ayn*] to work for change.[38]

Having catalogued the many enemies of Islam, the pamphlets assert that only by returning to the principles of Islam can the Muslim community regain the power to confront the forces arrayed against it. This vision of a restored *umma* is one not only of military and political strength but also of moral virtue. Among the central features of life in the Islamic world today, the pamphlets note, is the spread of all kinds of perversions (*fawahish*): moral deviations (*inhiraf*), vice (*radhila*), and depravity (*shudhudh*), perpetrated in the unbridled pursuit of material and sensual pleasures. The establishment of Islamic rule would restore the health of the *umma* by reviving the distinction between *haram* (what is forbidden) and *halal* (what is permitted), thus replacing materialist civilization with a moral civilization in which society's energies are directed toward noble ends.

Rather than provide a detailed blueprint for the construction of an Islamic state, the pamphlets hail Islam as an unqualified panacea for all the problems of the *umma* and the world at large, hastening a utopia in which all human needs will be met. As Yakan asserts,

All change-oriented movements to date have finished in terrible human tragedies and bloodshed. . . . The *umma* and the entire world
need an agenda of change that can guarantee it stability and well-
being and rid it of the present nightmare of misery and anxiety and
fear and deprivation. And this can be achieved only through Islamic
change.[39]

How is Islamic change to be achieved? Consistent with the views of the
Muslim Brotherhood, the pamphlets stress that the path to Islamic reform
begins with self-reform and proceeds in ever expanding circles to embrace
the *umma* and eventually humanity as a whole. The young Muslim who
seeks to transform society must therefore begin with himself.

The first step for the Muslim youth is to deepen his belief and develop
a "correct" understanding of Islamic precepts.[40] Girded by faith, he is next
exhorted to engage in a process of self-purification, or struggle against oneself
(*al-ijtihad ma'a al-nafs*). As *Duties of the Muslim Youth* maintains,

We must realize that our greatest enemy lies within . . . the self leans
toward evil and away from good, and hence we have been commanded
to purify and straighten it and guide it with a tight leash to the worship
of its Lord and Creator and prohibit it from its longings and wean it
from its pleasures, for if we neglect it, it will go astray, and we will
never conquer it after that.

In battling his own appetites and desires, the Muslim youth is advised to
follow the example set by the companions of the Prophet and the ancestors
(*al-aslaf*) and to put himself in an atmosphere in which he will be constantly
reminded of the rewards and punishments of the afterlife, such as through
the performance of the evening prayer and the reading of the Qur'an at
dawn. In this way, "the afterlife will influence this world and concentrate
our concerns into one united concern, and that is the fear of the Day of
Judgment."

The rejection of material and sensual pleasures is a recurring theme. The
young adult is advised to "stay away from foolishness and those who take
part in it, who are sick in their hearts and souls." Abstention from desired
things is bitter medicine, the pamphlet acknowledges, but it is necessary in
order to "cure the sickness of the heart."[41] The Muslim youth also is exhorted
to purify himself of sexual and material longings through immersion in Islamic study and prayer. Asceticism is thus presented as a defining virtue

of the committed Islamic life. Acknowledging that the adjustment to self-denial is difficult, the pamphlets advise the young Muslim to associate only with others equally committed, who will provide companionship and prevent him from lapsing back into his former ways.

Detachment from the temptations of the material and sensual world is both an end in itself and a means to increase one's capacity to influence others. In order to promote Islam as a worldview and a way of life, the pamphlets explain, the Muslim youth must set an example through his own behavior. As *Duties of the Muslim Youth* points out: "We must know that the method of the *da'wa* by example [*bi'l-qudwa*] is much stronger than by words, as was said long ago: the action of one man has a greater effect on one thousand men than the words of a thousand men [have] on one man."[42]

The *Da'wa* as Civic Obligation

Once he has applied Islamic principles to his own life, the Muslim youth is ready to spread the message of Islam to others. That is, he is ready to engage in the *da'wa fardiyya* (the individual *da'wa*) involving person-to-person transmission of the call to God. By accepting the *da'wa* as a personal mission, the pamphlets explain, the Muslim youth helps expand the Islamic movement. Beginning with family members, neighbors, and friends, he is urged to gradually widen his mission to his peers.

He who propagates the *da'wa*, or the *da'i*, must prepare himself fully for the task. Not only must he possess a comprehensive knowledge of Islam, but he also must be skilled in outreach. Several of the pamphlets offer practical advice to the novice *da'i*; indeed, two of them consist entirely of such guidance.[43] While they differ somewhat in their depiction of the sequence of steps to be followed, all insist that the *da'i* must be self-conscious and systematic in his contact with the uninitiated in order to achieve maximum effect. What advice is offered to the new *da'i* as he embarks on this important mission? The first point, acknowledged as critical by all the guidebooks, is to "know your audience." The *da'wa* is directed to all Muslims, yet the style and language in which it is presented must be tailored to each individual's social background, level of education, and personal circumstances. The successful *da'i* is one who approaches each person in a way that accords with his distinct mind-set and personality, selecting the ideas and methods of contact appropriate to each case.[44] In addition, before broaching the sensitive issue at hand, the *da'i* must cultivate a relationship with the individual in question, or "addressee." The *da'i* should demonstrate his empathy and concern for the addressee's problems and, when possible, help resolve them. As Yakan advises, "Feel his pain, try to understand what ails him, get to know his problems."[45] In this manner the *da'i* can increase the person's trust and heighten his receptivity to the message.

When the *da'i* broaches the subject of Islam, the pamphlets instruct, he is advised not to be too rigid in its presentation. As Yakan reminds the reader, "Too much harshness and rigidity can lead people to adhere even more stubbornly to their evil behavior, a result directly opposite to what is intended."[46] In addition, the *da'i* must anticipate questions and be prepared to address doubts and hesitations. As the pamphlets point out, society today is overrun by competing slogans, platforms, and agendas, each of which is attempting to attract people through various forms and methods of propaganda.[47] Amid all this confusion, the *da'i* must be prepared to debunk the claims of those who would distort the Islamist *da'wa*, reveal the shortcomings of other platforms, and provide a "correct understanding" of Islamic theory and practice. To assist in this task, Yakan's *How We Call to Islam* provides a critique of capitalism and socialism, supplemented by a recommended reading list.

The most systematic approach to the *da'wa* is elaborated by Mustafa Mashhur in *The Call to God*, which presents a step-by-step plan for propelling the noncommitted Muslim toward a full embrace of Islam. According to Mashhur, the first stage of the *da'wa* is building a relationship with the addressee in order to increase his receptivity to the message. The second stage is "awakening his dormant faith." Here Mashhur uses the metaphor of sleep to powerful effect:

> Many Muslims who are occupied by the affairs of the world and are distracted from worshiping and obeying God are like people who are fast asleep while a fire is coming closer to them and will devour them if they do not wake up. Among those sleepers are some people who are awake and watching the scene but are incapable of keeping the fire away from the sleepers. Thus duty requires them to awaken the sleepers so that they will realize the situation and move away from the fire. . . .
>
> But as often happens when you awaken a sleeper, he asks you to leave him alone so he can continue sleeping because he is enjoying it and doesn't want anyone to disturb him. He asks this while he is still asleep, because if he were truly awake and saw the fire, he would

rush out and escape, and if he claims he is awake, don't believe him, unless the claim is accompanied by his efforts to move away.

The second stage of the *da'wa* is deepening the nonobserver's sense of God's greatness and creativity, which can be done by commenting on the wonders of nature (for example, "how can plants grow from simple mud and water . . . and can scientists with all the knowledge at their disposal create a grain of wheat in their laboratories?"). Having awakened "faith in God and his unity and his power and his perfection," the addressee's heart will become open to knowledge of the Day of Judgment.

In the third stage, the *da'i* must help the addressee understand what in practice the obligation to obey God entails. At this point,

it is best to supply him with simple books about Islamic belief and worship and moral codes, invite him to attend some lessons and sermons, introduce him to good people, and keep him away from bad people . . . and that's how we create for him an environment in which to complete his new Islamic personality.

The fourth stage of the *da'wa* consists of instructing the addressee that worship in its full sense goes beyond the five pillars to include all aspects of life, such as "food, drink, clothing, knowledge, work, marriage, sports, and raising children." In all these areas, he must strive to turn everyday acts into acts of worship, so that "the whole world becomes a big *mihrab* (prayer niche)."

In the fifth stage, the *da'i* must impress on the addressee that "in our religion, it is not enough for us to be Muslims within ourselves." He should continue the conversation with the addressee in this way "until there is born within him feelings of civic responsibility toward Islam and Muslims." In particular, the *da'i* should point out that "the responsibility for establishing an Islamic state is not limited to the ruler or the *'ulama'* but is the responsibility of every Muslim man and woman present in this period."

At the sixth stage, the *da'i* must explain that the public obligations of the committed Muslim cannot be fulfilled in isolation but require that he link his efforts with those of an Islamic movement. "No individual alone can establish the Islamic state and return the caliphate; rather, there must be a collectivity [*gama'a*] to gather together all these individual efforts in order to fulfill this mighty task."

In the final stage of the *da'wa*, the *da'i* must answer the respondent's question: What movement should I join? At present, this is a critical issue, Mashhur notes, given the wide variety of Islamic groups in Egypt today, "each of which calls on youth to join their ranks and all of which carry the banner of Islam, and each of which has its own slogans and methods by which to attract youth." The addressee must be advised to investigate each group carefully and select the best one. Yet Mashhur anticipates the outcome, asserting that the only movement that has all the needed qualities is the Muslim Brotherhood.[48]

By participating in the call to God, the readers of such pamphlets are assured that they can help "change this bitter reality in which we live and establish the Islamic state."[49] They are not promised rewards, material or otherwise, in this life. On the contrary, the dangers of propagating the *da'wa*, including the risk of harassment, arrest, interrogation, or worse, are frankly acknowledged. Those who work for the Islamic cause must know that the path ahead will require personal sacrifice. As *Duties* declares,

> He who wants to proceed on this path must prepare himself to have much patience and great stamina and realize that he may die without seeing the victory of God. . . . He should know that the path is full of hardship and tears, that he may be imprisoned or fired from his work or even tortured or killed. All that may be done to him to force him to leave the path, and if he caves in, he will lose both in this world and the world to come; but if he continues on the path to the end, the outcome will be in paradise, God willing.[50]

In addition to the rewards of paradise, the looming arrival of the Day of Judgment, in which each person is held accountable for his actions, should impel youth to action. *Duties* advises,

> Imagine each one of us himself in the hands of God, when God holds him accountable and asks him what he did to raise his word and achieve his reign and free the conquered land of the Muslims. Will he say — "Oh Lord, I was not convinced that work on behalf of such goals was an individual obligation for me'" Or will he say: "Oh Lord, I didn't have the time to work for your sake?" Or will he say, "Oh Lord, I was a coward and afraid because I know that work on your behalf is arduous and full of thorns"? I warn myself and I warn you that if we don't work for Islam, we must expect the reckoning of God

and his Prophet, and that is in this life; in the world to come, the situation is even more terrible, and the punishment, even more severe.[51]

Given the enormity of the task ahead of him, the Muslim youth is advised not to work in isolation but to pursue his goals within a broader Islamic movement. Solidarity with committed peers will provide him with psychic and emotional support and strengthen his ability to cope with whatever hardships lie ahead. As Hilali writes,

> Experience demonstrates that the Muslim cannot continue to perform his obligations with continued strength and balance except under one condition, and that is the presence of a sound environment and a good milieu in which to join together to obey God and fulfill his commandments. And he must seek such a milieu, even if it consists of two people only. . . . And within the group, the love of God assumes a tangible form; its members rise up gradually until they reach the level of solidarity that the companions and the ancestors reached — the point at which if one put a piece of food in the mouth of his brother, he himself felt full, and if he needed money, he would put his hand in his brother's pocket without having to ask permission; and if one of his brothers was far away, he felt as if a cherished part of himself was missing.[52]

Conclusion

At the core of Islamist outreach was a massive ideological project to capture the hearts and minds of educated youth. Islamists active at the neighborhood level disseminated a particular "frame" of Islam emphasizing the obligation of all Muslims to participate in reforming society at large. The promotion of a new ethic of civic obligation differs profoundly from a more narrow appeal to the "rational" self-interests of potential recruits. In fact, Islamists called on graduates to struggle against the natural human inclination to seek pleasure, wealth, and power. As *Duties of the Muslim Youth* explains, "Human nature is intent on self-aggrandizement and vanity and love of this world and hatred of death, on greed and lustful desires and envy. Thus God has asked us to struggle against it."[53]

The presumption that movement participation is a form of rational, self-interested behavior has led many social movement scholars to underestimate the extent to which ideas influence action.[54] From a rational-actor perspective, the interests of potential challengers are rooted in objective conditions of exploitation. Individual interests or "preferences" are given, but rational actors may or may not choose to pursue them through collective action. Within this paradigm, ideological frames mediate the progression from preferences to behavior by shaping the perceived costs and benefits of different paths of action. In this way, they increase the likelihood of collective action when they raise popular expectations of success.

Islamist ideological outreach has done far more than alter the cost-benefit calculations of self-interested recruits. Rather than simply mediate the relationship between preferences and action, Islamist outreach has changed the preferences of educated youth. By promoting new values, identities, and commitments, the Islamists have created new motivations for action that transcend the bounds of narrow self-interest. They have influenced not only how individuals pursue their goals but also what those goals will be.

In recent years, movement scholars have begun to acknowledge the role of ideas in mobilization. Even so, much of the movement literature describes the construction, transmission, and reception of ideological frames as *psychological processes* involving change in individual perceptions.[55] The problem is that when we conceive of framing as a strictly psychological process, we fail to fully appreciate its *political* character. As Alison Brysk observed, oppositional frames typically challenge established canons and call into question the legitimacy of dominant institutions and elites. In this way, "counter-hegemonic" themes or ideas pave the way for broader instances of social and political change. As Brysk noted, "When power-holders lose legitimacy, other power-holders withdraw support, institutions lose cohesion and subordinates may directly confront authority figures. This can lead to attempts at various types of social change, from preemptive reform to civil disobedience to revolution."[56]

Eickelman and Piscatori claim that in the Muslim world, new Islamist intellectuals are challenging the exclusive authority of "official interlocutors" — the state and the clergy it appoints and approves — to define Islam to the mass public.[57] In Egypt, the new interpretations of Islam advanced by movement activists not only have cast doubt on the legitimacy of the established order but also have paved the way for new forms of civic engagement detached from — and opposed to — formal political institutions and elites.

This chapter discussed the content and mechanisms of Islamist ideological outreach but did not touch directly on the reasons for its success. To explain this success, we must shift our attention from the mobilizers to the mobilized, from the Islamist message to its reception. Why was the Islamist frame of civic obligation so enthusiastically embraced by so many educated, lower-middle-class youth? We explore this question next.

7   Explaining the Success of
Islamist Outreach

      The rise of Islamic activism among urban, educated youth in Egypt in the 1980s and early 1990s poses something of a puzzle for students of collective action. Under the shadow of Egypt's authoritarian state, even nonviolent, reformist Islamist groups like the Muslim Brotherhood remained technically illegal and subject to surveillance and harassment by the security police. An open affiliation with the Islamist cause entailed real risks, whereas the prospects of effecting change — at least in the immediate term — were remote. Under these seemingly unpropitious conditions, we might expect Egyptian graduates to reject the Islamist message. Why, then, did so many embrace it and ultimately act on it?

      To explain the success of Islamist outreach, we need to look more closely at the "micromechanisms of mobilization," that is, at how movement leaders forge and sustain linkages with potential recruits.[1] The mobilization literature contains at least two major theories of recruitment that draw on different assumptions about the motives behind collective action. Informed by a "rational actor" model of human behavior, one strand of the literature contends that movements attract new members by appealing to their individual self-interests. Movements do this by providing "selective incentives" — a range of material, psychological, and/or emotional benefits that are contingent on participation. From this viewpoint, *access to benefits* motivates potential participants to join a group or movement, and these benefits explain their continued involvement over time. Another strand of the literature contends that individuals often join groups or movements to express deeply held commitments, values, and beliefs. A movement may thus elicit participation as a response to a perceived moral duty or obligation, irrespective of the costs and benefits incurred by those involved.[2]

I argue here that both interests and ideas often motivate collective action but that their relative causal weight may shift over time as participants become increasingly integrated into movement networks. A close investigation of Islamic patterns of recruitment in three *sha'bi* neighborhoods of Cairo revealed that it was self-interest that induced many graduates to join the Islamic movement but that it was their integration into Islamist networks and subsequent absorption of new ideological commitments that paved the way for their participation in Islamist opposition politics.

The entry of graduates into the Islamic movement was typically a gradual process in which lower-risk forms of activism preceded higher-risk ones. Many graduates initially joined Islamic networks because of the various social, psychological, and emotional benefits conferred by participation, much as "rational actor" models of mobilization would predict. But while such benefits help explain the graduates' initial participation in the movement, they alone cannot explain their eventual progression to higher-risk, more overtly political forms of Islamic activism. What facilitated this progression was the graduates' embrace of an ideology that framed activism as a "moral obligation" demanding self-sacrifice and unflinching commitment to the cause of religious transformation. The positive reception of the Islamist message by Egypt's educated youth, however, was not a function of its intrinsic appeal. Rather, it hinged on a set of conditions external to the message itself, including (1) its close "fit" with the life experiences and beliefs of those graduates targeted for recruitment, (2) the credibility and effectiveness of its agents and modes of transmission, and (3) its reinforcement through intensive, small-group solidarity at the grass-roots level.

Networks and Selective Incentives

The entry of Egyptian graduates into the Islamic movement often began with participation in neighborhood-level Islamic networks and progressed (in some, but certainly not all, cases) to opposition activities associated with the movement's bid for political power. Interestingly, this progression conforms to patterns of recruitment observed elsewhere. For example, in his classic study of participation in the American civil rights movement, Doug McAdam noted that "extremely risky, time-consuming involvements . . . are almost always preceded by a series of safer, less demanding instances of activism."[3] The Islamist recruit typically followed just such a trajectory, proceeding from "safe, less demanding" forms of activism to more costly and potentially more dangerous ones.

Many graduates first got involved in the Islamic movement by participating in social or cultural activities sponsored by a neighborhood mosque or Islamic student association. For example, they began by attending religious lessons at a nearby mosque, joining an informal study group, or accompanying a friend or neighbor to special prayer services in observance of an Islamic holy day. Several factors diminished the perceived risks and enhanced the perceived advantages of such initial forms of participation. First, with few channels outside home and school for peer interaction, Islamic lessons, seminars, and prayer meetings offered some of the few socially sanctioned venues for graduates of both sexes to congregate outside the home. In addition, the religious character of such activities elevated their respectability and prestige. When asked to describe people active in local Islamic networks, the residents of *sha'bi* areas typically replied that they were simply "strongly attached to religion." The small activist mosques and those involved in them were referred to as *sunniyyin*, meaning those who follow the Sunna (path, way) of the Prophet and his companions. The term thus had the positive connotation of exemplary behavior and closeness to God.

Islamic patterns of recruitment drew on preexisting ties among relatives, friends, and neighbors.[4] This enabled Islamists to absorb the graduates into their circle on the basis of preestablished familiarity and trust and to deflect any suspicion that a dependence on strangers might have aroused. The initial costs of Islamist participation were lowered by the fact that they did not necessarily require breaking prior social ties. On the contrary, close social relationships between activist and nonactivist peers often continued. For example, my interview with one young woman who wore the *niqab* (the full veil covering the face and body) and gloves was interrupted by the unexpected arrival of a close female friend from the university, dressed in a T-shirt and jeans. In sum, the presence of Islamist networks at the local level where people lived, studied, and worked made them highly accessible and minimized the social distance between participants and nonparticipants. The result was that neighborhood residents viewed graduates' involvement in Islamist circles — and the heightened religiosity it was presumed to reflect — as a normal and unremarkable feature of local community life.

The social embeddedness of Islamic networks permitted a certain amount of flexibility and experimentation, enabling the graduates to "try out" different levels and forms of participation.[5] Furthermore, such networks provided opportunities for participation detached from the realm of *al-siyasa*, or high politics. It was well known in *sha'bi* neighborhoods that young people suspected of involvement in militant Islamic groups were vulnerable to the threat of arrest, detention, interrogation, and even torture or death. Moreover, state authorities were seen as often failing to discriminate between reformist and militant Islamist groups, lumping together those active in the Brotherhood, say, with those in Jihad. With their emphasis on incremental change at the local level rather than direct confrontation with the regime, Islamic communal networks were thus perceived by potential recruits and their families as less risky venues for social activity.

Islamic networks not only provided opportunities for comparatively low risk forms of participation that were sanctioned by the local community but also offered graduates a range of "selective incentives."[6] For instance, such networks served as channels for the distribution of goods and services and the exchange of favors and protection. Some of the Islamists I interviewed mentioned that they could turn to peers in the movement for help in securing a job or a visa to work abroad. An individual's participation in Islamist networks also might increase his or her chances of securing work in the Islamic parallel sector or enhance his or her family's access to the funds distributed by mosques or to subsidized day-care and health services.[7] Involvement in Islamist circles could even improve one's marriage opportunities. Islamist peers could vouch for the morals of unmarried men and women and expand their range of eligible mates by using family contacts beyond the neighborhood or even beyond Cairo. Indeed, several of the graduates I interviewed indicated that they had met, or planned to meet, a spouse through the mediation of their Islamist circle.

In addition to these tangible benefits, participation in Islamic networks conferred a range of psychological and emotional rewards that social movement scholars refer to as "solidary incentives."[8] Participation gave the graduates a feeling of belonging and an intimacy with peers based on shared commitments and routines. Indeed, the graduates commonly referred to others in their Islamic circle as *ikhwa*, "brothers and sisters," and the close bonds were evident in the warm hugs and embraces between members (of the same sex), the exchange of personal secrets and confidences, and the readiness to assist one another in times of need. In addition, participation offered recruits a sense of psychic empowerment, transforming poorly skilled graduates with bleak economic prospects into fellow soldiers in the noble task of Islamic reform.

Besides linking participation in Islamist networks with tangible and intangible benefits, Islamist outreach on the periphery created powerful pressures for social conformity, increasing the social and psychological costs of nonparticipation. This raises the question of whether Islamic outreach had a coercive aspect. Most Islamists insisted that they sought to bring about change through persuasion (*al-iqna'*) rather than by force. But the conditions under which persuasion acquires a coercive dimension are a subject of vigorous debate.

The role of coercion has been emphasized by critics of the Islamic movement, who maintain that young people in many *sha'bi* communities face intense peer pressure to conform to Islamic moral and social codes. The critics have also noted the marginalization of competing viewpoints and pointed to the fact that the Islamists had begun indoctrinating ever younger students, shifting from the university and secondary (grades 9 through 12) levels to the preparatory schools (grades 7 through 9). Several leftists I interviewed in one *sha'bi* neighborhood had witnessed this early indoctrination firsthand. As one observed: "The Islamic groups get to the students now when they are young — in preparatory school and in high school. They get them when they are young and impressionable, telling them this is *haram* [forbidden] and that is *halal* [permitted]."

Among the signs that Islamists were moving into the lower levels of the school system was the conflict that erupted in the Ministry of Education in 1994, when thousands of teachers were punitively transferred for allegedly disseminating "extremist" Islamic views in the classroom (for details, see chapter 5).

We must also determine whether there is a coercive dimension to ideological outreach in general. For example, we need to ask at what point forceful efforts at persuasion blur into "brainwashing," especially in situations in which conflicting views are absent or underrepresented. The claim that Islamists were "trapping" innocent youth through indoctrination was forcefully asserted by the Egyptian weekly *Akhir sa'a*:

> The private mosques have become the biggest snare of the youth, who comes originally to pray, but who, upon being ready to leave, is seized by an extremist as his next victim, who sits him down and whispers at him, and his nice-sounding, honeyed words have an effect, who promises him a straight path to heaven if he obeys the rulings of God (and the extremist takes it upon himself to interpret what they are), and warning of the suffering in hell if he disobeys. Then he suggests that the youth start attending daily religious lessons, and listen to the Friday

sermons, and invites him to eat dinner at his home, where the other members of the extremist group are waiting for him in order to complete his mobilization.[9]

In this way, the article concludes, the "unsuspecting youth, who started out just wanting to pray, ends up a member of a Shawqiyya or Ikhwaniyya or Gihadiyya or Salafiyya extremist group which are enemies of the state."

One need not take the appraisals of critics at face value to recognize that under certain conditions, Islamist ideology can be difficult to resist. In a social context in which a majority of the population are devout Muslims and other interpretations of Islam are not authoritatively presented, it may be difficult for a young man or woman to withstand the argument that "God requires you to pray or veil or fast" or "God requires you not to drink or smoke or interact with members of the opposite sex or socialize with non-Muslims."

Islamist outreach, therefore, generated significant pressures for social conformity. One example is the case of Salma, who was pressured to give up acting by female peers in her secondary school. Even the ostensibly generous act of presenting the *khimar* and several long-sleeved, ankle-length "Islamic" dresses to a young woman facing the momentous decision of whether or not to wear a veil can easily be viewed as a form of peer pressure. As one young woman in a neighborhood Islamic circle explained, "We buy the *khimar* for those who can't afford it, or one of us gets the material and another one sews it. When a woman is ready to make the decision, we try to get things ready very quickly, before she changes her mind."

Although less common, sometimes Islamists attempted to prohibit ostensibly non-Islamic behavior by force. The majority of Islamists active at the grassroots level rejected the use of physical force, emphasizing that true religious conduct must stem from inner conviction rather than external pressure. But more militant Islamist groups and factions were less hesitant about using force to achieve their goals.

Cases of physical coercion by Islamists were, not surprisingly, reported in detail in the official Egyptian press. For example, *Akhir sa'a* published the names of several mosques in Greater Cairo and Upper Egypt where Islamic militants had allegedly issued *fatwas* (religious rulings) banning the enjoyment of photography, music, films, and television.[10] During the 1980s and early 1990s, both the bombing of video stores, nightclubs, and other leisure establishments viewed as promoting moral decadence and the assassination of critics of the movement, including the well-known secular intellectual

Farag Fawda, leave no doubt that some Islamists were ready to brutally punish those seen as deviating from their version of Islamic belief and practice.

The social practice of parallel Islamic institutions could be seen as coercive as well. For example, Sami Zubaida argued that such institutions functioned as new vehicles of social control. "If the quest for civil society is one which seeks a framework for the exercise of human rights and social autonomies," he declared, "then the model presented by the Islamic sector falls short." Rather, the Islamist sector "reproduces under modern conditions the authoritarian and patriarchal framework of the associations of kinship, village and religious community" at a time when such communities have been weakened by socioeconomic change.[11] By enforcing a particular version of Islamic belief and conduct, Zubaida alleged, the institutions of the parallel Islamic sector simply substituted one form of social and ideological domination for another.

In sum, a range of positive and negative inducements facilitated the entry of graduates into Islamic communal networks on the periphery. While easing their initial entry into the movement, such interest-based appeals cannot explain the graduates' progression from lower-risk to higher-risk and more overtly political forms of Islamic activity. As a graduate proceeded from attending a collective prayer session or religious study group in his dorm or neighborhood to campaigning for an Islamist candidate or participating in sit-in strikes or demonstrations, the risks associated with participation increased. In such instances, in which the costs of participating could be absolute, a strictly "rational" or instrumental explanation for involvement does not suffice. Moreover, a focus on individual costs and benefits does not capture the ways in which participation in Islamic networks was subjectively experienced. In interviews, graduates in the movement repeatedly underscored the *normative* basis for their own actions, explaining that, self-interest aside, they were obligated to participate in the task of Islamic reform.

How can we come to terms with the causal role of ideological conviction? Whether conceived of as the duty to enlighten one's neighbors and friends or, more broadly, as the duty to participate in elections, peaceful demonstrations, and other forms of direct political action, the new Islamist ethic of civic obligation cannot simply be discounted as a "screen" behind which individual interests functioned. Rather, as Emirbayer and Goodwin have contended, we must take seriously the possibility that "it is historical actors' specifically normative commitments, rather than (or in addition to) their pursuit of material goals, that effectively drives their social movement participation."[12]

Acknowledging that "ideas matter" is only a starting point, for we still must determine how and why a certain set of ideas becomes the basis for collective action. Indeed, in mainstream social movement theory, the conditions for the successful construction, transmission, and reception of mobilizing beliefs and ideas have not yet been fully explored. For example, in *Freedom Summer*, his classic study of the American civil rights movement, Doug McAdam noted that an important process of *identity conversion* prepared recruits to participate in high-risk forms of activism, but he did not fully explain how and why young civil rights activists acquired their ideological affinities, or exactly how their integration into activist networks served to reinforce them.[13]

The question of why individuals find persuasive a particular call to action was raised by David Snow and Robert Benford:

> Why are potential constituents mobilized on some occasions while at other times framing efforts fall on deaf ears and may even be counterproductive? Under what conditions do framing efforts strike a responsive chord or resonate within the targets of mobilization? . . . What, in short, accounts for what might be termed *frame resonance?*[14]

To understand how certain frames acquire resonance in a given context, we need to shift our attention from the mobilizers to the mobilized. Building on Snow and Benford's ideas, we need to examine how a given ideology resonates with the life experience and broader belief system of potential recruits.

The Resonance of the Islamist Message

A central goal of Islamist outreach was to promote a new ethic of civic obligation, emphasizing the duty of every Muslim to participate in the task of Islamic reform, regardless of the benefits and costs incurred by those involved. Why were so many graduates ready to embrace — and act on — an ideology that stressed the primacy of the public good over the pursuit of private self-interest? First, Islamic mobilizers on the periphery adapted a respected cultural repertoire to new purposes. By framing their outreach as engaging in the *da'wa*, the Islamists endowed it with a cultural legitimacy that it otherwise would have lacked. Furthermore, the Islamist message resonated powerfully with the life experiences of recent graduates, as well as with prevailing themes in Egyptian popular culture. Finally, the graduates' reception of the Islamist message was enhanced by the credibility and efficacy of its agents and methods of transmission.

Many graduates from urban, lower-middle-class communities had profound grievances concerning their own limited prospects for advancement as well as what they perceived as the breakdown of fairness and accountability in society at large. Their search for solutions took different forms. Some graduates decided to emigrate, temporarily or permanently; others tried to develop the personal or social connections (*wasta*) needed to obtain a better job. Thus some (and perhaps even most) graduates confronted their circumstances with a hard-knocks pragmatism, not inclined to explore the causes of their diminished prospects or the policy changes needed to improve them.

The graduates' dissatisfaction could also, however, trigger a broader existential search for meaning that, in some instances, culminated in the embrace of Islam. Gamal, a graduate in a militant Islamic group explained, "Most people have problems and are looking for a solution. In the end, many find the solution in Islam." Or as Muhammad, another young Islamist, ventured, Islamist books and tapes "spoke to me." He recalled the period after he graduated from college:

> I felt lost at that period. After graduating, I had no goals, no direction.
> Actually, I felt it even during my years at the university. I didn't know
> my purpose in life. Before I became committed [*multazim*], I read
> Naguib Mahfuz, Taha Hussein, Tawfiq al-Hakim, and they all increased my confusion. They didn't speak from an Islamic point of view
> but from a Western conception of things.

Muhammad began to read Islamic books and listen to cassette tapes on the *da'wa* and started attending lessons at the Gam'iyya Shar'iyya mosque on Gala' Street in Ramses, which he referred to as the "mother" of that association's national network of mosques:

> I began to attend services at the mosque and to listen and read, and
> there were doubts and questions inside me. I looked for answers to
> them. Questions about God — why worship him, for example; he
> doesn't need us. The beginning and the end, my aim and my purpose
> in life — what was it?

Muhammad found in Islam the answers he was seeking. "There is a major difference between the committed and the uncommitted youth," he said. "The committed youth has a goal and a purpose; he wants to be a servant of God." In sum, the decision to commit one's life to the spread of Islam relieved the graduates' angst over their marginalized status and gave them a sense of higher purpose and significance. The appeal of Islamic ideology was thus magnified under socioeconomic conditions in which conventional routes of self-advancement were blocked.

Islamic ideology also built on, and responded to, the "culture of alienation" that prevailed among educated, lower-middle-class youth. To the many graduates struck by the juxtaposition of acute poverty and great wealth, who had read about drug dealers in parliament and allegations of corruption implicating senior government officials and their family members, who had themselves or knew someone who had been passed over for a job despite their qualifications because they did not have the right social connections, who had witnessed a high-school teacher distribute an exam in advance to students who had paid for it, who had seen a wealthy motorist violate traffic laws with impunity, or who had been arrested without having committed any crime, the single greatest problem facing Egyptian society was its *normlessness*.

According to many lower-middle-class graduates — including those with no political affiliations whatsoever — this crisis of morals (*azmat al-akhlaq*) was at the root of the country's current malaise. Unfettered by conscience, wealthy and powerful elites manipulated the system to their own advantage, with little concern for the less fortunate. As one graduate put it, "Here the rich eat the poor; the strong eat the weak." For graduates who had been socialized to view themselves as a meritocratic elite, perhaps the greatest source of bitterness was what they perceived as an erosion of the link between merit and reward. As noted earlier, the exhaustion of Egypt's statist economic model and the introduction of market reforms had diminished the value of graduate entitlements and augmented the importance of marketable skills and social connections linked to class background. To graduates without social connections or sufficient resources to acquire foreign-language and computer skills, the distribution of jobs and incomes in the liberalized economy appeared strikingly unfair. At the same time, many graduates saw the political system as dominated by Westernized politicians and military officials who were indifferent to popular suffering and — in the absence of effective mechanisms of oversight — both able and willing to exploit their offices for private gain.

The Islamist *da'wa* tapped into these grievances and portrayed Islam as the means to fundamentally transform the conditions in which they were rooted. Indeed, with its emphasis on collective adherence to a God-given moral code and collective responsibility for the public welfare, the *da'wa* projected a vision of Islamic rule that stood out as a striking reverse image of the status quo. Against the perceived reality of state elites preoccupied with self-enrichment and removed from popular needs and concerns, the *da'wa* conveyed the image of a leadership animated by its religious duty to safeguard the well-being of the Islamic *umma*. Against the perceived reality of a society of atomized individuals pursuing selfish aims, it offered the image of a moral community living in accordance with God's precepts. Perhaps most important — and here we must remember the self-image of the *muthaqqafīn* (cultured ones) — against the perceived reality of a society in which power and circumstance determined life chances, Islamist ideology projected the image of a society in which merit — both moral/spiritual and practical/professional — would be justly acknowledged and rewarded.

The diagnostic and prescriptive power of Islamic ideology, capable of revealing the causes of society's malaise and pointing the way to a solution, cannot be underestimated. This cognitive dimension helps explain why the Islamist message appealed to some of the more intellectually minded graduates, contrary to the stereotype of the typical Islamist as relatively unsophisticated.

One example of this intellectual cadre was Gamal, a graduate of middle-class background whose parents were committed Nasserists. Gamal grew up familiar with leftist thought, earned diplomas in several European languages, and, as a journalist for *Misr al-fatat* — a new, small-circulation Islamist newspaper — regularly reviewed excerpts from the foreign press, including *Le Monde*, *Newsweek*, and *Der Spiegel*. Gamal explained that he rejected Nasserism because it "lacked a coherent philosophical foundation." He found the answers he was seeking through an extensive reading of primary Islamic texts. "For every issue," he noted, "Islam offers a coherent analysis and set of principles. Take, for example, the issue of social justice." Gamal rejected the versions of Islam offered by the Muslim Brotherhood and other established groups and, with a small group of similarly minded peers, was working to formulate a "new trend" closer to the more radical distributive model of Islam found in Iran.

The emotive power of an ideology that appears capable of explicating and resolving society's most intractable problems calls to mind the resonance of Marxist ideas among young, lower-middle-class youth in interwar Europe.

Consider, for example, this passage from an autobiographical essay by Arthur Koestler:

> Tired of electrons and wave-mechanics, I began for the first time to read Marx, Engels and Lenin in earnest. By the time I had finished with *Feuerbach* and *State and Revolution*, something had clicked in my brain which shook me like a mental explosion. To say that one had "seen the light" is a poor description of the mental rapture which only the convert knows (regardless of what faith he has been converted to). The new light seems to pour from all directions across the skull; the whole universe falls into pattern by magic at one stroke. There is now an answer to every question, doubts and conflicts are a matter of the tortured past — a past already remote, when one had lived in dismal ignorance in the tasteless, colorless world of those who *don't know*. Nothing henceforth can disrupt the convert's inner peace and seren-ity — except the occasional fear of losing faith again, losing therefore what alone makes life worth living, and falling back into the outer darkness.[15]

With its emphasis on fairness and social justice, Islamic ideology gave voice to the moral outrage felt by those graduates who regarded themselves as unjustly deprived of their due rewards as an educated (that is, meritocratic, as opposed to class) elite. At the same time, it offered them a new conceptual language for understanding the predicament of contemporary Egyptian so-ciety, the vision of a better alternative, and an agenda for change — all in a single package.[16]

In concluding our discussion of Islamist ideology, let us examine the argument that it was actually "rational" for graduates to support the Islamic movement, as they believed it would promote their interests in the long run. That is, one could assert that it was not the Islamist ethic of civic obligation so much as the prospect of jobs and status in an Islamic order that motivated graduates to participate in the Islamic movement. In fact, it is impossible to determine precisely what share of graduate participation can be attributed to "duty" versus "interest." And yet, I would argue, this dichotomy misses the point, for in either case, the motivations for participation were created by Islamist ideological outreach. That is, in either case, it was Islamist ide-ology that motivated the graduates to shift from abstention to participation, whether by persuading them that their interests would be served by Islamic reform or by inducing them to act on the basis of normative commitments rather than self-interest. As noted earlier, however, when asked why they had become active in the Islamic movement, the graduates emphasized that they did so to fulfill a religious duty. A strictly interest-based account of Islamic activism would be forced to discount such responses as an expression of "false consciousness," that is, to claim that the graduates were not aware of the "real," interest-based motivations guiding their behavior. Yet if we accept the graduates' responses as a valid indicator of (at least some share of) their actual motivations, we must conclude that both ideas and interests played a causal role.

Communicating the Islamist Message: Its Agents and Methods of Transmission

The success of Islamist mobilization was due not only to the resonance of the Islamist message but also to the efficacy of its agents and methods of transmission. First, let us consider the agents, or social carriers, of the Islamist call to God: what qualities contributed to their success? As Brysk has argued, "Since the credibility of information is judged in part by the credibility of the source, we would expect speakers with greater social legitimacy to suc- ceed more often at persuading others."[17] Brysk contends that legitimacy is particularly strong for those "to whom society has already allocated a special protective or interpretive role," such as mothers, priests, warriors, and doctors.

In Egypt, the Islamists' successful appropriation of the authority to inter- pret sacred texts — an authority formerly monopolized by the state-appointed *'ulama'* — paved the way for the graduates' acceptance of their message. Sev- eral other factors enhanced the credibility and prestige of Islamist activists on the periphery. As noted earlier, those activists who had gained political skills and sophistication as Islamist student leaders in the 1970s became active in broader arenas of Egyptian public life in the 1980s and early 1990s. By then in their thirties and early forties, this "middle generation" of Islamic activists included several charismatic leaders who offered compelling role models for younger activists and provided intellectual, logistical, and moral support to outreach efforts on the periphery. Furthermore, while the coun- try's senior military and technocratic elites were generally of upper- or middle-class origin, this emerging "Islamic counter-elite" had its roots in the neighborhoods of Egypt's cities and provincial towns. Drawn from the same class and cultural background as those of the potential recruits, this middle generation of Islamists helped bridge the divide between elite and mass political culture, speaking the same language and having experienced the same deprivations as the audience to whom they appealed.

The graduates' internalization of Islamist values was further reinforced by their integration into local Islamist networks. According to McAdam, Tilly, and Tarrow, "the cultural construction of collective action is invariably a network — that is to say, a structural — process."[18] The Islamic networks of Egypt's *sha'bi* neighborhoods constituted the structural pathways for the transmission of Islamist ideas. At the same time, they facilitated the rise of new forms of intensive, small-group solidarity that reinforced the graduates' new Islamist commitments while simultaneously detaching them from the conventional socializing influences of family, neighbors, and peers. Islamic communal networks thus constituted a crucible for both the transmission of Islamist ideology and the development of new kinds of collective practice through which it was reinforced.

In sum, Islamist mobilization promoted ideological frames as much as, if not more than, appealing to graduates' self-interests. But the mobilizing power of Islamist frames was informed and constrained by the social and cultural environment in which they were propagated. Graduates became Islamists not because of the intrinsic appeal of the *da'wa* but because the networks for its transmission were deeply embedded in urban, lower-middle-class communities; its social carriers were familiar and respected; and its content resonated with the life experience and belief system of potential recruits.

The Impact of Islamic Mobilization

The Islamist project of ideological outreach created new motivations and venues for opposition activism under conditions of authoritarian rule. To what extent did this contribute to broader processes of social and political change?

When we talk about Islamic activism, we are actually referring to a wide range of activities with different political implications. As noted earlier, Islamic outreach was not the outcome of a unified campaign by a single group or movement but was a decentralized process involving discrete groups of Islamic actors with different goals and tactics. While all Islamist activists sought to promote Islamic change, they differed in their conception of the end point toward which society should be headed and the manner in which it should be pursued. Just as the goals and tactics of Islamists varied, so did the impact of their outreach. In some instances, the main result of Islamic outreach was to prompt new forms of social interaction at the local level. For Salma and her friends, for example, participation in Islamist networks meant higher levels of religious observance, such as the observance of extra fast days, the addition of extra *rak'as* (prayer sequences) to one's daily prayers, and the wearing of the *niqab* and other *nawafil* (ritual observances that exceed regular religious obligations and find favor in the sight of God). But even when such new commitments radically transformed a graduate's social relationships, they did not necessarily push him or her toward overt political engagement.

The graduates' involvement in local Islamic networks often instilled greater sympathy or identification with Islamist groups in the national political arena without leading to direct participation in politics. Indeed, many graduates active in Islamist networks, like their nonactive peers, continued to regard the realm of *al-siyasa*, or high politics, as dangerous and remote from the concerns of their daily lives. In such instances, Islamic outreach on the periphery fostered the development of a "supportive public" broadly sympathetic to the aims of the Islamic movement but not directly challenging the regime.

By contrast, exposure to the message of the Muslim Brotherhood or a militant Islamic opposition group more often led graduates into direct political involvement. We have no way to gauge what proportion of Egyptian graduates in Islamic networks in the 1980s and early 1990s identified with the Brotherhood, Jihad, or any other group aspiring to a more extensive transformation of society and state. My own impression is that the majority of graduates involved in Islamist networks in Greater Cairo were politically unaffiliated, while among those who were affiliated, the vast majority identified with the Muslim Brotherhood.

As noted earlier, the *da'wa* of the Brotherhood stressed that every Muslim had a personal responsibility for the state of the Islamic *umma* and the world at large. How did this Islamic ethic of civic obligation translate into practice? As Tarrow, Tilly, and other social movement scholars have noted, the forms that civic engagement assumes depend on the "repertoires of contention" available at a given place and time.[19] In Egypt in the 1980s and early 1990s, the activities of young Islamists affiliated with the Muslim Brotherhood included (but were not limited to) attending (or helping organize) Islamic seminars, plays, and public prayer sessions; voting for (or running as) Brotherhood candidates in student union, faculty club, professional association, or parliamentary elections; distributing campaign literature and running errands during the lead-up to electoral campaigns; and participating in peaceful marches, sit-ins, and demonstrations. In addition, Brotherhood-affiliated youth worked in Islamic bookstores, publishing houses, health clinics, schools, banks, investment houses, and manufacturing companies.[20]

Islamist outreach on the periphery helped give rise to a new Islamic community, encompassing a committed core of Islamist activists and a broader base that I have termed a "supportive public." Despite differences in their levels of political involvement, all the members of this community were part of a new Islamic political discourse and culture. Indeed, the impact of Islamist outreach on Egyptian culture and values was deeper and more extensive than its impact on existing relations of domination and power.

But Gramsci's insight holds: cultural and ideological change can pave the way for change in relations of power by undermining the legitimacy of ruling institutions and elites and justifying collective resistance to them. It is not wholly accurate to describe the new Islamic subculture as "counterhegemonic," since it was not uniformly oppositional in its content or impact. Nevertheless, it contained several elements that reinforced the disengagement of educated youth from the symbols and structures of Egypt's formal political institutions and elites.

Inside the Islamist Worldview

The integration of graduates into Islamist social networks enhanced their receptivity to an Islamist perspective on everything from the nature of the political system to such issues as veiling, education, marriage, sex, and death. Hence the most fundamental change produced by Islamic mobilization on the periphery is what we might call a "transvaluation of values," that is, a reordering of the priorities that guide individual action.

This culture shift had numerous manifestations. For example, in a social milieu in which a secular university degree (*shahada*) had long been coveted as both a status symbol and an instrument of career advancement, the Islamist subculture diminished the relative value attached to secular knowledge gained through formal education and increased that of religious knowledge gained informally through self-study and group lessons at private mosques. My conversations with a group of young veiled women in one *sha'bi* neighborhood typified this trend. As one young woman told me, "Knowledge for us is knowledge of religion. Religion includes and encompasses all other kinds of knowledge."

In agreement, another young woman added, "That's right — did you know that all of modern scientific knowledge was already known and can be found in the Qur'an?"

When asked what kind of books they read, several of the women replied that they read only religious books; two sisters were especially proud of their extensive Islamic book collection. As one of them told me,

> We read what we respect — religion only. It is a question of priorities. Rather than waste time reading novels or other books, we read religious books. Novels and other nonreligious books can be read too, so long as they don't contain anything against religion — stories about sex are forbidden, for example. If there was time after religion, we'd read other books, but there's never enough time for religion, is there?

Or as another woman later commented: "Why waste time going to a film, when we can go the mosque and take religious lessons?"

A parallel change can be seen in the devaluation of a university education and white-collar employment as appropriate goals, for either oneself or one's marriage partner. Young women in particular began to question the pursuit of a university degree that would equip them only for jobs that, by strict Islamist standards, were inappropriate. The young veiled women just cited shared the view that a woman's first priority was at home. As one of them declared, a woman should work only if four conditions were met: she wasn't needed at home, her work had an inherent value, her husband approved, and the job did not require mixing with members of the opposite sex. Two examples of "appropriate work" for women were jobs in health and teaching that provided services to women and children only.

The devaluation of secular university degrees enabled lower-middle-class graduates to rationalize their decision to opt out of a system that relegated them to the lower rungs anyway. Reflecting the debilitated state of public schooling in urban, lower-middle-class neighborhoods, many of the veiled young women I interviewed had received low scores on their college-entrance exams, thus limiting their career options. As Amina recalled,

> I originally intended to go to university but when I received my *magmu'* [total exam score], the only thing it allowed me to enter was commerce. So I refused. Why go into commerce — a field for which

there is no need? Only in medicine and teaching, where women can teach girls, is there a need for women to work. So I gave it up.

Similarly, young women began adjusting their expectations regarding the education level and jobs of potential marriage partners. For decades, urban, lower-middle-class women and their parents favored suitors with a white-collar job, which they associated with job security and a higher social status. From an Islamist perspective, the women I interviewed stressed, the great value placed on white-collar work was unwarranted. As one young woman said,

Why does the ordinary youth want to wait for a government job? For the social status. But now even he is forced to find work elsewhere. In Islam, work is obligatory. But it can be any work, as long as it is honest. My cousin is a law graduate, but he sells perfume at a kiosk on the street. There's no shame in that. The important thing is not how much prestige is involved or how much he earns. The important things is to earn a living legitimately, not earn it through stealing, drugs, or other illegal activities.

Among the positions some Islamists did not consider religiously permissible were jobs in banks that charged interest and jobs in the tourism industry.

In all three of the *sha'bi* neighborhoods where I conducted my fieldwork, graduates active in Islamic networks spoke of adjusting their expectations. For example, Mona, who wears the *khimar*, explained that five years ago she had hoped to go to university. Now that she had finally completed secondary school (it took her several extra years because she left school and later returned), she wanted to continue learning, "but not necessarily for a degree. Degrees aren't what matters. What counts is learning. I could study at home, and Ahmad [her fiancé] could bring me books."

What about her fiancé? Mona responded:

Ahmad, who never even finished *i'dadi* [junior high school], knows so much about Islam! I am constantly amazed — I ask him, how did you learn so much? He learned from the mosque, from lessons, from other people who are committed. I respect that more than people who have degrees. I'd rather have someone like Ahmad than an engineer or doctor who didn't know anything about Islam.

In addition, graduates in Islamic networks asserted their self-conscious rejection of the materialist values pervading the surrounding secularized Egyptian society. As Amina explained, "The ordinary Muslim needs to earn more money than the committed Muslim, because his needs for material things [*istilzamatu*] are greater." Frequently cited was the contrast between the lavish dowries, furniture, and consumer durables expected by ordinary brides and grooms and the far more modest requirements of partners committed to Islam. As Muhammad observed,

> For us to get married, we need only the simplest things — for example, a little room in our parent's apartment is enough. The pressure to get everything at once is not present in a *multazim* family. The truly Muslim woman knows she is like a queen in the house; she doesn't need material things. If a woman sets a fixed amount of money for the engagement gift as a condition of marriage, how can that be love?

As their expectations regarding higher education, career advancement, and material wealth diminished, so too did the graduates' feelings of disappointment and frustration. When asked what problems they faced as young adults at the start of their lives, most of the graduates active in Islamic networks responded that they did not have any problems. As one young veiled woman told me, "We don't consider ourselves to have any problems. You should talk to the ordinary youth if you want to know about problems." Several young women nodded in agreement. One expressed a different view. Acknowledging the difficulties of daily life, she noted: "We struggle, but we regard it as a test of our faith."

Leaders in the Islamic movement echoed the idea that society's main problems were not a matter of resources but of values. In the spring of 1990, I interviewed Kamal Habib, an Islamic militant who had been imprisoned for his leadership role in the Jihad organization,[21] which, he proudly reminded me, "was the one that assassinated Anwar Sadat." His comments in this regard were striking:

> As a graduate, I don't have any problems. We need very little, live life simply, don't need fancy cars and apartments and all that. I married a woman from the university. We live very simply, but we don't feel poor. Society imposes shackles on people; it pressures them to worry about clothes and apartments and money. . . .
>
> We in the organization do not need to have dowries or expensive

parties or anything like that to get married. I found an apartment in [a *sha'bi* neighborhood]. From the organization, I had twenty-one volunteers helping me find a cheap apartment. That's the meaning of Islamic solidarity [*al-takaful al-islami*].

The problem is that we are not living an Islamic reality. The definition of a society's problems depends on the nature of that society. It's not just a question of resources. In the 1970s, many private luxury apartments remained vacant while other people could not find housing. That was during Sadat's time, may God destroy him. People's values got all shaken up [*zalzilit qiyam in-nas*].

In their deliberate rejection of values widely held in their own communities, young Islamists often faced intense opposition from their parents. Several graduates mentioned that their parents initially balked at their decision to adhere to a strict Islamic way of life. For example, several young women noted that their parents had opposed their decision to cover their face with the *niqab* or to wear gloves; others mentioned their parents' strenuous resistance to the idea of marriage without a generous dowry. In order to proceed with their plans, the graduates were often forced to defy their parents' authority. Nevertheless, the graduates I interviewed emphasized that respect for one's parents was important. As one female graduate explained, "We can't blame them for thinking as they do, because they grew up in a different environment." Or as Muhammad noted, "If my parents told me to do something that went against God's laws, I wouldn't do it. But I wouldn't curse them for it." One solution to parental resistance was to encourage parents to come to the mosque and talk things over with the imam. Salma, who wears the *niqab*, noted that her mother objected to the idea at first. But she agreed to attend the prayer services led by the charismatic young imam at the "Sunni" mosque in her neighborhood. After hearing the imam's sermons, Salma said, her mother became reconciled to her decision. The Islamist subculture thus produced a subtle reversal of authority relations in the family, encouraging adolescents — backed by local, self-trained Islamist authorities — to challenge their parents' dictates and "correct" their faulty understanding of Islam.

The Islamist rejection of values dominant in Egyptian popular culture occurred under a distinct set of circumstances. It took place at a time when many students failed to receive the scores they needed to enter the academic field of their choice, when formal education no longer guaranteed permanent employment, and when "respectable" jobs were in increasingly short supply. Furthermore, it occurred at a time when the lifestyle that many residents in *sha'bi* communities sought for themselves or their children — a lifestyle associated with the possession of expensive consumer goods — was increasingly out of reach. Rather than promising the satisfaction of material needs, the Islamist movement promoted detachment from them as an emblem of moral superiority.

In sum, the Islamist reordering or "transvaluation" of values lessened the graduates' frustration not by providing the means to satisfy their aspirations for middle-class status, jobs, and lifestyles but by promoting life goals more readily fulfilled within existing resource constraints. By redefining what should be valued, the Islamist movement offered many young Egyptians a "solution" to the problems they faced in everyday life. This "solution" extended to the most basic of human needs. For example, Muhammad explained that for men who wanted to get married but had no resources, Islam offered a cure for sexual frustration: fasting and prayer were advised as a means to "decrease the longing." Here, too, Islam offered a way out of psychic distress that took into account existing structural constraints, in this instance, the limited opportunities for sexual expression outside marriage.

Islamic outreach also enhanced the graduates' relative position in existing social and political hierarchies of power. First, their embrace of Islamic commitments augmented the graduates' sense of their own moral authority vis-à-vis non-Islamist parents, neighbors, and peers. Paradoxically, by adopting the strict behavioral code of the "committed Muslim," the graduates were freer to flout the strictures of traditional *sha'bi* social conventions that limited their choice and autonomy in other ways. This type of empowerment was particularly important to young lower-middle-class women, whose freedom of movement and control over education, career, and marriage decisions were often sharply restricted by conservative *sha'bi* social codes. By adopting "correct" Islamic behavior, young women gained an aura of respectability that enabled them to move more freely in public spaces without fear of social sanction. In addition, they were able to invoke their "rights in Islam" as a means to mobilize social pressure against parents or spouses who mistreated them.[22]

Further, Islamic outreach reshaped popular political culture by altering the graduates' relationship to the authoritarian state. Islamist ideology challenged the prevailing climate of fear and passivity by exhorting graduates to obey a higher authority, regardless of the sanctions they would incur as a result. The embrace of Islamist commitments was thus a form of psychic empowerment. "The committed Muslim is not afraid of anything except God,"

Muhammad noted. "He doesn't fear death." Moreover, struggles in this life were viewed as a test of faith to be welcomed by the believer. The point to be made here is not that all graduates active in the Islamic movement were ready to sacrifice their lives for the cause but that a firm belief in the righteousness of their mission and its backing by God enabled many of them to overcome the paralyzing fear that inhibits protest in authoritarian settings. By stressing the fleeting and ephemeral nature of life on earth in comparison with eternal life in the world to come, the Islamist message — more, perhaps, than leftist and other secular ideologies — reduced the potency of the regime's threats to citizens' physical and material comfort and well-being.

In addition to helping graduates overcome fear, the *da'wa* (particularly in the version propagated by the Muslim Brotherhood) challenged the dominant trend of noninvolvement in public life. Against the "rational" idea that voting and other forms of political action were a waste of time, the Brotherhood *da'wa* asserted that every Muslim must contribute to the task of Islamic social and political reform. As one young activist said, "The young person who is religious is the one who is interested in the affairs of society — Islam requires it." Or as another put it: "An observant Muslim will not be quiet when she sees oppression or wrongdoing going on around her." By promoting a new ethic of civic obligation, the *da'wa* helped convert a passive political stance to an active one.

Islamic outreach also generated a widespread sense of optimism about the future. As a young Islamist working in an Islamic bookstore told me: "If you talk to ordinary youth, you will find that they are negativists "*salbiyyin*"; they are miserable and they complain a lot and they feel that nothing can be done. But Muslim youths are positive thinking."

In interview after interview, graduates in the Islamic movement stressed that the committed Muslim is positive thinking (*igabi*), a term connoting optimism and faith in the future: "Others despair and complain, but we are positive thinkers." Notwithstanding the hardships and difficulties Islamists faced during this period, the influence of Islam as a global force was destined to expand. As Kamal Habib predicted, "The future is with us. The *sha'bi* neighborhoods are our base, because they didn't change when the upper classes began to imitate the West. . . . American society is in decline. All societies pass through phases, they rise and fall. Now is a period of transition. Soon Islam will be resurgent."

I asked, "You mean those who are now in prison will one day be the ones in power?" and he responded, "Yes, exactly. When I get out, we can talk about it some more."[23]

Other Islamic activists, whether militant or reformist, expressed the same faith in Islam's inevitable advance. Western societies were in a state of decay, as demonstrated by their high rates of crime, teen pregnancy, and drug use; the breakdown of the family; and the presence of homelessness and poverty amid great wealth. Only Islam could offer humankind the moral and spiritual framework it needed, and in time this would be obvious to all. As one young Islamist journalist predicted,

> First Islam will spread through the neighborhoods, and then to Egyptian society as a whole, and then to the Egyptian state, and then to other Muslim countries, and then to countries in which Muslims were formerly the rulers, and then to other parts of the world, including Europe and the United States.

I had already moved to another question when I realized he had not finished. "And then it will spread to other planets in the solar system, and eventually it will spread to the entire universe."

The idea that the future belongs to Islam was forcefully expressed in a play performed at the Engineers' Association Sporting Club in the spring of 1991. As an indication of the larger cultural change that Islamic outreach has engendered, the play and the circumstances surrounding it are worth describing in some detail.

Situated along the banks of the Nile in the wealthy neighborhood of Zamalek, the Engineers' Association Sporting Club, equipped with a playground, sports grounds, and café, has historically offered a site of leisure for affluent, Westernized engineers and their families. But when the association came under Islamist leadership in the mid-1980s, the Sporting Club acquired a different hue. One Friday evening in the spring of 1991, the club became the venue for the performance of an Islamic play. An audience of about 300 attended, with women seated on the right of the central aisle and men seated on the left. All the women in attendance were veiled, whether in the simple *higab* or the more "religiously correct" *khimar* or *niqab*.

Performed by young male engineers, the play was loosely based on religious stories set before the advent of Islam.[24] In the first story, a young man refuses to renounce his faith in the one God and declare his obeisance to the pharaoh. Enraged, the pharaoh tries to kill him in a variety of ways, from burning him to burying him to drowning him, but each time the young man manages to survive. In the end, he says to the pharaoh, "If you want to kill me, you can, but you must say 'In the name of God.'" Exasperated, the pharaoh repeats the words, and only this time does he manage to kill him. At this point, however, the pharaoh's own guards become believers and revolt against him.

The second story is about a confrontation across a crevice, or dry riverbed between a king and his ministers and the believers in one God. When the believers refuse to renounce their beliefs, the king's officials throw them into the crevice where a fire burns. Hence the believers are martyred by a king who refuses to acknowledge the sovereignty of a higher power.

Both stories tellingly focused on the oppression of righteous believers by an arrogant ruler and his obsequious advisers. Even though they were dressed in toga-style costumes suggestive of ancient times, the actors took pains to demonstrate the relevance of the drama to the present day. In his mannerisms, body language, and verbal expressions, one of the pharaoh's advisers bore an unmistakable resemblance to the then minister of education, Fathi Surur, and other actors similarly aped well-known political figures, to the delighted guffaws and snickers of the crowd.

The most memorable moment of the evening occurred after the play had ended. After taking their bows, the actors joined hands on stage and summoned the audience to join them in song. "The Islamic awakening, it is coming, it is coming," the crowd sang in unison. The lead actor, standing in the middle of the stage, reached out for a small child seated in the front row and placed him on his shoulders. A Qur'an was placed in one of the child's hands and a sword in the other. The actor crossed the child's hands over his head, and the singing reached a peak: "The Islamic awakening, it is nearly here, it is around the corner." Outside the walls of the club, on the wide boulevards that curve along the Nile, affluent Egyptians in Western clothes strolled in the twilight, oblivious to what was going on inside.

Ideologized Islam provided Egyptians with a radically different vantage point from which to view the political system and their role within it. This break in consciousness was one of the Islamist movement's main goals and, to the extent that it succeeded at the collective level, one of its greatest achievements. Zenab, a female Islamic activist, made the point quite clearly:

The government keeps people running after a morsel of bread. Therefore they aren't free to think, to question, to challenge anything. Most people never escape from that circle. They are too busy running after money or lurching from one crisis to another. But we [Islamists] stand outside the circle and are trying to bring other people out of it as well.

In a second interview, Zenab returned to this theme, noting that "most people lack the means to think critically" and that "the Muslim Brotherhood gives them those tools."

Zenab's idea of "breaking out of the circle" exhibits some striking parallels with Vaclav Havel's notion of "living within the truth."[25] To both Zenab and Havel, ruling elites implicate citizens in their own domination by sapping them of the ability to challenge dominant beliefs and norms. Both held the view that a change in consciousness — in how individuals perceive and relate to the world — was necessary before they could aid in their own liberation from oppression. Before conditions were ripe for broader social change, both Zenab and Havel stressed, the individual must live in accordance with his or her own inner convictions. "At a minimum, a Muslim must be honest," Zenab stated, just as Havel called on individuals to live as close to the truth as possible.

Here the similarity ends. Whereas Havel wrote of "truth" with a small "t" and viewed liberation as freedom from the constraints of all ideologies, Zenab and other Islamists in Egypt retained their belief in the existence of a transcendent Truth with redeeming power. While Havel and the other "antipoliticians" of eastern Europe aimed to liberate the individual from the noose of a suffocating orthodoxy, the Islamists promised relief from moral anarchy by establishing a community united in adherence to God's laws.

The graduates in Islamic networks consciously tried to separate themselves from secularizing and Westernizing influences in society. As one remarked, "We isolate ourselves from bad people." Other graduates active in the movement told me they had been advised not to associate with Egyptian Copts; others had been warned against contact with foreigners. Moreover, several graduates emphasized that all of Egypt's leaders, laws, and social customs had been shaped by imported ideas and institutions that were not suitable for a Muslim society. Muhammad pointed out that many of Egypt's laws were borrowed from France and the United States; Zenab noted that most of the country's leaders were trained in foreign schools. The solution, they maintained, was to achieve greater self-sufficiency within the Islamic community. As one veiled young woman noted, "If I had a disagreement with a friend, I wouldn't consult the French laws used in this country; instead, I would consult with someone from our circle."

Islamist mobilization on the periphery has created nothing less than a "counter-society" detached from the mainstream social and political order. To reduce the spirit of this community to one of opposition would be to understate its creative, experimental, and comprehensive character. What defined the Islamic movement was less its opposition to a given regime or set of policies than its efforts to construct, from the bottom up and over time, a new kind of society inspired by Islamist ideals.

One of the reasons that Islamist outreach on the periphery was tolerated in the 1980s and early 1990s was that the Mubarak regime failed to fully appreciate its political significance. Indeed, activism in ostensibly nonpolitical settings on the periphery can, under certain conditions, challenge incumbent elites closer to the center of national politics. The next chapter explains how the Muslim Brotherhood tapped into a "premobilized" support base to win control of several of Egypt's national professional associations.

8 From the Periphery to the Center

The Islamic Trend in Egypt's Professional Associations

From Mobilization to Political Change

Islamic mobilization in Egypt occurred on the periphery of the formal political system in settings removed from state control. Mobilization also was a decentralized process involving thousands of Islamic activists scattered across the neighborhoods of Cairo's cities and provincial towns. Indeed, those engaged in Islamist outreach at the local level had diverse affiliations, and many of them had no direct relationship to the realm of high politics, or *al-siyasa*. How, then, did mobilization on the periphery affect national political institutions and elites?

Mobilization can yield very different results. In some instances, its impact is purely local and social, whereas in others, it can culminate in the overthrow of a country's most senior leaders. Of particular interest here is the question of when and how mobilization can contribute to a *peaceful* turnover of power. Given the centrality of competitive elections as a mechanism for alternating power without violence, a key question is when and how mobilization can affect contestation through the ballot box. In general, we can hypothesize that the impact of mobilization hinges on (1) the "openness" of the formal political system to electoral contestation and (2) the capacity of opposition parties to convert mobilized support into votes.

The effect of mobilization on formal political institutions and elites depends in part on the openness of the political system. For comparison, we can distinguish among three types of systems: "open" systems, which permit the free formation of political parties and unrestricted contestation among them for the most senior positions of power (for example, democracies); "closed" authoritarian systems, which prohibit independent parties and are devoid of any meaningful contestation for power; and "semi-open" authoritarian systems, in which political contestation occurs within limits set by the regime. In the contemporary Muslim Middle East, we might characterize Turkey as an "open" system (qualified by the military's sporadic intervention in the political process); Syria, Iraq, Libya, and Saudi Arabia as "closed" systems; and Egypt, Algeria, Morocco, Jordan, and Kuwait as "semi-open" systems. In the last category, the most senior power holder (whether a king, amir, or president) is typically not subject to direct popular elections. Yet members of the country's national representative bodies — such as parliament and interest groups representing labor, business, and the professions — are chosen through elections involving some measure of real competition.

In "closed" systems, no nationally organized opposition party or movement can aggregate citizens' preferences and channel them into a peaceful contest for political power. With the electoral option closed off, mobilization is likely to pose little or no direct threat to incumbent political elites unless, as in Iran in the late 1970s, it is so massive and widespread as to eject them by force. The key point is that in closed authoritarian systems, mobilization will not lead to a peaceful and legal turnover of power *unless* it induces the incumbent regime to change the rules of the game, that is, unless it induces a transition from a closed system to a semi-open or an open one.

By contrast, both open and semi-open systems contain arenas in which organized opposition groups can compete for political power. In Turkey, for example, the Islamist Refah (Welfare) Party took part in competitive elections for parliament in 1995 and won a plurality of the vote, leading to the appointment of the party's leader, Necmettin Erbakan, as prime minister.[1] In Jordan and Kuwait, Islamists compete legally and openly for seats in parliament. In Egypt, the Muslim Brotherhood, the country's largest Islamist political organization, still does not have legal party status. Nevertheless, in the 1980s and early 1990s, Brotherhood candidates ran as independents in parliamentary elections and as an organized bloc in elections for leadership of several of Egypt's major national professional associations. In open and semi-open systems, the potential thus exists for formally organized opposition groups to tap into support mobilized on the periphery and channel it into electoral contests closer to the political center.

The progression from mobilization to nonviolent political change depends not only on the openness of the political system but also on the strength of the linkages between opposition parties and members of the mass public. In authoritarian regimes, opposition parties are often "salon" parties with little or no connection to a popular base. As noted earlier, none of Egypt's legal opposition parties has a strong presence at the grassroots level. Had the Muslim Brotherhood in Egypt been a typical "salon" party, its ability to tap into Islamist sentiment on the periphery would have been limited. But unlike other opposition groups, the Brotherhood did in fact succeed in cultivating a popular base, largely owing to the bridging function performed by its middle-generation activists. From the mid-1980s to the mid-1990s, such activists represented the Brotherhood in parliament and the professional associations while remaining part of a broader network of Islamic activists engaged in outreach at the grassroots level. They were thus uniquely situated to channel support mobilized on the periphery into electoral contests at or near the center of national politics.

This chapter traces the Muslim Brotherhood's electoral ascent in Egypt's professional associations and discusses how it transformed them into major sites of Islamist political experimentation.[2]

The Islamic Trend in Egypt's Professional Associations: An Overview

On September 11, 1992, the Islamic Trend (al-Tayyar al-islami), as the Muslim Brotherhood faction was known, won control of the Lawyers' Association, defeating its rivals in free and competitive elections. The Islamic Trend's victory in one of the country's last remaining strongholds of liberal and leftist opinion brought shock and soul-searching among the nation's secular politicians and intellectuals. The election revealed little about the preferences of the majority of Egyptian lawyers, since only about 10 percent of the association's 140,000 members voted. What it did indicate — along with the Islamic Trend's victories in the associations of doctors, scientists, engineers, and other professions in the 1980s and early 1990s — was the growing alienation of the country's educated middle class from the country's veteran politicians and the emergence of the Islamic Trend as their only credible alternative.

By permitting a genuine process of political contestation in Egypt's national professional associations (while prohibiting it in parliament), the Mubarak regime may have wagered that it could accommodate the opposition's demands for representation without jeopardizing its own hold on power. To some extent, this strategy succeeded, at least in the short term. In exchange for the right to participate through legal channels, the country's largest opposition movement agreed to play by the regime's rules and refrained from directly challenging its power in the street. As a result of this tacit arrangement, however, the regime ultimately ceded control of some of the country's highest-profile institutions to opposition forces committed to an Islamic transformation of Egyptian society and state. Under Islamist control, these associations became important sites of social and political experimentation, enabling the emerging "Islamic counter-elite" to demonstrate its leadership abilities, promote a new Islamic subculture, and expand its base of support within Egypt's "new middle class."

The Islamists won elections in several of Egypt's leading professional associations by capitalizing on the discontent of new members whose ambitions for middle-class jobs and status had failed to materialize. Many of these graduates had already been incorporated into Islamist networks on university campuses and in residential neighborhoods. Hence they formed a "premobilized constituency" that Brotherhood candidates could tap in elections for control of the associations' boards.

To place these developments in historical context, let us begin by examining the evolution of Egypt's professional associations since the Nasser era.

Arenas of Contestation "by Default": The Politicization of Egypt's Professional Associations

The political role of the professional associations, or syndicates (al-niqabat al-mihaniyya), has significantly changed since the Nasser era. During the 1950s and 1960s, the associations were pillars of the corporatist system of interest representation established by Nasser. Within this framework, each broad occupational group was represented by a single national peak-organization licensed by the state and subject to its control. Because corporatist laws prohibited the existence of more than one interest group in the same profession, the associations became the sole legal representative of professional interests.

During the Nasser era, the associations served primarily as vehicles of co-optation and control, enabling the regime to distribute benefits to a strategic middle-class constituency while containing their political activity within official channels. Most associations retained their nonconfrontational character under Sadat. Dominated by competing sectoral blocs and cliques, the associations were vulnerable to state manipulation, enabling Sadat to "re-

ward the more loyal associations and divide the more unruly ones."[3]
Throughout the Sadat era, the majority of professional associations retained
their docile character, with two notable exceptions: by the mid-1970s, the
Journalists' and Lawyers' Associations had emerged as centers of independent leftist and liberal political opinion and, as such, were among the few
mainstream political organizations to openly criticize the regime's policy.

The professional associations assumed a much higher political profile
under President Mubarak. Whether because of an inadvertent retreat by the
state or a deliberate attempt to broaden "safety-valve" channels for dissent,
Mubarak allowed candidates affiliated with the Muslim Brotherhood to
openly compete against government and secular opposition candidates for
control of the associations' executive boards. Under the banner of the Islamic
Trend (al-Tayyar al-islami) or the Islamic Voice (al-Sawt al-islami), the
Brotherhood ran its own list of candidates in several professional association
elections. Though still subject to corporatist legislation and dependent on
state funds, the associations thus became sites of relatively free and fair contestation "by default."[4]

At the beginning of the 1990s, there were twenty-one professional associations in Egypt.[5] Historically, the most active and independent have been the
well-established associations (typically founded before 1952) representing the
free professions such as law, journalism, and medicine. Given the high status
of professionals in Egypt, the associations are often described as representing
the "vanguard" or "elite" of Egypt's broad technical and salaried white-collar
middle class. Despite their continued status as elite institutions, the social
composition of the professional associations has changed dramatically over
time. In particular, the skyrocketing university enrollments of the late 1970s
and early 1980s and the subsequent rise in the number of graduates with
professional degrees have transformed the associations into mass institutions
whose members vary widely by income, occupational status, and worldview.

From Elite to Mass Institutions: Egypt's Professional
Associations Under Mubarak

By the early 1990s, membership in Egypt's professional associations had
grown to slightly more than 2 million members. In most associations, membership was open to all holders of professional degrees, which, depending
on the field of study, required four to six years of university education.[6] Most
graduates joined their association shortly after graduation, because mem-

bership was a prerequisite for employment in most fields and it offered access to benefits like secondary pensions, subsidized health insurance, and help in obtaining visas to work abroad. In most professions, degree holders were eligible for association membership regardless of their current employment status. As a result — and critical to our purposes here — most associations included not only acting professionals but also graduates who were working outside their profession and those who were unemployed.[7]

The entry of thousands of new graduates led to a dramatic expansion in the size of the professional associations in the decade between the mid-1970s and the mid-1980s. The parameters of this growth can only be estimated, as most associations do not regularly update their membership data. Even so, the membership data for the country's eight largest professional associations highlight the aggregate trends (see table 8.1).

Membership in Egypt's professional associations expanded rapidly in the 1970s, at a rate of about 12 percent a year, and continued to grow, a bit more slowly but from a much larger base, between 1978 and 1991. This pattern reflects the accelerated growth in university enrollments during the Sadat era, which continued, albeit at a slower pace, through the mid-1980s under Mubarak.

The sketchiness of the available data makes it difficult to determine the share of youth (al-shabab, usually defined as members aged thirty-five or younger) in the total association membership. However, a close look at membership data from three associations — commercial employees, engineering, and medicine — gives us a rough sense of their numerical weight and, by inference, their potential power as a voting bloc (see table 8.2).

In order to assess the political clout of any subgroup in a professional association, we must first distinguish between formally registered and active members. Because association membership lists were not regularly updated, they typically included the names of deceased persons as well as those who had moved abroad. In addition, they included members who had not paid their dues and thus did not have the right to vote in association elections. According to association officials, in the early 1990s roughly one-half to two-thirds of all registered members in the three associations surveyed were "active members"; that is, they resided in the country and had paid their dues in full and therefore had the right to vote.[8]

Moreover, at least half — and as many as two-thirds — of the active members in the three professional associations surveyed were recent graduates under the age of thirty-five. The preponderance of younger members was a direct outcome of the rapid expansion of Egypt's system of higher education

TABLE 8.1 Change in Aggregate Professional Association Membership

	1963	1971	1978	1991
Medicine	11,538	11,848	34,170	100,200
Law	6,872	9,816	13,283	130,000
Journalism	1,166	1,503	1,999	5,000
Engineering	18,387	36,774	95,039	192,550
Agronomy	11,277	36,370	94,262	250,000
Education	120,477	190,740	290,450	750,000
Commerce	n/a	n/a	108,831	310,000
Pharmacy	3,191	5,520	13,150	30,000
Total	174,332	294,206	651,184	1,767,750
Change	*100.00*	*168.76*	*373.53*	*1,114.01*

Av. annual growth per interval (%)	*1963–71*	*1971–78*	*1978–91*
	6.8	12	8

Sources: Data on association membership between 1962 and 1978 are from Robert Bianchi, "Islam and Democracy in Egypt," *Current History*, February 1989, 95. Membership data for 1991 are from Amani Qandil, "Al-Niqabat al-mihaniyya fi Misr wa-'amaliyyat al-tahawwul al-dimuqrati" [Professional Groups in Egypt and the Process of Democratic Transformation], paper presented at the Conference on Democratic Challenges in the Arab World (Cairo: Center for Political and International Development Studies, September 1992). (I compared Qandil's figures with those in other sources, including the *Arab Strategic Report* of 1991 and membership data provided to me by association officials. While Qandil's figures were generally supported by such other sources, her estimate of the Lawyers' Association membership appeared inflated, and so I lowered it to the more conservative 130,000. Integrating different data sets is inherently problematic yet serves to highlight general trends.)

in the 1970s and 1980s. Important to our purposes, many of those graduates entering the professional associations in the Mubarak era were from non-elite backgrounds. In the tight job market of the 1980s and early 1990s, such graduates were at a distinct economic disadvantage, relative to both older professionals and upper-class graduates from the same age cohort. Given their bleak employment and earning prospects, such graduates comprised a large share of what Mustafa Kamil al-Sayyid called the "new poor" of the middle classes.[9] As a distinctive group, we might characterize them as Egypt's professional underclass, the "lumpen intelligentsia" or the "lumpen elite."

TABLE 8.2 Estimated Total Membership, Active Membership, and Active Members Under the Age of 35 in Selected Professional Associations, 1990

Profession	Total	Est Active Members	Members <35 yrs (%)
Commerce	307,500	170,000–200,000	60–75
Engineering	186,000	120,000	60
Medicine	90,000	45,000–60,000	50–65

Sources: Data on membership in the Commercial Employees' Association were obtained from three sources—a report prepared by staff members for the association's Sixteenth General Assembly, 1990; a study of association membership cited in the pamphlet "Syndicates and Society" (in Arabic) distributed by the leftist-liberal bloc at the General Assembly meeting in March 1990 and also cited in *al-Ahali*, March 21, 1990; and interviews with association officials. Engineers' Association membership data are from the association's computerized database. Doctors' Association membership data were compiled from the *Arab Strategic Report*, 1988; Ministry of Health records; and interviews with association leaders. Official association estimates were compared with those cited in Amani Qandil, "The Islamic Trend in Interest Groups in Egypt," *Qadaya fikriyya*, October 1989, 162–68; and in *al-Ahram al-iqtisadi*, April 18, 1988.

The absorption of thousands of new graduates with limited earning and employment prospects transformed the associations from elite institutions with relatively small, privileged memberships into mass institutions marked by sharp generational and class cleavages. Such changes reflect the pyramidal structure of Egypt's "new middle class," with a small, predominantly older upper stratum at its apex and a growing pool of young, economically disadvantaged degree holders at its base. Through the mid-1980s, the social and economic grievances of this large bloc of new members were largely ignored by old-guard association leaders. The consequences of this neglect suddenly became apparent in the mid-1980s, when the Islamic Trend contested elections in the professional associations for the first time.

The Electoral Rise of the Islamic Trend

The professional associations were one of the few sites of unrestricted political contestation in Egypt in the 1980s and early 1990s. As a result, the stunning electoral victories that the Islamists achieved there are of particular significance. Indeed, such victories provide a clear indication of the Islamists' unrivaled ability to mobilize educated, urban voters, an ability that is obscured in parliamentary elections in which the participation of Islamist groups is restricted and the overwhelming majority of educated, urban citizens do not vote.

In 1984, the Brotherhood-affiliated Islamic Trend entered the Doctors' Association elections as an organized bloc for the first time. Shortly thereafter, it ran its own list of candidates in the Engineers', Dentists', Scientists', Agronomists', Pharmacists', Journalists', Commercial Employees', and Lawyers' Association elections.[10] The Islamic Trend's early victories prompted the formation of countervailing blocs representing secular opposition candidates and/or "national" candidates backed by the government. At the same time, traditional electoral lists based on sector or workplace (for example, the army engineers' list in the Engineers' Association, or the Qasr al-'Ayni — Cairo's largest public hospital — list in the Doctors' Association), typically headed by a senior government official, remained a factor, as did candidates running as independents.

Before charting the electoral rise of the Islamic Trend in several professional associations, a caveat about available electoral data is in order. Most published studies derive their association election results from newspaper reports, even though such reports often conflict. Coverage of association elections, particularly when they register large gains for opposition candidates, is conspicuously thin in the government press, forcing us to rely on opposition newspapers whose reporting may be colored by their political agendas. The associations themselves are, in principle, the best source of information, yet in many instances their staff members have been unwilling or unable to provide an accurate chronology of election results for successive years. Moreover, since all candidates technically ran as independents, official association records usually identified winning candidates by name only, rather than by platform or list. Interpreting the results is further complicated by the fact that the political orientations of candidates were not always visible. As Islamic Trend activists explained, some candidates with Islamist sympathies chose not to affiliate with the Brotherhood list, even though they supported the Brotherhood agenda.

In most professional associations, half the seats of the governing board are up for election once every two years, and the association president, or *naqib*, is elected every four years. In the larger associations, such as those of the commercial employees and engineers, elections also are held for positions on the boards of the association's occupational branches (*shu'ab*). The pattern that emerged during the 1980s was for opposing blocs to compete for seats on the executive boards and for all sides to endorse a government candidate, such as a minister or other high-ranking government official, for *naqib.* This arrangement guaranteed that the association would have a powerful patron who could represent its interests in high-level policy decisions and secure its share of public revenues for housing, land, and services.

The Islamic Trend initially won its largest victories in the associations representing the technical professions of medicine, pharmacy, and engineering, scoring more modest gains in the associations of journalism and law, and barely penetrating the large associations of commerce, agriculture, and teaching. Let us look more closely at the Islamic Trend's electoral performance.

The Doctors' Association is a particularly striking case in which the Islamic Trend outperformed its rivals by ever increasing margins (see table 8.3).

The Islamic Trend entered the Doctors' Association elections as an organized bloc in 1984, but according to its secretary general and a Brotherhood activist, 'Abd al-Mun'im Abu-l-Futuh, association elections had in-

TABLE 8.3 Islamic Trend Performance in the Doctors' Association, 1980–1992

Year	Reg. Members	Votes Cast	Part Rate	% votes to Islamic Trend
1980	(40,000)	4,500	11	n/a
1982	50,000	4,400	9	n/a
1984	60,000	12,600	21	5,000 (40% of votes)
1986	70,000	11,800	17	6,000 (51% of votes)
1988	80,000	19,100	24	12,000 (63% of votes)
1990	90,000	21,000	23	15,000 (71% of votes)
1992	100,200	28,000–30,000*	29	

*estimated

Note: Participation rates here are based on the total number of registered members. Although it may be more useful to determine voter turnout based on active membership, only a few associations have reliable data on active membership, and they generally are available only for recent years.

Sources: Data compiled from "The Doctors' Association Elections Between Yesterday and Today," *al-Atibba'* [the journal of the Doctors' Association], vol. 11, August 1992; *al-Ahrar,* April 7, 1986; *al-Ahram al-iqtisadi,* April 23, 1990; *al-Nur,* May 2, 1990; Amani Qandil, "Al-Niqabat al-mihaniyya fi Misr wa-'amaliyyat al-tahawwul al-dimuqrati" [Professional Groups in Egypt and the Process of Democratic Transformation], paper presented at the Conference on Democratic Challenges in the Arab World (Cairo: Center for Political and International Development Studies, September 1992); and the section on associations in *Al-Umma fi'am* [*The Umma in a Year, 1990–1991*] (Mansoura: Wafa' Publishers, 1992), 246. When the data conflicted, I gave priority to official association data.

cluded individual candidates sympathetic to the Brotherhood for much longer. What distinguished the 1984 elections, he stressed, is that for the first time some lists were organized on an ideological basis rather than along workplace or sectoral lines.[11]

In the 1984 elections, the Islamic Trend won seven of the twenty-five seats on the Doctors' Association executive board, and by 1990 it controlled twenty of twenty-five, after deliberately choosing not to contest the remaining seats in order to accommodate representatives of other groups. Coincident with the electoral rise of the Islamic Trend in the 1980s was a steady rise in voter turnout. While the number of registered doctors doubled from 1980 to 1988, the number of voters more than quadrupled during the same period. Looking at a somewhat longer time span, we find that aggregate participation more than tripled, rising from 9 percent of total members in 1982 to about 30 percent in 1992. Assessing voter turnout on the basis of active membership yields even higher participation rates. For example, in 1990 association records indicate that 45,500 doctors had the right to vote and thus that 46 percent, or nearly half, of all active members participated in that year's elections.[12] Such turnout rates, Islamist association officials were quick to point out, far exceeded typical participation rates in general parliamentary elections. The Islamic Trend's rapid electoral ascent in the Doctors' Association occurred against a backdrop of intense competition among three voting blocs: Islamic, leftist-liberal, and a progovernment list dominated by the Ministry of Health, in an association in which, according to informed observers, nearly one-third of the members are Coptic Christians. The presence of several competing blocs may help explain the association's high voter turnout and why, as this competition intensified, the turnout increased over time. In a context of rising participation, the Islamic Trend captured a large share of the new votes. Furthermore, candidates and observers from across the political spectrum contend that the bulk of these votes came from young graduates who entered the association in the late 1970s and 1980s.

The Islamic Trend also won decisive electoral victories in the Engineers', Pharmacists', and Scientists' Associations. The Islamic Trend entered the Engineers' Association for the first time in 1985, with the blessing of the association's longtime president, the construction industry magnate Osman Ahmad Osman.[13] But the Islamic Trend did not achieve its first major victory until 1987, when it won forty-five of sixty-one seats on the association's executive board, defeating the association's most powerful sectoral blocs in a hotly contested election. In 1991, in elections for *majalis al-shu'ab*, the executive boards of the association's occupational branches (electrical, mechanical, civil, and so on), the Islamic Trend contested forty-six of fifty seats and won all forty-six by margins of at least five to one relative to its closest competitors.[14]

In interpreting these results, we must remember that as in the other professional associations, most members of the Engineers' Association do not vote. In the 1991 elections, about 13 percent of the total membership, or an estimated 20 percent of active members, voted in the Engineers' Association elections. Such rates demonstrate that Islamic Trend victories drew on the support of a politicized minority against a backdrop of widespread passivity and alienation.

According to the assistant secretary general and Brotherhood activist Abu-l-'Ila Madi Abu-l-'Ila, voting rates in 1987, 1989, and 1991 were higher in the rural provinces than in Cairo and were especially high among association members aged thirty-five or younger. Youth were heavily represented among voters, he noted, because they made up a large share of the association body and had the greatest need for the association's help to find work, secure housing, and generate enough savings to get married. As in the Doctors' Association, observers across partisan lines noted that younger engineers tended to vote at a higher rate for the Islamic Trend. According to Madi, who served for several years as the association's election coordinator, of the roughly 4,000 engineers who voted in the Greater Cairo area in 1989, about 3,000 were under the age of thirty-five. Of this group, about 2,800 voted for the Islamic Trend.[15]

While the Islamists achieved striking electoral gains in some associations, they barely made any inroads in others. As of the early 1990s, the Islamic Trend had yet to establish a tangible presence in the large professional associations of teachers, agronomists, and veterinarians. In general, such occupations fall near the bottom of Egypt's professional hierarchy and are characterized by low wages, poor working conditions, and low social status. Yet rather than serving as vehicles of political dissent, their associations have tended to function as arms of the state bureaucracy. The internal regulations of the 750,000-member teachers' union, for example, automatically designate the minister of education as its president.

Corporatist legislation helps explain why sympathy for the Islamic Trend among rank-and-file association members, which according to informed observers is substantial, has not translated into successful electoral campaigns to win control of their boards. In addition, the vast majority of teachers, agricultural workers, and veterinarians are state employees. Satisfaction of their economic demands thus depends on the cooperation of state authorities, and the economic dependence of teachers and other state employees appears to have encouraged a focus on bread-and-butter issues favoring collaboration rather than confrontation with the state.[16]

By comparison, the associations of the "free professions" — medicine, engineering, journalism, and law — have traditionally exhibited greater political independence. During the 1970s, the Journalists' and Lawyers' Associations were leading sites of opposition to Sadat's open-door economic policy and rapprochement with Israel. By contrast, for most of Sadat's tenure, the Engineers' and Doctors' Associations were dominated by sectoral blocs and interests tied to the state.[17] Beginning in the mid-1980s, however, the elite technical associations moved to the foreground of political activism under the leadership of the Islamic Trend. One reason the elite professional associations encouraged independent political expression was that they represented professionals working outside the state sector of the economy. Although a majority of doctors worked in public-sector hospitals and clinics, a large proportion supplemented their low public salaries through a second job in the private sector, which in many cases supplied the bulk of their income. Among the new sources of employment for young doctors were the Islamic-run clinics and hospitals that had proliferated in the lower-middle-class neighborhoods of Egypt's cities and provincial towns.

Members of the free professions also enjoyed special prestige and visibility as the vanguard of the country's intelligentsia, independent of their employment and earning power. This arguably granted them a degree of immunity from state harassment. In addition, their socialization as an educated elite fostered a collective sense of social responsibility as advocates of the Egyptian people (al-sha'b) at large. This self-perception helped fuel a tradition of political activism in the university student unions and later in the professional associations as well.

Differences in legislation, membership profiles, and political subtraditions explain why some associations were more receptive to Islamic activism than others. In some cases, however, it was a crisis of leadership at the apex of the association establishment that created an opening for the Islamists' bid for power.

Perhaps the best evidence of the contingent and changing "structures of opportunity" for Islamic activism in the professional associations was the Islamic Trend's surprise victory in the Lawyers' Association elections of September 1992. For decades, the Lawyers' Association had been dominated by secular liberal and leftist leaders. The former gained respect for their outspoken defense of civil liberties, democracy, and the rule of law, while the latter developed a reputation for their staunch nationalist opposition to Sadat's economic and political opening to the West.

During the Mubarak era, intense political and legal disputes among rival cliques in the association attenuated its role as a gadfly for liberal and national causes. By the early 1990s, chronic infighting between supporters of the longtime president, Ahmad Khawaga, and those of his rivals had paralyzed the association board. Having gained public visibility through their work on the association's committees for civil liberties and Islamic law, Brotherhood activists capitalized on the growing frustration and disgust felt by many lawyers toward the association's veteran leaders. Hence the 1992 elections were probably as much an indication of disaffection from incumbent political elites as of growing support for the Islamic Trend.

In such settings as the Doctors', Engineers', and Lawyers' Associations, how did the Islamic Trend gain the support of young professionals? In their analysis of the Lawyers' Association elections of 1992, secular observers emphasized the Islamists' superior organization, financing, and electoral tactics, all of which enabled them to derive maximum leverage from the support of a politicized minority.[18]

The growing support for the Islamic Trend in the professional associations was not simply the result of election-day maneuvers. It was more fundamentally due to the new kinds of elite-mass linkages forged by Islamists on the periphery and sustained by Brotherhood leaders as elected association officials. As I will argue, such linkages were aided by the social, cultural, and generational proximity of Islamist Trend leaders to the associations' young, lower-middle-class base; the Islamic Trend's sponsorship of new programs and services; the appeal of a platform deliberately short on programmatic detail and long on the call for a return to morals (*akhlaq*) and accountability in Egyptian public life; and the development of new models of political leadership and community that sharply contrasted with the policies and practices of state elites.

From the Universities to the Professional Associations: The "Middle Generation" of Islamic Activists

It is striking how many of the Islamist student leaders of the 1970s resurfaced in the 1980s and early 1990s as Brotherhood candidates in the professional associations, as well as in the university faculty clubs and in parliament. A few notable examples include Dr. 'Isam al-'Iryan, amir[19] of the

Islamist student association (*gama'a*) in the Faculty of Medicine at Cairo University, who was elected the youngest member of parliament in 1984 and was a board member of the Doctors' Association; Dr. 'Abd al-Mun'im Abu-l-Futuh, president of the university-wide student union at Cairo University in 1975/76, who was elected secretary general of the Doctors' Association in 1988; Dr. Hilmi Gazzar, former "amir of amirs," who was elected assistant secretary general of the Giza branch of the Medical Doctors' Association in 1984; and Abu-l-'Ila Madi Abu-l-'Ila, amir of the Islamist student Association in the Faculty of Engineering at Minya University, who was elected assistant secretary general of the Engineers' Association in 1988.[20]

Joining the Muslim Brotherhood created new strategic opportunities for Islamic student leaders. In particular, it enabled them to continue their activities after graduation as representatives of an organization that was de facto tolerated, even though it was denied legal status. The most important outlet for such postgraduate activism was the professional associations. As 'Abd al-Mun'im Abu-l-Futuh explained, "It is natural that people with opinions want to participate in institutions, to have a role. After graduation, such students looked for a place to continue their activity. Given the restrictions on party activity, many of them turned to the professional associations."[21] Closer in age, class background, and experience to recent university graduates than were the old-guard association officials, this new generation of Islamic leaders managed to a large extent to bridge the traditional divide between elite and mass political culture. As Dr. Hilmi Gazzar observed, "We were *shabab* [youth] just like them and faced similar struggles; some of us made it, but others didn't. I have younger friends, and I ask them what problems they are dealing with; I want to know." As he noted:

> Before, the association leaders sat in their offices and expected the doctors to come to them. This was a mistake. We [the Islamic Trend] go to the doctors, go down to the workplace, the hospitals, and clinics, to ask doctors about their problems and complaints. The questionnaire we distributed to identify the major problems [that] doctors face confirmed that there's a generational dimension. Younger doctors face more problems. For example, the quality of medical education has declined sharply in recent years, owing to the increase in enrollments. There used to be one professor to every ten to fifteen students; now thousands of students are attempting to receive an education in the same faculties. Hence there is no real opportunity for practical training.[22]

Similarly, Abu-l-'Ila Madi Abu-l-'Ila, assistant secretary general of the Engineers' Association, observed:

> Up to 1985, the people who ran the association were viewed by most engineers as bureaucrats who were simply not interested in the problems of members. . . . There used to be a total separation [*infisal tamm*] between the leaders and the members. They [the former association leaders] did not know what it was like to suffer from unemployment or a housing shortage or riding the buses — but we are like the ordinary engineers; we have the same living standards, or even lower. The younger members see that I can relate, that I can understand their problems. Hence they feel less of a gap between the leaders and the members.[23]

The changes wrought by the Islamic leadership once they occupied a majority of seats on the associations' executive boards were both practical and symbolic. First, the style of leadership changed. Protocols insulating association leaders from the rank-and-file were abandoned, and, as Madi emphasized, "Now a young member can come in and find someone who will listen to him, who will take him seriously. That in itself counts." The regular interruption of office business hours for prayers, during which all members present — from the secretary general down to the unemployed graduates — stood together in one line in the direction of Mecca, reinforced the symbolic equality between unequals on the ladder of income and status, emphasizing that all present were equal before God.

In addition to developing a more responsive and egalitarian leadership style, Islamic Trend leaders turned the associations into a showcase for concrete distributional initiatives targeted at the large pool of recent graduates at their base. For example, in 1988 in a series of well-publicized events, several Islamic-run associations directed national attention to the problems of unemployment and low wages among educated youth. The Engineers' Association held a conference focused on the more than 20,000 predominantly young engineers without work, and the Doctors' Association conducted a survey of nearly 25,000 doctors in twelve governorates, in which 84 percent of those interviewed claimed that their salaries were not enough to cover their living costs. Having declared the period from 1988 to 1990 as a time to focus on "improving the incomes and living standards of young doctors," in 1990 the Doctors' Association followed up its initial survey with a series of investigative visits to document wages and working conditions in public and private hospitals and clinics.[24]

By reinvigorating existing programs and establishing new ones, the associations' Islamic leadership tried to address the needs of new members. For example, they organized advanced training courses, offered health and "emergency" insurance, extended low-interest loans to help young members get married and/or establish their own small businesses, and facilitated the purchase of consumer durables and furniture on long-term installment plans. In addition, they demanded a reduction in university enrollments to alleviate the labor surplus and lobbied for the establishment of liaison offices to help Egyptian professionals obtain work in other Arab states. Such initiatives were enumerated in the associations' official journals and Islamic Trend campaign literature, such as the green-and-white handbook distributed during the Engineers' Association elections in February 1991, entitled "The Engineers' Association 1987–1991: Achievements and Statistics."

While the Islamic Trend highlighted the positive impact of its projects, critics emphasized their flaws. For example, in a series of articles published in the leftist newspaper *al-Ahali* in the spring of 1990, a doctor from Minya lamented the high price of an apartment or clinic in the Doctors' Towers, owned by an Egyptian-Saudi financial group with ties to the Muslim Brotherhood and promoted by the medical association's Islamic-run board. "As such units are beyond the dreams of young doctors," he writes, "we must ask, who exactly does the association serve?"[25]

Both leftists and Islamists active in the associations claimed to understand the urgent needs and concerns of young professionals and to be capable of defending their interests. More broadly, both groups emphasized their status as political outsiders, distinguishing themselves from the old-guard association officials whom Islamists and leftists alike portrayed as tainted by chronic factional struggles, nondemocratic decision making, the use of union office for self-enrichment, and a penchant for "big receptions and fancy cars." Yet despite their alleged commitment to the associations' younger members, the magnitude of existing needs far exceeded the resources or capacities of either opposition bloc. In private conversations, Islamic Trend leaders admitted that only a small proportion of association members had benefited from their housing, education, and employment initiatives. They explained that the state, and not the associations, was the only institution capable of launching programs on the scale necessary to make a real impact. In this context, the programs and services initiated by Islamic leaders had a chiefly symbolic value, demonstrating the intent, if not the actual means, to meet the needs of the associations' rank and file.

As the leaders of large, public institutions, Islamic Trend officials had to cultivate and maintain relationships with government ministries, local government authorities, and public and private financial institutions. Nonetheless, they succeeded in preserving their reputation as uncompromising critics of — and a moral alternative to — the very system with which, as association officials, they were forced to cooperate.

In shifting from amirs to association officials, the middle-generation Islamists moved closer, in appearance and in practice, to the norms of the status quo. Gone in most cases were the untrimmed beards of their defiant student days; instead, most were clean shaven or had neatly trimmed beards and wore standard Western- or civil-service-style suits. From modest dormitory rooms, they had moved into the air-conditioned offices of the association headquarters, where they supervised a large staff, received visitors from the provinces, were interviewed by journalists, and met with other association or party leaders to coordinate strategy on issues of shared concern. Such contrasts graphically illustrate their shift from direct confrontation with the regime to a cautious and grudging accommodation. Nonetheless, the antiestablishment aura remained in reputation, rhetoric, and, to some extent, reality.

For example, in the early 1990s, Dr. 'Abd al-Mun'im Abu-l-Futuh, secretary general of the Doctors' Association, was still widely admired for his bold verbal challenge to Anwar Sadat in a televised meeting between the president and student union leaders back in the late 1970s. In response to a long-winded speech by Sadat on the country's progress toward democracy, 'Abd al-Mun'im pointed out the gap between the president's rhetoric and actual conditions, provoking an outraged and shaken Sadat to shout — "Stop where you are!" (qif 'andak), a phrase gleefully quoted in opposition circles for years afterward. Likewise, young engineers recalled with pride that shortly after Sadat's assassination, the assistant secretary general of their association had headed the most-wanted list of "terrorists" published in the Egyptian press.[26]

In speeches, statements, and association meetings, Islamic Trend leaders regularly criticized the regime, particularly for its violations of human rights and restriction of political freedoms, including the right of opposition parties to compete openly for political power. They also denounced the harassment and torture of suspected members of underground militant Islamic groups and called for a repeal of the emergency laws which had remained in effect since Sadat's assassination in 1981. In the early 1990s, Islamic Trend leaders also convened joint association conferences to protest Egypt's military involvement in the Gulf War, demand political reforms, and challenge recent government efforts to violate the associations' autonomy. Islamic Trend leaders pointed out that such dissent was tolerated as long as it remained confined to association headquarters. As one leader put it, "The regime allows us to do what we want within our four walls, as long as it retains control of the street."[27]

In sum, while developing an institutional base in the professional associations, Islamic Trend leaders managed to navigate between mainstream and opposition circles — close enough to the state to deliver on their promises yet far enough away to maintain the antisystem credentials that were one of the main sources of their appeal.

In contrast to the Islamic Trend, the Egyptian left experienced a painful decline in the 1980s and early 1990s and is still attempting to sort out its lessons. By the mid-1980s the Egyptian left had fragmented into rival Nasserist, social-democratic, Marxist, and Communist factions. Dispirited and demoralized, leftists have tried to recast their image against the backdrop of widespread disenchantment with socialism and other "Western" solutions to the country's predicament. While emphasizing the financial and social constraints under which they operated, they also acknowledged such internal problems as a rigid and dogmatic leadership, competition among rival ideological blocs and personalities, and insufficient outreach at the grassroots level.

On top of these problems was the less tangible, but no less real, problem of a loss of self-confidence. As Ashraf Hilmi, a leftist candidate in the 1991 Engineers' Association elections, explained, "We have recently succumbed to political defeatism [ihbat siyasi] as a result of our failures and defeats." Is there a new leftist generation? "Yes, but [unlike the generation of the late 1960s and early 1970s], it has no experience of struggles." There is a growing leftist presence in the engineering faculty at Ein Shams University, he noted, but it has not yet effectively challenged the Islamic Trend. "First we must defeat them in the student associations, then in the professional associations, and then in the People's Assembly."[28]

Explaining Islamist Electoral Victories in the Professional Associations

The Islamist mobilization of young professionals began in the dorm rooms and study halls of Egyptian university campuses, at student union meetings, book fairs, prayer sessions, and Islamic study groups. The Islamists' victories in the professional associations were thus the culmination of nearly a decade of grassroots Islamic outreach, which created a popular base receptive to the Brotherhood's platform of Islamic reform. As the leftist union activist Ashraf Hilmi aptly characterized it, "You raise Ikhwani [Brotherhood] students in the university, then five years later you have an electoral base for the professional associations. It's like planting seeds on a farm."

Beyond the walls of the universities, Islamic outreach in urban lower-middle-class neighborhoods contributed to the formation of a constituency on which Brotherhood candidates could draw in association elections. In a context in which most professionals did not vote, a key question was how the Muslim Brotherhood managed to challenge prevailing patterns of political alienation and abstention. Through outreach on the periphery, Islamic activists promoted a new valuation of participation in public life. Challenging attitudes of apathy and defeatism, they instructed graduates that Islam demands al-ijabiyya (positive thinking), fueled by faith in not only the possibility but also the inevitability of a victory for the Islamic cause. Voting was presented as a wajib dini (religious obligation), and the importance of the associations was emphasized, if only as a conduit of benefits and an arena in which Islamic reform could be achieved incrementally from the bottom up.

In cultivating a new participatory ethic, the Islamists emphasized two distinctions. First, they contrasted the relative freedom of association elections, and hence the greater authenticity of their results, with the regime-controlled elections for parliament. As evidence, they noted that unlike the parliamentary elections, association elections were overseen by judges or Islamist-led election committees.[29] Second and, more important, the Islamic Trend was portrayed as qualitatively different from government and leftist candidates in moral terms. Making constant reference to the other-worldly motivations that distinguished them from secular rivals, Islamists claimed the Brotherhood would root out the corruption, influence peddling, and self-promotion of politics as usual.

Another factor that contributed to the success of the Islamic Trend was its command of electoral organization and tactics. Although association elections offered all ideological and sectoral blocs an equal opportunity to reach out to potential supporters, the contrast between the campaigns launched by the Islamic Trend and those of its rivals was striking.

The Lawyers' Association elections of September 1992 are a case in point. These elections registered the growing frustration of lawyers toward veteran leaders who seemed out of touch and hopelessly paralyzed by factional rivalry. Numerous proposals and recommendations put forward between 1989 and 1992 to improve the incomes and work conditions of young lawyers were never acted on by the association board, even after a public conference on the subject was held in 1990.[30] Another indication of the growing alienation of association members from their elected leadership was the fact that more than two-thirds of them had not paid their annual membership dues and thus had forfeited the right to vote.

When the Islamic Trend entered the Lawyers' Association elections, few observers thought it would win. But under the symbolic leadership of lawyer Sayf al-Islam Banna (son of Hasan al-Banna, founder of the Muslim Brotherhood), the Islamic Trend managed to turn the growing discontent to its own advantage, relying on electoral tactics it had successfully used elsewhere. In order to gain maximum leverage, the Islamic Trend organized its candidates on a single list, presenting a united front in the posters and campaign literature distributed before the election. By contrast, candidates on the left dissipated their energies by running on different platforms or as independents.

Second, to ensure high turnout rates, the Islamic Trend provided special services to its supporters. It was rumored that the Islamic Trend paid the overdue membership fees of up to 3,000 lawyers shortly before election day, a tactic it allegedly used in other associations as well.[31] On the day of the election, the Islamic Trend reserved a room at the association's Cairo branch office to serve as the headquarters for its ongoing campaign activities, which included distributing campaign literature and supplying food and drinks (one account mentions "iced rose water") to its supporters.[32] Last but not least, the Islamic Trend campaign received help from a large corps of volunteers from the association's Islamic Law committee, which, under the supervision of Mukhtar Nuh, a lawyer and Brotherhood activist, included more than 4,000 young lawyers by 1992.

On election day, roughly 14,000 lawyers voted, representing about one-third of the active members and 10 percent of all registered association members. The Islamic Trend's electoral strategies clearly paid off, enabling it to win sixteen of the twenty-four seats on the governing board and roughly half the votes cast, with the rest distributed among lists representing liberal, Marxist, Nasserist, and government candidates. The inability of such forces to launch effective campaigns of their own made the Islamic Trend's task that much easier. As one leftist journalist commented, the ruling National Democratic Party was "virtually absent from the election struggle, as if it were in a different country, despite the large number of NDP members in the association and the large number of its candidates for the governing board." Unlike the Islamic Trend, it ran "without planning or communication or coordination." In addition to defeating its secular rivals, the Islamic Trend defeated a competing Islamic list identified with the militant Jihad organization, which failed to gain a single seat on the board.[33]

Parallel trends were evident in other associations. At the Engineers' Association headquarters on election day in February 1991, groups of Islamist volunteers (some obviously too young to be engineers), wearing green smocks imprinted with the words "Islam Is the Solution," stood at the entrance to the voting booths, distributing campaign materials for the Islamic Voice.[34] Some carried posters and signs, and at times broke out into chants, like "Oh Muslim Brothers, wake up and renew our Islam as it was in the days of old." Strung across the entrance to the association, dominating the hundreds of smaller election posters representing other groups, hung a large, dark blue banner emblazoned with the words "The Islamic Voice."

Likewise, at the Commercial Employees' Association elections in 1989, Islamic Trend supporters congregated at the entrance to the voting booths, distributing literature, singing, and exhorting people to vote for candidates on the Islamic list. As one "nationalist" (qawmi)[35] candidate recalled, "I had supporters come to vote for me, who knew my record of service to the association. But how could I compete when an Islamic Trend supporter questioned a voter as he entered the booth — 'Are you going to vote for God?'"

The high abstention rates in professional association elections in the 1980s and early 1990s indicate that the majority of professionals, including those with serious grievances, had yet to be convinced that the associations had anything to offer them or deserved any claim on their loyalties. Many members regarded participation in association elections as a waste of time and viewed all candidates as essentially alike, as all seeking "positions" (manasib) in order to enhance their private wealth and power. Commenting on the Islamist victory in the Lawyers' Association elections, secular political activists, journalists, and intellectuals decried the prevailing mood of political defeatism (al-salbiyya), apathy (al-la-mubalah), and alienation (al-ightirab) that infects much of the professional middle class in Egypt today.

The victories of the Islamic Trend thus reflect the yawning gap between the country's dominant political culture and an emergent Islamist subculture marked by confidence in the efficacy of participation and the potential for meaningful reform under Islamic auspices. The results of my informal survey of young engineers confirm these trends. With the help of two Egyptian research assistants during the association elections of February 1991, I in-

terviewed ninety-six young engineers either shortly before or immediately
after they cast their vote at the Engineers' Association national headquarters
in Cairo. All those interviewed had graduated between 1980 and 1990 and
so were around twenty-three to thirty-four years old.

A minority of the engineers we interviewed had come to vote for personal
acquaintances or had been "ordered" by their company or army unit to vote
for a specific list. Other engineers chose not to identify the name of the list
they had voted for. Of those engineers who did express a voting preference
on political-ideological grounds, the majority supported the Islamic trend.
The engineers' reasons for supporting Islamic Trend candidates varied, from
the candidates' proven commitment to solving the problems of young engineers to faith in their personal integrity. The following quotations offer a
cross section of their views:

> I voted for the Islamic Trend; they have given the association new life;
> before they entered the elections, we didn't even know where the
> association was!

> The Islamic Voice has high principles and also experience. Before they
> became dominant in 1987, the association was run by thieves, who
> used to steal association funds for their own uses.

> I am ready to support any trustworthy candidate, and the activities of
> the Islamic Trend candidates prove they are trustworthy.

> The Islamic Voice has some great achievements, like the project of
> consumer durables, the health-care project, and the summer vacation
> houses.

> We want honest people who are able to help us, provide us with ser-
> vices, and can be trusted not to steal.

> I chose the Islamic Trend because they are honest and interested in
> reforming the country. By contrast, the leftists are interested only in
> obtaining positions and material benefits for themselves.

> I voted for the Islamic Voice. They are the only [political] trend in the
> elections — either you elect them or you elect individuals. The com-

munists and the leftists are in general not accepted. I support the Islamic trend, and especially the Ikhwan [Muslim Brotherhood], because they are moderate, far from extremism, and they have a future-oriented point of view.

I chose the Islamic Voice. They represent me completely. I have a sense of Islamic belonging. There's nothing called "political Islam" or "extremist Islam." Islam is Islam.

I gave my vote to the Islamic Trend. I believe in their principles, which are close to my own. They look after the public welfare. I don't know them personally, but I trust them. They have an active conscience [*damir sahi*].

These quotations indicate that support for the Islamic trend did not derive solely or even primarily from its distribution of material goods and services to an aggrieved constituency. Rather, they suggest the importance of the perceived moral superiority of Islamic Trend candidates, who were viewed as "loyal," "trustworthy," "honest," and "upright." In an environment in which the realm of *al-siyasa*, or high politics, has long been associated in the public mind with the self-interested pursuit of power, with factional infighting and party strife, Islamic Trend candidates successfully presented themselves as "above politics," motivated solely by a religiously informed sense of civic duty.

It is noteworthy that very few Islamic Trend supporters explicitly mentioned their support for the organization's political goals, that is, for the application of Islamic law as the basis for reorganizing state and society. Therefore, the commitment of Islamic Trend voters to establishing an Islamic state remains open to question. The appeal of the Islamic platform appeared to stem instead from the voters' perception of Islam as a restraint on the unbridled pursuit of self-interest and of Islamist candidates as worthy of the public trust.

This trust was similarly emphasized by Islamist candidates as the foundation of their popular support. In evaluating the Nasser era, Madi acknowledged that the former president had distributed valuable goods and services to the middle and lower classes. And yet, he argued, Nasser never achieved genuine political support. "I benefited from him isn't the same as he represents me," Madi concluded.[36]

From Mobilization to Countermobilization: The Regime Strikes Back

While the Brotherhood's move from the periphery toward the center enhanced its political influence, it also exposed the organization and its leaders to new risks. As the locus of Islamic activity shifted from decentralized and ostensibly nonpolitical settings to the large, national associations of the country's professional elite, the stakes of Islamic mobilization rose. At the same time, the early 1990s saw a sharp increase in violence by militant Islamic groups. Beginning around 1992, the Mubarak regime seized the offensive and initiated a series of actions designed both to root out the country's underground militant Islamic cells and to stem the growing influence and power of the nonviolent Muslim Brotherhood.

As part of this "authoritarian reversal," the regime's toleration of Brotherhood activity in the professional associations came to an abrupt end. On February 16, 1993, a new law for professional associations was hastily proposed and passed in parliament by the ruling National Democratic Party (NDP) majority. Entitled the Law to Guarantee Democracy Within the Professional Syndicate Associations, it established minimum participation rates for association elections (50 percent of all members in the first round, 33 percent in the second), which, if not met, would void the election results and subject the association to supervision by a panel of appointed judges. Backers of the law insisted that mandating higher levels of participation in association elections would prevent the associations' "organized minority" from dominating their "silent majority." Yet the law's critics, including journalists, opposition party leaders, and association officials across the ideological spectrum, condemned the law as a transparent attempt to dislodge Islamic leaders and return the associations to state control.

As the primary target of the law, the Islamist-run boards of the country's professional associations were at the forefront of protest against it. In the months after the law was passed, the boards of the Lawyers', Engineers', and Doctors' Associations organized demonstrations and work stoppages, drafted petitions to the speaker of parliament, and sponsored special plenary sessions and joint conferences to communicate their objections to a broader audience. Such activities included two demonstrations in front of the Cairo headquarters of the Engineers' Association on February 19 and March 5. At one demonstration, an estimated 15,000 professionals listened as association officials condemned the law, the ruling party, and the Mubarak regime for violating the association's freedoms.[37] Huge swathes of black cloth were hung across the entrance to the building. Posters depicting the powerful earthquake that had shaken Cairo the previous October protested "the earthquake of February 16" and "the assassination of the professional associations in Parliament," followed by the phrase *al-baqa' li-llah*, a phrase used to console the bereaved. By rallying their supporters into the street around the Engineers' Association headquarters, Islamic Trend leaders flexed their political muscle yet also demonstrated their capacity for self-restraint. On this and subsequent occasions, Islamic Trend leaders deliberately chose to avoid a major escalation of conflict that could have led to a violent showdown with the regime. Instead, they assumed the moral high ground, fighting the new restrictions by mobilizing public opinion against them and challenging their constitutionality in the courts. At the same time, they redoubled their mobilization efforts to raise voter turnout rates to the required levels.[38]

The government's efforts to dislodge the Brotherhood from the associations took other forms as well. For example, shortly after imposing new rules for association elections, the regime accused the Islamist boards of the Engineers' and Lawyers' Associations of financial mismanagement. Under the shadow of these allegations, the Engineers' Association was placed under official custodianship in May 1993, and its executive board was later dissolved and replaced by court-appointed administrators. In January 1995, the Lawyers' Association was also placed under government supervision.

The regime's assault on the Islamist-controlled professional associations was part of a broader campaign to stem the Brotherhood's growing influence in Egyptian public life. In addition to reimposing state control over major *sites* of Brotherhood activism, the regime also tried to paralyze the movement's leading *agents*. In a wave of arrests beginning in 1995 and continuing through 1996, the regime imprisoned many of the dynamic middle-generation leaders who had spearheaded the Brotherhood's entry into the professional associations. The defendants were tried in military courts and sentenced to three to five years of hard labor. In addition, the government waged a massive media campaign to turn potential *targets* of mobilization against the Brotherhood. In public speeches and interviews, President Mubarak and other senior government officials repeatedly referred to the Brotherhood as an "illegal organization," accused it of seeking to overthrow the government, and claimed that the Brotherhood and underground terrorist groups were "two faces of the same coin." As a result of the regime's systematic campaign against the Muslim Brotherhood, by the late 1990s the professional associations had ceased to function as centers of Islamist initiative;

many of the associations' most popular and dynamic Islamist leaders were in prison; and the Brotherhood's public image as a force for peaceful reform had been severely tarnished. The regime justified its campaign against the Brotherhood on security grounds, alleging, for example, that it maintained close ties with underground militant Islamist groups. Yet arguably the main objective of the campaign was "to prevent another Algeria," that is, to prevent the nonviolent wing of the Islamic movement from expanding its popular base and peacefully challenging the country's authoritarian elites.

Conclusion

Islamic mobilization on the periphery was not subject to centralized co-ordination and control by leaders of the Muslim Brotherhood, nor did it inevitably redound to their benefit. But the Muslim Brotherhood was the main beneficiary of decentralized outreach efforts, because it was able to aggregate citizens' newfound Islamist sympathies and channel them into electoral campaigns in national-level organizations closer to the political center. The rise of the Islamic Trend in Egypt's professional associations was part of a broader process of Islamic institution building that altered the landscape of Egyptian public life in the 1980s and early 1990s. Rather than contest state power directly, the Muslim Brotherhood gradually appropriated public space from the bottom up. Initially, the Brotherhood's participation in the professional associations appeared to fit both the regime's and the Islamists' objectives. Opening restricted channels for participation enabled the Mubarak regime to incorporate Islamic "moderates" while preserving its monopoly on power. By giving mainstream, nonviolent Islamists a stake in the system, the regime could induce them to play by its rules, restricting their participation to issuing statements and holding seminars while continuing to limit their access to the mass public. According to this tacit arrangement, the associations' political autonomy was respected while the regime retained control of the street.

At the same time, control of Egypt's professional associations gave Brotherhood activists an opportunity to hone their leadership skills and broaden their base of support. Although the capacity of the Brotherhood-run associations to address the real-life problems of recent graduates remained limited, the rhetorical emphasis on youth, backed in part by projects still in their infancy, had a symbolic importance independent of the benefits actually distributed. Against the backdrop of a seemingly out-of-touch military-bureaucratic state, the Islamic Trend portrayed itself as the successor to a more humane and responsive political tradition that could be traced back to the exemplary rule of *al-khulafa' ar-rashidun*, the rightly guided caliphs of the first Islamic state.

The image of the Islamic Trend as a servant of the public interest was reinforced in the days after the devastating earthquake of October 1992, when Doctors' Association volunteers arrived first on the scene in some of the worst-hit areas, setting up tents and distributing food, blankets, and medical care to the victims. Reacting to such initiatives, the Egyptian government complained, in the telling words of Interior Minister Muhammad 'Abd al-Halim Musa, "What is going on here? Do we have a 'state within the state' "?[39]

Interestingly enough, the words of the interior minister find an echo in the Islamists' own conception of their mission. Rather than challenge state power directly, the Islamic Trend was deliberately creating new models of political leadership and community on the ground. As Madi and his colleagues put it in 1991, "We are creating islands of democracy in a sea of dictatorship."

One can seriously question whether Islamist political experimentation in the associations was democratic, at least in the liberal sense of the word, given that the Islamist agenda balances individual rights against individual obligations within a framework of Islamic law. The key point here, however, is that intermediary associations formally attached to the state became important sites of political innovation — perhaps the equivalent of the "parallel polis" that emerged under Communism in Eastern Europe and challenged its official norms and practices well before the system collapsed. What Guiseppe Di Palma wrote about dissenters in Communist Eastern Europe rings true for Egypt as well:

> Perhaps their main strength in the long run — a feature revealed after the fact — was precisely that their intent was not at all to conspire in the way that underground parties and movements conspire against more labile authoritarian regimes. Rather, they sought to build, slowly and by the power of example, a parallel society.[40]

9 Cycles of Mobilization Under Authoritarian Rule

The rise of Islamic activism in Egypt is often portrayed as an expression of "real-life" grievances by educated, lower-middle-class youth. A closer analysis, however, suggests that grievance-based explanations of Islamic activism are not sufficient. In authoritarian settings, in which the risks of participating in an opposition movement are high and the prospects of effecting change are, at best, uncertain, even the most aggrieved citizens may retreat into self-preserving silence. Hence the burden is on movement organizers to create the motivations and venues for political protest and, in so doing, enable citizens to overcome the powerful psychological and structural barriers to participation erected by the authoritarian state.

The central purpose of this book was, first, to explain how the leaders of the nonviolent wing of Egypt's Islamic movement managed to mobilize educated, urban youth into politics and, second, to propose a broader set of hypotheses concerning the *conditions*, *dynamics*, and *outcomes* of mobilization in authoritarian settings more generally. Let us review the main findings of this book in each of these areas.

The Structural Potential for Mobilization in Authoritarian Settings

My first aim was to specify the conditions under which the mobilization of citizens by opposition groups becomes possible in authoritarian settings. Moving beyond the conventional "democratic-authoritarian" distinction, I argued that authoritarian regimes differ in their propensity and capacity to control potential *agents, sites,* and *targets* of mobilization. Furthermore, an authoritarian regime's propensities and capacities for societal control are not fixed but can change over time. That is, when a regime's control over society weakens, the structural potential for mobilization perforce expands.

In Egypt, the rise of Islamic activism occurred at a particular historical moment when the "revolutionary" regime of 1952 ran out of steam. As the regime's distributional, mobilizational, and coercive capacities diminished, the structural opening for mobilization widened. As state entitlements lost value, serious grievances emerged among those sectors of society whose status and livelihood depended on them most. At the same time, processes of economic and political liberalization initiated by the regime for its own purposes broadened the resources and institutional space available for opposition outreach to aggrieved groups.

The opening of Egypt's authoritarian system was an uneven process that privileged some institutional arenas and actors over others. In order to accommodate citizens' growing demands for political expression without jeopardizing its grip on power, the Mubarak regime tolerated the emergence of new space on the periphery while retaining tight control over political contestation at the center. The result was to shift the locus of political dynamism from formal institutions at the center to ostensibly marginal and "nonpolitical" sites on the periphery. Much to the regime's chagrin, however, the vast and decentralized network of Islamist institutions on the periphery offered ideal sites for political outreach and organization. As Doug McAdam and other social movement scholars observed years ago, "nonpolitical" groups and organizations can provide the setting for the production of collective *political* action. Consider, for example, the crucial role of black churches in the development of the civil rights movement.[1] My purpose in this book was not simply to extend the coverage of "nonpolitical" settings to authoritarian contexts but also to explain why regime-led processes of political and economic liberalization may end up privileging nonpolitical sites on the periphery over formal political arenas at the center.

Even if the (deliberate or inadvertent) retreat of the authoritarian state from previous attempts at societal control explains how mobilization by opposition groups becomes possible, it does not explain how and why such mobilization occurred. In order to understand the progression from opportunities to outcomes, we must acknowledge the crucial role of human agency. That is, we need to identify the strategies employed by movement organizers to mobilize citizens into politics and also the reasons that their strategies succeed or fail. Therefore, we need to shift our focus from the macrostructural environment to the microdynamics of movement outreach and organization.

The Micromechanisms of Mobilization

Informed by a "rational-actor" model of human behavior, much of the American social movement literature focuses on interests as motives for collective action. There is no doubt that an appeal to the interests of potential recruits helped ease graduates' entry into the Islamic movement in Egypt and has sustained their involvement over time. Participation in Islamic social networks increased graduates' access to a wide range of benefits, from help in obtaining a visa or job to the emotional satisfaction derived from intensive bonds of friendship and trust. But the Egyptian case also suggests that interest-based appeals cannot explain graduates' progression from initial, lower-risk forms of participation to higher-risk and more overtly political ones. This progression hinged on the graduates' embrace of a *normative commitment* to political action and on their integration into movement networks in which this commitment could be reinforced. Hence it was as much through a massive project of ideological outreach as through an appeal to the graduates' interests that movement organizers converted lower-middle-class graduates from targets of recruitment into agents of Islamic reform.

This book also contends that to acknowledge the mobilizing power of ideas is not enough. Rather, we need to investigate how movement "frames" are socially constructed and to explain how and why a particular frame motivates political action in a given place and time. Building on Snow and Benford's analysis of framing and on Brysk's "symbolic politics" approach, I argued that successful ideological outreach requires a resonant message, credible messengers, and effective mechanisms of transmission. What makes a message "resonant," messengers "credible," and mechanisms "effective" is context specific, contingent on the life experiences of the citizens whom a movement has targeted for recruitment as well as on the cultural and institutional environment in which they are embedded. While elements of the local context diminish the mobilizing power of some ideas, they amplify the potency of others.

In concluding this section, we might ask to what extent the rise of opposition activism in Egypt was an outcome of religion. In the social movement field, the role of religion in the formation of motivations and venues for opposition activism has not been fully explored.[2] As a preliminary step, we can think of religious (or, more broadly, cultural) institutions and ideas as potential resources in the struggles between regimes and opposition movements for legitimate authority and power. Yet we cannot move from deep structures of religious institutions and beliefs to outcomes without acknowledging the intervening role of human agency. Cultural beliefs about the sacred, divinity, and the afterlife can be mobilized by both defenders and opponents of the established order. Likewise, cultural repertoires of behavior like the da'wa can be used by different actors for opposing ends. Whether or not such cultural resources are used, and used effectively, depends on the creative and persuasive abilities of those engaged in political struggle.

The rise of opposition activism in Mubarak's Egypt was not inevitable, nor was it inevitable that such activism should assume an Islamic form. That there is nothing "natural" about the success of Islamist outreach in a Muslim country is indicated by the dominance of leftist movements in the Arab world as recently as the 1960s and early 1970s. That the reform-minded Islamists mobilized far greater support than their secular — as well as more militant Islamist — rivals was the result of discrete features of movement leadership, strategy, and ideology, elements far more specific than "Islam."

Mobilization and Political Change: The Question of Impact

The path from mobilization to political change is not a direct or an inexorable one. For mobilization to facilitate an electoral change of power requires the presence of a centralized party organization able to convert mobilized support into electoral gains. Although denied legal party status, Egypt's Muslim Brotherhood can be seen as a "proto-party" that formed an institutional bridge between mobilizers on the periphery and electoral contests closer to the political center. The Brotherhood's ability to perform this bridging function hinged on the effective leadership of a new generation of Islamic leaders. While serving as the Brotherhood's representatives in the professional associations, these leaders remained connected to Islamic mobilizers at the grassroots level. Thus they were strategically positioned to channel support mobilized on the periphery into challenges to the associations' veteran elites.

This book focused on the rise of Islamic activism in Egypt from 1984 to 1994, during which time overt support for the Muslim Brotherhood among young professionals reached its height. Having investigated the rise of Islamic activism, we must, in conclusion, attempt to make sense of its subsequent decline. As Sidney Tarrow has pointed out, movement challenges to the established order typically provoke a response from allies and adversaries and ultimately from the state. As the number of actors involved increases and their interactions become more numerous and complex, movement organizers lose control over the course of events, and the outcome is determined through political struggle.[3]

Tarrow's work focused on cycles of organized protest rather than the more diffuse forms of activism at issue here. But the gist of his argument still holds: that a movement's very success can lead to instances of countermobilization by its opponents, altering the environment in which the movement arose. One sees precisely such a dynamic in Egypt and elsewhere in the Arab world, where Islamic mobilization has created a massive backlash by incumbent authoritarian elites.

A classic cycle of mobilization and countermobilization has been taking place in Egypt since 1992. While the Brotherhood's foray into the professional associations enhanced its leaders' visibility and influence, it also exposed them to greater risks. By channeling support on the periphery into electoral victories closer to the political center, such leaders ultimately transgressed the limits of the regime's tolerance. The Brotherhood's victories in the associations thus triggered a crackdown that reversed many of the gains it had made in the preceding decade.

Beginning in 1992, the Mubarak regime launched an assault on the Muslim Brotherhood that has continued through the present day. During the latter half of the 1990s, the regime arrested and imprisoned scores of leading Brotherhood activists, forced the organization out of the associations, and sought to destroy its reputation by accusing it of having ties with extremist Islamic groups. The Brotherhood's striking reversal of fortunes after 1992 raises some important questions about a movement's ability to sustain its influence over time. After a decade of self-confident expansion, why was the Brotherhood so vulnerable to attack? As has been stressed throughout this book, in authoritarian settings a movement's impact depends in large part on the orientations, strategies, and capacities of the regime's leaders. Opposition movements are able to challenge a particular aspect of the status quo because the regime tolerates it, does not know about it, does not fully appreciate its significance, or is simply unable to stop it. Islamist participation in the Egypt's political system in the 1980s and early 1990s was possible for the first two reasons: because the regime was willing to accommodate opposition forces as long as they did not appear to threaten its grip on power and because the regime initially underestimated the political significance of Islamist organization and outreach on the periphery. Once regime leaders concluded that Islamic mobilization was a political threat, their patience quickly evaporated. While this explains why the regime *chose* to move against the Brotherhood, the question remains — why was it *able* to do so?

We can speculate that a movement's vulnerability to a regime's counter-attack is greatest when authoritarian elites are unified and their coercive apparatus is intact and when public support for the movement is limited to a narrow segment of society. When ruling elites are divided and/or their coercive abilities are compromised (for example, after a defeat in war), their ability to contain an opposition movement is diminished. But when such a movement has managed to mobilize a large and cross-class base of support, even a unified and coherent authoritarian regime may be unable to quell it through repression.

Consider, for example, the Iranian revolution. In the 1970s, the Pahlevi regime had a fully "closed" political center, eliminating the electoral option as a route to political change. But partly because of their long-standing in-stitutional autonomy and prestige, the Shi'i clergy were able to mobilize a broad-based popular coalition against the shah. Ultimately, support for the Islamic movement expanded beyond the seminary students at its core to encompass broader sectors of society, including industrial workers and the lumpen proletariat at the base of the social pyramid. At the same time, the revolution gained the support of the *bazaaris*, or commercial bourgeoisie, and established an alliance of convenience with secular opposition groups representing white-collar and professional sectors of the middle class. With this broad base of support, Khomeini was able to oust the shah from power.

Like Iran under the shah, most authoritarian regimes in the contemporary Sunni Muslim Arab world are headed by unified ruling elites with large and cohesive security agencies at their disposal. But in most of the Sunni Muslim world, the dominant strand of the Islamic movement is reformist rather than revolutionary in orientation and has yet to expand its base of support beyond its core constituency of urban, middle-, and lower-class students and professionals.

In Egypt, the Muslim Brotherhood does not have strong ties to industrial workers and has only a limited presence among the semiliterate urban and rural poor. At the same time, ideological and class differences separate the Brotherhood from regime elites and members of the secular opposition. Elsewhere around the globe, the reluctance of authoritarian leaders to cede power to their opponents was eased by the presence of a "safe" opposition party which, it was believed, could safeguard the interests of those exiting power. By contrast, with its commitment to the application of Islamic law and repeated, if vague, references to ending corruption and achieving social justice, the Muslim Brotherhood is regarded with suspicion by the military and bureaucratic elites at the apex of the Egyptian state.

If ideology and interests separate Egypt's leading opposition movement from its most senior power holders, they also have distanced the Islamists from important segments of the business and professional upper-middle class who are more secular in orientation and whose economic interests align them with the status quo. The mistrust with which many secular Egyptians view the reformist wing of the Islamic movement is exacerbated by the presence of a militant Islamic fringe whose intolerance of dissenting viewpoints and use of violence have stigmatized the entire movement and fanned fears of a radical Islamic takeover. It can be argued that a similar "guilt by association" has hindered reformist Islamist movements in Tunisia and Morocco. And in Algeria, the intense suspicion with which the Islamic Salvation Front was regarded by secular middle- and upper-class groups contributed to its isolation when it was targeted for repression in 1992.

The failure of the Muslim Brotherhood in Egypt to move beyond its core constituency has hampered its ability to sustain its momentum over time. Lacking ties to the masses and distrusted by members of the country's senior political and economic elites, the Brotherhood was vulnerable to a counterattack by the regime. In addition, having been trained for peaceful forms of oppositional activity within legal channels, the Brotherhood's own activist cadres were ill prepared for a direct confrontation with the regime during a period of authoritarian reversal.[4] Accustomed to a strategy of gradual reform, such cadres merely lapsed from action to inaction, unwilling or unable to adopt more radical tactics when legal channels of protest were closed off.

In headlong retreat from the liberal reforms of the 1980s, the Mubarak regime has closed off former sites of independent political activity and, to some extent, retargeted strategic urban, lower-middle-class groups for incorporation and control. Besides asserting administrative control over the country's professional associations and student unions, the regime has accelerated its program to incorporate private mosques into the mosque network supervised by the Ministry of Religious Endowments. At the same time, the regime has expanded its own direct outreach to marginalized youth. For example, it has sent "religious caravans" of senior Muslim clergy into the provinces to admonish youth to refrain from politics, while areas that were centers of Islamic activism, such as the Cairo neighborhood of Imbaba, have been targeted for economic development. Having moved from a "hege-monic" to a "liberalizing" phase in the 1970s and 1980s, the regime has arguably shifted toward a new form of hegemony since the early 1990s, albeit one oriented less to mass mobilization and social change than to demobil-ization and control.

Islam and the State: Confrontation or Convergence?

The Mubarak regime's offensive against "opposition Islam" is only one dimension of its complex relationship with Islamic institutions and actors in Egypt today. At the same time that it has forced the Brotherhood to the sidelines, it has tolerated — and, some would say, encouraged — a greater role for the Muslim religious establishment in various spheres of Egyptian public life. For example, the regime has allowed senior *'ulama'* affiliated with al-Azhar, the country's leading institution of Islamic learning, to assume a proactive role as "guardians of the *shari'a*," granting them the authority to censor intellectual and artistic production and participate in the formation of government policy. More broadly, the regime has tolerated — if not en-couraged — the growing influence of conservative Muslim clergy within the judiciary, the educational system, and the state-run media. While using the vast coercive apparatus at its disposal to demobilize autonomous Islamic groups perceived as capable of challenging its power, the regime has per-mitted a remarkable degree of Islamic penetration of the state apparatus, what critics have described as a "revolution by stealth."[5]

As contradictory as these two strands of regime policy appear, they are, in fact, intimately related. Recognizing the potency of Islamic symbols in contests over political power, the regime has granted the Muslim clergy a privileged role in the establishment in order to boost its own Islamic cre-dentials. Rather than head off opposition Islam through a principled defense of secularism and liberalism, the country's leaders have enlisted Islam as a means of securing the regime's survival.

The Muslim clerics who address the masses in government mosques and on state-controlled television are often more conservative, and thus more critical of the pluralism of values and lifestyles in contemporary Egyptian society, than many of the Islamists in organized opposition groups. That is, many of the clerics with official endorsement are more "radical" than the Brotherhood in their efforts to bring Egyptian society into conformity with a rigid and highly conservative interpretation of Islamic law. From the regime's perspective, however, the key distinction is that such clerics seek societal rather than political change. And unlike members of the Muslim Brotherhood, they are viewed as incapable of (and uninterested in) mobilizing an organized challenge to the regime's power.

The Mubarak regime's relationship with Islamic actors and institutions in Egypt has two seemingly contradictory dimensions: the regime uses the state apparatus to contain autonomous Islamic opposition groups while at the same time permitting the "creeping Islamization" of the state itself. The results may preserve the regime, but only at the cost of conceding enormous terrain to some of the most intolerant elements in the Islamic establishment. Continuity at the level of the regime is thus accompanied by a constriction of the terrain for unorthodox thought and expression.

The resulting paradox is that as the state has escalated its assault on Islamic opposition groups, it has become incrementally more Islamic itself. In sum, Egypt does not appear to be on the path to democratization, nor is it suspended in some sort of authoritarian deep freeze. Rather, we find a complex dialectic of contestation and co-optation linking the regime with a diverse set of religious actors. The outcome of this process remains open-ended, to be shaped by the future decisions of regime leaders, establishment '*ulama*', and Islamic counter-elites. But in the short term, the prospects for a deepening of democracy, secular liberalism, and pluralism in Egypt are not promising.

Islamic Experimentation and Political Change

Even when they do not lead directly to regime change, new forms of political activism can reshape authoritarian polities in profound ways. For example, they can change citizens' basic orientations to the public sphere. As de Weydenthal wrote with regard to dissident groups in Eastern Europe:

> They all shared a common denominator in their implicit or explicit attempts to broaden and intensify public participation in social affairs. Furthermore, by conducting these efforts through groups and individuals operating outside the existing power structures and officially sanctioned procedures, as well as by insisting that such activities merely represented the legitimate exercise of rights belonging to all citizens, the dissidents introduced an element of inherent pluralization into East European politics.[6]

By introducing new values and developing new repertoires of personal and collective action, movements can pave the way for broader instances of citizen engagement in public affairs.

In some cases, the new forms of participation that emerge in authoritarian settings may contribute to the formation of a democratic civil society; in other cases, they may lay the groundwork for new forms of authoritarian domination. To assess their long-term impact, we need to investigate the values that inform the new groups and movements and the ways in which they interact with other independent political forces and with incumbent elites. Rather than conceptualizing the Islamists as protagonists in some dichotomous battle between authoritarianism and democracy, I propose that we take more seriously their creative — and thus both liberating and coercive — powers. Just as authoritarian regimes can assume many forms, so too can the alternatives that surface in their midst.

In regard to the model of state and society currently proposed by Egypt's Islamists, both as it is being incubated in peripheral settings and as it might manifest itself were they to assume power, there are grounds for both optimism and concern. Whether their ascent to power would bring about greater (or less) respect for democracy, human rights, and the rule of law is difficult to predict, as the Islamists' commitments to such goals are evolving and have yet to be fully tested in practice. But one thing is certain. The degree to which Islamists incorporate such priorities into their political practice will depend less on fixed doctrinal imperatives than on their evolving relationships with other social and political forces. Indeed, the most effective way for the Mubarak regime to encourage the Islamists to become more democratic is for it to become more democratic itself.

Postscript

The Muslim Brotherhood and the Mubarak Regime, 1995–2001

The events covered in this book ended in the mid-1990s, when the Mubarak regime launched a major counter-initiative against the Muslim Brotherhood. Mubarak's assault on the Brotherhood represents an abrupt departure from the grudging toleration accorded nonviolent Islamist groups during the first decade of his rule. Beginning around 1993, against a backdrop of mounting violence by Islamic militants, the regime began to denounce the Brotherhood as an "illegal organization" with "ties to extremist groups." A glance at the charges brought against Brotherhood leaders suggests, however, that the regime found them threatening *not because they were terrorists but because they were not*. Indeed, I would contend that it was the Brotherhood's electoral takeover of Egypt's professional associations — and its growing credibility as a moderate and responsible opposition in Egyptian society at large — that prompted the regime to move against it. As Egyptian observers noted at the time, regime leaders wanted "to prevent another Algeria," that is, to prevent a nonviolent Islamic movement with popular support from challenging their power at the ballot box.[1]

The Regime's Offensive

The regime's campaign against the Muslim Brotherhood proceeded along several fronts. First, scores of the Brotherhood's most dynamic leaders were imprisoned in successive waves of arrests. In 1995, the regime detained eighty-one of the Brotherhood's leading activists, including former members of parliament, university professors, association officials, and businessmen. The defendants were tried in military court, and fifty-four of them received sentences of up to five years with hard labor. Those who received the maximum sentence included two of the Brotherhood's most influential "middle-generation" leaders — 'Isam al-'Iryan (former member of parliament and assistant secretary general of the Doctors' Association) and 'Abd al-Mun'im Abu-l-Futuh (secretary general of the Doctors' Association and secretary general of the Federation of Arab Doctors). Both 'Iryan and Abu-l-Futuh were charged with "directing an illegal organization aiming to impede the rule of law and the Constitution." They also were charged with providing financial assistance to the families of terrorists and using their association positions to help Islamic militants abroad.[2]

Since 1995, hundreds more Brotherhood activists have been detained, and many have received prison sentences after trials in military court.[3] In one high-profile case, in October 1999, security officers raided the Engineers' Association office in Maadi, a southern suburb of Cairo, where a group of Brotherhood leaders active in the professional associations had assembled to coordinate future plans. The sixteen leaders arrested at the meeting (in addition to four seized at their homes) — including prominent members of the Lawyers', Engineers', Doctors', Pharmacists', and Veterinarians' Associations — were charged with "belonging to a secret outlawed group," "planning to overthrow the system of government," and "infiltrating the professional associations to undermine security in the country."[4] Following a prolonged trial, the Supreme Military Court announced its verdict on November 19, 2000: three of the accused were sentenced to five years in prison; twelve were sentenced to three years; and five were declared innocent. The most prominent of those sentenced was Mukhtar Nuh, a former member of parliament and treasurer of the Lawyers' Association, who received three years in prison.[5]

The arrest and imprisonment of prominent Brotherhood activists accomplished several ends. First, it increased the risks of Islamist political activity and created a powerful deterrent to it. Second, the prolonged trials covered by the media — with newspapers carrying photos of the accused in prison cages — allowed the regime to rehearse its charges against the Muslim Brotherhood before the educated public. In this way, the regime hoped to transform the Brotherhood's image from that of a moderate and responsible opposition to that of a radical organization opposed to the constitution and subverting the public order. Indeed, it is only if and when such an image conversion has occurred that the activities for which Mukhtar Nuh and his

counterparts were charged — that is, their attempts to "infiltrate" the professional associations, spread their ideas, and recruit new members — acquire
a sinister hue. Finally, the arrests prevented some of the Brotherhood's most
charismatic figures from running in upcoming parliamentary and professional association elections. Citizens convicted of a crime in Egypt are
barred from political activity not only for the duration of their trial and prison
term but also for several years thereafter. It thus appears to be no coincidence
that the October 1999 arrests of Mukhtar Nuh and nineteen other association activists took place only a few days after the country's highest court lifted
the sequestration of the Lawyers' Association, thereby paving the way for
new elections within six months. As Diya' Rashwan, an analyst at the al-
Ahram Center for Political and Strategic Studies observed, the aim of the
crackdown was "to prevent the organization from effectively taking part in
the next association elections by depriving it of activists who enjoy credibility
within association circles."[6] In addition, the Supreme Military Court delayed
its verdict until November of the following year, thus preventing Nuh and
his codefendants from running in the parliamentary elections scheduled for
that month. According to the same logic, dozens more Brotherhood activists
were arrested in the period leading up to the parliamentary elections and
again in April 2001 just before the elections for the Shura Council.[7]

In addition to targeting Brotherhood leaders for arrest, the regime reim-
posed its control over those arenas of civil society that had become important
sites of Islamic political experimentation in the preceding decade. During
the mid-1990s, the regime tightened its control over association elections
and placed both the Engineers' and Lawyers' Associations under judicial
sequestration (see chapter 8). The regime also blocked Islamist candidates
from participating in student union elections. For example, in 1998, opposition newspapers reported that security forces had arrested hundreds of Islamists from at least five universities in the run-up to the student elections
scheduled for that November.[8] In addition, the government began to subsidize non-Islamist societies on campus, and according to one report, administrators at one university in Upper Egypt began to hand out monthly
cash allowances to needy students as a means of deterring extremism.[9]

The regime also tried to establish greater control over local institutions
on the periphery that had served as sites of Islamist outreach. A January 1996
law mandated that all private mosques be placed under the control of the
Ministry of Religious Endowments (Awqaf), and then in April of that year
the People's Assembly passed a law prohibiting any charitable association
from receiving foreign funds, with the intent of cutting the flow of funds to

Islamic associations from the Gulf.[10] In 1999, the People's Assembly passed the Law on Civil Associations and Institutions (law 153), which strengthened the government's oversight of nongovernmental organizations (NGOs), for example, requiring all NGOs to report their board members' names and sources of funding.[11] Although law 153 was subsequently overturned in court on a technicality, the other laws have remained in force.

The Brotherhood Under Siege

Under mounting pressure from the government's security forces and subject to a widening web of administrative and political restrictions, the Muslim Brotherhood entered a period of retrenchment. Through the end of the 1990s, the Brotherhood maintained a low profile, refraining from statements and activities that might trigger another round of repression. At the same time, the crisis in the Brotherhood's relations with the regime led to a wave of soul-searching and introspection, prompting some of the middle generation's "rising stars" to openly criticize the organization's old guard. In particular, the middle-generation leaders accused the aging leaders who dominated the Guidance Bureau of being autocratic, ideologically rigid, and obsessed with internal unity and discipline at the cost of suppressing constructive debate. In addition, they castigated the old guard for remaining aloof from — and hostile to — other political trends, isolating the Brotherhood from potential allies and rendering it more vulnerable to repression. Finally, while the Brotherhood's senior leaders vowed to stay the course, some of its middle-generation activists became even more convinced that the Brotherhood needed to shed the handicaps of illegality and gain acceptance as a legitimate political actor.[12]

The growing tensions between the Brotherhood's old guard and middle-generation leaders came to a head in 1996. First, the death of eighty-three-year-old Supreme Guide Hamid Abu Nasr in January of that year raised the issue of succession. According to media reports, Ma'mun Hudeibi — the Brotherhood's official spokesman and allegedly the real power in the Guidance Bureau — hastily announced at Abu Nasr's funeral the appointment of seventy-six-year-old Mustafa Mashhur as the organization's new supreme guide, rousing the indignation of middle-generation leaders who felt that regular elective procedures had been flouted.[13] That same month, the Brotherhood's senior leaders were caught off guard when a prominent group of middle-generation leaders headed by the thirty-eight-year-old Islamist engineer Abu-l-'Ila Madi announced their intention to form a new party, the Wasat (Center) Party. Including three Copts among its founders, the Wasat Party claimed to represent something new, in Madi's words, "a civic platform based on the Islamic faith, which believes in pluralism and the alternation of power."[14]

The Wasat Party initiative received extensive coverage in the Arab and Western media, with commentators debating whether it constituted an effort to establish a Brotherhood party by disguise or, rather, as Madi insisted, was a separate initiative expressing the views of its founders.[15] At first the regime assumed that the Wasat Party was simply a front for the Brotherhood. On April 3, Madi and two other cosponsors of the party were among thirteen Brotherhood leaders arrested and charged by the Higher State Security Prosecution Office with "belonging to an illegal organization," "preparing anti-regime publications," "carrying out political activities without permission," and "attempting to form the Wasat Party as a front for the banned Muslim Brotherhood." In August, after almost five months in detention and a trial in military court, eight of the defendants received prison sentences, and five — including the three Wasat Party founders — were acquitted.[16] As Madi explained, the government authorities eventually realized not only that the Wasat Party was independent of the Brotherhood but also that the Brotherhood's old guard bitterly opposed it as an affront to their own power.[17]

The official reaction of the Brotherhood leadership to the Wasat Party was indeed negative. Madi's announcement brought a prompt condemnation from Hudeibi and other veteran leaders on the Brotherhood's Guidance Bureau, and that spring Hudeibi ordered all Brotherhood members who had joined the new party to withdraw immediately or face expulsion.[18] In response, Madi and twelve other prominent middle-generation leaders announced their resignation from the Brotherhood in August, to be joined by three others in November.

At one level, the schism in the Brotherhood's leadership ranks signaled a power struggle between two generations — between the senior power holders, now their seventies and early eighties, who dominated the Guidance Bureau, and the middle generation, now in their forties, who had joined the Brotherhood in the late 1970s and spearheaded its entry into parliament and the professional associations in the 1980s and early 1990s. On another level, the schism reflected a conflict between two visions of the Brotherhood's future, one emphasizing continuity with the past and the other seeking to push the Brotherhood toward a more "modern" interpretation of Islam on such sensitive issues as women's and minority rights, as well as toward greater pragmatism and flexibility in its relations with the outside world. While support for such competing visions did not fall strictly along generational lines, it was the "rising stars" of the middle generation who were the most vocal proponents of change.

As part of the fallout from the confrontation between Madi and Hudeibi over the Wasat Party initiative, the Brotherhood's middle-generation leaders have split into two camps. While broadly similar in orientation and goals, they differ in their relationship to the Brotherhood's old guard and in their assessment of whether — under the latter's sway — the Brotherhood is truly capable of reform.

The Wasat Party Islamists

The first group of middle-generation leaders are those who broke off from the Muslim Brotherhood in 1996 to form the Wasat Party. Among the most prominent leaders of this group are engineers Abu-l-'Ila Madi and Salah 'Abd al-Karim, lawyer 'Isam Sultan, and publisher Muhammad 'Abd al-Latif. Since their falling-out with Ma'mun Hudeibi and other members of the Guidance Bureau in 1996, this group has stayed away from the Brotherhood. Under the banner of the Wasat Party, they have tried to "modernize" the Islamic reform agenda and lay out a set of detailed political, social, and economic programs for public scrutiny and debate.[19] Citing the model of legal Islamic parties in Turkey, Jordan, Yemen, Malaysia, and elsewhere, they have affirmed their commitment to full organizational transparency and accountability and have vigorously pursued the legal recognition needed to participate fully and openly in the country's political life.

In 1996 and again in 1998, the Wasat Party founders submitted their application to the Shura Council's Political Parties' Committee; on both occasions, their bid for a license was rebuffed, and on appeal, the committee's decision was upheld in court.[20] Although their efforts to obtain legal party status so far have failed, the Wasat group has gained the support of some prominent secular journalists, intellectuals, and political figures who see them as representing a moderate and enlightened form of political Islam. Building on patterns of cooperation forged during their years as association leaders, the Islamists of the Wasat camp have met with secular opposition leaders in various NGO-sponsored seminars, "salons," and conferences to discuss such sensitive issues as the scope for intellectual, religious, and political freedom; the status of women and minorities; and the proper role of *shari'a* in the formation of the country's legal codes. While some fundamental differences of opinion remain, the Wasat Islamists and the proponents of secular democracy have found some areas of common ground and have begun to develop relationships of familiarity and trust.

Such relationships have paved the way for two crosspartisan initiatives. In 1998, a group of twenty-two would-be publishers, including Islamists, Nasserists, and liberals, applied for permission to form a new newspaper, known as *al-Mustaqbal* (*The Future*). The list of applicants included Wasat Party founders (and former Brotherhood activists) Abu-l-'Ila Madi, 'Isam Sultan, Tawfiq al-Shawi, and Salah 'Abd al-Karim, plus Muhammad Salim al-'Awwa, an independent Islamist thinker with close ties to the Wasat group. The list also included several secular intellectuals and journalists and a well-known actor. As Diya' Rashwan, a political scientist who is generally considered a Nasserist, noted, "We all are different, but we agree on goals and principles and we accept our differences."[21]

With that application still pending, a slightly different mix of Wasat Party Islamists and secularists submitted an application to the Ministry of Social Affairs for permission to form a new association (*gam'iyya*). In April 2000 they achieved a modest breakthrough when their application was approved. According to chairman Muhammad Salim al-'Awwa, the new association, known as the Egyptian Society for Culture and Dialogue, "supports the culture of dialogue in a society in which violence prevails."[22] Its charter calls for holding seminars and conferences, conducting and publishing original research, and assisting in other ways to strengthen the values of intellectual pluralism and cultural opening and to encourage the country's development in various fields.

The Wasat Party founders claim that they will eventually apply for party status a third time; meanwhile, they are concentrating their energies on the new association. For example, in November 2000, the association sponsored a panel discussion on the "al-Aqsa" Palestinian uprising and its implications for the Arab-Islamic world and its relations with the West. Held at the headquarters of the Journalists' Association in downtown Cairo, the event was attended by about 200 guests and was followed by a lively question-and-answer session. Critics allege that in their shift from grassroots organization and outreach to holding seminars, the middle-generation leaders of the Wasat camp have abandoned their ties with — and influence over — the mass public. In reply, 'Isam Sultan, secretary general of the new association, stated that at the present time, securing a legal foothold was simply a higher priority. "Once we have legitimacy, we can concern ourselves with mobilization," he explained, noting as an aside that "anyway, mobilization comes easy to us."[23]

The "Prison Team" Returns

While some middle-generation leaders have left the Muslim Brotherhood to forge their own path, others have chosen to remain in the Brotherhood fold. The latter group includes two prominent activists affiliated with the Doctors' Association — 'Abd al-Mun'im Abu-l-Futuh and 'Isam al-'Iryan. Both returned to the Brotherhood in 2000 after five years in prison and, with the status of "martyrs," resumed active roles in the organization. Abu-l-Futuh, who suffered a heart attack while in prison, is the secretary general of the Doctors' Association and the secretary general of the Federation of Arab Doctors. Allegedly a member of the Guidance Bureau, he is on good terms with the Brotherhood's old guard and also commands the respect of its younger members. Furthermore, amid rumors about the deteriorating health of Supreme Guide Mustafa Mashhur, Abu-l-Futuh has emerged as a possible candidate for his successor.[24] 'Isam al-'Iryan, assistant secretary general of the Doctors' Association, has also resumed a major role in the Brotherhood since his release from prison. Although unwilling to say so on record, it is widely reported that 'Iryan masterminded the Brotherhood's successful electoral campaign in the parliamentary elections of November 2000.[25]

In public statements and interviews, Abu-l-Futuh and 'Iryan deny the existence of generational and ideological schisms within the Brotherhood, claiming that any internal disagreements are limited to nonessential issues. Yet media reports allege that while in prison, Abu-l-Futuh, 'Iryan, and Ibrahim al-Za'farani (a third imprisoned Brotherhood leader) issued statements harshly critical of Counselor Ma'mun Hudeibi and Guidance Bureau Secretary Ahmad Sharaf's handling of the Wasat Party case.[26] Moreover, since his release, Abu-l-Futuh has openly advocated the Brotherhood's reconstitution as an open and transparent political party. As he told the journal *al-Majallah* in the spring of 2001,

We hope that the government would lift the ban on the Muslim Brotherhood and allow us to form a legal party to present a respectable example. We are banned from doing that openly. We want the news of our meetings to be in all the newspapers and the media and for anyone to be allowed to attend them and present his views and criticisms. The government should give us a license to carry out our activity openly and benefit from the criticism of others.[27]

What role the Brotherhood's middle-generation leaders play in high-level decision making is hard to gauge, as is their ability to promote what the Arabic-language journal *al-Watan al-'arabi* has dubbed an "ideological and operational Brotherhood perestroika." Yet with Mashhur, Hudeibi, and other senior leaders in their late seventies and early eighties, a turnover of power is inevitable in the near future. There is a good chance that power will pass first to veteran leaders only slightly younger than — and still fiercely loyal to — the old guard. One member of this "half generation," medical professor Mahmud 'Izzat Ibrahim, who is sixty-five, has been cited as a possible successor to the post of supreme guide. Yet the odds are that the Brotherhood's politically dynamic and skilled middle generation will gain influence over time. In the future, the accession of a middle-generation leader to the position of supreme guide could pave the way for the Brotherhood's reconciliation with the Wasat group. Given the respect he commands in both Brotherhood and Wasat Party circles, 'Abd al-Mun'im Abu-l-Futuh is particularly well suited for this bridging role.

Now that nearly a decade has passed since the Mubarak regime launched its campaign against the Muslim Brotherhood, we might ask to what extent it managed to eliminate the Brotherhood as a major force in Egyptian public life. There is no doubt that the regime pushed the Brotherhood into a period of retrenchment and exacerbated tensions within it, causing an unprecedented schism in its leadership ranks. But despite the determination of Egypt's authoritarian leaders to weaken the Brotherhood as an opposition force, they failed to prevent its recent comeback. As noted earlier, in the elections of November 2000 the Brotherhood won seventeen seats, making it the largest opposition bloc in parliament. Then in February 2001, when the Lawyers' Association held competitive elections after a hiatus of five years, the Brotherhood won every seat it contested, gaining control of one-third of the seats on the association's board.[28]

Such developments suggest that an authoritarian regime's own democratic pretensions may restrict the amount of coercion it is prepared to deploy in suppressing nonviolent opposition groups. Unlike the leaders of Syria and Iraq — or, for that matter, unlike Nasser — President Mubarak claims to be leading his country on a gradual path to democracy. And as I will elaborate, even in the absence of effective institutional constraints on its power, an authoritarian regime's pursuit of democratic legitimacy may force it to accommodate opposition actors that it could suppress by force.

Democratic Pretensions and Authoritarian Control

Governed by emergency laws for more than twenty years, Egypt is hardly a model of democracy. But like other authoritarian regimes in the developing world, the Mubarak regime is militarily and economically dependent on Western governments, which monitor its adherence to global democratic norms. Without exaggerating the amount of external pressure it confronts, or underestimating its readiness to defy such pressure when it believes its own interests are at stake,[29] it is safe to say that the Mubarak regime is sensitive about its image abroad and that this concern affects the formation of domestic policy. For example, it was widely reported that the regime was embarrassed by media reports on the great amount of electoral violence and fraud during the parliamentary elections of 1995, as well as by the fact that the elections left the ruling National Democratic Party in control of 94 percent of parliament's 454 seats. The unrepresentative and illegitimate character of the parliament was underscored in the summer of 2000, when four of its members were convicted of bank fraud and Egypt's Supreme Constitutional Court ruled that the results of the previous two elections were invalid because they did not receive full judicial supervision. In response, President Mubarak recalled parliament from its summer recess, passed a major reform of the country's electoral laws, and vowed that the next elections would be fully free and fair. As he declared on September 20 at a meeting of National Democratic Party leaders: "The People's Assembly elections will mark a new departure, affirming that Egypt is a democratic state."[30] It was thus with great fanfare that the regime arranged for the first time for judicial supervision of the country's parliamentary elections.

The regime's management of the November 2000 elections bears the imprint of its conflicting desires for democratic credibility and authoritarian control. On the one hand, the elections were substantially freer and fairer than those of the recent past. Candidates representing a wide range of political trends, including the Muslim Brotherhood, participated in the elections as independents. Furthermore, judges scrupulously monitored the casting of ballots in the country's 10,000 polling stations, making the outcome less vulnerable to fraud than any other in Egypt's history.[31] Indeed, the regime sought maximum credit for judicial supervision, as demonstrated by the stream of self-congratulatory statements issued by Egyptian government officials and reported in the official press. For example, on December 16, the state-run *Egyptian Gazette* quoted the boast by Speaker of Parliament Fathi Surur that "Egypt is leading the world in this respect."[32]

While tolerating the Brotherhood's participation in the elections, the regime intervened to limit its electoral gains. Scores of Brotherhood activists
were arrested in the lead-up to the election period. During the elections
themselves, plainclothes security agents harassed Brotherhood supporters in
several districts and, in some instances, physically blocked them from entering the polling stations.[33] Noting the regime's dependence on security
thugs to prevent Islamist victories, Egyptians wryly observed at the time that
the elections were "clean on the inside and dirty on the outside." The results
of the elections likewise suggest a balancing of regime objectives. On the
one hand, the legitimacy of the new parliament was enhanced by the fact
that the number of seats gained by opposition parties increased from thirteen
to thirty-four, with seventeen seats for the Muslim Brotherhood alone. On
the other hand, the NDP and its allied independents retained a comfortable
85 percent majority, with 388 of 444 seats under their control.[34]

The regime's efforts to suppress the country's nonviolent Islamist opposition
have also been reined in by the judiciary, which still has a substantial degree
of independence despite fifty years of authoritarian rule. In recent years, the
courts have ruled against the government in a number of important decisions.
For example, in June 2000, the Constitutional Court struck down the government's new restrictive Law on Civil Associations and Institutions (law 153 of
1999) on procedural grounds.[35] Then in October of that year, the country's
highest administrative court upheld a lower court decision repealing the sequestration of the Lawyers' Association, setting the stage for new elections.
After a series of postponements, the elections were held in February 2001,
and the Brotherhood won one-third of the seats on the executive board. A
court ruling also cleared the way for judicial supervision of the parliamentary
elections of November 2000, hampering the regime's ability to restrict Islamist
gains through outright fraud.

We must be careful, however, not to exaggerate the judiciary's power. If
Egypt's judges have limited the regime's freedom of maneuver, it is only
because the regime has chosen to honor their decisions. Here, too, we must
conclude that it was the regime's own pretensions to democracy and the
rule of law — rather than the presence of the judiciary as an effective institutional constraint on regime power — that created opportunities for the officially vilified Muslim Brotherhood to resume its participation in Egyptian
public life.

The Brotherhood's strong performance in Egypt's latest parliamentary and
professional association elections hints at its enduring mobilizing power. But
its conduct in these elections also reveals a new pattern of self-restraint. This

leads us to a final observation: repression did not propel the Brotherhood toward radicalization. On the contrary, its leaders have emerged from the most recent crisis determined to avoid another confrontation with the regime and anxious to present the Brotherhood as a moderate and responsible opposition that poses no threat to the public order.

Evidence of this trend can be discerned in the subtle changes that distinguish the Brotherhood's recent electoral campaigns from those of earlier years. For example, the Brotherhood fielded 156 candidates in the parliamentary elections of 1995 but only 76 candidates in 2000. This reduction enabled the Brotherhood to concentrate on traditional areas of its strength (for example, Cairo and Delta towns rather than Upper Egypt) but also to avoid districts where it would have to run against prominent NDP politicians. In addition, in most districts the Brotherhood did not run well-known leaders but instead chose young individuals with good local reputations and no records of detention or arrest. The Brotherhood's reliance on candidates unknown outside their own districts prompted accusations that it was fielding "secret candidates" whose ties with the Brotherhood were not obvious to voters. This approach, however, can also be seen as an attempt by the Brotherhood to allay the regime's fears and lessen the chances that its candidates would end up in prison.[36]

The Brotherhood took similar steps in the Lawyers' Association elections of February 24, 2001. In order to avoid embarrassing the regime (and alarming the secular opposition) with another electoral sweep, the Brotherhood contested only eight of the twenty-four seats on the association's executive board. In addition, it allied itself with secular candidates and studiously avoided any association with the handful of candidates known to have ties with Jihad and the Islamic Group.[37]

The Brotherhood has also toned down its confrontational rhetoric vis-à-vis the regime. After the elections of November 2000, Brotherhood leaders made the case that their popular mandate entitled them to legal party status. Yet as Abu-l-Futuh stressed in an interview with *al-Hayat*, even if the Brotherhood is not granted a license, it will continue to act within the framework of the constitution and the rule of law. As he explained: "What the Muslim Brotherhood suffered in the past years and our stand in the recent elections provide clear evidence that we prefer the public interest to self-interest. As much as we are interested in participating in political action, we care for the country's security and peace."[38]

Whether the moderation of the Brotherhood's strategy and rhetoric is merely a sophisticated tactic to gain support or reflects a genuine shift in priorities is an open question. Regardless of the motives behind it, this trend toward moderation has not increased the Brotherhood's prospects for legal recognition, which leads us back to the observation with which this postscript began. The Mubarak regime moved against the Brotherhood in the mid-1990s not because it was violent or antidemocratic but because after a decade of growing influence, it had emerged as a viable competitor for political power. In the coming years, President Mubarak and his senior advisers will continue to place a premium on political stability as they continue with the implementation of painful economic reforms. If recent trends are any indication, the regime will most likely permit the chastened Brotherhood to assume a marginal role in public life. But it will almost certainly prohibit the conversion of either the Muslim Brotherhood or the Wasat group into legal political parties that could challenge its power at the ballot box. To ensure that the Brotherhood — which retains strong ties to the mass public — does not regain its former influence, the regime will continue to harass its leaders, impede its efforts at organization and outreach, and attack its moderate image in the official press.

With President Mubarak set to finish his fourth consecutive term in office in 2005, change may be on the horizon. Rather than seek a fifth term at age seventy-seven, Mubarak may instead cede power to a designated successor. According to widespread rumor, the most likely candidate for this role is Mubarak's son Gamal, who will be forty-one when his father's current term expires. In any event, it will be Mubarak's successor who will have to decide whether to perpetuate the "managed politics" of recent decades or to attempt the fuller integration of Egypt's Islamist groups. At the same time, it remains to be seen whether the Brotherhood will stick to its highly conservative Islamic agenda or move toward a conception of Islam more consistent with global democratic norms. As we noted, the democratic evolution of Egypt's largest opposition group would do little to enhance its immediate prospects for inclusion. In the longer run, though, the democratic evolution of the Brotherhood could matter a great deal, for it could pave the way for the rise of a united democratic front encompassing secular and Islamist groups alike. The prospects for such a coalition remain too slim to warrant optimism, but they are sufficient to allow for hope. In particular, they permit us to envision possibilities for Egypt's future that transcend the bleak choice between secular and religious variants of authoritarian rule. W*Allah yahdi 'l-gami'*.

Notes

1. Introduction

1. Al-Zawahiri, a physician by training, is suspected of being the mastermind of the September 11 attacks on the World Trade Center and the Pentagon. He is a senior adviser to bin Laden and has been living in exile in Afghanistan since the mid-1990s. Muhammad 'Atef allegedly served as bin Laden's chief military adviser and assisted in the training of terrorist operatives. Both Al-Zawahiri and 'Atef were indicted in a U.S. federal court for their role in the 1998 attacks on American embassies in Kenya and Tanzania. 'Atef was reportedly killed in an American military raid on an al-Qa'ida base in Afghanistan; Al-Zawahiri remains at large.

2. For a discussion of how the terrorist activities of Egyptian militants have alienated the Egyptian public, see Fawaz A. Gerges, "The End of the Islamist Insurgency in Egypt?: Costs and Prospects," *Middle East Journal* 4 (fall 2000) 593–94.

3. Sami Zubaida, "Islam, the State and Democracy: Contrasting Conceptions of Society in Egypt," *Middle East Report* 22, no. 179 (November/December 1992): 8.

4. Malcolm Kerr, "Egypt," in *Education and Political Development*, ed. James S. Coleman (Princeton, N.J.: Princeton University Press, 1965), 188–89.

5. See Brenda Gazzar, "The Ballot and the Bullet," *Cairo Times*, November 2–8, 2000; Amil Khan, "Violent Clashes Continue to Mar Egypt Elections," *Middle East Times*, November 12–18, 2000; and "Killings Mar Egyptian Elections," BBC World Service, November 14, 2000.

6. Currently, all candidates in Egyptian parliamentary elections run as independents, but some identify with a particular political party or faction. Brotherhood-

affiliated candidates won 17 seats. The Wafd Party won 7 seats, the leftist Tagammu' 6, the Nasserist Party 3, and the Liberal Party 1.

7. Egyptian luminaries of the Islamist movement include Hassan al-Banna, Sayyid
Qutb, Muhammad al-Ghazzali, and Yusuf al-Qaradawi.

8. The literature on the Iranian revolution includes studies informed by social
movement theory and, in particular, by theories of revolution. By contrast,
research on Islamic movements in the Arab world has only recently begun to
build on — and contribute to — theoretical developments in the social movement field.

9. See, for example, Quintan Wiktorowicz, *The Management of Islamic Activism:
The Salafis, the Muslim Brotherhood, and State Power in Jordan* (Albany: State
University of New York Press, 2000). See also Quintan Wiktorowicz, ed., *Is-
lamic Activism: A Social Movement Approach* (forthcoming).

10. Doug McAdam, Sidney Tarrow, and Charles Tilly called for "a cautious and
anti-imperialist enlargement of attention from what we know about particular
forms of contention in democratic polities to broader scope and types of contentious politics." See Doug McAdam, Sidney Tarrow, and Charles Tilly, "A
Comparative Synthesis on Social Movements and Revolution: Towards an Integrated Perspective" (paper presented at the annual meeting of the American
Political Science Association, San Francisco, 1996), 25. Likewise, a major volume published that year notes: "The new comparative riches available to movement scholars are based almost exclusively on research rooted in core democracies and focused primarily on contemporary movements." See Doug
McAdam, John D. McCarthy, and Mayer N. Zald, *Comparative Perspectives
on Social Movements: Political Opportunities, Mobilizing Structures and Cultural Framings* (Cambridge: Cambridge University Press, 1996), 2.

11. See, for example, the second edition of Sidney Tarrow's *Power in Movement:
Social Movements and Contentious Politics* (Cambridge: Cambridge University
Press, 1998); and Doug McAdam, Sidney Tarrow, and Charles Tilly, *The Dynamics of Contention* (Cambridge: Cambridge University Press, 2001). Both
are synthetic works of social movement theory that integrate research on social
movements outside the West.

12. As of this writing, one of the few studies of Islamic activism regularly cited in
the mainstream social movement literature is Charles Kurzman's "Structural
Opportunity and Perceived Opportunity in Social Movement Theory: The Iranian Revolution of 1979," *American Sociological Review* 61 (1996): 153–70.

13. Tarrow, *Power in Movement*, 4.

14. As used here, *opposition activism* can assume an infinite variety of forms, from
attendance at an antiregime lecture or sermon, to participation in a nonviolent
rally or demonstration, to acts of armed resistance. Hence apart from the question of whether or not citizens join an opposition movement is the question of
why their participation assumes a particular form.

15. The literature on Islamic movements is dominated by article-length studies published in journals or in edited volumes. For example, see John Esposito, ed., *Political Islam: Revolution, Radicalism or Reform?* (Boulder, Colo.: Lynne Rienner, 1997); and Joel Beinin and Joe Stork, eds., *Political Islam: Essays from Middle East Report* (Berkeley and Los Angeles: University of California Press, 1997). The literature also contains some book-length studies, which range from in-depth studies of particular Islamic groups to works that are more synthetic and comparative. Two recent studies of contemporary Islamic activism, both written by journalists, are particularly valuable. See Anthony Shadid, *Legacy of the Prophet: Despots, Democrats and the New Politics of Islam* (Boulder, Colo.: Westview Press, 2001); and Geneive Abdo, *No God but God: Egypt and the Triumph of Islam* (Oxford: Oxford University Press, 2000). Important scholarly works include those by Dale F. Eickelman and James Piscatori, *Muslim Politics* (Princeton, N.J.: Princeton University Press, 1996); and François Burgat and William Dowell, *The Islamic Movement in North Africa*, Middle East Monograph Series (Austin: Center for Middle Eastern Studies, University of Texas, 1993).

16. See, for example, Burgat and Dowell, "Islamism as the Language of Political Reaction to Western Cultural Domination," 63–85, in *The Islamic Movement in North Africa*. See also Leila Hessini, "Wearing the Hijab in Contemporary Morocco: Choice and Identity," in *Reconstructing Gender in the Middle East: Tradition, Identity and Power*, eds. Fatma Muge Gocek and Shiva Balaghi (New York: Columbia University Press, 1994).

17. For an influential early study in this vein, see Philip S. Khoury, "Islamic Revivalism and the Crisis of the Secular State in the Arab World," in *Arab Resources*, ed. Ibrahim Ibrahim, 213–34 (Washington D.C.: Center for Contemporary Arab Studies, Georgetown University, 1983). Other examples of the "political economy" perspective include Mark Tessler, "The Origins of Popular Support for Islamist Movements: A Political Economy Analysis," occasional papers for the Center for International Studies, University of Wisconsin at Milwaukee and Marquette University, December 1993. In a later work, Tessler reiterates his main arguments but grants a secondary causal role to organizational and ideological factors. See Mark Tessler, "The Origins of Popular Support for Islamist Movements: A Political Economy Analysis," in *Islam, Democracy, and the State in North Africa*, ed. John P. Entelis, 93–126 (Bloomington: Indiana University Press, 1997). See also Saad Eddin Ibrahim, "The Changing Face of Islamic Activism: How Much of a Threat?" Paper presented to the workshop U.S.–Egyptian Relations After the Cold War, National Defense University, Washington, D.C., April 28–29, 1994. Ibrahim contends that the "inner logic" of the recent wave of Islamic activism in Egypt is similar to that of such activism elsewhere, with "politicized Islam as an idiom for expressing profound worldly grievances" (13).

18. Such insights figure prominently in the "resource mobilization" and "political process" models that dominate the mainstream American social movement literature. For a review of the former, see Aldon D. Morris and Cedric Herring, "Theory and Research in Social Movements: A Critical Review," in *Annual Review of Political Science*, vol. 2, ed. Samuel Long (Norwood, N.J.: ABLEX, 1987), 137–98. For an early and influential formulation of the "political process" approach, see Doug McAdam, *Political Process and the Development of Black Insurgency, 1930–1970* (Chicago: University of Chicago Press, 1982).

19. Such environmental factors are explored in the social movement literature on "political opportunity structures." See, for example, the contributions to "Part I: Political Opportunities" in McAdam, McCarthy, and Zald, eds., *Comparative Perspectives on Social Movements*, particularly McAdam's chapter "Conceptual Origins, Current Problems, Future Directions," 23–40.

20. For example, they may launch a media campaign against it, pressure its political and financial patrons to defect, and/or exploit existing legislation (for example, zoning laws) to limit its room to maneuver.

21. The difference between democratic and authoritarian regimes in this regard is actually a matter of degree. First, some forms of protest that are presently tolerated in Western democracies were repressed in earlier periods, such as during war or social unrest. Second, some contemporary democracies ban political organizations on the grounds that their agendas violate the constitution, for example, neo-Nazi groups in Germany or the KACH Party in Israel. Finally, in the United States, where radical groups have generally not been banned outright, federal authorities have conducted covert operations to investigate and disrupt groups deemed subversive of the public order. Two prominent examples are the McCarthy era's anticommunist investigations and the FBI's COINTELPRO campaign against the Black Panthers. Regarding the latter, see Hugh Pearson, *The Shadow of the Panthers: Huey Newton and the Price of Black Power in America* (Reading, Mass.: Addison-Wesley, 1994); and Ward Churchill and Jim Vander Wall, *The COINTELPRO Papers: Documents from the FBI's Secret Wars Against Domestic Dissent* (Boston: South End Press, 1990).

22. For a discussion of why the Nasserist model of state-led development failed to become self-sustaining, see John Waterbury, *The Egypt of Nasser and Sadat: The Political Economy of Two Regimes* (Princeton, N.J.: Princeton University Press, 1983); Raymond A. Hinnebusch Jr., *Egyptian Politics Under Sadat* (Boulder, Colo.: Lynne Rienner, 1988), 11–39; and Joel S. Migdal, *Strong Societies and Weak States: State-Society Relations and State Capabilities in the Third World* (Princeton, N.J.: Princeton University Press, 1988), 181–205.

23. McAdam, McCarthy, and Zald, eds., *Comparative Perspectives on Social Movements*, 8.

24. Tarrow, *Power in Movement*, 76.

25. This core-periphery distinction parallels Alfred Stepan's distinction between "political society" and "civil society." See Alfred Stepan, *Rethinking Military Politics: Brazil and the Southern Cone* (Princeton, N.J.: Princeton University Press, 1988), 3–7.

26. Strong rational-actor assumptions inform the influential "resource mobilization" and "political process" models of social movement participation, particularly before the latter was modified to incorporate attention to cultural and ideological factors.

27. Social movement scholars highlight the provision of "selective incentives" as a means to overcome the "free-rider" problem identified by Mancur Olson. See Mancur Olson Jr., *The Logic of Collective Action* (Cambridge, Mass.: Harvard University Press, 1965). For further discussion of selective incentives, see William Gamson, *The Strategy of Social Protest* (Homewood, Ill.: Dorsey Press, 1975), 66–71. See also McAdam, *Political Process*, 45–46; and Debra Friedman and Doug McAdam, "Collective Identity and Activism: Networks, Choices and the Life of a Social Movement," in *Frontiers in Social Movement Theory*, ed. Aldon D. Morris and Carol McClurg Mueller, 158–66 (New Haven, Conn.: Yale University Press, 1992). For a discussion of the use of selective incentives by Islamic groups, see Alan Richards and John Waterbury, *A Political Economy of the Middle East* (Boulder, Colo.: Westview Press, 1996), 349–50.

28. For the distinction between "high risk/high cost" and "low risk/low cost" activism, see Doug McAdam, "Recruitment to High-Risk Activism: The Case of Freedom Summer," *American Journal of Sociology* 92 (July 1986): 64–90. See also Doug McAdam, *Freedom Summer* (New York: Oxford University Press, 1988).

29. For an elaboration of the new synthetic theoretical approach to social movements, see the introduction to Doug McAdam, *Political Process and the Development of Black Insurgency, 1930–1970*, 2nd ed. (Chicago: University of Chicago Press, 1999). See also McAdam, McCarthy, and Zald, eds., *Comparative Perspectives on Social Movements*; Doug McAdam, Sidney Tarrow, and Charles Tilly, "Toward an Integrated Perspective on Social Movements and Revolution," in *Comparative Politics: Rationality, Culture, and Structure*, eds. Mark Irving Lichbach and Alan S. Zuckerman, 142–73 (Cambridge: Cambridge University Press, 1997); and Tarrow, *Power in Movement*.

30. See Robert D. Benford and David A. Snow, "Framing Processes and Social Movements: An Overview and Assessment," *Annual Review of Sociology* 26 (2000): 611–39; see also David A. Snow and Robert D. Benford, "Ideology, Frame Resonance and Participant Mobilization," in *International Social Movement Research. From Structure to Action: Comparing Social Movement Across Cultures*, edited by Bert Klandermans, Hanspeter Kriesi, and Sidney Tarrow, vol. 1 (Greenwich, Conn.: JAI Press, 1988); and David A. Snow et al., "Frame

Alignment Processes, Micromobilization, and Movement Participation," *American Sociological Review* 51 (1986): 464–81.

31. Robert Benford, "An Insider's Critique of the Social Movement Framing Perspective," *Sociological Inquiry* 67 (November 1997): 414–18.

32. For a similar argument concerning the link between informality and the evasion of state control, see Wiktorowicz, *The Management of Islamic Activism*, 6–10.

33. See Tarrow, *Power in Movement*, "Cycles of Contention" (ch. 9), 141–60.

34. My research permit from the Ministry of Higher Education explicitly prohibited the use of questionnaires and recording equipment (and also prohibited the taking of notes!) Not only was the conduct of a random, large-n survey illegal but also given the sensitivity of questions about oppositional affiliations and activities, it was unlikely to produce reliable results. Egyptian colleagues replied with unrestrained derision to the idea of asking informants "their true opinion of President Mubarak" or "whether they were involved in any illegal organizations or activities."

35. To protect the anonymity of my respondents, I do not identify the neighborhoods by name; individual respondents are referred to by pseudonyms.

36. The interviews were open-ended and varied in scope depending on the circumstances in which they were conducted. In some cases I interviewed the same individual several times; in others, circumstances required that I interview several activists at the same time.

37. In two neighborhoods, my access to Islamist networks hinged on my longstanding relationships with families who introduced me to neighbors, relatives, and peers active in the Islamic movement. Without such relationships, which dated back to 1986, it would have been difficult, if not impossible, to establish the levels of intimacy and trust on which both my interviews and participant-observation relied. In the third neighborhood, my access to Islamist movement organizers and constituents stemmed from the contacts I made as a volunteer teacher at a neighborhood community center.

38. See Alexander George and Timothy J. McKeown, "Case Studies and Theories of Organization Decision-Making," *Advances in Information Processing in Organizations*, vol. 2 (Greenwich, Conn.: JAI Press, 1985).

2. Nasser and the Silencing of Protest

1. Raymond A. Hinnebusch Jr., *Egyptian Politics Under Sadat: The Post-Populist Development of an Authoritarian-Modernizing State* (Boulder, Colo.: Lynne Rienner, 1988), 2.

2. See John Waterbury, *The Egypt of Nasser and Sadat: The Political Economy of Two Regimes* (Princeton, N.J.: Princeton University Press, 1983); and John

Waterbury, "The 'Soft State' and the Open Door: Egypt's Experience with Economic Liberalization, 1974–1984," *Comparative Politics*, October 1985, 65–81.

3. Hinnebusch, *Egyptian Politics Under Sadat*, 29–35.
4. The term "social contract" is widely used in the literature on Egypt. See, for example, Khalid Ikram, "Meeting the Social Contract in Egypt," *Finance and Development*, September 1981, 30–33. See also a discussion of the social contract in Diane Singerman, *Avenues of Participation: Family, Politics and Networks in Urban Quarters of Cairo* (Princeton, N.J.: Princeton University Press, 1985), 244–45.
5. Haggai Erlich, *Students and University in 20th Century Egyptian Politics* (London: Frank Cass, 1989), 176.
6. Mahmoud A. Faksh, "The Consequences of the Introduction and Spread of Modern Education: Education and National Integration in Egypt," *Middle Eastern Studies* 16 (May 1980): 48.
7. Mahmoud 'Abdel-Fadil, "Educational Expansion and Income Distribution in Egypt, 1952–1977," in *The Political Economy of Income Distribution in Egypt*, ed. Gouda 'Abdel-Khalek and Robert Tignor (New York: Holmes & Meier, 1982), 353.
8. Waterbury, *The Egypt of Nasser and Sadat*, 222.
9. Clement Henry Moore, *Images of Development: Egyptian Engineers in Search of Industry* (Cambridge, Mass.: MIT Press, 1980), 6, 68.
10. Cited in 'Abdel-Fadil, "Educational Expansion and Income Distribution in Egypt," 352.
11. Interview with Ibrahim Hilmi 'Abd al-Rahman, spring 1991.
12. Nazih Ayubi, *Bureaucracy and Politics in Contemporary Egypt* (London: Ithaca Press, 1980), 241; and 'Abdel-Fadil, "Educational Expansion and Income Distribution in Egypt," 358.
13. 'Abdel-Fadil, "Educational Expansion and Income Distribution in Egypt," 358.
14. This pattern was not new but was built on precedents from the liberal era. Following a wave of student political unrest, a law was passed in 1949 providing free tuition for the first two years of academic secondary school to students scoring above a certain grade in their primary examinations. Then, in what Kerr termed a "demagogic bid," the Wafd government in 1950 decreed free secondary tuition for all, regardless of grades. Attuned to the overwhelming popular demand for higher education, Nasser expanded the formula to include education at the university level. See Malcolm Kerr, "Egypt," in *Education and Political Development*, ed. James S. Coleman (Princeton, N.J.: Princeton University Press, 1965), 176.
15. Erlich, *Students and University*, 177.

16. 'Abdel-Fadil, "Educational Expansion and Income Distribution in Egypt," 352–54.

17. This expansion was fueled by the nationalization measures of 1961, which brought under state control about 80 percent of all nonagricultural activities, including all major firms in industry, finance, and construction. See Saad Eddin Ibrahim, *The New Arab Social Order* (Boulder, Colo.: Westview Press, 1982), 380.

18. Ayubi, *Bureaucracy and Politics in Contemporary Egypt*, 250–51, table 4. Similarly, John Waterbury notes that the civil service (exclusive of the public sector) grew by 7.5 percent per year between 1962 and 1971, compared with an annual growth rate of 2.2 percent of the national workforce. See Waterbury, *The Egypt of Nasser and Sadat*, 242, table 11.2.

19. Interview with Kamal ed-Din Hussein, January 1991.

20. Interview with Ibrahim Hilmi 'Abd al-Rahman, April 1991.

21. Ayubi, *Bureaucracy and Politics in Contemporary Egypt*, 242, 355–66. With access to government jobs determined strictly by formal degrees, the *ta'yin* policy was a particular boon to university-educated women, 70 percent of whom obtained state employment. See Moore, *Images of Development*, 131.

22. Robert Mabro, *The Egyptian Political Economy* (Oxford: Clarendon Press, 1974), 209–10, 227.

23. See the discussion of "solidarism" in Alan Richards and John Waterbury, *A Political Economy of the Middle East* (Boulder, Colo.: Westview Press, 1996), 277–78, 309–22.

24. Ahmad Abdalla, *The Student Movement and National Politics in Egypt* (London: Al-Saqi Books, 1985), 139.

25. Abdalla, *The Student Movement*, 124–29; and Erlich, *Students and University*, 174–81.

26. Faksh, "The Consequences of the Introduction and Spread of Modern Education," 51–52.

27. Erlich, *Students and University*, 185. See also Abdalla, *The Student Movement*, 127–29.

28. Kerr, "Egypt," 188–89.

29. Ibrahim, *The New Arab Social Order*, 381–83.

30. Kerr, "Egypt," 187.

31. See Abdalla, *The Student Movement*, 123–25; Faksh, "The Consequences of the Introduction and Spread of Modern Education," 49–51; Erlich, *Students and University*, 187–90; and Kerr, "Egypt," 192–93.

32. Abdalla, *The Student Movement*, 149–50.

33. Ibid., 216.

34. Ibid., 158–59.

35. Theda Skocpol, *States and Social Revolutions* (Cambridge: Cambridge University Press, 1979).

3. Educated and Underemployed

1. For an early discussion of the "new middle class," see Manfred Halpern, *The Politics of Social Change in the Middle East and North Africa* (Princeton, N.J.: Princeton University Press, 1963).
2. There is a voluminous literature on the causes and consequences of the Egyptian *infitah*. For a particularly cogent analysis, see John Waterbury, "'The Soft State' and the Open Door: Egypt's Experience with Economic Liberalization, 1974–1984," *Comparative Politics*, October 1985, 65–83.
3. In 1974, exogenous resources constituted no more than 6 percent of GDP; by 1980/81, their share had risen to 45 percent. See Ragui Assaad and Simon Commander, *Egypt: The Labour Market Through Boom and Recession* (Washington, D.C.: International Bank of Reconstruction and Development, 1990), 6. Also cited in Waterbury, "'The Soft State,'" 68.
4. Assaad and Commander, *Egypt*, 3, table 1. Between 1974 and 1983, Egypt's budget deficit averaged about 22 percent of GDP.
5. For comparison, note that before economic liberalization, from 1960 to 1976, Egypt's labor force grew by an average of 2.2 percent per year, while state employment grew by 7.5 percent. See Heba Handoussa, *The Burden of Public Service Employment and Remuneration: A Case Study of Egypt* (Geneva: International Labor Organization, 1988), 32.
6. Ragui Assaad, "The Employment Crisis in Egypt: Trends and Issues" (unpublished manuscript, September 1993), table 6.
7. Reliable data on graduate appointments are available only beginning with the class year of 1977. See Nader Fergany, "Design, Implementation and Appraisal of the October 1988 Round of the LFSS," CAPMAS Labor Information System Project, 1990, 22.; Handoussa, *The Burden*, 11, tables 2.2 and 2.3.
8. Nagib Hasan Ghayta, "Ba'd mazahir al-khalal fi suq al-amal al-misri" [Some Manifestations of Imbalance in the Egyptian Labor Market] (unpublished manuscript in Arabic, Ministry of Labor Force, 1987), 28, table 13. Ghayta notes that in 1987 "degree holders represented more than half of all applicants and appointees" (29).
9. Handoussa, *The Burden*, 23 and 25, table 4.3.
10. For estimates of redundant state employment in the 1970s, see Nazih Ayubi, "Bureaucratic Inflation and Administrative Inefficiency: The Deadlock in Egyptian Administration," *Middle East Studies* 18 (July 1982): 289; John Waterbury, *The Egypt of Nasser and Sadat: The Political Economy of Two Regimes* (Princeton, N.J.: Princeton University Press, 1983), 246; World Bank, *Egypt: Alleviating Poverty During Structural Adjustment* (Washington, D.C.: World Bank, 1991), 46. By the late 1970s, evidence of the distortions caused by the guaranteed employment scheme began to generate calls for reform, but few changes were actually implemented, with one important exception. In 1978,

the regime issued law 48, allowing public-sector enterprises to set their own hiring levels, thereby effectively removing them from the Ministry of Labor Force's centralized manpower allocation scheme. Employment growth in the public-enterprise sector slowed as a result, leaving the government to absorb the bulk of the new graduates. For additional information, see Assaad and Commander, *Egypt*, 11, table 2.

11. Heba Handoussa, "Crisis and Challenge: Prospects for the 1990s," in *Employment and Structural Adjustment: Egypt in the 1990s*, ed. Heba Handoussa and Gillian Potter (Cairo: American University in Cairo Press, 1991), 3.

12. On wage trends during this period, see Assaad and Commander, *Egypt*, 13.

13. Assaad and Commander, *Egypt*, app., table 1.

14. Handoussa, *The Burden*, 3.

15. World Bank, *Egypt*, 96; Assaad and Commander, *Egypt*, 2.

16. Assaad and Commander, *Egypt*, 2–3; Alan Richards, "The Political Economy of Dilatory Reform," *World Development* 29 (December 1991): 1724.

17. Richards, "The Political Economy," 1724.

18. World Bank, *Egypt*, 103.

19. President Mubarak's May Day speech, May 3, 1989; in FBIS-NES-89–084.

20. Assaad, "The Employment Crisis in Egypt," table 6. In 1991, state employment continued to represent roughly one-third (33.4 percent) of total employment and slightly more than half (54.8 percent) of total domestic employment outside agriculture.

21. Assaad and Commander, *Egypt*, 25.

22. For growth of the graduate pool, see Assaad and Commander, *Egypt*, 17; and Ragui Assaad, "Structural Adjustment and Labour Market Reform" (unpublished manuscript, May 1993), table 7. See also Handoussa, *The Burden*, 10, table 5.

23. Ghayta, "Some Manifestations of Imbalance," pp. 29–30; Cabinet Information Support Center, internal memorandum, 1991.

24. Information on extending the time lag was supplied by the staff of the Office of Graduate Administration, Ministry of Manpower and Training.

25. See Nader Fergany, "A Characterization of the Employment Problem in Egypt," in *Employment and Structural Adjustment: Egypt in the 1990s*, ed. Heba Handoussa and Gillian Porter (Cairo: American University in Cairo Press, 1991), 41, table 5. Data on migration remain sketchy. Other studies set the number of Egyptian migrant workers at 2 million. See *al-Ahram*, May 1, 1990; and *Egyptian Gazette*, May 5, 1990. Indeed, estimates as high as 3.8 million have been cited in the Egyptian press; see *al-Ahram*, June 2, 1990.

26. Handoussa, "Crisis and Challenge," 6.

27. Assaad, "The Employment Crisis in Egypt," 16, n. 30.

28. The lower unemployment rate yielded by the Labor Force Sample Survey (LFSS) in 1991 was due less to improvements in the economy than to differences

in the measurement techniques. See Fergany, "A Characterization," 27–29, 45–46.

29. Interviews with Robert Ford and Gina Abercrombie-Winstanley, U.S. embassy, Cairo, spring 1991.

30. Personal communication with members of the Engineers' Association Executive Board, fall 1990.

31. See Sa'd Mujahid al-Raghi and 'Ali 'Abd al-Fattah Hashim, eds., "Al-Bitala bayn al-muhandisiin: Al-taqat al-mu'attala fi al-mujtama' al-misri — al-mushkila wa al-hall" [Unemployment Among Engineers — Idle Resources in Egyptian Society — The Problem and the Solution], Conference proceedings, Engineers' Association, Scientific Committee, 1989.

32. Translated and reprinted in the English section of al-Ahram al-iqtisadi, October 17, 1994.

33. For example, in the spring of 1989, Cairo University's Faculty of Economics sponsored a public conference, "Unemployment in Egypt," and in the fall, the Egyptian Association of Political Economy and Statistics sponsored a conference, "Human Resources and Unemployment." In early 1990, Cairo University's Center for Political Research and Studies held a forum, "University Education Policy: Its Political and Economic Dimensions."

34. Since 1989, articles on unemployment have appeared frequently in al-Ahram al-iqtisadi, al-Ahram, al-Akhbar, al-Wafd, and al-Ahali, to name only the most prominent examples. Al-Ahram al-iqtisadi featured at least seven major articles on unemployment in 1989 alone; see the issues of February 13, June 13, July 24, August 28, November 20, and December 11, 1989.

35. Al-Ahram al-iqtisadi, July 31, 1989.

36. See, for example, the president's Labor Day May Day speech (May 1, 1989).

37. Speech at Alexandria University, July 18, 1992, in FBIS-NES-92–139, July 20, 1992, p. 8.

38. The same logic informed the regime's retreat from other elements of the "social contract" in a period of economic adjustment. As Alan Richards observed, the government has reduced subsidies "gradually and by stealth." Richards, "The Political Economy," 1724. For example, the government reduced the cost of bread subsidies by shrinking the size of the standard loaf from 60 to 130 grams, thus tripling the cost per calorie to the household. World Bank, Egypt, 106.

39. World Bank, Egypt, 47. The same point is made by Assaad and Commander, Egypt, 16.

40. Assaad and Commander, Egypt, app., table 1.

41. World Bank, Egypt, 117.

42. In 1980, 47.9 percent of graduates applied for government jobs; in 1981, 39 percent; in 1982, 30.8 percent; and in 1983, 30.0 percent. The data on the total number of university graduates per class year are from the Supreme Council of Universities Handbook, March 1993; and the CAPMAS Statistical Yearbooks,

1987 and 1990. Information on the number of applicants per class year was provided by the staff of the Office of Graduate Administration, the Ministry of Manpower and Training, spring 1990.

43. See Ministry of Social Affairs, in conjunction with the North-South Consultants' Exchange, "Unemployed Graduates in the Governorate of Beni Suef: Survey of Conditions and Needs" (Cairo: Ministry of Social Affairs, 1991); see also Assaad, "Structural Adjustment and Labour Market Reform," table 2.

44. See, for example, *Egyptian Gazette*, May 12, 1991, which quotes the executive director for the Middle East at the International Monetary Fund.

45. Interview with Minister 'Atif 'Ibed, June 5, 1991.

46. Interview with a senior official in the CAOA, spring 1991.

47. The Supreme Council of Universities includes the president and a dean from each university. It prides itself on its independence, from both the government and the demands of individual universities or faculties. Nevertheless, by law the president of the council is the minister of education, which effectively limits the council's autonomy from the state. It is my understanding that the decisions of the council's executive board are generally binding but that the minister may request certain adjustments to accommodate political considerations.

48. *Al-Ahram*, June 2, 1991.

49. This official had no sooner finished speaking when, as if on cue, a female employee working in his division knocked on the door. After apologizing for the interruption, she proudly announced that her son had just passed the university entrance exam. She offered us chocolates from a box she was carrying and then continued to proceed door by door to share the good news.

50. Interview with CAOA official, spring 1991.

51. Mohaya Zaytoun, "Earnings," CAPMAS Labour Information System Project, 1990, 44–46.

52. Conducted in three stages in 1990 and 1991, the purpose of the Needs Assessment Survey was to identify the qualifications and skills that personnel managers of private firms sought in graduate applicants. By mid-1991, sixty-one firms had participated in the survey, most of which were joint ventures or foreign-owned firms based in Cairo.

53. Bonuses and allowances for entry-level engineers and geologists were not specified in the section of the survey available to me, so I estimated them based on ratios of bonus/allowance to salary for other categories of employees.

54. The fair is sponsored by the university's Alumni and Trustee Affairs Office.

55. See Office of Alumni Affairs, *December 1990 Employment Fair: Job Openings*, American University in Cairo, December 8, 1990.

56. *Caravan*, December 16, 1990, 6.

57. This was the average monthly family income reported by the graduates interviewed. Staff members of a community center located in one *sha'bi* neighborhood confirmed that this income level was typical for families in the area.

58. Prospective employers confirm the tight competition for white-collar jobs. For example, Fu'ad Hashim, president of the Arab Investment Bank, recalled that in 1991 the bank advertised five vacant positions and received more than 800 applications. The bank was forced to set up a committee to review all the applicants, "costing us a lot of time and money." For this reason, he noted, "we normally don't fill jobs by way of an open search" but, rather, by word of mouth. Interview with Fu'ad Hashim, spring 1991.

59. *Al-Wafd*, March 10, 1990.

60. See, for example, "The Search for a Vacant Position: A Difficult Task: Secretary and House-Director Positions . . . A Back Door to Moral Deviance!" *al-Wafd*, November 6, 1990; "Who Will Save Them from Fake Advertisements?" *al-Wafd*, November 1988; "Youth Are Bewildered . . . Between the Ministry of Manpower and Illusory Openings," *al-Wafd*, June 17, 1988; and "Youth Employment Companies," *Sabah al-khayr*, February 28, 1991.

61. *Al-Wafd*, November 6, 1990.

62. See, for example, "The Degree Complex Is Behind the Labor Crisis in Egypt!" *al-Akhbar*, December 17, 1988.

63. Based on interviews with officials at the Cairo branch of the Commercial Employees' Association, winter 1990.

64. See *Uktobar*, May 20, 1990; *al-Nur*, July 22, 1990; *al-Wafd*, April 25, 1989; *al-Wafd*, June 17, 1990; *Sabah al-khayr*, May 10, 1990.

65. *Akhir sa'a*, January 31, 1990.

66. For a discussion of popular Egyptian engagement and marriage protocols, indicating the expenses incurred by the bride and groom and the savings mechanisms used to meet them, see Diane Singerman, *Avenues of Participation: Family, Politics and Networks in Urban Quarters of Cairo* (Princeton, N.J.: Princeton University Press, 1995), ch. 3, "Reproducing the Family," 74–131.

67. Interview with Fu'ad Hashim, Arab Investment Bank, spring 1991.

68. *Al-Watan*, January 31, 1988.

4. Parties Without Participation

1. On the gap between the revolutionary goals and capacities of such regimes, see Joel S. Migdal, *Strong Societies and Weak States: State-Society Relations and State Capabilities in the Third World* (Princeton, N.J.: Princeton University Press, 1988).

2. For a discussion of "limited pluralism," see Juan Linz, "Totalitarian and Authoritarian Regimes," in *Macropolitical Theory*, vol. 3 of *Handbook of Political Science*, eds. Fred I. Greenstein and Nelson W. Polsby (Reading, Mass.: Addison-Wesley, 1975), 264–66.

3. Law 40 prohibited the formation of parties on grounds of religion, class, or geographic affiliation. In addition, it stated that parties in Egypt should not conflict with the *shari'a* as the principal source of legislation; the principles of the July 23 and May 15 revolutions; or the preservation of national unity, social peace, socialist gains, or the democratic socialist system. See Mona Makram Ebeid, "The Role of the Official Opposition," in *Egypt Under Mubarak*, eds. Charles Tripp and Roger Owen (New York: Routledge, 1990), 27.

4. Raymond A. Hinnebusch Jr., *Egyptian Politics Under Sadat: The Post Populist Development of an Authoritarian-Modernizing State* (Boulder, Colo.: Lynne Rienner, 1988), 160.

5. This term is part of the Egyptian lexicon and may be translated as denied legal status, denied legal recognition, or denied legitimacy. See part 4, "Al-Quwa al-mahjuba 'an al-shar'iyya" [The Forces Denied Legal Status], in *Al-Taqrir al-stiratiji al-'arabi* [*The Arab Strategic Report*], ed. al-Sayyid Yasin, for successive years, 1987 through 1991 (Cairo: Al-Ahram Center for Political and Strategic Studies, 1989), 510–42.

6. The center right, the Liberal Party (Hizb al-ahrar), was created from the "rightist" platform in the Arab Socialist Union; the center left, the Socialist Labor Party (Hizb al-'amal al-ishtiraki), was created in 1978 as an alternative to the more genuinely oppositionist NPUP. See Hinnebusch, *Egyptian Politics Under Sadat*, 158–71.

7. In the 1976 elections, the government's "Misr Arab Socialist" Party received 81 percent, or 280 of a total of 344 seats, while the right gained 12 seats, the left 4, and independents 48. In 1979, the renamed National Democratic Party (NDP) won 92 percent of the seats in parliament, plus most of the 30 seats reserved for women candidates. See Hinnebusch, *Egyptian Politics Under Sadat*, 159; Nazih Ayubi, "Government and State in Egypt Today," in *Egypt Under Mubarak*, eds. Charles Tripp and Roger Owen (New York: Routledge, 1990), 8–9.

8. Hinnebusch, *Egyptian Politics Under Sadat*, 183–85.

9. See Sa'd ed-Din Ibrahim's review of the president's remarks at the Cairo book fair in *al-Ahram al-iqtisadi*, February 12, 1990. See also the president's May Day speech of 1989, FBIS-NES-89–084, May 3, 1989.

10. Among the most significant decisions taken during Mubarak's decade were those of the Supreme Constitutional Court declaring the existing electoral laws to be unconstitutional.

11. Raymond A. Hinnebusch Jr., "The Formation of the Contemporary Egyptian State from Nasser and Sadat to Mubarak," in *The Political Economy of Contemporary Egypt*, ed. Ibrahim Oweiss (Washington, D.C.: Center for Contemporary Arab Studies, Georgetown University), 196.

12. The six major parties were the National Democratic Party, the New Wafd Party, the (increasingly Islamist) Labor Party, the National Progressive Unionist Party

(also known as Al-tagammu'), the Liberal (Ahrar) Party, and the newly formed Arab Democratic Nasserist Party.

13. Under the Political Parties Law, the Shura Council's Committee for Political Party Affairs is empowered to legalize new parties. The committee has seven members: the chairman, who is the speaker of the Shura Council; the ministers of justice, interior, and people's assembly affairs; and three additional members appointed by the president. During the 1980s, the committee rejected petitions for the formation of about ten parties. Groups whose petitions are denied can appeal the decision in an administrative appeals court.

14. Michael Hudson, "After the Gulf War: Prospects for Democratization in the Arab World," *Middle East Journal* 45 (summer 1991): 408.

15. "Limited" or "restricted pluralism" (*al-ta'addudiyya al-muhaddada* or *al-muqayyada*) are terms regularly applied to the Egyptian political system in Egyptian scholarly and media commentary, as well as in Western scholarship. See for example, Ashraf Hussein, "Al-Musharaka al-siyasiyya wa'l-intikhabat al-barlamaniyya" [Political Participation and Parliamentary Elections], in *Al-Intikhabat al-barlamaniyya fi Misr: Dirasat intikhabat 1987* [*Parliamentary Elections in Egypt: Study of the 1987 Elections*], ed. Ahmad Abdalla (Cairo: Al-Ahram Center for Political and Strategic Studies, 1990), 38.

16. FBIS-NES-89–084; May 3, 1989. See also the interview with President Mubarak in *al-Ahram*, reprinted in FBIS-NES-92–028, February 11, 1992.

17. FBIS-NES-92–139, July 20, 1992. See also Sa'd ed-Din Ibrahim's editorial on President Mubarak's remarks at the twenty-second Cairo International Book Fair, *al-Ahram al-iqtisadi*, February 12, 1990.

18. This statement applies to recent liberalizing experiments in other Arab states as well. See Rex Brynen, Bahgat Korany, and Paul Noble, eds., *Comparative Experiences*, vol. 2 of *Political Liberalization and Democratization in the Arab World* (Boulder, Colo.: Lynne Rienner, 1998), 217–72; see also John P. Entelis and Lisa J. Arone, "Algeria in Turmoil: Islam, Democracy and the State," *Middle East Policy* 1 (1992): 27.

19. Yasin, *Arab Strategic Report*, 1988, 478.

20. *Al-Ahram al-iqtisadi*, April 23, 1990. For a similar argument, see the column by satirist Mahmud al-Sa'dani in *al-Ahram*, May 9, 1990.

21. Interview with Rif'at Sa'id, Tagammu' party headquarters.

22. See especially the *Arab Strategic Report*, 1988, which, more than other volumes, addresses these issues directly in "The Parties and the Party System," 475–79. Another source is the new Islamist annual yearbook, *The Umma in a Year*. For example, see "Political Forces in Egyptian Society," in *Al-Umma fi 'am: Taqrir hawli 'an al-shu'un al-siyasiyya wa'l-iqtisadiyya al-misriyya* [*The Umma in a Year, 1990–1991: An Annual Report on Egyptian Political and Economic Affairs*], eds. Mahmud Abdalla 'Akif and Muhammad Hazim Ghurab (Mansoura: Wafa' Publishers, 1992), 97–134.

23. Party officials interviewed were Rif'at Sa'id, chairman of the party's Executive Council (Tagammu'); Magdi Hussein (Labor Party); Mahmud Abaza, chairman of the Wafd Party's Youth Committee; and a second Wafd party official who asked not to be identified. The Labor Party was suspended by the Shura Council's Political Parties' Committee in May 2000.

24. Interview with Mahmud Abaza, spring 1991. Reliance on this "middle generation" of activists was stressed by leaders in the other opposition parties as well.

25. Though somewhat active through the mid-1980s, the NPUP's organization, the Association of Progressive Youth (Ittihad al-shabab al-taqaddumi) has atrophied since that time. The Labor Party also has a youth movement and issues statements in its name. According to Magdi Hussein, the movement has a presence on university campuses and sponsors activities for students during the summer recess.

26. Yasin, *Arab Strategic Report*, 1988, 475.

27. This point was made by Rif'at Sa'id, chairman of the executive board of the NPUP, who noted that such problems are found in other parties as well.

28. The Islamist yearbook *The Umma in a Year* for 1990/91 cites the following figures on party membership: 160,000 for al-Wafd, 100,000 for the Labor Party, 80,000 for the NPUP, and 45,000 for al-Ahrar. In an interview, Magdi Hussein, a senior party official of the Labor Party, also estimated the party's membership to be 100,000.

29. Interview with Egyptian political scientist and leftist political activist Ahmad Abdalla, September 21, 1994.

30. The only exception was from May 1980 to October 1981, the period just before Sadat's assassination.

31. Interview with independent leftist Farid Zahran, director of the press service Sharikat al-mahrusa, spring 1991; this phrase was used by others as well.

32. Circulation data provided by Wafd Party officials, spring 1991.

33. Interview with Mahmud Abaza, secretary of youth for the Wafd Party, spring 1991.

34. The figure for the mid-1980s is from Ebeid, "The Role of the Official Opposition," 37. According to Ahmad Abdalla, by the mid-1990s its circulation had fallen to roughly 18,000. Interview with Ahmad Abdalla, September 21, 1994.

35. 'Adil Hussein, who also served as the secretary general of the Labor Party, died of a stroke on March 15, 2001.

36. The lower figure is from Arthur S. Banks, ed., *Political Handbook of the World, 1994–95* (New York: CSA Publishers, 1995); the higher figure is from the *Europa World Yearbook, 1994* (London: Europa Publications, 1995).

37. Interview with Magdi Hussein, at the headquarters of the Labor Party and the *al-Sha'b* newspaper, Sayyida Zeinab, Cairo, spring 1991. *Al-Sha'b* was shut down by the government in the spring of 2000.

38. A Wafd Party official noted that the number of newspapers that the party printed was determined by its advertising revenues: "If we had more revenue, we'd print more." By contrast, he noted, the government newspapers could operate at a loss by tapping into public revenues. Magdi Hussein of the Labor Party noted that the government pressures those advertisers that constitute the party's main source of finance.

39. See Yasin, *Arab Strategic Report*, 1988, 477; and Hussein, "Political Participation and Parliamentary Elections," 49. Hussein notes that "the existing legal framework within which the parties operate limits the reach of party activities to their headquarters and newspapers."

40. Interview with Magdi Hussein, Labor Party headquarters.

41. Yasin, *Arab Strategic Report*, 1988, 477.

42. Based on my own observation in Ezbekiyya, 1990.

43. Interview, spring 1991.

44. Interview, fall 1990.

45. David C. Schwartz, *Political Alienation and Political Behavior* (Chicago: Aldine, 1973), ix, 7.

46. For a discussion of the presumed causal flow from social conditions to political attitudes to political behavior, see Schwartz, *Political Alienation and Political Behavior*, ch. 1.

47. William Kornhauser, *The Politics of Mass Society* (New York: Free Press, 1959). For a discussion of Kornhauser's and other theories of alienation, see John Milton Yinger, "Anomie, Alienation and Political Behavior," in *Handbook of Political Psychology*, ed. Jeanne N. Knutson (San Francisco: Jossey-Bass, 1973), esp. 186–93.

48. Although his approach to the study of alienation differs from my own, Schwartz makes a similar point; see his *Political Alienation and Political Behavior*, 11.

49. For further discussion of the phenomenon of political alienation in the Arab world, see Mark Tessler, "Alienation of Urban Youth," in *Polity and Society in Contemporary North Africa*, eds. I. William Zartman and William Mark Habeeb (Boulder, Colo.: Westview Press, 1993), 71–101.

50. Ahmad Abdalla, *The Student Movement and National Politics in Egypt* (London: Zed Books, 1985), 232.

51. See Sa'd Ibrahim Gom'a, *Al-Shabab wa'l-musharaka al-siyasiyya* [*Youth and Political Participation*] (Cairo: Al-Thaqafa Publishers, 1984), 157, 192–93. Gom'a's survey results are presented in abridged form in Abdalla, *The Student Movement*, 232, 233. Abdalla also cites a survey conducted at Alexandria University in the early 1980s indicating that "91 percent of youth do not participate in political activity." See Fayiz Zayid et al., "Why Do Youth Not Participate in Political Activity?" *Sawt al-shabab*, April 1, 1985.

52. My interviews with graduates affiliated with Islamist and leftist groups are cited in later chapters.

53. Partly because of the different circumstances in which they were conducted, the interviews varied in length and content. Although there were several questions I asked all respondents, each interview took an idiosyncratic course dictated by the specific preoccupations of the informant himself or herself. The loose format of the interviews precludes a numerical summary of results. But to a greater degree than would have been possible with a formal survey, this format allowed me to tune into issues and concerns that the informants identified as important, rather than allow a questionnaire to guide my inquiry in a preset direction.

54. The names of all respondents have been changed to protect their anonymity.

55. Robert Springborg, *Mubarak's Egypt: Fragmentation of the Political Order* (Boulder, Colo.: Westview Press, 1989), 148.

56. During the many hours I was stuck in Cairo traffic jams, I queried scores of taxi drivers regarding their opinions on a variety of political subjects. I do not have information about their class or educational backgrounds. However, I have included their comments when they were particularly vivid and also representative of themes echoed by the graduates in my sample.

57. See Yinger, "Anomie, Alienation, and Political Behavior," 173. Durkheim describes "anomie" as "a state of de-regulation." See Emile Durkheim, *Suicide: A Study in Sociology* (New York: Free Press, 1951), ch. 5.

58. A single candidate for the position of president is nominated by the NDP-controlled parliament and submitted to the electorate for approval in a popular referendum.

59. See, for example, the edited volumes on the elections of 1984, 1987, and 1990 published by the al-Ahram Center for Political and Strategic Studies; see also Ahmad Abdalla, ed., *Al-Intikhabat al-barlamaniyya fi Misr: Dirasat intikhabat 1987* [*Parliamentary Elections in Egypt: A Study of the 1987 Elections*] (Cairo: Center for Arab Research, Sina Publishers, 1990).

60. Hussein, "Political Participation and Parliamentary Elections." Hussein's figures are supported by other sources; for example, see Ali ed-Din Hilal, ed., *Intikhabat Majlis al-Sha'b 1987: Dirasa wa-tahlil* [*The People's Assembly Elections, 1987: Study and Analysis*] (Cairo: Al-Ahram Center for Political and Strategic Studies, 1988), 130.

61. Saad Eddin Ibrahim, "Civil Society and Electoral Politics in Egypt," *Civil Society* 4 (December 1995): 4.

62. The percentage of adult citizens registered to vote was 43.8 in 1974, 48.1 in 1976, and 54.6 in 1983. See Hussein, "Political Participation and Parliamentary Elections," 46. Ahmad Abdalla notes that roughly half of all adults are not registered to vote. See Ahmad Abdalla, "Parliamentary Elections in Egypt: Which Elections? Which Parliament? Which Egypt?" in *Al-Intikhabaat al-barlamaniyya fi Misr: Diraasat intikhabat 1987* [*Parliamentary Elections in Egypt: Study of the 1987 Elections*], ed. Ahmad

Abdalla (Cairo: Al-Ahram Center for Political and Strategic Studies, 1990), 292.

63. Hussein, "Political Participation and Parliamentary Elections," 47, citing table 6 in *Intikhabat Majlis al-Sha'b 1984: Dirasa wa-tahlil* [*The People's Assembly Elections, 1984: Study and Analysis*], ed. Ali ed-Din (Cairo: Al-Ahram Center for Political and Strategic Studies, 1986), 233.

64. For a discussion of the ratio of eligible to registered voters, see Hussein, "Political Participation and Parliamentary Elections," 46.

65. Salwa Sha'rawi Gom'a, "An Explanation of Voting Behavior: A Comparative Study of the District of East Cairo and the Governorate of Suez," in *The People's Assembly Elections: 1987*, 49.

66. Study cited by Mustafa Kamal al-Sayyid, "Intikhabat Majlis al-Sha'b 'am 1987: Dalalat al-intikhabat" [The People's Assembly Elections for 1987: Evidence from the Elections], in *The People's Assembly Elections, 1987*, 130.

67. Interview published in *al-Musawwar*, June 26, 1987. Cited by al-Sayyid, "Intikhabat Majlis al-Sha'b 'am 1987," 141, n. 13.

68. It won 280 of 344 seats in 1976, 389 of 448 seats in 1984, 309 of 448 seats in 1987, 255 of 444 seats in 1990, and 317 of 444 seats in 1995.

69. These percentages are approximate, as the reported number of candidates who were not on the NDP slate but joined the NDP majority after the elections varies somewhat. The question of independents was not an issue before 1987, because until then, all candidates were required to run on a party list. For more on the 1995 elections, see Ibrahim, "Civil Society," 4.

70. This law was rescinded in 1990.

71. The president is allowed by the constitution to appoint up to ten members of parliament. In addition, until 1986, thirty seats were guaranteed to women, which in practice added to the NDP majority. Law 188 of 1986 declared the allocation of seats to women to be unconstitutional. See Charles Tripp and Roger Owen, eds., *Egypt Under Mubarak* (New York: Routledge, 1989), 27–38.

72. Hasan Abu l-'Inan, "The Computer of the Ministry of Interior . . . Innocent of the Accusation of Forgery," *al-Ahram*, April 14, 1987. For a typical allegation of election fraud perpetrated by computer, see *al-Sha'b*, April 12, 1987. Both are cited in Springborg, *Mubarak's Egypt*, 180, n. 107. Springborg also quotes (190) from an editorial by Mustafa Amin in *al-Akhbar*, April 12, 1987.

73. For further discussion of allegations of electoral fraud, see Springborg, *Mubarak's Egypt*, 190.

74. Springborg, *Mubarak's Egypt*, 189.

75. Interview with Rif'at al-Sa'id, fall 1990.

76. Springborg, *Mubarak's Egypt*, 189.

77. Gom'a, "An Explanation of Voting Behavior," 51.

78. In 1990, all the major opposition parties except for the NPUP boycotted the elections on the grounds that existing electoral laws were unconstitutional. In

1995, the electoral law stipulated that all candidates must run as independents. Before the election many Brotherhood candidates were arrested, and others were subject to severe harassment. After 1987, therefore, the Brotherhood has not freely participated as an organized bloc in parliamentary elections.

79. Ayubi, "Government and State in Egypt Today," 14.
80. For a nuanced elaboration of this argument, see Abdalla, "Parliamentary Elections in Egypt," 292–95.
81. *Al-Yasar*, January 1991.
82. Hussein, "Political Participation and Parliamentary Elections," 45.

5. The Parallel Islamic Sector

1. Initially coined by Peter Eisinger in the early 1970s, the concept of political opportunity structures has been further elaborated by Charles Tilly, Doug McAdam, Sidney Tarrow, and other advocates of a "political process" model of social movements. See, for example, Sidney Tarrow, *Power in Movement: Social Movements, Collective Action and Protest*, 2nd ed. (Cambridge: Cambridge University Press, 1998), 71–90.
2. Doug McAdam, "Conceptual Origins, Current Problems, Future Directions," in *Comparative Perspectives on Social Movements: Political Opportunities, Mobilizing Structures, and Cultural Framings*, eds. Doug McAdam, John D. McCarthy, and Mayer N. Zald (Cambridge: Cambridge University Press, 1996), 27.
3. See ibid., 7.
4. See the discussion of "substitute spaces and actors" in authoritarian regimes in Manuel Antonio Garreton, "Political Processes in an Authoritarian Regimes: The Dynamics of Institutionalization and Opposition in Chile, 1973–1980," in *Military Rule in Chile: Dictatorship and Opposition*, eds. Samuel Valenzuela and Arturo Valenzuela (Baltimore: Johns Hopkins University Press, 1985), 168.
5. John L. Esposito, *Islam and Politics* (Syracuse, N.Y.: Syracuse University Press, 1984), 213.
6. Esposito, *Islam and Politics*, 214. See also Raymond A. Hinnebusch Jr., *Egyptian Politics Under Sadat: The Post-Populist Development of an Authoritarian-Modernizing State* (Boulder, Colo.: Lynne Rienner, 1988), 205.
7. Giles Kepel, *Muslim Extremism in Egypt: The Prophet and the Pharaoh* (Berkeley and Los Angeles: University of California Press, 1993), 134–35; and Ahmad Abdalla, *The Student Movement and National Politics in Egypt, 1923–1970* (London: Al-Saqi Books, 1985), 226–27.
8. Heba Handoussa, "Crisis and Challenge: Prospects for the 1990s," in *Employment and Structural Adjustment: Egypt in the 1990's*, eds. Heba Handoussa and Gillian Potter (Cairo: American University in Cairo Press, 1991), 3.

9. Nader Fergany, "A Characterization of the Employment Problem in Egypt," in *Employment and Structural Adjustment: Egypt in the 1990's*, eds. Heba Handoussa and Gillian Potter (Cairo: American University in Cairo Press, 1991), 3. The figure for 1968 is from Sa'd Eddin Ibrahim, *The New Arab Social Order* (Boulder, Colo.: Westview Press, 1982), 63.

10. Alan Richards and John Waterbury, *A Political Economy of the Middle East: State, Class and Economic Development* (Boulder, Colo.: Westview Press, 1990), 390, table 14.5.

11. Robert Springborg, *Mubarak's Egypt: Fragmentation of the Political Order* (Boulder, Colo.: Westview Press, 1988), 47; see also Richard Moench, "Oil, Ideology and State Autonomy in Egypt," *Arab Studies Quarterly* 10 (1988): 186.

12. Samia Sa'd Imam, *Man yamluk Misr? Dirasa tahliliyya li-usul nukhbat al-infitah al-ijtima'iyya, 1974–1980* [*Who Owns Egypt?: An Analytical Study of the Social Origins of the Infitah Elite, 1974–1980*] (Cairo: Dar al-mustaqbal al-'arabi, 1987), 205, 211, 280–309. Cited in Moench, "Oil, Ideology and State Autonomy in Egypt," 187.

13. Hamied N. Ansari, "The Islamic Militants in Egyptian Politics," *International Journal of Middle East Studies* 16 (March 1984): 129. The estimate cited is from *al-Gumhuriyya*, September 8, 1981.

14. FBIS, September 30, 1994, 17; from *al-Musawwar*, September 23, 1994.

15. "From Here Extremism Begins; the Independent Mosques," *Akhir sa'a*, December 2, 1992. The journal reported the number of government mosques as 13,000.

16. Middle East Watch, *Human Rights Conditions in the Middle East in 1993* (New York: Human Rights Watch, 1994), 25. This estimate is regularly cited by Egyptian and Western scholars.

17. For more on this broader phenomenon, see Denis J. Sullivan, *Private Voluntary Organizations in Egypt: Islamic Development, Private Initiative, and State Control* (Gainesville: University of Florida Press, 1994).

18. Ashraf Hussein, "Political Participation and Parliamentary Elections," in *Al-Intikhabat al-barlamaniyya fi Misr: Dirasat intikhabat* [*Parliamentary Elections in Egypt: A Study of the 1987 Elections*], ed. Ahmad Abdalla (Cairo: Al-Ahram Center for Arab Studies, Sina Publishers, 1990), 298. See also Sarah Ben-Nefissa Paris, "Le Mouvement associatif égyptien et l'Islam: Éléments d'une problématique," *Maghreb-Mashrek*, no. 135 (January/February 1992): 19–36; and Sami Zubaida, "Islam, the State and Democracy: Contrasting Conceptions of Society in Egypt," *Middle East Report* 22 (November/December 1992): 2–10.

19. Ashraf Hussein estimated the number of PVOs in Egypt in the early 1990s at 15,000. See Ashraf Hussein, "Private Voluntary Organizations and the Legal Obstacles to Their Formation and Activities," in *Humum Misr wa-azmat al-'uqul al-shabba* [*The Concerns of Egypt and the Crisis of Young Minds*], ed.

Ahmad Abdalla (Cairo: Al-Jil Center for Youth and Sociological Studies, 1994), 297. In *Private Voluntary Organizations in Egypt*, Sullivan cites an estimate of 14,000. By contrast, Egyptian government and party leaders have offered estimates as high as 30,000. See Ben-Nefissa Paris, "Le Mouvement associatif égyptien et l'Islam," 27, 33.

20. Ben-Nefissa Paris, "Le Mouvement associatif égyptien et l'Islam," 27.

21. Sa'd Eddin Ibrahim, "The Changing Face of Islamic Activism: How Much of a Threat?" (paper presented to the workshop U.S.–Egyptian Relations After the Cold War, National Defense University, Washington, D.C., April 28–29, 1994), 5.

22. Sullivan, *Private Voluntary Organizations in Egypt*, 81.

23. Hussein, "Political Participation and Parliamentary Elections," 298–300; and Zubaida, "Islam, The State and Democracy," 7. According to law 32, all PVOs must apply to the governorate branch of the Ministry of Social Affairs for a permit to raise funds. Most non-Islamic PVOs have limited independent resources and rely on government subsidies. The major exception are those that receive foreign aid, for example, from the U.S. Agency for International Development, the Ford Foundation, and Western European governments.

24. Sullivan, *Private Voluntary Organizations in Egypt*, 70–72.

25. Interview with Ashraf Hussein, Cairo, May 1993.

26. As Springborg observed: "The Islamic financial sector, consisting of Islamic banks and investment companies, as well as organizations that collect *zakat* [Islamic personal income tax], has contributed to the growth of an Islamic social sector, which includes facilities for the provision of health, educational and welfare services" (Springborg, *Mubarak's Egypt*, 224–25).

27. Ben-Nefissa Paris, "Le Mouvement associatif égyptien et l'Islam," 33.

28. Sullivan explains the system of fees at the hospital affiliated with the Mosque of Sayida Zeinab and notes that it forms part of a network of eighteen mosque-hospitals in the Cairo area (*Private Voluntary Organizations in Egypt*, 69). He also describes the fee structure at the main branch of the Islamic Medical Society (79–80).

29. Ben-Nefissa Paris, "Le Mouvement associatif égyptien et l'Islam," 34. This point was also stressed in an interview with Ashraf Hussein, Cairo, May 1993.

30. Springborg, *Mubarak's Egypt*, 53. Other estimates of their assets are even higher. For example, Moench noted that the assets of the Islamic investment companies were estimated by the *Middle East Times* at $20 billion and by *al-Ahali* at $60 billion ("Oil, Ideology and State Autonomy in Egypt," 186). For more on the Islamic investment companies, see Alain Roussillon, "Sociétés islamiques de placement de fonds et 'ouverture economique,'" Dossiers du CEDEJ, March 1988, Cairo.

31. Interview with 'Abd al-Mun'im Salim, *Liwa' al-islam* office, Cairo, May 1991.

32. Interview with Ashraf Hussein and 'Adil Sha'ban, Cairo, May 1993. They allege that the photograph was actually the work of an artist, who threatened to sue the bookstore to secure his share of the profits.

33. Interview with Ashraf Hussein and 'Adil Sha'ban, Cairo, May 1993.

34. *Akhir sa'a*, December 2, 1992. The exact term used was "white weapons," referring to knives, sticks, and the like.

35. Robert Bianchi, "Islam and Democracy in Egypt," *Current History*, February 1989, 93–94.

36. Ibid., 93–95, 104.

37. *Akhir sa'a*, December 2, 1992, 12–13.

38. See Sullivan, *Private Voluntary Organizations in Egypt*, 13.

39. *Akhir sa'a*, December 2, 1992, 12–13.

40. Based on an interview in the spring of 1991 with an Islamist activist who was active in the al-Rahma mosque in Talbiyya, which the government accused of being a center for prohibited activities. It was transferred to the Ministry of Religious Endowments, and a group of Islamists, including my informant, raised the issue in court.

41. *Akhir sa'a*, December 2, 1992, 12–13. In sharp contrast to graduates in other fields, who must wait many years for appointment, the graduates of religious studies at al-Azhar University are able to secure government jobs immediately after graduation, indicating the labor shortages in this field.

42. FBIS, September 30, 1994; *al-Musawwar*, September 23, 1994.

43. Ibid.

44. According to the government officials I interviewed, such socialization is minimal or nonexistent except in such centralized elite agencies as the Auditing Office, the Ministry of Finance, and the Ministry of Foreign Affairs.

45. Hinnebusch makes a parallel argument (*Egyptian Politics Under Sadat*, 262–63).

46. Given the absence of survey data on such issues, there is no way to determine the levels of private religious observance and/or sympathy for Islamist goals among Egyptian civil servants in the 1980s and early 1990s. One relevant observation that I and my colleagues noted was the predominance of veiling among female civil servants, to the point that unveiled women constituted a distinct minority in many government offices.

47. Ben-Nefissa Paris, "Le Mouvement associatif égyptien et l'Islam," 26; see also Zubaida, "Islam, The State and Democracy," 6. According to decree 859 of 1985, thirteen of the seventeen associations declared to be in the general interest were Islamic in character.

48. Ben-Nefissa Paris, "Le Mouvement associatif égyptien et l'Islam," 32. Ben-Nefissa Paris cites a series of articles published in the leftist journal *al-Ahali* in July 1991. Such favoritism was also noted by Hussein, "Political Participation

and Parliamentary Elections," 298, and was emphasized by him in an interview, May 1993.

49. *Akhir sa'a*, December 2, 1992.

50. Springborg, *Mubarak's Egypt*, 50–52.

51. Chris Hedges, "In Islam's War, Students Fight on the Front Line," *New York Times*, October 4, 1994; see also the interview with Hussein Ahmad Amin in *Civil Society* 3 (September 1994).

52. According to Liberty for the Muslim World, an Islamist research institute based in London, such teachers were suspected of belonging to the Brotherhood or sympathizing with them. They were either shifted to administrative jobs or transferred from their towns and villages to distant locations. The most noteworthy case, the report mentions, was that of the winner of the republic's First Teacher Award, who was "rewarded for his outstanding record with a transfer from his home in Menoufia to Damanhour." See "Liberty: Escalating Tension Between Government and Ikhwan in Egypt Leads to Algerian Syndrome," *Liberty for the Muslim World*, August 9, 1995.

53. See "Liberty: Escalating Tension Between Government and Ikhwan," and "Lawlessness in the Nile Basin: Who Runs Egypt, Government or Mafia?" *Liberty for the Muslim World*, October 20, 1995. This estimate of the number of political prisoners is cited in both reports.

54. Sidney Tarrow, "States and Opportunities: The Political Structuring of Social Movements," in *Comparative Perspectives on Social Movements: Political Opportunities, Mobilizing Structures and Cultural Framings*, eds. Doug McAdam, John D. McCarthy, and Mayer N. Zald (Cambridge: Cambridge University Press, 1996), 43.

55. I define an Islamist political opposition group as one that aspires to gain control of government, by either violent or peaceful means and either in the present or at some time in the future. Such groups can assume a variety of forms, ranging from underground cells to political parties.

56. The classic study of the Muslim Brotherhood before 1952 is by Richard P. Mitchell, *The Society of the Muslim Brothers* (Oxford: Oxford University Press, 1969). The membership estimates cited here are from p. 328.

57. Mitchell, *The Society of the Muslim Brothers*, 234–41.

58. Ibid., chs. 2 and 3. The secret apparatus (*al-jihaz al-sirri*) was known internally as "the special section" (*al-nizam al-khass*) and was inspired by the idea of jihad (30–32).

59. Raymond Baker, *Sadat and After: Struggles for Egypt's Political Soul* (Cambridge, Mass.: Harvard University Press, 1990), 246.

60. There is little published information on the Brotherhood's organization and membership at the regional level. See the discussion of internal Brotherhood elections in the leftist journal *Roz al-Yusuf*, April 6, 1992 (cited in FBIS-NES-

92–072, April 14, 1992), and February 6, 1995, 20–21 (cited in FBIS-NES-95–028, February 10, 1995).

61. For more information on the militant wing of the Islamic movement, see Mary Anne Weaver, A *Portrait of Egypt: A Journey Through the World of Militant Islam* (New York: Ferrar, Straus & Giroux, 1999); see also Nemat Guenena and Sa'd Eddin Ibrahim, "The Changing Face of Egypt's Islamic Activism" (unpublished paper, September 1997), 35, 50–51.

62. Telephone interview with an editor at the World Islam Studies Enterprise (WISE), Tampa, Florida, September 5, 1995.

63. When asked about their intellectual influences, Brotherhood activists in the early 1990s most frequently cited the works of the organization's founder, Hasan al-Banna, as well as the works of Sayyid Qutb. In addition, they cited the works of such leading contemporary Islamic scholars as Yusuf al-Qaradawi and Sheikh Muhammad al-Ghazzali. It is only since the mid-1990s that the Brotherhood's agenda has been noticeably influenced by the new Islamist intellectuals, who propose a more liberal interpretation of Islam. For more on the new Islamist political discourse, see Gudrun Kramer, "Islamist Notions of Democracy," in *Political Islam: Essays from Middle East Report*, eds. Joel Beinin and Joe Stork (Berkeley and Los Angeles: University of California Press, 1997), 71–82; and Yvonne Yazbeck Haddad, "Islamists and the Challenge of Pluralism" (occasional papers for Center for Contemporary Arab Studies) (Washington, D.C.: Georgetown University, 1995).

64. I have no hard data on the distribution of votes between Ikhwani and Jihadi Islamic groups in student elections; however, in interviews, numerous observers, including many Islamists, emphasized the electoral strength of "jihadist" groups in Upper Egypt's main universities.

65. Ibrahim, "The Changing Face of Islamic Activism."

66. Headed by Supreme Guide Hamid Abu Nasr, an octogenarian in poor health, the Brotherhood's senior leadership included several other old-guard veterans with long-standing family and personal ties to the organization: Mustafa Mashhur, Ma'mun al-Hudeibi, and Sayf al-Islam Banna (son of the Brotherhood's founder). When Supreme Guide Abu Nasr's health deteriorated in the early 1990s, a succession struggle ensued in this inner circle, and after Abu Nasr's death, Mustafa Mashhour assumed the position of supreme guide, with Ma'mun Hudeibi as first deputy. See *Roz al-Yusuf*, April 6, 1992 (cited in FBIS-NES-92–072; April 14, 1992); and *Roz al-Yusuf*, February 6, 1995, 20–21 (cited in FBIS-NES-95–028; February 10, 1995).

67. The activities of the *gama'at* in the 1970s are well documented. See Kepel, *Muslim Extremism in Egypt*; Abdalla, *The Student Movement and National Politics in Egypt*; and Haggai Erlich, *Students and University in 20th Century Egyptian Politics* (London: Frank Cass, 1989). For an insider's account, see

Badr Muhammad Badr, *Al-Jama'at al-islamiyya fi jami'at Misr: Haqa'iq wa-watha'iq* [*The Islamic Student Associations in Egyptian Universities: Facts and Documents*] (Cairo: Published privately, 1989).

68. Kepel, *Muslim Extremism in Egypt*, 134–35; Abdalla, *The Student Movement and National Politics in Egypt*, 226.

69. Kepel, *Muslim Extremism in Egypt*, 139.

70. Ibid., 141.

71. Kepel, *Muslim Extremism in Egypt*, 144; Abdalla, *The Student Movement and National Politics in Egypt*, 226–27.

72. The *gama'at* were independent associations organized by faculty, with membership open to any Muslim student who "committed himself to Islamic behavior." In general, there were no formal membership dues or rosters listing members' names, making it hard to determine their actual numbers. In each faculty the group was headed by an "amir" and a "*shura* council." The amirs of every faculty comprised the university's *shura* council, which set the general course of Islamic activities on campus, reaching decisions by majority vote. This *shura* council was led by an "amir of amirs," chosen by his peers for his leadership abilities, his personal integrity, and his commitment to Islam. See Badr, "The Islamic Association in Egypt's Universities."

73. The Sunna are the sayings and actions of the Prophet and his companions.

74. This incident was reported in *al-Akhbar*, February 2, 1977. It is mentioned by Badr, *The Islamic Student Associations in Egyptian Universities*, 228 and 280, n. 12. The incident was also recalled with obvious satisfaction by many Islamists I interviewed.

75. Student union election results are from *Al-Umma fi 'am: Taqrir hawli 'an al-shu'un al-siyasiyya wa'l-iqtisadiyya al-misriyya* [*The Umma in a Year, 1990–1991: An Annual Report on Egyptian Political and Economic Affairs*], eds. Mahmud Abdalla 'Akif and Muhammad Hazim Ghurab (Mansoura: Wafa' Publishers, 1992), 278.

76. See *The Umma in a Year, 1990–1991*, 281–82; see also Chris Hedges, "Egypt Cracking Down on Islamic Student Groups," *New York Times*, November 28, 1993.

77. For further information on government intervention in student union politics in the early 1990s, see *The Umma in a Year, 1990–1991*, 277–81. See also "Liberty: Escalating Tension Between Government and Ikhwan," Badr Muhammad Badr, "Crisis in the Universities Due to the Student Elections: Judges Stop the Student Elections to Remove the Islamic Candidates," *al-Mujtama'*, November 22, 1994, 42–43; and Cherif Cordahi, "Egypt: Islamicists, Authorities Battle to Control Student Unions," *Interpress Service*, December 2, 1994.

78. Based on in-depth interviews with Badr Muhammad Badr, Hilmi Gazzar, Abu-l-'Ila Madi Abu-l-'Ila, 'Isam al-'Iryan, 'Abd al-Mun'im Abu-l-Futuh, and other middle-generation leaders in the Islamist movement.

6. *"The Call to God"*

1. As Zald notes, "Behavior entails costs; therefore grievances or deprivation do not automatically or easily translate into social movement activity, especially high-risk social movement activity." Mayer N. Zald, "Looking Backward to Look Forward: Reflections on the Past and Future of the Resource Mobilization Research Program," in *Frontiers in Social Movement Theory*, eds. Aldon Morris and Carol McClurg Mueller (New Haven, Conn.: Yale University Press, 1992), 326.

2. Alison Brysk writes, "Changes in roles, values and collective identity often lead directly to mobilization." See "Hearts and Minds: Bringing Symbolic Politics Back In," *Polity* 27 (summer 1995): 580.

3. Doug McAdam, John D. McCarthy, and Mayer N. Zald, "Introduction: Opportunities, Mobilizing Structures, and Framing Processes—Toward a Synthetic, Comparative Perspective on Social Movements," in *Comparative Perspectives on Social Movements: Political Opportunities, Mobilizing Structures, and Cultural Framings*, eds. Doug McAdam, John D. McCarthy, and Mayer N. Zald (Cambridge: Cambridge University Press, 1996), 6.

4. David Snow and Robert D. Benford, "Ideology, Frame Resonance and Participant Mobilization," in *International Social Movement Research. From Structure to Action: Comparing Social Movement Across Cultures*, eds. Bert Klandermans, Hanspeter Kriesi, and Sidney Tarrow, vol. 1 (Greenwich, Conn.: JAI Press, 1988), 198.

5. McAdam, McCarthy, and Zald, eds., "Introduction," 6.

6. See Diane Singerman, *Avenues of Participation: Family, Politics and Networks in Urban Quarters of Cairo* (Princeton, N.J.: Princeton University Press, 1995). See also Andrea B. Rugh, *Family in Contemporary Egypt* (Cairo: American University in Cairo Press, 1985); Guilain Denoux, "State and Society in Egypt," *Comparative Politics*, April 1988, esp. 371–72; and Nadia Khoury-Dagher, "Households and the Food Issue in Cairo: The Answers of Civil Society to a Defaulting State," unpublished manuscript, CIRED, Paris, n.d.

7. Interview with the Egyptian psychologist Dr. Muhammad Sha'lan; spring 1991.

8. The only "hard" evidence available concerns the geographic distribution of Islamic militants. See the map of Greater Cairo in Giles Kepel, *Muslim Extremism in Egypt: The Prophet and the Pharaoh* (Berkeley and Los Angeles: University of California Press, 1985), 222, indicating the location of the defendants' homes and the types of neighborhood. See also Hamied Ansari, "The Islamic Militants in Egyptian Politics," *International Journal of Middle East Studies* 16 (March 1984): 132–33. Ansari observes, "A breakdown of the Tanzim members by provinces and areas may be most revealing. . . . Within Greater Cairo, the major areas of concentration were Mataria, Zeitun, Rod al-Farag and al-Sahel. All constitute the northern belt which 'has been the receptacle

for most of the twentieth-century rural migrants' . . . . By contrast no evidence of significant militant activities was found in the older and more stable communities in the popular sections of the city, such as Misr al-Qadima or Sayyida Zeinab." My own impression, based on repeated visits to eight *sha'bi* neighborhoods in Cairo, is that nonmilitant Islamist outreach is concentrated in this third type of neighborhood as well.

9. Kepel, *Muslim Extremism in Egypt*, 217–18. In "The Islamic Militants in Egyptian Politics," Ansari also emphasizes the receptivity of rural migrants to the Islamist message.

10. As the leftist tradition of community activism has died out, the *buluкat* neighborhoods have become more "open" to Islamic activity. As my informant explained, the arrest of scores of leftist community organizers between 1978 and 1981 broke the continuity of a leftist presence in his neighborhood. "By the time we got out of prison," he recalled, "we found that Islamist groups had taken over." Interview, January 31, 1991.

11. These neighborhoods were chosen on practical grounds, that is, on the basis of where, as a result of my prior relationship with resident families, I had the greatest access to Islamist networks. To protect my informants, I have not mentioned the names of the neighborhoods.

12. See Denis J. Sullivan, *Private Voluntary Organizations in Egypt: Islamic Development, Private Initiative, and State Control* (Gainesville: University of Florida Press, 1994), ch. 3; also interviews with Islamist officials of the Medical Association at its Cairo headquarters, spring 1991. Such officials emphasized the growing importance of secondary employment in private health clinics, and Islamic clinics in particular, as a way for young doctors working in the government health sector to supplement their modest incomes.

13. While a majority of formally trained sheikhs who serve as *du'at* are politically compliant, a minority of them have become known for their independent and sometimes highly critical views of the regime. Such sheikhs are typically affiliated with independent mosques. A well-known example is Imam 'Abd al-Rashid Saqr, who was imprisoned several times in the 1980s for his "political sermons" at the Salah ad-Din mosque near the University Bridge in Cairo. It was widely alleged in Islamic circles that Saqr was banned from giving sermons because he was too *sarih* (frank, candid) and *gari'* (outspoken) for the government's tastes.

14. Dale Eickelman and James Piscatori, *Muslim Politics* (Princeton, N.J.: Princeton University Press, 1996), 72.

15. The following section draws on the results of open-ended interviews I conducted with two dozen Islamic activists in three *sha'bi* neighborhoods, as noted earlier. A large majority of these Islamists identified with the reformist strand of the movement.

16. The verse ends, "and that is the weakest form of faith." This last part was almost always left out by graduates citing the verse.

17. Other Islamists noted that a first contact might entail offering to help a neighbor or peer find a solution to a personal problem, for example, helping him make the contacts needed to secure a visa to travel abroad or to find employment.

18. All names have been changed to protect my informants.

19. Mustafa Mashhur, *Al-Da'wa ila-Allah: Al da'wa al-fardiyya* [*The Call to God: The Individual Da'wa*] (Cairo: Islamic Center for Studies and Research / Dar al-Tawzi' wa'l-Nashr al-Islamiyya, 1981), 8.

20. Interview, spring 1991. The survey had been conducted as part of his master's thesis on the Islamic press, which he had not yet completed.

21. The term *al-sunna* both refers the way or path of the Prophet and serves as the collective plural of Sunni, an individual follower of the Prophet's path.

22. The mosque was reputed to be affiliated with the Salafiyya movement, which promotes adherence to the lifestyle of the *aslaf* (ancestors) — that is, of the Prophet, his family, and his righteous companions.

23. Despite this expression of skepticism, the young woman had decided to wear the *khimar*, had begun to attend religious lessons on a weekly basis, and had started to question her previous ambition to obtain a secular university degree.

24. One purchases a membership (*ishtirak*) for a nominal amount, entitling one to borrow as many books and tapes as one would like. I also heard from one of the young women I interviewed that the Islamic bookstore where she works lends books to graduates who cannot afford them.

25. A young Islamist purchased several such tapes for me outside an independent mosque in one *sha'bi* neighborhood. The tapes, which cost a few pounds each, were of very poor recording quality. I do not know where and by whom they were manufactured.

26. Eickelman and Piscatori, *Muslim Politics*, 122.

27. The most extensive study of Islamic book production in Egypt is by Yves Gonzalez-Quijano, "Les Gens du livre: Champ intellectuel et édition dans l'Égypte républicaine (1952–1993)" (Ph.D. diss., l'Institut d'études politiques de Paris, 1994).

28. Interview with staff member at an Islamic bookstore, Sayyida Zeinab, Cairo, spring 1991.

29. For further discussion of such "Islamic books," see Eickelmann and Piscatori, *Muslim Politics*, 40–41.

30. Magdi al-Hilali, *Wajibat al-shabab al-muslim* [*The Duties of the Muslim Youth*] (Shubra: Dar al-Manar, 1987); Fathi Yakan, *Al-Shabab wa'l-taghyir* [*Youth and Change*, 1987] and *Kayf nad'u ila al-Islam* [*How We Call to Islam*, n.d.], both in Nahw wa'y islami series (Beirut: Mu'assasat al-Risala); Mashhur, *The Call to God*; and Hasan al-Banna, *Ila al-Tullab* [*To Students*] and *Ila al-Shabab, wa-*

ila al-talaba khassatan [*To Youth and Especially to Students*], both in Mukhtar al-da'wa series (Alexandria: Dar al-Da'wa, n.d.).

31. This section discusses the common themes of these pamphlets in narrative form. Individual sources are identified by the number assigned to them in the preceding list.

32. 1, pp. 16–21 and 3, p. 23.

33. 5, pp. 9–10.

34. 4, p. 18.

35. 3, pp. 15–16.

36. 5, pp. 14–16. The idea of the *da'wa* as a *fard 'ayn* is also repeated in other pamphlets. See, for example, 1, p. 46, and 3, p. 16. Elsewhere it is described as a *wajib shar'i* (duty under Islamic law). See 2, p. 17, and 3, p. 32.

37. Other pamphlets likewise emphasize the special obligations of youth. See 1, p. 5, 60–61; also 5, pp. 5–6.

38. 1, pp. 44–46. For similar views, see 2, pp. 12–17, 27–30; 3, pp. 49–51; and 5, p. 6.

39. 2, p. 25.

40. See 3, p. 23, and 1, pp. 16–21.

41. 1, pp. 22–28.

42. See 1, p. 43; also 6, p. 24.

43. The two pamphlets are *How We Call to Islam* by Fathi Yakan and *The Call to God: The Individual Da'wa* by Mustafa Mashhur.

44. 3, pp. 21, 29; see also p. 40 where Yakan invokes the Prophet's teaching: "Preach to the people in accordance with their mental faculties [*khatibu 'n-nasa 'ala qadri 'uqulihim*].

45. 3, p. 40.

46. 3, p. 41. For a similar argument, see 1, p. 41.

47. See 3, p. 40, and 4, pp. 7–8.

48. See 4, pp. 12–27.

49. See 1, p. 46.

50. See 1, pp. 53–54.

51. See 1, pp. 46–47.

52. See 1, pp. 56–57; also 3, p. 25.

53. 1, p. 23.

54. Doug McAdam clearly stated the rationalist assumptions underlying prevailing theories of social movement formation: "Both the resource mobilization and political process perspectives locate social movements squarely within the realm of rational political action. In contrast to institutionalized politics, social movements are simply "politics by others means," often the *only* means open to relatively powerless challenging groups." See Doug McAdam, "Micromobilization Contexts and Recruitment to Activism," in *International Social Movement Research. From Structure to Action: Comparing Social Movement*

Across Cultures, eds. Bert Klandermans, Hanspeter Kriesi, and Sidney Tarrow, vol. 1 (Greenwich, Conn.: JAI Press, 1988), 127–28.

55. Note, for example, the preface to Morris and Mueller, eds., *Frontiers in Social Movement Theory*, which states that "the essays in this volume represent a first step toward the development of a social psychology that is appropriate for and complementary to the structural-political framework of RM" (ix).

56. Brysk, "Hearts and Minds," 581.

57. Eickelman and Piscatori, *Muslim Politics*, 72.

7. Explaining the Success

1. Doug McAdam, "Micromobilization Contexts and Recruitment to Activism," in *International Social Movement Research. From Structure to Action: Comparing Social Movement Across Cultures*, eds. Bert Klandermans, Hanspeter Kriesi, and Sidney Tarrow, vol. 1 (Greenwich, Conn.: JAI Press, 1988), 151.

2. According to Benford and Snow, movement leaders can mobilize individuals into politics by issuing a "call to arms" or rationale for collective action, a process they describe as "motivational framing." See Robert D. Benford and David A. Snow, "Framing Processes and Social Movements: An Overview and Assessment," *Annual Reviews in Sociology* 26 (2000): 611–39.

3. Doug McAdam, *Freedom Summer* (New York: Oxford University Press, 1988), 51.

4. The role of preexisting kinship, neighborhood, or village ties in channeling individuals into opposition movements has been noted elsewhere as well. See, for example, Timothy Wickham-Crowley, *Guerrillas and Revolution in Latin America* (Princeton, N.J.: Princeton University Press, 1992), 138–40.

5. Although I have no way to estimate how often this occurred, and there were considerable pressures militating against it, I learned of several cases in which graduates experimented with Islamic activism and then gave it up. For example, Salma, who now wears the *niqab*, explained that at an earlier stage in her life she tried wearing the veil, "but I wasn't ready and I gave it up." Similarly, Muhammad explained that he went through a phase of intense religious observance, involving regular attendance at dawn prayers and religious lessons, but subsequently abandoned such activities in order to concentrate on his search for a job.

6. The provision of selective incentives is seen as a way to overcome the "free-rider problem" identified by Mancur Olson. See William Gamson, *The Strategy of Social Protest* (Homewood, Ill.: Dorsey Press, 1975), 66–71; Debra Friedman and Doug McAdam; "Collective Identity and Activism: Networks, Choices and the Life of a Social Movement," in *Frontiers in Social Movement Theory*, eds. Aldon Morris and Carol McClurg Mueller (New Haven, Conn.: Yale University Press, 1992), 161; and Doug McAdam, *Political Process and the*

Development of Black Insurgency, 1930–1970 (Chicago: University of Chicago Press, 1982), 45–46. Drawing on such insights, John Waterbury and Alan Richards emphasized that small group size and selective incentives enabled Islamic groups to overcome the free-rider problem. See Alan Richards and John Waterbury, *A Political Economy of the Middle East* (Boulder, Colo.: Westview Press, 1996), 349–50.

7. Formally, of course, it was not necessary to participate in Islamist religious and social activities in order to utilize Islamist services; in practice, however, acquiring allies and patrons in Islamist circles increased one's access to resources in the parallel Islamic sector.

8. See for example, McAdam, *Political Process*, 45.

9. "From Here Extremism Begins: The Independent Mosques," *Akhir sa'a*, December 2, 1992, pp. 12–13.

10. *Akhir sa'a*, December 2, 1992, pp. 12–13.

11. Sami Zubaida, "Islam, the State and Democracy: Contrasting Conceptions of Society in Egypt," *Middle East Report* 22 (November/December 1992): 9.

12. Mustafa Emirbayer and Jeff Goodwin, "Network Analysis, Culture, and the Problem of Agency," *American Journal of Sociology* 99 (May 1994): 1433. Similarly, Alison Brysk argues that "changes in roles, values, and collective identity often lead directly to mobilization." See Alison Brysk, "Hearts and Minds: Bringing Symbolic Politics Back In," *Polity* 27 (summer 1995): 580.

13. While highlighting the strengths of *Freedom Summer*, Emirbayer and Goodwin note: "If there is a weakness to McAdam's analysis of *Freedom Summer*, it lies in his insufficient attention to precisely this element of normative commitment to cherished ideas. . . . McAdam might have provided a more convincing account than he does of the cultural and political idioms of the day—not all of which, after all, were supportive of racial equality—and examined how and why certain of them came to have such a powerful resonance for so many people, especially young, relatively affluent college students, precisely at that specific historical juncture." Emirbayer and Goodwin, "Network Analysis, Culture, and the Problem of Agency," 1433.

14. David A. Snow and Robert D. Benford, "Ideology, Frame Resonance, and Participant Mobilization," in *International Social Movement Research. From Structure to Action: Comparing Social Movement Across Cultures*, eds. Bert Klandermans, Hanspeter Kriesi, and Sidney Tarrow, vol. 1 (Greenwich, Conn.: JAI Press, 1988). The authors attribute frame resonance to four factors: (1) the robustness and completeness of the framing effort, for example, its internal consistency; (2) the relationship of the frame to the broader belief system; (3) the relevance of the frame to the participants' life world; and (4) timing in "cycles of protest" (198–99).

15. Arthur Koestler, "The Initiates," in *The God That Failed*, ed. Richard Crossman (New York: Bantam Books, 1949), 18–19.

16. In Snow and Benford's terms, the *da'wa* succeeded in accomplishing "diagnostic, prognostic, and motivational framing tasks." For further discussion of these tasks, see Snow and Benford, "Ideology, Frame Resonance, and Participant Mobilization," 200–4.
17. Brysk, "Hearts and Minds," 577.
18. Doug McAdam, Sidney Tarrow, and Charles Tilly, "A Comparative Synthesis on Social Movements and Revolution: Towards an Integrated Perspective" (paper presented at the annual meeting of the American Political Science Association, September 1996), 16. The authors credit this insight to Mustafa Emirbayer and Jeff Goodwin. See Emirbayer and Goodwin, "Network Analysis, Culture, and the Problem of Agency."
19. For a discussion of "repertoires of contention," see Charles Tilly, *The Contentious French* (Cambridge, Mass.: Harvard University Press, 1986); and Sidney Tarrow, *Power in Movement: Social Movements, Collective Action and Politics,* 2nd ed. (Cambridge: Cambridge University Press, 1998), 29–42.
20. The repertoires of Islamic militants, which already have been described by others, will not be covered here except to note that they ranged from the distribution of services to the deployment of force against government and civilian targets.
21. Kamal al-Sa'id Habib was one of the leaders of the Jihad organization and was in charge of weapons recruitment. He was sentenced by the Supreme State Security Court to ten years of prison and hard labor plus five additional years. See *al-Ahram,* January 10, 1984; and Nemat Guenena, "The 'Jihad': An 'Islamic Alternative' in Egypt," Cairo Papers in Social Science, no. 9, monograph 2 (summer 1986): 50, 99.
22. In one instance, a group of young Islamist women in one *sha'bi* neighborhood responded with indignation to a neighbor's report that her husband had beaten her and threatened to throw their colicky infant out the window. "He has no right to treat you like that," said one of the Islamists. "Tell him to read this!" and here, she picked up a book on the rights and duties of women in Islam. If he didn't shape up, the Islamist women promised the neighbor, they would contact the local imam and have him issue a stern warning to her husband.
23. Kamal Habib was released from prison several years later. Since that time, he has renounced the use of violence and is working to form a political party calling for application of Islamic law.
24. The play drew on two separate religious stories. The first was a story about three characters — a young man, a monk, and a magician — which is well known both inside and outside Islamist circles. The second, known as "Ashab al-ukhdud," or "People of the Trench," is mentioned briefly in the Qur'an (Q 85: 4–8).
25. Jan Vladislav, ed., *Vaclav Havel: Living in Truth* (London: Faber & Faber, 1986), esp. "The Power of the Powerless," 36–122.

8. From the Periphery to the Center

1. Erbakan assumed the post of prime minister in June 1996, but his tenure as prime minister was cut short when he was forced to step down under military pressure in June 1997. Then in January 1998 the Refah Party itself was banned by the Turkish Constitutional Court. After the ban, a new Islamist party, the Virtue Party, was established by former Refah members.

2. For an earlier discussion of this subject, see Carrie Rosefsky Wickham, "Islamic Mobilization and Political Change: The Islamist Trend in Egypt's Professional Associations" in *Political Islam: Essays from Middle East Report*, eds. Joel Beinin and Joe Stork (Berkeley and Los Angeles: University of California Press, 1997), 120–35.

3. Robert Bianchi, *Unruly Corporatism* (Oxford: Oxford University Press, 1989), 93.

4. That Egypt's professional associations provided an outlet for opposition groups denied legal recognition, particularly for the Islamists, has been noted by numerous Egyptian scholars and association activists. See, for example, the section on professional associations in al-Sayyid Yasin, ed., *Al-Taqrir al-istiratiji al-'arabi* [*The Arab Strategic Report*] for successive years, 1987 through 1991. (Cairo: Al-Ahram Center for Political and Strategic Studies).

5. Mustafa Kamal al-Sayed, "A Civil Society in Egypt?" *Middle East Journal* 47 (spring 1993): 232.

6. Unlike in the United States, in some fields a professional degree is awarded after four years of undergraduate study. An engineering degree requires five years of study, and a medical degree requires six.

7. There are some exceptions to this general rule; for example, membership in the Journalists' Association is open only to graduates who can supply proof that they are employed as journalists. According to the young lawyers I interviewed in May 1993, the Lawyers' Association required graduates to obtain full-time work in the legal profession within five years of graduation in order to retain their membership eligibility.

8. In some associations, the proportion of active membership constitutes an even smaller share of the total. For example, several newspaper reports alleged that only 44,000, or roughly one-third of the Lawyers' Association members, had paid their dues and had the right to vote in the 1993 elections.

9. Mustafa Kamal al-Sayed, "The Islamic Movement in Egypt: Social and Political Implications," in *The Political Economy of Contemporary Egypt*, ed. Ibrahim Oweiss (Washington, D.C.: Center for Contemporary Arab Studies, Georgetown University, 1990), 237.

10. Technically all candidates run as independents, although for campaign purposes, they may appear in a single list, which is printed and distributed to voters before and on election day. In interpreting these figures, note that the associ-

ation president is elected only once every four years and that half the association board is renewed every two years. Years in which there are presidential elections generally have a higher turnout than other years. In the Doctors' Association, presidential elections years included 1984, 1988, and 1992.

11. Interview with 'Abd al-Mun'im Abu-l-Futuh, secretary general of the Medical Doctors' Association, June 9, 1991, Cairo.

12. *Al-Atibba'*, no. 11, August 1992.

13. Osman's close personal and business ties with the Muslim Brotherhood may help explain his readiness to accommodate the Islamic Trend's entry into association politics. The tacit cooperation between Osman and the Islamic Trend soon became strained, however, when pressure rose on Osman and his allies on the executive board amid allegations of financial abuses and the mishandling of association funds. Besides establishing a foothold in the Engineers' Association with Osman's support, the Islamic Trend was ultimately able to capitalize on his decline by juxtaposing its own "clean" credentials against the abuses associated with his tenure. Despite the Islamic Trend's antiestablishment rhetoric, it has in practice been prepared to ally with powerful statist interests when this was expedient and to challenge them when circumstances changed.

14. Based on official association elections results provided to me by association officials. For 1987 results, see also the *Arab Strategic Report*, 1988, 499.

15. Election participation rates and results are based on association records and interviews with Abu-l-'Ila Madi Abu-l-'Ila, assistant secretary general and chairman of the association's election steering committee, December 1990–March 1991.

16. See the section on the Egyptian Teachers' Union in the *Arab Strategic Report*, 1987; and Amani Qandil, "Al-Niqabat al-mihaniyya fi Misr wa-'amaliyyat al-tahawwul al-dimuqrati" [Professional Groups in Egypt and the Process of Democratic Transformation], paper presented at the Conference on Democratic Challenges in the Arab World (Cairo: Center for Political and International Development Studies, September 1992), 6–7.

17. In a partial exception to this rule, the Engineers' Association organized a "national front" in the early 1970s under the leadership of the association president, 'Abd al-Khaliq al-Shinnawi. Headed by an alliance of leftist and liberal forces, the executive board demanded greater association autonomy, voiced support for student demonstrators, and criticized the slow pace of democratic reform. This brief show of political independence was cut short, however, when Sadat reorganized the association and replaced its leadership in 1974. See Bianchi, *Unruly Corporatism*, 115.

18. See, for example, the commentary on the elections in the leftist newspaper *al-Ahali*, September 23, 1992.

19. *Amir* was the term for leader favored by Islamic student groups over more secular terms as *qa'id*, *ra'is*, and *za'im*. In each faculty, the Islamic student

association or *gama'a* was headed by an *amir* and a *shura* council. The *amirs* of every faculty constituted the *shura* council of the university, which elected an *"amir of amirs"* on the basis of his personal integrity, leadership abilities, and commitment to Islam.

20. For an overview of *gama'at* activity on university campuses in the 1970s, see Badr Muhammad Badr, *Al-Jama' at al-islamiyaa fi jami'at Misr: Haqa'iq wa-watha'iq* [*The Islamic Associations in Egyptian Universities: Facts and Documents*] (Cairo: published independently, 1989). Part memoir and part analysis, this study was written by a journalist and former Islamic student activist who writes for several Islamist newspapers in Egypt and the Gulf.

21. Interview with 'Abd al-Mun'im Abu-l-Futuh, secretary general of the Doctors' Association, May 1991.

22. Interview with Hilmi Gazzar, Doctors' Association, Giza Branch office, May 1991.

23. Interview with Abu-l-'Ila Madi Abu-l-'Ila, Engineers' Association headquarters, December 1990.

24. For further information on the Engineers' Association study of unemployed engineers, see al-Raghi Sa'd Mujahid and 'Ali 'Abd al-Fattah Hashim, eds., "Al-Bitala bayn al-muhandisiin: Al-Taqat al-mu'attala fi al-mujtama' al-misri — Al-Mushkila wa al-hall" [Unemployment Among Engineers: Idle Resources in Egyptian Society — The Problem and the Solution] Conference Proceedings (Cairo: Engineers' Association, 1989). The results of the Doctors' Association surveys are covered in the *Arab Strategic Report*, 1988, 496–97, and the *Arab Strategic Report*, 1990, 454, as well as in the Islamic opposition press.

25. *Al-Ahali*, March 21 and April 11, 1990.

26. As several young engineers proudly exclaimed, he was *"al-irhabi al-awwal"* (the first terrorist). In fact, this is a slight embellishment of actual events. According to Madi, a week after Sadat's assassination, the Egyptian press published photos of five "terrorists" allegedly involved in plotting his death under the headline "WANTED." Madi's name and photo were second, after 'Abbud al-Zumur, the leader of the militant Jihad organization. In fact, Madi had not been involved in the assassination plot, but he went into hiding after the report appeared in order to avoid arrest. Charges against him in the case were later dropped.

27. It appears, however, that in certain cases there were limits to what the regime was ready to tolerate within the associations as well. For example, the Engineers' Association planned to hold a conference, Torture in Egypt, at its headquarters in January 1990 and was prevented from doing so by state security forces, who barricaded the entrance to the building.

28. Interview on June 24, 1991, with Ashraf Hilmi, engineer and leftist candidate in the Engineers' Association elections of February 1991.

29. See, for example, coverage of the Lawyers' Association elections in *al-Sha'b*, September 25, 1992. It is worth noting that the fairness and integrity of the Islamist electoral committees were acknowledged even by their rivals.

30. See the *Arab Strategic Report*, 1990, 455.
31. Progovernment candidates have also allegedly used this tactic, both in the lead-up to the Lawyers' Association elections of 1992 and in other association elections as well.
32. In other association elections, the Islamic Trend provided free transportation to voters from their workplace or residence. I do not know if these services were provided in the Lawyers' Association elections, but it is likely that they were.
33. This section on the Lawyers' Association elections draws on several sources. In English, see Nabil 'Abd al-Fattah, "Islamist Success in Bar Association Vote Viewed," *The Middle East*, December 1992; and Scott Matton, "Islam by Profession," *The Middle East*, December 1992. In Arabic, see 'Abd al-Salam Rizq, "The Lawyers' Association: Where To?" *al-Ahali*, September 23, 1992; as well as the acidic exchange between Islamic activist 'Isam al-'Iryan and leftist leader Rif'at al-Sa'id, and the commentary by Lutfi Wakid in the September 23, 1992, issue of *al-Ahali*. See also coverage of the lawyers' elections in *al-Sha'b*, September 1992, and the series of articles by the journalist and leftist activist Amina Shefiq in *al-Ahram*, October 5 and 19, 1992.
34. In the Engineers' Association, the Brotherhood list is officially known as the Islamic Voice (al-Sawt al-islami) rather than the Islamic Trend (al-Tayyar al-islami).
35. The "national list" in the Commercial Employees' Association was described by its opponents as the progovernment list. However, candidates on the list whom I interviewed stressed their independence and emphasized that unlike their more ideologically minded rivals, they advocated pragmatic steps to improve the public welfare.
36. Interview with Abu-l-'Ila Madi Abu-l-'Ila at the Engineers' Association headquarters, December 24, 1990.
37. As one Brotherhood activist organizing the demonstration noted with some pride, "We even condemned Mubarak by name!"
38. The new association law and responses to it are analyzed in *al-Hayat*, February 15, 17, and 22; in the Egyptian magazine *Uktobar*, February 28, 1993; and in the Egyptian opposition press. For further discussion of the law, see *al-Mujtama' al-madani*, the Arabic edition of *Civil Society* 3 (March 1993). The law is also discussed in the official association journals; for example, see the April 1993 issues of *al-Atibba'* [*Doctors*] and the May 1993 issue of *al-Muhandisun* [*Engineers*].
39. *New York Times*, October 21, 1992.
40. Guiseppe Di Palma, "Legitimation from the Top to Civil Society: Politico-Cultural Change in Eastern Europe," in *Liberalization and Democratization*, ed. Nancy Bermeo (Baltimore: Johns Hopkins University Press, 1992), 72.

9. Cycles of Mobilization

1. Doug McAdam, "Micromobilization Contexts and Recruitment to Activism," in *International Social Movement Research. From Structure to Action: Comparing Social Movement Across Cultures*, eds. by Bert Klandermans, Hanspeter Kriesi, and Sidney Tarrow, vol. 1 (Greenwich, Conn.: JAI Press, 1988), 135.
2. See Christian Smith, "Introduction: Correcting a Curious Neglect, or Bringing Religion Back In," in *Disruptive Religion: The Force of Faith in Social Movement Activism*, ed. Christian Smith (New York: Routledge, 1996), 1–25.
3. See the discussion of "cycles of protest" in Sidney Tarrow, *Power in Movement: Social Movements, Collective Action and Politics*, 2nd ed. (Cambridge: Cambridge University Press, 1998), 24–25, 141–60.
4. I thank Ahmad Abdalla for this insight.
5. Mary Anne Weaver, "Letter from Cairo: Revolution by Stealth," *New Yorker*, June 8, 1998.
6. Jan de Weydenthal, "The Character of East European Dissent During the Late 1970s," in *Dissent in Eastern Europe*, ed. Jane Leftwich (New York: Praeger, 1983), 146.

Postscript

1. For a discussion of the Egyptian government's "Algeria complex," see Mona Makram Ebeid, "Democratization in Egypt: The 'Algeria Complex,'" *Middle East Policy* 3 (1994): 119–26.
2. Middle East News Agency (MENA) report, November 23, 1995; see also *al-Ahram*, October 11, 1995, and statements by the Egyptian Interior Ministry reported by Agence France Presse, January 23, 1995, and *al-Watan al-'arabi*, December 13, 1996.
3. According to Brotherhood estimates, in August 2000, about 1,300 people had already been arrested in that year alone. See Susan Sachs, "War on Fundamentalism Silences Dissent in Egypt," *International Herald Tribune*, August 5, 2000.
4. Mona el-Tahawy, "Egypt Cracks Down on Islamist Activists," *The Guardian*, October 23, 1999.
5. *Akhir sa'a*, November 22, 2000; see also MENA news report of November, 19, 2000, excerpted by BBC Monitoring Middle East — Political, supplied by BBC Worldwide Monitoring.
6. *The Guardian*, October 23, 1999.
7. United Press International, "Egypt's Islamists Blast Government for Election Ban," September 19, 2000; Amnesty International, Egypt: Run-up to Shura Council Election Marred by Wave of Arrests," May 15, 2001.
8. Simon Apiku, "Islamists Barred from Student Elections," *Middle East Times*, November 8, 1998.

9. E. S. McKee, "Fading Fundamentalists," *Jerusalem Report*, July 17, 2000. See also Apiku, "Islamists Barred from Student Elections." Asyut University was cited in this regard.

10. See Steve Negus, "Down but Not Out: The Muslim Brotherhood Keep a Low Profile, but Their Main Activity — Charity Work — Still Goes On," *Cairo Times*, April 3, 1997. Under article 4 of a 1992 law, the use of foreign funds is permitted only if approved by the Ministry of Social Affairs.

11. Sachs, "War on Fundamentalism Silences Dissent in Egypt."

12. See Muhammad Salah, "The Muslim Brotherhood Confronts Its Worst Internal Conflict," *al-Wasat*, November 18, 1996.

13. See Andrew Hammond, "Brotherhood Crisis Takes on New Proportions," *Middle East Times*, December 7, 1996. See also *al-Wasat*, November 18, 1996.

14. Andrew Hammond, "New Center Party Takes State by Surprise," *Middle East Times*, January 21–27, 1996; David Gardner, "Battles Won, but Not the War," *Financial Times*, May 20, 1996.

15. Early Arabic-language coverage of the Wasat Party initiative included reports in *al-Hayat*, January 18, 1996; *al-Wasat*, January 22, 1996; and *al-Mujtama'*, January 23, 1996. For subsequent analysis in English, see Andrew Hammond, "Reconstructing Islamism," *Middle East Times*, September 29–October 5, 1996; Nabil 'Abd al-Fattah, "Politics and the Generations' Battle," *al-Ahram Weekly*, October 17–23, 1996; and Amira Howeidy, "Brotherhood Torn by Unprecedented Schism," *al-Ahram Weekly*, November 12–26, 1996.

16. *Qadaya dawliyya*, August 26, 1996.

17. Interview with Abu-l-'Ila Madi Abu-l-'Ila, Cairo, November 6, 2000.

18. Commenting on their reaction, Salah wrote, "The old guard of the Brotherhood sought to crush the party and block it from obtaining legal status to an even greater degree than the government," *al-Wasat*, November 18, 1996, 24.

19. For the latest elaboration of the Wasat Party platform, see Salah 'Abd al-Karim, *Awraq hizb al-Wasat al-misri* [*The Papers of the Egyptian Wasat Party*] (1998).

20. The first application was submitted on January 10, 1996, and the Political Parties' Committee ruled against them on May 18, 1996. Acting as lawyer for the Wasat group, Muhammad Salim al-'Awwa submitted an appeal to the Political Parties' Tribunal, and on May 9, 1998, the tribunal ruled against them. Two days later, on May 11, 1998, Madi submitted papers for al-Wasat al-Misri (the Egyptian Wasat Party), with a new platform and an expanded list of members. On September 21, 1998, the committee ruled against them, and on June 5, 1999, the verdict was upheld by the Political Parties Tribunal.

21. Amira Howeidy, "Newspaper for the Mainstream," *al-Ahram Weekly*, August 14, 1997.

22. "The Little NGO That Could," *Cairo Times*, April 13–19, 2000.

23. Interview with 'Isam Sultan, Cairo, November 14, 2001.

24. See *al-Majallah*, March 17, 2001. The article notes that the most likely successor, however, is Ma'mun Hudeibi, who enjoys "total control of MB affairs
and is considered the effective initiator of all its activities."

25. When I asked 'Isam al-'Iryan to clarify his formal responsibilities in the Brotherhood, he turned to a colleague and said jokingly, "I could get another five years
if I answered that question!" Interview with 'Isam al-'Iryan, November, 2000.

26. See articles in *al-Ahali*, October 16, 1996, and *al-Watan al-'arabi*, December
13, 1996.

27. *Al-Majallah*, March 17, 2001.

28. *Cairo Times*, February 20 and 27, 2001; Roula Khalaf, "Egypt Survey," *Financial Times*, May 9, 2001; *Middle East Economic Digest*, March 9, 2001.

29. One recent court case subjected the Mubarak regime to an outpouring of
international censure. On May 21, 2001, an Egyptian state security court sentenced Saad Eddin Ibrahim — a prominent Egyptian American sociologist and
director of the Ibn Khaldun Center for Development Studies — to seven years
of prison with hard labor on dubious charges ranging from accepting money
from foreign sources without the government's permission to defaming the
country's reputation. It is telling that the regime moved to punish Ibrahim after
he brought to international attention such embarrassing domestic conditions
as discrimination against Coptic Christians and electoral fraud. See Mary Anne
Weaver, "Egypt on Trial," *New York Times Magazine*, June 17, 2001; see also
Amnesty International; "Egypt: Human Rights Defenders Saad Eddin Ibrahim
and His Colleagues Must Be Released," June 20, 2001.

30. "Special Report: Mubarak Faces Test of Legitimacy," *Middle East Economic
Digest*, October 13, 2000.

31. Indeed, the elections were spaced out over three days to comply with a court
ruling mandating judicial supervision, since Egypt did not have enough judges
to cover all the country's polling stations at once.

32. Cited in Amil Khan, "Government Blames Opposition for Egypt's Poor Elections Results," *Middle East Times*, December 22, 2000, 1.

33. Amil Khan, "Elections Marred by Government Meddling," *Middle East Times*,
November 5–11, 2000; "Mubarak's Party Maintains Comfortable Majority in
Parliament," Deutsche Presse–Agentur, November 15, 2000.

34. Khalaf, "Egypt Survey." In what was interpreted as a major defeat for the NDP,
its own candidates won only 175 of 444 seats; 65 percent of the NDP deputies
in the outgoing parliament were defeated. The remainder of the NDP bloc in
the 2000 parliament is composed of 213 independents who joined the NDP
after the elections. See also Gamal Esam el-Din, "The New Equation," *al-
Ahram Weekly*, November 16–22, 2000.

35. Human Rights Watch, *Human Rights Watch World Report 2001: Events of 2000*
(New York: Human Rights Watch, 2001); see also Paul Schemm, "Survival
Mode," *Cairo Times*, August 10–16, 2000.

36. See *al-Musawwar*, November 3, 2000; *al-Hayat*, September 14, 2000; McKee, "Fading Fundamentalists."
37. Khalaf, "Egypt Survey"; *Middle East Economic Digest*, March 9, 2001; *al-Sharq al-awsat*, March 1 and 30, 2001.
38. *Al-Hayat*, December 2, 2000.

Bibliography

English- and French-Language Sources

'Abd al-Fattah, Nabil. "Islamist Success in Bar Association Vote Viewed." *The Middle East*, December 1992.

———. "Politics and the Generations' Battle." *Al-Ahram Weekly*, October 17–23, 1996.

Abdalla, Ahmad. *Parliamentary Elections in Egypt: What Elections . . . What Parliament . . . and Which Egypt?* Amsterdam: Amsterdam Middle East Papers, vol. 1, no. 3, 1995.

———. "Popular Participation in the Cairo District of Ain el-Sera: 1958–1984." In NGO Participation in African Development. Brussels: Union of International Associations, 1986.

———. *The Student Movement and National Politics in Egypt, 1923–1970.* London: Al-Saqi Books, 1985.

'Abdel-Fadil, Mahmoud. "Educational Expansion and Income Distribution in Egypt, 1952–1977." In *The Political Economy of Income Distribution in Egypt*, edited by Gouda 'Abdel-Khalek and Robert Tignor. New York: Holmes & Meier, 1982.

———. *The Political Economy of Nasserism: A Study in Employment and Income Distribution Policies in Urban Egypt, 1952–1972.* Cambridge: Cambridge University Press, 1980.

'Abdel-Khalek, Gouda, and Robert Tignor, eds. *The Political Economy of Income Distribution in Egypt.* New York: Holmes & Meier, 1982.

'Abdel-Malek, Anouar. *Egypt: Military Society.* New York: Vintage Books, 1968.

Abdo, Geneive. *No God but God: Egypt and the Triumph of Islam.* Oxford: Oxford University Press, 2000.

Abed-Kotob, Sana. "The Accommodationists Speak: Goals and Strategies of the Muslim Brotherhood of Egypt." *International Journal of Middle East Studies* 27 (1995): 321–40.

Aggag, Karim. "A Civil Society in the Arab World." *Civil Society*, June 1992.

Ahmad, Akbar, and Hastings Donnan. *Islam, Globalization and Postmodernity*. London: Routledge, 1994.

American University in Cairo. "December 1990 Employment Fair: Job Openings." Cairo: Office of Alumni Affairs, American University in Cairo, December 8, 1990.

Amin, Galal. "Migration, Inflation and Social Mobility." In *Egypt Under Mubarak*, eds. Charles Tripp and Roger Owen. London: Routledge, 1989.

———. "Migration, Inflation and Social Mobility: A Sociological Interpretation of Egypt's Current Economic and Political Crisis." Paper presented at the Conference on Politics and the Economy in Egypt Under Mubarak, School of Oriental and African Studies, London, May 18, 1987.

Amnesty International. "Egypt: Grave Human Rights Abuses amid Political Violence." Amnesty International Index MDE, December 3, 1993.

———. "Egypt: Human Rights Defenders Saad Eddin Ibrahim and His Colleagues Must Be Released." Amnesty International, June 20, 2001.

———. "Egypt: Run-up to Shura Council Election Marred by Wave of Arrests." Amnesty International, May 15, 2001.

Anderson, Lisa. "The State in the Middle East and North Africa." *Comparative Politics* 20 (October 1987): 1–18.

Ansari, Hamied N. "The Islamic Militants in Egyptian Politics." *International Journal of Middle East Studies* 16 (March 1984).

Apiku, Simon. "Islamists Barred from Student Elections." *Middle East Times*, November 8, 1998.

———. "Moderate Islamist Party Rebuffed Again." *Middle East Times*, June 10–16, 1999.

Asad, Talal, and Roger Owen, eds. *The Middle East*. New York: Monthly Review Press, 1983.

Assaad, Ragui. "The Employment Crisis in Egypt." Unpublished manuscript, September 1993.

———. "Labour Underutilization and Segmented Labour Markets: The Case of Egypt." In *Conference Proceedings, Unemployment in Egypt*, First Conference of the Economics Department, Cairo University, 1989.

———. "Structural Adjustment and Labor Market Reform." Unpublished manuscript, May 1993.

Assaad, Ragui, and Simon Commander. *Egypt: The Labour Market Through Boom and Recession*. Washington, D.C.: World Bank, May 1990.

Ayubi, Nazih. "Bureaucracy and Development in Egypt Today." Unpublished manuscript. University of Exeter, 1988.

————. *Bureaucracy and Politics in Contemporary Egypt*. London: Ithaca Press, 1980.

————. "Bureaucratic Inflation and Administrative Inefficiency: The Deadlock in Egyptian Administration." *Middle East Studies* 18 (July 1982).

————. "Government and the State in Egypt Today. In *Egypt Under Mubarak*, eds. Charles Tripp and Roger Owen. London: Routledge, 1989.

————. "The Political Revival of Islam: The Case of Egypt." *International Journal of Middle East Studies* 12 (December 1980).

————. "The Politics of Militant Islamic Movements in the Middle East." *Journal of International Affairs* 36 (fall/winter 1982–83).

Baker, Raymond. *Sadat and After: Struggles for Egypt's Political Soul*. Cambridge, Mass.: Harvard University Press, 1990.

Banks, Arthur S., ed. *Political Handbook of the World, 1994–95*. New York: CSA Publishers, 1995.

Beblawi, Hazem. "The Rentier State in the Arab World." In *The Arab World*, edited by Giacomo Luciani. Berkeley and Los Angeles: University of California Press, 1990.

Beinin, Joel. "Formation of the Egyptian Working Class." *Middle East Report* 94 (1981).

————. "Labor, Capital and the State in Nasserist Egypt: 1952–1961." *International Journal of Middle East Studies* 21 (February 1989).

Beinin, Joel, and Joe Stork, eds. *Political Islam: Essays from Middle East Report*. Berkeley and Los Angeles: University of California Press, 1997.

Benford, Robert D. "An Insider's Critique of the Social Movement Framing Perspective." *Sociological Inquiry* 54 (1997): 409–30.

Benford, Robert D., and David A. Snow. "Framing Processes and Social Movements: An Overview and Assessment." *Annual Review of Sociology* 26 (2000): 611–39.

Ben-Nefissa Paris, Sarah. "Le Mouvement associatif égyptien et l'Islam: Éléments d'une problematique." *Maghreb-Mashrek*, January/February 1992, 19–36.

Bermeo, Nancy, ed. *Liberalization and Democratization*. Baltimore: Johns Hopkins University Press, 1992.

Bianchi, Robert. "Islam and Democracy in Egypt." *Current History* 88 (February 1989): 93–97.

————. *Unruly Corporatism: Association Life in Twentieth Century Egypt*. Oxford: Oxford University Press, 1989.

British Embassy. "Employment in Egypt." British Embassy Report, May 1989.

————. "The Salary Structure and Employment Policies of the Egyptian Government." British Embassy Report, November 1984.

Brynen, Rex, Bahgat Korany, and Paul Noble, eds. *Political Liberalization and Democratization in the Arab World*. Vol. 1. Boulder, Colo.: Lynne Rienner, 1995.

————, eds. *Political Liberalization and Democratization in the Arab World*. Vol. 2, *Comparative Experiences*. Boulder, Colo.: Lynne Rienner, 1998.

Brysk, Alison. "Hearts and Minds: Bringing Symbolic Politics Back In." *Polity* 27 (summer 1995): 559–86.

Burgat, François, and William Dowell. *The Islamic Movement in North Africa*. Middle East Monograph Series. Austin: Center for Middle Eastern Studies, University of Texas, 1993.

Campagna, Joel. 1996. "From Accommodation to Confrontation: The Muslim Brotherhood in the Mubarak Years." *Journal of International Affairs* 50 (summer 1996).

Cassandra. "The Impending Crisis in Egypt." *Middle East Journal* 49 (winter 1995).

Center for Human Rights Legal Aid. *Egyptian Politics: The Fiction of a Multiparty System*. Cairo: Center for Human Rights Legal Aid, October 1996.

Churchill, Ward, and Jim Vander Wall. *The* COINTELPRO Papers: Documents from the FBI's Secret Wars Against Domestic Dissent. Boston: South End Press, 1990.

Cohen, Jean L. 1985. "Strategy or Identity: New Theoretical Paradigms and Contemporary Social Movements." *Social Research* 52 (winter 1985): 664–716.

Coleman, James S., ed. *Education and Political Development*. Princeton, N.J.: Princeton University Press, 1965.

Cooper, Mark. "Egyptian State Capitalism in Crisis: Economic Policies and Political Interests." In *The Middle East*, edited by Talal Asad and Roger Owen. New York: Monthly Review Press, 1983.

Cordahi, Cherif. "Egypt: Islamicists, Authorities Battle to Control Student Unions." Interpress Service, December 2, 1994.

Coulam, Robert, and Richard A. Smith, eds. *Advances in Information Processing in Organizations*. Vol. 2. Greenwich, Conn.: JAI Press, 1985.

Crossman, Richard, ed. *The God That Failed*. New York: Bantam Books, 1949.

Curry, Jane Leftwich, ed. *Dissent in Eastern Europe*. New York: Praeger, 1983.

Darnovsky, Marcy, Barbara Epstein, and Richard Flacks, eds. *Cultural Politics and Social Movements*. Philadelphia: Temple University Press, 1995.

Denoux, Guilain. "State and Society in Egypt." *Comparative Politics*, April 1988.

el-Din, Gamal Esam. "The New Equation." *Al-Ahram Weekly*. November 16–22, 2000.

———. "Open Letter to Yusuf Wali." *Middle East Times*, August 14–20, 1990.

Di Palma, Guiseppe. "Legitimation from the Top to Civil Society: Politico-Cultural Change in Eastern Europe." In *Liberalization and Democratization*, edited by Nancy Bermeo. Baltimore: Johns Hopkins University Press, 1992.

Durkheim, Emile. *Suicide: A Study in Sociology*. New York: Free Press, 1951.

Ebeid, Mona Makram. "Democratization in Egypt: The 'Algeria' Complex." *Middle East Policy* 3 (summer 1994): 119–26.

———. "Egypt: 2000 Parliamentary Elections." *Middle East Policy* 8 (June 2001).

———. "The Role of the Official Opposition." In *Egypt Under Mubarak*, edited by Charles Tripp and Roger Owen. London: Routledge, 1989.

Eckstein, Susan, ed. *Power and Popular Protest*. Berkeley and Los Angeles: University of California Press, 1989.

"Egypt: People's Assembly Elections Result in Victory for NDP." *Middle East Economics Digest*, December 21, 1990.

Egyptian Organization for Human Rights. "Armed Violence in Egypt: Facts and Conclusions: An EOHR Report." *Civil Society*, no. 10, October 1992.

Eickelman, Dale F., and James Piscatori. *Muslim Politics*. Princeton, N.J.: Princeton University Press, 1996.

Emirbayer, Mustafa, and Jeff Goodwin. "Network Analysis, Culture, and the Problem of Agency." *American Journal of Sociology* 99 (1994).

Entelis, John P., ed. *Islam, Democracy, and the State in North Africa*. Bloomington: Indiana University Press, 1997.

Entelis, John P., and Lisa J. Arone. "Algeria in Turmoil: Islam, Democracy and the State." *Middle East Policy* 1 (1992): 23–35.

Erlich, Haggai. *Students and University in 20th Century Egyptian Politics*. London: Frank Cass, 1989.

Escobar, Arturo, and Sonia E. Alvarez. *The Making of Social Movements in Latin America: Identity, Strategy and Democracy*. Boulder, Colo.: Westview Press, 1992.

Esposito, John. *Islam and Politics*. Syracuse, N.Y.: Syracuse University Press, 1984.

———, ed. *Political Islam: Revolution, Radicalism or Reform?* Boulder, Colo.: Lynne Rienner, 1997.

Europa Publications. *Europa World Yearbook, 1994*. London: Europa Publications, 1995.

Fahmy, Ninette S. "The Performance of the Muslim Brotherhood in the Egyptian Syndicates: An Alternative Formula for Reform?" *Middle East Journal* 52 (autumn 1998): 551–62.

Faksh, Mahmoud. "The Consequences of the Introduction and Spread of Modern Education: Education and National Integration in Egypt." *Middle Eastern Studies* 16 (May 1980).

Fergany, Nader. "A Characterization of the Employment Problem in Egypt." In *Employment and Structural Adjustment: Egypt in the 1990's*, edited by Heba Handoussa and Gillian Porter. Cairo: American University in Cairo Press, 1991.

———. "Design, Implementation and Appraisal of the October 1988 Round of the LFSS." CAPMAS Labor Information System Project, 1990.

———. "Employment and Unemployment in the Domestic Economy." Preliminary report, CAPMAS Labor Information System Project, December 1990.

———. "Recent Trends in Open Unemployment: Egypt, 1989–1992." *Research Notes*. Cairo: Al-Mishkat Center for Research and Training, 1993.

Friedman, Debra, and Douglas McAdam. "Collective Identity and Activism: Networks, Choices and the Life of a Social Movement." In *Frontiers in Social Movement Theory*, edited by Aldon D. Morris and Carol McClurg Mueller. New Haven, Conn.: Yale University Press, 1992.

Gamson, William A. *The Strategy of Social Protest*. Homewood, Ill.: Dorsey Press, 1975.

Gardner, David. "Battles Won, but Not the War." *Financial Times*, May 20, 1996.

Garreton, Manuel Antonio. "Political Processes in an Authoritarian Regime: The Dynamics of Institutionalization and Opposition in Chile, 1973–1980." In *Military Rule in Chile: Dictatorship and Opposition*, edited by Samuel Valenzuela and Arturo Valenzuela. Baltimore: Johns Hopkins University Press, 1985.

Gaventa, John. *Power and Powerlessness: Quiescence and Rebellion in an Appalachian Valley*. Champaign-Urbana: University of Illinois Press, 1980.

Gazzar, Brenda. "The Ballot and the Bullet." *Cairo Times*, November 2–8, 2000.

Geertz, Clifford. *The Interpretation of Cultures*. New York: Basic Books, 1973.

———. *Islam Observed: Religious Development in Morocco and Indonesia*. Chicago: University of Chicago Press, 1968.

"A Gentle Middle Eastern Islam?" *The Economist*, January 29, 2000.

George, Alexander, and Timothy J. McKeown. "Case Studies and Theories of Organizational Decision-Making." In *Advances in Information Processing in Organizations*, edited by Robert Coulam and Richard A. Smith. Vol. 2. Greenwich, Conn.: JAI Press, 1985.

Gerges, Fawaz A. "The End of the Islamist Insurgency in Egypt? Costs and Prospects." *Middle East Journal* 4 (fall 2000) 593–94.

Gerth, H. H., and C. Wright Mills, eds. *Max Weber: Essays in Sociology*. New York: Oxford University Press, 1980.

Gilsenan, Michael. *Recognizing Islam: Religion and Society in the Modern Arab World*. New York: Pantheon Books, 1982.

Gocek, Fatima, and Shiva Balaghi, eds. *Reconstructing Gender in the Middle East: Tradition, Identity and Power*. New York: Columbia University Press, 1994.

Goffman, Erving. *Frame Analysis*. New York: Harper-Colphon, 1974.

Gonzalez-Quijano, Yves. "Les Gens du livre: Champ intellectuel et édition dans l'Égypt républicaine (1952–1993)." Ph.D. diss., l'Institut d'études politiques de Paris, 1994.

Greenstein, Fred I., and Nelson W. Polsby, eds. *Handbook of Political Science*. Vol. 3, *Macropolitical Theory*. Reading, Mass.: Addison-Wesley, 1975.

Guazzone, Laura, ed. *The Islamist Dilemma: The Political Role of Islamist Movements in the Contemporary Arab World*. Reading, UK: Ithaca Press, 1995.

Guenena, Nemat. "The 'Jihad': An 'Islamic Alternative' in Egypt." Cairo Papers in Social Science, no. 9, monograph 2. Cairo: American University in Cairo Press, 1986.

Guenena, Nemat, and Saad Eddin Ibrahim. "The Changing Face of Egypt's Islamic Activism." Unpublished paper, September 1997.

Gurr, Ted. *Why Men Rebel*. Princeton, N.J.: Princeton University Press, 1970.

Haddad, Yvonne Yazbeck. "Islamists and the Challenge of Pluralism." Occasional papers for Center for Contemporary Arab Studies. Washington, D.C.: Georgetown University, 1995.

Halpern, Manfred. *The Politics of Social Change in the Middle East and North Africa.* Princeton, N.J.: Princeton University Press, 1963.

Hammond, Andrew. "Brotherhood Crisis Takes on New Proportions." *Middle East Times,* December 7, 1996.

———. "New Center Party Takes State by Surprise." *Middle East Times,* January 21–27, 1996.

———. "Reconstructing Islamism." *Middle East Times,* September 29–October 5, 1996.

Handoussa, Heba. *The Burden of Public Service Employment and Remuneration: A Case Study of Egypt.* International Labor Organization (ILO) monograph. Geneva: International Labor Organization, 1988.

———. "Crisis and Challenge: Prospects for the 1990s." In *Employment and Structural Adjustment: Egypt in the 1990s,* edited by Heba Handoussa and Gillian Potter. Cairo: American University in Cairo Press, 1991.

Handoussa, Heba, and Gillian Potter, eds. *Employment and Structural Adjustment: Egypt in the 1990s.* Cairo: American University in Cairo Press, 1991.

Hanninen, S., and L. Paldan, eds. *Rethinking Marx.* Berlin: Argument-Sonderband AS 109, 1984.

Hansen, Bent. *Egypt and Turkey: The Political Economy of Poverty, Equity and Growth.* World Bank Comparative Studies. Oxford: Oxford University Press, 1991.

Hansen, Bent, and Sami Radwan. *Employment Opportunities and Equity in a Changing Economy: Egypt in the 1980s.* Geneva: International Labor Organization, 1932.

Hedges, Chris. "Egypt Cracking down on Islamic Student Groups." *New York Times,* November 28, 1993.

———. "In Islam's War, Students Fight on the Front Line." *New York Times,* October 4, 1994.

Hessini, Leila. "Wearing the Hijab in Contemporary Morocco: Choice and Identity." In *Reconstructing Gender in the Middle East: Tradition, Identity and Power,* edited by Fatima Gocek and Shiva Balaghi. New York: Columbia University Press, 1994.

Hinnebusch, Raymond A. Jr. *Egyptian Politics Under Sadat: The Post-Populist Development of an Authoritarian-Modernizing State.* Boulder, Colo.: Lynne Rienner, 1988.

———. "The Formation of the Contemporary Egyptian State from Nasser and Sadat to Mubarak." In *The Political Economy of Contemporary Egypt,* edited by Ibrahim Oweiss. Washington, D.C.: Center for Contemporary Arab Studies, Georgetown University, 1990.

Howeidy, Amira. "Brotherhood Torn by Unprecedented Schism." *Al-Ahram Weekly,* November 12–26, 1996.

———. "Newspaper for the Mainstream." *Al-Ahram Weekly,* August 14, 1997.

———. "'Wasset' by Any Other Name." *Al-Ahram Weekly*, May 14, 1998.

Hudson, Michael. "After the Gulf War: Prospects for Democratization in the Arab World." *Middle East Journal*, 45 (summer 1991).

Human Rights Watch. *Human Rights Watch World Report 1995: Events of 1994.* New York: Human Rights Watch, 1995.

———. *Human Rights Watch World Report 2001: Events of 2000.* New York: Human Rights Watch, 2001.

Hussein, Mahmoud. *La Lutte de classes en Égypte, 1945–1970.* Paris: Maspero, 1971.

Huwaidi, Amirah. "Islamists and Secularists to Publish New Weekly." *Civil Society*, September 1997.

Ibrahim, Ibrahim, ed. *Arab Resources*. Washington, D.C.: Center for Contemporary Arab Studies, Georgetown University, 1983.

Ibrahim, Saad Eddin. "Anatomy of Egypt's Militant Islamic Groups: Methodological Note and Preliminary Findings." *International Journal of Middle East Studies* 12 (1980): 423–53.

———. "The Changing Face of Egypt's Islamic Activism: How Much of a Threat?" Paper presented to the workshop U.S.–Egyptian Relations After the Cold War, National Defense University, Washington, D.C., April 28–29, 1994.

———. "The Changing Face of Islamic Activism." *Civil Society* 4 (1995).

———. "Civil Society and Electoral Politics in Egypt." *Civil Society* 4 (December 1995).

———. "Egypt's Islamic Activism in the 1980s." *Third World Quarterly* 10 (April 1988): 632–57.

———. *The New Arab Social Order.* Boulder, Colo.: Westview Press, 1982.

———. "Social Mobility and Income Distribution in Egypt, 1952–1977." In *The Political Economy of Income Distribution in Egypt*, edited by Gouda 'Abdel-Khalek and Robert Tignor. New York: Holmes & Meier, 1982.

Ikram, Khalid. "Meeting the Social Contract in Egypt." *Finance and Development*, September 1981.

Ismael, Tareq Y., and Rif'at Sa'id. *The Communist Movement in Egypt: 1920–1988.* Syracuse, N.Y.: Syracuse University Press, 1990.

Jankowski, James. *Egypt's Young Rebels: "Young Egypt" 1933–1952.* Stanford, Calif.: Hoover Institution Press, 1973.

———. "The Social Basis of Egyptian Arabism." Unpublished manuscript.

Johnston, Hank, and Bert Klandermans, eds. *Social Movements and Culture.* Vol. 4, *Social Movements, Protest, and Contention.* Minneapolis: University of Minnesota Press, 1995.

Joint-Venture Companies. "Wage Survey." Cairo: Joint-Venture Companies, 1989.

Karawan, Ibrahim A. "Re-Islamization Movements According to Kepel: On Striking Back and Striking Out." *Contention* 2 (1992).

Kepel, Giles. *Muslim Extremism in Egypt: The Prophet and the Pharaoh.* Berkeley and Los Angeles: University of California Press, 1993.

Kerr, Malcolm. "Egypt." In *Education and Political Development*, edited by James S. Coleman. Princeton, N.J.: Princeton University Press, 1965.

Khalaf, Roula. "Egypt Survey." *Financial Times*, May 9, 2001.

Khan, Amil. "Elections Marred by Government Meddling." *Middle East Times*, November 5–11, 2000.

———. "Government Blames Opposition for Egypt's Poor Elections Results." *Middle East Times*, December 22, 2000.

———. "Killings Mar Egyptian Elections." BBC World Service, November 14, 2000.

———. "Violent Clashes Continue to Mar Egypt Elections." *Middle East Times*, November 12–18, 2000.

Khoury, Philip S. "Islamic Revivalism and the Crisis of the Secular State in the Arab World." In *Arab Resources*, edited by Ibrahim Ibrahim. Washington, D.C.: Center for Contemporary Arab Studies, Georgetown University, 1983.

Khoury-Dagher, Nadia. "Households and the Food Issue in Cairo: The Answers of Civil Society to a Defaulting State." Unpublished manuscript. Paris: CIRED (International Research Center on Environment and Development, n.d.).

Kitschelt, Herbert P. "Political Opportunity Structures and Political Protest: Anti-Nuclear Movements in Four Democracies." *British Journal of Political Science* 16 (1986).

Klandermans, Bert. "The Formation and Mobilization of Consensus." In *International Social Movement Research. From Structure to Action: Comparing Social Movement Across Cultures*, edited by Bert Klandermans, Hanspeter Kriesi, and Sidney Tarrow. Vol. 1. Greenwich, Conn.: JAI Press, 1988.

Klandermans, Bert, Hanspeter Kriesi, and Sidney Tarrow, eds. *International Social Movement Research. From Structure to Action: Comparing Social Movement Across Cultures*. Vol. 1. Greenwich, Conn.: JAI Press, 1988.

Knutson, Jeanne N., ed. *Handbook of Political Psychology*. San Francisco: Jossey-Bass, 1973.

Koestler, Arthur. "The Initiates." In *The God That Failed*, edited by Richard Crossman. New York: Bantam Books, 1949.

Korayem, Karima. "Government Policies and the Labour Market in Egypt." Memo no. 1393. Cairo: Institute of National Planning, Arab Republic of Egypt, February 1984.

Kornhauser, William. *The Politics of Mass Society*. New York: Free Press, 1959.

Kramer, Gudrun. "Islamist Notions of Democracy." In *Political Islam: Essays from Middle East Report*, edited by Joel Beinin and Joe Stork. Berkeley and Los Angeles: University of California Press, 1997.

Kurzman, Charles. "Structural Opportunity and Perceived Opportunity in Social Movement Theory: The Iranian Revolution of 1979." *American Sociological Review* 61 (1996): 153–70.

Larana, Enrique, Hank Johnston, and Joseph R. Gusfield, eds. *New Social Movements: From Ideology to Identity*. Philadelphia: Temple University Press, 1994.

"Lawlessness in the Nile Basin: Who Runs Egypt, Government or Mafia?" *Liberty for the Muslim World*, October 20, 1995.

"Liberty: Escalating Tension Between Government and Ikhwan in Egypt Leads to Algeria Syndrome." *Liberty for the Muslim World*, August 9, 1995.

Lichbach, Mark Irving, and Alan S. Zuckerman, eds. *Comparative Politics: Rationality, Culture, and Structure*. Cambridge: Cambridge University Press, 1997.

Luciani, Giacomo, ed. *The Arab World*. Berkeley and Los Angeles: University of California Press, 1990.

Linz, Juan. "Totalitarian and Authoritarian Regimes." In *Handbook of Political Science*. Vol. 3, *Macropolitical Theory*, edited by Fred I. Greenstein and Nelson W. Polsby. Reading, Mass.: Addison-Wesley, 1975.

Lipsky, Michael. *Protest in City Politics*. Chicago: Rand-McNally, 1970.

"The Little NGO That Could." *Cairo Times*, April 13–19, 2000.

Lockman, Zachary. *Workers and Working Classes in the Middle East*. Albany: State University of New York Press, 1994.

Lukes, Steven. *Power: A Radical View*. London: Macmillan, 1974.

Mabro, Robert. *The Egyptian Economy, 1952–1972*. Oxford: Clarendon Press, 1974.

Mainwaring, Scott, and Eduardo Viola. "New Social Movements, Political Culture and Democracy in Brazil and Argentina in the 1980's." *Telos* 61 (fall 1984).

Mannheim, Karl. *Ideology and Utopia*. New York: Harcourt Brace, 1936.

Matton, Scott. "Islam by Profession." *The Middle East*, December 1992.

McAdam, Douglas. *Political Process and the Development of Black Insurgency, 1930–1970*. Chicago: University of Chicago Press, 1982.

———. "Conceptual Origins, Current Problems, Future Directions." In *Comparative Perspectives on Social Movements: Political Opportunities, Mobilizing Structures, and Cultural Framings*, edited by Douglas McAdam, John D. McCarthy, and Mayer N. Zald. Cambridge: Cambridge University Press, 1996.

———. *Freedom Summer*. New York: Oxford University Press, 1988.

———. "Micromobilization Contexts and Recruitment to Activism." In *International Social Movement Research. From Structure to Action: Comparing Social Movement Across Cultures*, edited by Bert Klandermans, Hanspeter Kriesi, and Sidney Tarrow. Vol. 1. Greenwich, Conn.: JAI Press, 1988.

———. *Political Process and the Development of Black Insurgency, 1930–1970*. Chicago: University of Chicago Press, 2nd ed., 1999.

———. "Recruitment to High-Risk Activism: The Case of Freedom Summer." *American Journal of Sociology* 92 (July 1986): 64–90.

McAdam, Douglas, John D. McCarthy, and Mayer N. Zald. "Introduction: Opportunities, Mobilizing Structures, and Framing Processes — Toward a Synthetic, Comparative Perspective on Social Movements." In *Comparative Perspectives on Social Movements: Political Opportunities, Mobilizing Structures, and Cultural Framings*, edited by Douglas McAdam, John D. McCarthy, and Mayer N. Zald. Cambridge: Cambridge University Press, 1996.

―――. "Social Movements." In *The Handbook of Sociology*, edited by Neil J. Smelser. Beverly Hills, Calif.: Sage, 1988.

―――, eds. *Comparative Perspectives on Social Movements: Political Opportunities, Mobilizing Structures and Cultural Framings*. Cambridge: Cambridge University Press, 1996.

McAdam, Douglas, Sidney Tarrow, and Charles Tilly. "A Comparative Synthesis on Social Movements and Revolution: Towards an Integrated Perspective." Paper presented at the annual meeting of the American Political Science Association, San Francisco, 1996.

―――. *The Dynamics of Contention*. Cambridge: Cambridge University Press, 2001.

McCarthy, John D., and Mayer N. Zald. "Resource Mobilization and Social Movements: A Partial Theory." *American Journal of Sociology* 82 (1977): 1212–41.

McKee, E. S. "Fading Fundamentalists." *The Jerusalem Report*, July 17, 2000.

Mead, Donald C. *Growth and Structural Change in the Egyptian Economy*. Homewood, Ill.: Irwin, 1967.

Melucci, Alberto. *Nomads of the Present*. London: Hutchinson, 1989.

Middle East Watch. *Behind Closed Doors: Torture and Detention in Egypt*. New York: Human Rights Watch, 1992.

―――. "Egypt: Human Rights Abuses Mount in 1993." New York: Human Rights Watch, 1993.

―――. *Human Rights Conditions in the Middle East in 1993*. New York: Human Rights Watch, 1994.

Migdal, Joel S. "The State in Society: An Approach to Struggles for Domination." In *State Power and Social Forces: Domination and Transformation in the Third World*, edited by Joel S. Migdal, Atul Kohli, and Vivienne Shue. Cambridge: Cambridge University Press, 1994.

―――. *Strong Societies and Weak States: State-Society Relations and State Capabilities in the Third World*. Princeton, N.J.: Princeton University Press, 1988.

Migdal, Joel S., Atul Kohli, and Vivienne Shue, eds. *State Power and Social Forces: Domination and Transformation in the Third World*. Cambridge: Cambridge University Press, 1994.

Ministry of Social Affairs, in conjunction with the North-South Consultants' Exchange. "Unemployed Graduates in the Governorate of Beni Suef: Survey of Conditions and Needs." Cairo: Ministry of Social Affairs, 1991.

"Mission Impossible: Youth on a Hot Tin Roof." Letter to the Editor. *Egyptian Gazette*, May 12, 1991.

Mitchell, Richard P. *The Society of the Muslim Brothers*. Oxford: Oxford University Press, 1969.

Moench, Richard U. "Oil, Ideology and State Autonomy in Egypt." *Arab Studies Quarterly* 10 (1988): 176–92.

Moore, Clement Henry. *Images of Development: Egyptian Engineers in Search of Industry*. Cambridge, Mass.: MIT Press, 1980.

Morris, Aldon D., and Cedric Herring. "Theory and Research in Social Movements: A Critical Review." *Annual Review of Political Science*. Vol. 2. Norwood, N.J.: ABLEX, 1987.

Morris, Aldon D., and Carol McClurg Mueller, eds. *Frontiers in Social Movement Theory*. New Haven, Conn.: Yale University Press, 1992.

Mouffe, Chantal. "Hegemony and New Political Subjects: Toward a New Concept of Democracy." In *Marxism and the Interpretation of Culture*, edited by C. Nelson and L. Grossberg. Champaign-Urbana: University of Illinois Press, 1988.

————. "Towards a Theoretical Interpretation of New Social Movements." In *Rethinking Marx*, edited by S. Hanninen and L. Paldan. Berlin: Argument-Sonderband AS 109, 1984.

"Mubarak Faces Test of Legitimacy" (special report). *Middle East Times*. October 13, 2000.

"Mubarak's Party Maintains Comfortable Majority in Parliament." *Deutsche Presse–Agentur*, November 15, 2000.

Mueller, Carol McClurg. "Building Social Movement Theory." In *Frontiers in Social Movement Theory*, edited by Aldon D. Morris and Carol McClurg Mueller. New Haven, Conn.: Yale University Press, 1992.

Muslim Brotherhood. *Muslim Women in the Muslim Society*. Cairo: Muslim Brotherhood, 1994.

Myrdal, Gunnar. *Asian Drama*. New York: Pantheon Books, 1968.

Najjar, Fauzi. "Elections and Democracy in Egypt." *American-Arab Affairs*, no. 29 (1989): 96–113.

Negus, Steve. "Down but Not Out: The Muslim Brotherhood Keep a Low Profile, but Their Main Activity — Charity Work — Still Goes On." *Cairo Times*, April 3, 1997.

Nelson, C., and L. Grossberg, eds. *Marxism and the Interpretation of Culture*. Champaign-Urbana: University of Illinois Press, 1988.

Nordlinger, Eric A. 1987. "Taking the State Seriously." In *Understanding Political Development*, edited by Myron Weiner and Samuel Huntington. Boston: Little Brown, 1987.

Norton, Augustus Richard. "The Future of Civil Society in the Middle East." *Middle East Journal* 47 (spring 1993).

Oberschall, Anthony. *Social Conflict and Social Movements*. Englewood Cliffs, N.J.: Prentice-Hall, 1973.

Office of Alumni Affairs. *December 1990 Employment Fair: Job Openings*. American University in Cairo, December 8, 1990.

Olson, Mancur Jr. *The Logic of Collective Action*. Cambridge, Mass.: Harvard University Press, 1965.

Ost, David. *Solidarity and the Politics of Anti-Politics: Opposition and Reform in Poland Since 1968*. Philadelphia: Temple University Press, 1990.

Oweiss, Ibrahim M., ed. *The Political Economy of Contemporary Egypt*. Washington, D.C.: Center for Contemporary Arab Studies, Georgetown University, 1990.

Pearson, Hugh. *The Shadow of the Panthers: Huey Newton and the Price of Black Power in America*. Reading, Mass.: Addison-Wesley, 1994.

Posusney, Marsha Pripstein. "Collective Action and Workers' Consciousness in Contemporary Egypt." In *Workers and Working Classes in the Middle East*, edited by Zachary Lockman. Albany: State University of New York Press, 1994.

———. "Irrational Workers: The Moral Economy of Labor Protest in Egypt." *World Politics* 46 (1993): 83–120.

Ramet, Sabrina Petra. *Social Currents in Eastern Europe: The Sources and Consequences of the Great Transformation*. Durham, N.C.: Duke University Press, 1995.

Reid, Donald. "The Rise of Professional Organizations in Modern Egypt." *Comparative Studies in Society and History* 16 (1971).

Richards, Alan. "The Political Economy of Dilatory Reform: Egypt in the 1980s." *World Development* 19 (December 1991): 1721–30.

———. "Ten Years of Infitah: Class, Rent and Policy Stasis in Egypt." *Journal of Development Studies*, July 1987.

Richards, Alan, and John Waterbury. *A Political Economy of the Middle East: State, Class, and Economic Development*. Boulder, Colo.: Westview Press, 1990.

———. *A Political Economy of the Middle East*. Boulder, Colo.: Westview Press, 1996.

Rignall, Karen. "The Egyptian Social Fund for Development: Strategies of Compensation During Structural Adjustment." Senior thesis, Princeton University, 1992.

Rosen, Lawrence. *Bargaining for Reality: The Construction of Social Relations in a Muslim Community*. Chicago: University of Chicago Press, 1984.

Roussillon, Alain. "Sociétés islamiques de placement de fonds et 'ouverture économique.'" Cairo: Dossiers du Cedej, March 1988.

Rugh, Andrea B. *Family in Contemporary Egypt*. Cairo: American University in Cairo Press, 1985.

Sachs, Susan. "War on Fundamentalism Silences Dissent in Egypt." *International Herald Tribune*, August 5, 2000.

Salame, Ghassan, ed. *Democracy Without Democrats?: The Renewal of Politics in the Muslim World*. London: I. B. Tauris, 1994.

al-Sayed, Mustafa Kamal. "A Civil Society in Egypt?" *Middle East Journal* 47 (spring 1993).

———. "The Islamic Movement in Egypt: Social and Political Implications." In *The Political Economy of Contemporary Egypt*, edited by Ibrahim Oweiss. Washington, D.C.: Center for Contemporary Arab Studies, Georgetown University, 1990.

————. *Society and Politics in Egypt: The Role of Interest Groups in the Egyptian Political System, 1952–1981.* Cairo: Dar al-mustaqbal al-'arabi, 1983.

Schemm, Paul. "Survival Mode." *Cairo Times,* August 10–16, 2000.

Schwartz, David C. *Political Alienation and Political Behavior.* Chicago: Aldine, 1973.

Shadid, Anthony. *Legacy of the Prophet: Despots, Democrats and the New Politics of Islam.* Boulder, Colo.: Westview Press, 2001.

al-Sharqawi, Souad. "Uprooting Terrorism." *Civil Society,* May 1993.

Singerman, Diane. *Avenues of Participation: Family, Politics and Networks in Urban Quarters of Cairo.* Princeton, N.J.: Princeton University Press, 1995.

Skocpol, Theda. *States and Social Revolutions.* Cambridge: Cambridge University Press, 1979.

Slater, David. "New Social Movements and Old Political Questions: Rethinking State-Society Relations in Latin American Development." *Journal of International Political Economy,* spring 1991.

Smelser, Neil J., ed. *The Handbook of Sociology.* Beverly Hills, Calif.: Sage, 1988.

Smith, Christian. "Introduction: Correcting a Curious Neglect, or Bringing Religion Back In." In *Disruptive Religion: The Force of Faith in Social Movement Activism,* edited by Christian Smith. New York: Routledge, 1996.

Smith, Christian, ed. *Disruptive Religion: The Force of Faith in Social Movement Activism.* New York: Routledge, 1996.

Snow, David A., and Robert D. Benford. "Ideology, Frame Resonance and Participant Mobilization." In *International Social Movement Research. From Structure to Action: Comparing Social Movement Across Cultures,* edited by Bert Klandermans, Hanspeter Kriesi, and Sidney Tarrow. Vol. 1. Greenwich, Conn.: JAI Press, 1988.

Snow, David A., E. Burke Rochford Jr., Steven K. Worden, and Robert D. Benford. "Frame Alignment Processes, Micromobilization, and Movement Participation." *American Sociological Review* 51 (1986): 464–81.

"Special Report: Mubarak Faces Test of Legitimacy." *Middle East Economic Digest,* October 13, 2000.

Springborg, Robert. *Mubarak's Egypt: Fragmentation of the Political Order.* Boulder, Colo.: Westview Press, 1989.

Starrett, Gregory. *Putting Islam to Work: Education, Politics, and Religious Transformation in Egypt.* Berkeley and Los Angeles: University of California Press, 1998.

Stepan, Alfred. *Rethinking Military Politics: Brazil and the Southern Cone.* Princeton, N.J.: Princeton University Press, 1988.

————, ed. *Democratizing Brazil: Problems of Transition and Consolidation.* Oxford: Oxford University Press, 1989.

Stokes, Gale. *The Walls Came Crumbling Down: The Collapse of Communism in Eastern Europe.* Oxford: Oxford University Press, 1993.

Sullivan, Denis J. "Ameliorating the Social Costs of Economic Reform: The Social Fund for Development in Egypt." Paper presented at the Middle East Studies Association Conference, Research Triangle Park, N.C., November 1993.

————. *Private Voluntary Organizations in Egypt: Islamic Development, Private Initiative, and State Control.* Gainesville: University of Florida Press, 1994.

Sullivan, Denis J., and Sana Abed-Kotob. *Islam in Contemporary Egypt: Civil Society vs. the State.* Boulder, Colo.: Lynne Rienner, 1999.

Sunar, Ilkay. "The Politics of State Interventionism in 'Populist' Egypt and Turkey." Paper presented at the Middle East Studies Association Conference, Washington, D.C., November 1991.

el-Tahawy, Mona. "Egypt Cracks down on Islamist Activists." *The Guardian,* October 23, 1999.

Tarrow, Sidney. *Power in Movement: Social Movements, Collective Action and Politics.* Cambridge: Cambridge University Press, 1994.

————. *Power in Movement: Social Movements and Contentious Politics.* 2nd ed. Cambridge: Cambridge University Press, 1998.

————. "States and Opportunities: The Political Structuring of Social Movements." In *Comparative Perspectives on Social Movements: Political Opportunities, Mobilizing Structures and Cultural Framings,* edited by Douglas McAdam, John D. McCarthy, and Mayer N. Zald. Cambridge: Cambridge University Press, 1996.

Tessler, Mark. "Alienation of Urban Youth." In *Polity and Society in Contemporary North Africa,* edited by I. William Zartman and William Mark Habeeb. Boulder, Colo.: Westview Press, 1993.

————. "The Origins of Popular Support for Islamic Movements: A Political Economy Analysis." Occasional Papers Series, Center for International Studies, University of Wisconsin Press, 1993.

————. "The Origins of Popular Support for Islamist Movements: A Political Economy Analysis." In *Islam, Democracy, and the State in North Africa,* edited by John P. Entelis. Bloomington: Indiana University Press, 1997.

Thelen, Kathleen, Sven Steinmo, and Frank Longstrech, eds. *Structuring Politics: Historical-Institutionalism in Comparative Analysis.* Cambridge: Cambridge University Press, 1992.

Tilly, Charles. *The Contentious French.* Cambridge, Mass.: Harvard University Press, 1986.

————. *From Mobilization to Revolution.* New York: McGraw-Hill, 1978.

Tismeanu, Vladimir. *Reinventing Politics: Eastern Europe from Stalin to Havel.* New York: Free Press, 1992.

Touraine, Alain. *The Voice and the Eye: An Analysis of Social Movements.* Cambridge: Cambridge University Press, 1981.

Tripp, Charles, and Roger Owen, eds. *Egypt Under Mubarak.* London: Routledge, 1989.

United Press International. "Egypt's Islamists Blast Government for Election Ban."
    September 19, 2000.
U.S. Embassy. "Egyptian Economic Trends." U.S. Embassy Report, Cairo, 1991.
————. "Foreign Economic Trends and Their Implications for the United States:
    Report for the Arab Republic of Egypt." U.S. Embassy Report, April 1991.
Valenzuela, Samuel, and Arturo Valenzuela, eds. *Military Rule in Chile: Dictatorship
    and Opposition*. Baltimore: Johns Hopkins University Press, 1985.
Vatikiotis, P. J. *Nasser and His Generation*. London: Crohm Helm, 1978.
Vladislav, Jan, ed. *Vaclav Havel: Living in Truth*. London: Faber & Faber, 1986.
Waldman, Peter. "As Egypt Suppresses Muslim Brotherhood, Some Fear Backlash."
    Wall Street Journal, December 8, 1995.
Waterbury, John. *The Commander of the Faithful: The Moroccan Political Elite: A
    Study in Segmented Politics*. New York: Columbia University Press, 1970.
————. *The Egypt of Nasser and Sadat: The Political Economy of Two Regimes*.
    Princeton, N.J.: Princeton University Press, 1983.
————. *A Political Economy of the Middle East*. Boulder, Colo.: Westview Press,
    1996.
————. "The 'Soft-State' and the Open Door: Egypt's Experience with Economic
    Liberalization, 1974–1986." *Comparative Politics*, October 1985, 65–83.
"We Are a Civil Party with an Islamic Identity." Interview with Abu 'Ila Madi Abu
    'Ila and Rafiq Habib. *Middle East Report*, April–June 1996.
Weaver, Mary Anne. "Egypt on Trial." *New York Times Magazine*, June 17, 2001.
————. "Letter from Cairo: Revolution by Stealth." *New Yorker*, June 8, 1998.
————. *A Portrait of Egypt: A Journey Through the World of Militant Islam*. New
    York: Ferrar, Straus & Giroux, 1999.
Weber, Max. "The Social Psychology of the World Religions." In *Max Weber: Essays
    in Sociology*, edited by H. H. Gerth and C. Wright Mills. New York: Oxford
    University Press, 1980.
Weiner, Myron, and Samuel Huntington, eds. *Understanding Political Development*.
    Boston: Little Brown, 1987.
de Weydenthal, Jan B. "The Character of East European Dissent During the Late
    1970's." In *Dissent in Eastern Europe*, edited by Jane Leftwich Curry. New
    York: Praeger, 1983.
Wickham, Carrie Rosefsky. "Islamic Mobilization and Political Change: The Islamist
    Trend in Egypt's Professional Associations." In *Political Islam: Essays from the
    Middle East Report*, edited by Joel Beinin and Joe Stork. Berkeley and Los
    Angeles: University of California Press, 1997.
Wickham-Crowley, Timothy. *Guerrillas and Revolution in Latin America*. Princeton,
    N.J.: Princeton University Press, 1992.
Wiktorowicz, Quintan. *Islamic Activism: A Social Movement Approach*. Forth-
    coming.
————. *The Management of Islamic Activism: The Salafis, the Muslim Brotherhood,
    and State Power in Jordan*. Albany: State University of New York Press, 2000.

World Bank. "Arab Republic of Egypt: Current Economic Situation and Economic Reform Program." World Bank Report, October 22, 1986.

———. *Arab Republic of Egypt: Current Economic Situation and Growth Prospects.* Washington, D.C.: World Bank, October 1983.

———. *Arab Republic of Egypt: Economic Management in a Period of Transition.* Vol. 11, *Human Resources.* Washington, D.C.: World Bank, May 8, 1978.

———. *Arab Republic of Egypt: Issues of Trade Strategy and Investment Planning.* Washington, D.C.: World Bank, January 1983.

———. *Egypt: Alleviating Poverty During Structural Adjustment.* World Bank Country Study. Washington, D.C.: World Bank, 1991.

———. "Meeting Basic Needs in Egypt: Mission Report." World Bank Report, November 15, 1979.

———. *World Development Report, 1993.* New York: Oxford University Press, 1993.

Yazbeck, Yvonne. "Islamists and the Challenge of Pluralism." Occasional Papers. Washington, D.C.: Center for Contemporary Arab Studies, Georgetown University, 1995.

Yinger, John Milton. "Anomie, Alienation and Political Behavior." In *Handbook of Political Psychology,* edited by Jeanne N. Knutson. San Francisco: Jossey-Bass, 1973.

Zald, Mayer N. "Looking Backward to Look Forward: Reflections on the Past and Future of the Resource Mobilization Research Program." In *Frontiers in Social Movement Theory,* edited by Aldon D. Morris and Carol McClurg Mueller. New Haven, Conn.: Yale University Press, 1992.

Zartman, I. William, and William Mark Habeeb, eds. *Polity and Society in Contemporary North Africa.* Boulder, Colo.: Westview Press, 1993.

Zaytoun, Mohaya. "Earnings." Preliminary report I/3 of the CAPMAS Labour Information System Project, December 1990.

———. "Earnings and the Cost of Living: An Analysis of Recent Developments in the Egyptian Economy." In *Employment and Structural Adjustment: Egypt in the 1990s,* edited by Heba Handoussa and Gillian Potter. Cairo: American University in Cairo Press, 1991.

———. "Earnings, Subsidies and Cost of Living: An Analysis of Recent Developments in the Egyptian Economy." Working paper, Cairo, December 1988.

Zubaida, Sami. "Islam, the State and Democracy: Contrasting Conceptions of Society in Egypt." *Middle East Report* 22 (November/December 1992): 2–10.

Arabic-Language Sources

(Note: The titles of Arabic-language newspaper and journal articles are given in English translation only.)

'Abd al-Fattah, Nabil, ed. *Taqrir 'an al-hala al-diniyya fi Misr: 1995* [*Report on Religious Conditions in Egypt: 1995*]. Cairo: Al-Ahram Center for Political and Strategic Studies, 1998.

————, ed. *Taqrir 'an al-hala al-diniyya fi Misr, al-'adad al-thani* [Report on Religious Conditions in Egypt, volume two]. Cairo: Al-Ahram Center for Political and Strategic Studies, 1998.

'Abd al-Karim, Salah. *Awraq hizb al-Wasat al-misri* [*The Papers of the Egyptian Wasat Party*]. 1998.

'Abd al-Magid, Wahid. ed. *Al-Taqrir al-istiratiji al-'arabi: 1999* [*The Arab Strategic Report: 1999*]. Cairo: Al-Ahram Center for Political and Strategic Studies, 2000.

Abdalla, Ahmad. "Al-Intikhabat al-barlamaniyya fi Misr: Ayy intikhabat wa-ayy barlaman wa-ayyat Misr? [Parliamentary Elections in Egypt: Which Elections, Which Parliament, Which Egypt?]. In *Al-Intikhabat al-barlamaniyya fi Misr: Dirasat intikhabat 1987* [*Parliamentary Elections in Egypt: A Study of the 1987 Elections*], edited by Ahmad Abdalla. Cairo: Center for Arab Research, Sina Publishers, 1990.

————. *Humum Misr wa-azmat al-'uqul al-shabbah* [*The Concerns of Egypt and the Crisis of Young Minds*]. Cairo: Al-Jil Center for Sociological and Youth Studies, 1993.

————, ed. *Al-Intikhabat al-barlamaniyya fi Misr: Dirasat intikhabat 1987* [*Parliamentary Elections in Egypt: A Study of the 1987 Elections*]. Cairo: Center for Arab Research, Sina Publishers, 1990.

"Appointment of Some Graduates of 1984 and Later Years." *Al-Ahram*, March 13, 1991.

Badr, Badr Muhammad. *Al-Jama'at al-islamiyya fi jami'at Misr: Haqa'iq wa-watha'iq* [*The Islamic Student Associations in Egyptian Universities: Facts and Documents*]. Cairo: Published privately, 1989.

————. "Crisis in the Universities Due to the Student Elections: Judges Stop the Student Elections to Remove the Islamic Candidates." *Al-Mujtama'*, November 22, 1994.

al-Banna, Hasan. *Ila al-Shabab, wa-ila al-talaba khassatan* [*To Youth and Especially to Students*]. Mukhtar al-Da'wa series. Alexandria: Dar al-Da'wa, n.d.

————. *Ila al-Tullab* [*To Students*]. Mukhtar al-Da'wa series. Alexandria: Dar al-Da'wa, n.d.

Commercial Employees' Association. "Report of the General Assembly." Cairo: Commercial Employees' Association, Cairo, 1990.

"The Degree Complex Is Behind the Labor Crisis in Egypt!" *Al-Akhbar*, December 17, 1988.

"The Doctors' Association Elections Between Yesterday and Today." *Al-Atibba'*, August 1992.

Fayyad, Nasir. "Civil Servants and University Graduates . . . Street Peddlers." *Al-Wafd*, June 17, 1990.

"From Here Extremism Begins: The Independent Mosques." *Akhir sa'a*, December 2, 1992.

Ghayta, Nagib Hasan. "Ba'd mazahir al-khalal fi suq al-'amal al-misri" [Some Manifestations of Imbalance in the Egyptian Labor Market]. Cairo: Ministry of Manpower and Training, 1987.

Gom'a, Sa'd Ibrahim. *Al-Shabab wa'l-musharaka al-siyasiyya* [*Youth and Political Participation*]. Cairo: Al-Thaqafa Publishers, 1984.

Gom'a, Salwa Sha'rawi. "Da'irat Madinat Nasr" [The Electoral District of Medinat Nasr]. In *Intikhabat Majlis al-Sha'b: 1990* [*The People's Assembly Elections: 1990*], edited by Ali ed-Din Hilal and Osama al-Ghazzali Harb. Cairo: Al-Ahram Center for Political and Strategic Studies, 1992.

———. "Tafsir al-suluk al-intikhabi: Dirasa muqarana li-Da'irat Sharq al-Qahira wa-Muhafazat al-Suwees" [An Explanation of Voting Behavior: A Comparative Study of the District of East Cairo and the Governorate of Suez]. In *Intikhabat Majlis al-Sha'b: 1987* [*The People's Assembly Elections: 1987*], edited by Ali ed-Din Hilal. Cairo: Al-Ahram Center for Political and Strategic Studies, 1988.

"Graduate . . . The Labor Market Needs Him Immediately!" *Al-Ahram*, November 5, 1990.

Haluda, 'Awad Mukhtar. "Al-Bitala fi Misr: Qiyasha wa-asalib 'ilajiha" [Unemployment in Egypt: Its Indicators and Ways to Address It]. Paper presented at the Conference on Human Resources and Unemployment, fourteenth annual conference of Egyptian economists, Cairo, November 1989.

Hilal, Ali ed-Din, ed. *Intikhabat Majlis al-Sha'b 1984: Dirasa wa-tahlil* [*The People's Assembly Elections, 1984: Study and Analysis*]. Cairo: Al-Ahram Center for Political and Strategic Studies, 1986.

———, ed. *Intikhabat Majlis al-Sha'b 1987: Dirasa wa-tahlil* [*The People's Assembly Elections, 1987: Study and Analysis*]. Cairo: Al-Ahram Center for Political and Strategic Studies, 1988.

Hilal, Ali ed-Din, and Osama al-Ghazzali Harb, eds. *Intikhabat Majlis al-Sha'b 1990: Dirasa wa-tahlil* [*The People's Assembly Elections, 1990: Study and Analysis*]. Cairo: Al-Ahram Center for Political and Strategic Studies, 1992.

al-Hilali, Magdi. *Wajibat al-shabab al-muslim* [*The Duties of the Muslim Youth*]. Shubra: Dar al-Manar, 1987.

Hilmi, Shukri 'Abbas. "Iqtisadiyyat al-ta'lim al-jami'i fi Misr" [The Economics of University Education in Egypt]. Paper presented at the Conference on University Education Policy, Center for Political Research and Studies, Cairo University, January 1990.

Hussein, Ashraf. "Al-Gam'iyyat al-ahliyya wa'l-mu'awiqat al-qanuniyya li-nash'atiha wa-nashatiha" [Private Voluntary Organizations and the Legal Obstacles to Their Formation and Activities]. In *Humum Misr wa-azmat al-'uqul al-shabba* [*The Concerns of Egypt and the Crisis of Young Minds*], edited by Ahmad Abdalla. Cairo: Dar al-Tiba'a al-Mutamayyiza, 1994.

———. "Al-Musharaka al-siyasiyya wa'l-intikhabat al-barlamaniyya" [Political Participation and Parliamentary Elections]. In *Al-Intikhabat al-barlamaniyya fi Misr: Dirasat intikhabat* [*Parliamentary Elections in Egypt: A Study of the 1987 Elections*], edited by Ahmad Abdalla. Cairo: Al-Ahram Center for Arab Studies, Sina Publishers, 1990.

Imam, Samia Saʻd. *Man Yamluk Misr' Dirasa tahliliyya li-usul nukhbat al-infitah al-ijtimaʻiyya, 1974–1980* [Who Owns Egypt? An Analytical Study of the Social Origins of the Infitah Elite, 1974–1980]. Cairo: Dar al-Mustaqbal al-ʻArabi, 1986.

"Inheriting Positions Is Prohibited, But . . . ." *Al-Nur*, February 6, 1991.

Ismaʻil, Muhammad Mahrus. "Al-Taʻlim al-ʻali wa'l-bitala fi Misr" [Higher Education and Unemployment in Egypt]. Paper presented at the fourteenth annual conference of Egyptian economists, Cairo, November 1989.

Kamil, Samia Mustafa. "Al-Taʻlim — Suq al-ʻamal — Bataalit al-mutaʻlimin" [Education — Labor Market — Educated Unemployment]. In *Al-Bitala fi Misr: Al-Mu'tamar al-awwal li-Qism al-Iqtisad, 1989* [Unemployment in Egypt: The First Conference of the Faculty of Economics, 1989], edited by Salwa Sulayman. Cairo: Faculty of Economics and Political Science, Cairo University, 1989.

Khawaga, Layla Ahmad. "Dirasa tahliliyya li-zahirat al-bitala al-safira wa-ʻalaqatiha bi-haykal suq al-ʻamal fi Misr" [Analytic Study of the Phenomenon of Open Unemployment and Its Relation to the Labor Market in Egypt]. In *Al-Bitala fi Misr: Al-Mu'tamar al-awwal li-Qism al-Iqtisad, 1989* [Unemployment in Egypt: The First Conference of the Faculty of Economics, 1989], edited by Salwa Sulayman. Cairo: Faculty of Economics and Political Science, Cairo University, 1989.

Mashhur, Mustafa. *Al-Daʻwa ila-Allah: Al daʻwa al-fardiyya* [The Call to God: The Individual Daʻwa]. Cairo: Islamic Center for Studies and Research, Dar al-Tawziʻ wa'l-Nashr al-Islamiyya, 1981.

Mustafa, Hala. *Al-Islam al-siyasi fi Misr: Min harakat al-islah ila jamaʻat al-ʻunf* [Political Islam in Egypt: From a Reform Movement to Associations of Violence]. Cairo: al-Ahram Center for Political and Strategic Studies, 1992.

Nasir, Nasir Abdalla, and Sabir Muhammad ʻAbdu Ribh. "Al-Waʻy al-siyasi li'l-murashshahin: Dirasa maydaniyya ʻala ʻayyina min al-murashshahin fi baʻd dawa'ir Muhafazat Sohag" [Political Awareness of Candidates: A Field Study of a Sample of Candidates in Certain Districts of Sohag Governorate]. In *Intikhabat Majlis al-Shaʻb 1990: Dirasa wa-tahlil* [The People's Assembly Elections, 1990: Study and Analysis], edited by Ali ed-Din Hilal and Osama al-Ghazzali Harb. Cairo: Al-Ahram Center for Political and Strategic Studies, 1992.

"A Practical Plan to Solve the Problems of Youth and End Graduate Unemployment — The Path of Sohag." *Al-Akhbar*, April 25, 1991.

"The Problems of Youth in the Desert." *Al-Musawwar*, July 7, 1989.

Qandil, Amani. "Al-Niqabat al-mihaniyya fi Misr wa-ʻamaliyyat al-tahawwul al-dimuqrati" [Professional Groups in Egypt and the Process of Democratic Transformation]. Paper presented at the Conference on Democratic Challenges in the Arab World. Cairo: Center for Political and International Development Studies, September 1992.

————. "The Islamic Trend in Interest Groups in Egypt." *Qadaya Fikriyya*, October 1989.

al-Raghi, Sa'd Mujahid, and 'Ali 'Abd al-Fattah Hashim, eds. "Al-Bitala bayn al-muhandisiin: Al-Taqat al-Mu'attala fi al-mujtama' al-misri — Al-Mushkila wa al-hall" [Unemployment Among Engineers: Idle Resources in Egyptian Society — The Problem and the Solution]. Conference Proceedings. Cairo: Engineers' Association, 1989.

Rizq, 'Abd al-Salam. "The Lawyers' Association: Where To?" *Al-Ahali*, September 23, 1992.

Rumayh, Tal'at. *Al-Wasat wa'l-ikhwan* [*The Wasat and the Brotherhood*]. Cairo: Jaffa Center for Studies and Research, 1997.

Safti, Ahmad, and Sami al-Sayyid Fathi. "Tahlil jawanib al-'a'id wa'l-taklifa al-ijtima'iyya li'l-ta'lim al-jami'i" [A Social Cost-Benefit Analysis of University Education]. Paper presented at the Conference on University Education Policy. Cairo: Center for Political Research and Studies, Cairo University, January 1990.

Salah, Muhammad. "The Muslim Brotherhood Confronts Its Worst International Conflict." *Al-Wasat*, November 18, 1996.

al-Sayyid, Mustafa Kamal. *Al-Mujtama' wa'l-Siyasa fi Misr: Dawr Jama'at al-masalih fi al-nizam al-siyasi al-misri, 1952–1981* [*Society and Politics in Egypt: The Role of Interest Groups in the Egyptian Political System, 1952–1981*]. Cairo: Dar al-mustaqbal al-'arabi, 1983.

————. "Intikhabat Majlis al-Sha'b 'am 1987: Dalalat al-intikhabat" [The People's Assembly Elections for 1987: Evidence from the Elections]. In *Intikhabat Majlis al-Sha'b 1987: Dirasa wa-tahlil* [*The People's Assembly Elections in April 1987*], edited by Ali ed-Din Hilal. Cairo: Al-Ahram Center for Political and Strategic Studies, 1987.

"The Search for a Vacant Position: A Difficult Task: Secretary and House-Director Positions . . . A Back Door to Moral Deviance!" *Al-Wafd*, November 6, 1990.

"Small Projects: A Slogan That Lacks Serious Implementation." *Al-Wafd*, March 10, 1991.

Sulayman, Salwa, ed. *Al-Bitala fi Misr: Al-Mu'tamar al-awwal li-qism al-iqtisad, 1989* [*Unemployment in Egypt: The First Conference of the Faculty of Economics, 1989*]. Cairo: Faculty of Economics and Political Science, Cairo University, 1989.

al-Tahawi, Muna. "Tahlil zahirat al-bitala bayn al-muta'allimin fi Misr" [Analysis of the Phenomenon of Educated Unemployment in Egypt]. In *Al-Bitala fi Misr: Al-Mu'tamar al-awwal li-qism al-iqtisad, 1989* [*Unemployment in Egypt: The First Conference of the Faculty of Economics, 1989*], edited by Salwa Sulayman. Cairo: Faculty of Economics and Political Science, Cairo University, 1989.

"27,000 Exceptional Hires." *Al-Ahram*, February 10, 1991.

"232,000 Appointed, Including 52,000 Exceptional Hires." *Al-Ahram*, February 16, 1991.

Al-Umma fi 'am: Taqrir hawli 'an al-shu'un al-siyasiyya wa'l-iqtisadiyya al-misriyya [*The Umma in a Year, 1990–1991: An Annual Report on Egyptian Political and Economic Affairs*], edited by Mahmud Abdalla 'Akif and Muhammad Hazim Ghurab. Mansoura: Wafa' Publishers, 1992.

Al-Umma fi 'am: Taqrir hawli 'an al-shu'un al-siyasiyya wa'l-iqtisadiyya al-'arabiyya [*The Umma in a Year, 1991–1992: An Annual Report on Arab Political and Economic Affairs*], edited by Mahmud Abdalla 'Akif. Mansoura: Wafa' Publishers, 1993.

"Who Will Save Them from Fake Advertisements?" *Al-Wafd*, November 1988.

Yakan, Fathi. *Al-Shabab wa'l-taghyir* [*Youth and Change*]. Nahw wa'y islami series. Beirut: Mu'assasat al-Risala, 1987.

———. *Kayf nad'u ila al-Islam* [*How We Call to Islam*]. Nahw wa'y islami series. Beirut: Mu'assasit al-Risala, n.d.

Yasin, 'Ali. "Diary of an Unemployed Graduate and the Journey in Search of a Job." *Al-Wafd*, March 10, 1990.

Yasin, al-Sayyid, ed. *Al-Taqrir al-istiratiji al-'arabi* [*The Arab Strategic Report*]. Cairo: Al-Ahram Center for Political and Strategic Studies, 1987–91.

"Youth Are Bewildered . . . About the Ministry of Manpower and Illusory Openings." *Al-Wafd*, June 17, 1988.

"Youth Projects: Ink on Paper." *Al-Akhbar*, March 29, 1990.

Zayid, Fayiz, et al. "Why Do Youth Not Participate in Political Activity?" *Sawt al-Shabab*, April 1, 1985.

Personal Interviews, January 1990–June 1991 (interviewees' positions at the time of the interview)

Abaza, Mahmud. Youth secretary, Wafd Party

'Abd al-Karim, Salah. Editor in chief, *al-Muhandisun* (official Engineers' Association magazine)

'Abd al-Quddus, Muhammad. Islamist author and journalist

'Abd al-Rahman, Ibrahim Hilmi. Former minister of planning

'Abd al-Salam, Hasan. General director, Technical Office, Central Agency for Organization and Administration (CAOA)

Abdalla, Ahmad. Independent political science researcher and scholar

'Abdel-Fadil, Mahmud. Economist, Cairo University

Abercrombie-Winstanley, Gina. Cultural affairs officer, U.S. embassy

Abu al-Yazid, Ahmad. Director, Small Business Program, Center for Development Studies (CDS), Cairo

Abu-l-Futuh, 'Abd al-Mun'im. Secretary general, Medical Doctors' Association

Abu-Gharib, Muhammad. General manager, Cabinet Information and Decision Support Center

Abu-l-'Ila, Abu-l-'Ila Madi. Assistant secretary general, Engineers' Association

'Ali, Fawzi 'Atiyya. Director, Office of the President, Central Agency for Organization and Administration (CAOA)

Amin, Galal. Economist, American University in Cairo

al-'Asqalani, Raga'. Director, Public Relations Office, Ministry of Manpower and Training

'Awad, Ibrahim Mahmud. Director of studies and research, General Administration of Graduates, Ministry of Manpower and Training

'Awda, Gihad. Political scientist, al-Ahram Center for Political and Strategic Studies

Badr, Badr Muhammad. Journalist

Bashir, Tahsin. Independent consultant

al-Bayyumi, Hisham. Political activist, Association of Progressive Youth (Ittihad al-shabab al-taqaddumi)

Bilal, 'Abd al-Hamid. General director, Office of the Minister, Ministry of Manpower and Training

Bishri, Muhammad. Treasurer, Engineers' Association

Bourne, John. Political affairs officer, British embassy

Dessouki, 'Ali ed-Din Hilal. Political scientist and director, Center for Political Research and Studies, Cairo University

Fergany, Nadir. Statistician, Central Agency for Public Mobilization and Statistics (CAPMAS), and director, CAPMAS Labor Information System Project

Ford, Robert. Economic affairs officer, U.S. embassy

Ga'far, Salah. Journalist, *al-Ahali*

Gazzar, Hilmi. Assistant secretary general, Medical Doctors' Association, Giza Branch

al-Ghazzali, 'Abd al-Hamid. Professor of economics, Cairo University

Ghunem, Fathi. First undersecretary of state for cultural affairs and missions, Ministry of Higher Education

al-Gibali, 'Abd al-Fattah. Economist, al-Ahram Center for Political and Strategic Studies

Ginena, Ni'mat. Independent researcher

al-Gohary, Kamal. First undersecretary, Ministry of Higher Education

Habib, Kamal. Member, Jihad

Handusa, Hiba. Economist and vice provost, American University in Cairo

Hanna, Milad. Member, Engineers' Association Executive Board

Harb, Osama al-Ghazzali. Associate director, al-Ahram Center for Political and Strategic Studies

Hasan, Baha' ed-Din. Director, Egyptian Organization for Human Rights (EOHR)

Hashim, Fu'ad. President, Arab Investment Bank

Hatim, Mirvat. Economic affairs officer, U.S. embassy

Hilmi, Ashraf. Engineer and leftist candidate, Engineers' Association

Hosni, Hasan. Director, Labor Force Planning Division, Central Agency for Organization and Administration (CAOA)

Hussein, Ashraf. Researcher, Center for Arab Studies

Hussein, Kamal ed-Din. Former minister of education

Hussein, Magdi. Activist, Labor Party (Hizb al-'amal)

Hussein, Shawqi. Dean, Faculty of Commerce, Cairo University

'Ibed, 'Atif. Minister of cabinet affairs and state minister of administrative devel-
    opment

Ibrahim, Sa'd ed-Din. Sociologist and director, Ibn Khaldun Center for Develop-
    ment Studies

al-'Iryan, 'Isam. Member, Medical Doctors' Association Executive Board

Kazim, Husen Ramzi. Director, Central Agency for Organization and Administration
    (CAOA)

al-Khalifa, Muhammad. Journalist, al-Wafd

Mahfuz, Muhammad Amin. Director, General Administration of Graduates, Min-
    istry of Manpower and Training

Mahmud, Mustafa. Physician and founder of the Mustafa Mahmud Mosque and
    Hospital

Malt, Sayyid. General director, Commercial Employees' Association, Giza branch

Mubarak, Hisham. Lawyer, Egyptian Organization for Human Rights (EOHR)

Muhammaden, Isma'il. Director of personnel, Mobil Oil

Mukhtar, Muhammad. Undersecretary of state for research, Central Agency for Or-
    ganization and Administration (CAOA)

Mursi, Salah. Secretary general, Supreme Council of Universities

Murtaghy, Nagla'. Director, Youth Entrepreneurship Society (YES)

Mustafa, Hala. Researcher, al-Ahram Center for Political and Strategic Studies

Osman, Osman Muhammad. Researcher, Institute of National Planning

Qandil, Amani. Political scientist and researcher, National Center for Sociological
    and Criminological Studies

Qasim, Sharif. Chairman of Youth Committee, Commercial Employees' Association

al-Qinawi, Kamal. General director of public relations, Ministry of Manpower and
    Training

Raghi, Sa'd. Professor of engineering and chairman of the Engineers' Association
    Committee on Engineering Education

Rashid, Mu'tasim. Adviser to the governor of Cairo

Raslan, Osama. Secretary general, Cairo branch of the Medical Doctors' Association

Sa'id, Rif'at. Chairman of the executive board, Tagammu' Party

Salim, 'Abd al-Mun'im. Editor in chief, Liwa' al-islam

Salim, 'Imad. Independent scholar and researcher

Salim, Muhammad 'Atiyya. Undersecretary of state for labor utilization, Ministry of
    Manpower and Training

al-Sayyid, Mustafa Kamal. Political scientist, Cairo University

Schleiker, Ronald. Political affairs officer, U.S. embassy

Sha'ban, 'Adil. Researcher, Center for Arab Studies

Shafiq, Amina. Journalist, *al-Ahali*
Sha'lan, Muhammad. Psychiatrist
Sharif, Hisham. Director, Cabinet Information and Decision Support Center
Sharif, Khalid. Economist, World Bank
Sharif, Raghi. Director of research, Supreme Council of Universities
Sidqi, Salah. Secretary general, Commercial Employees' Association
Tahir, Khalid. First Undersecretary, Ministry of Manpower and Training
Thabit, Ahmad. Independent political science researcher and scholar
Wisner, Frank. U.S. ambassador to Egypt
Yasin, 'Ali. Journalist, *al-Wafd*
Zahran, Farid. Director, Sharikat al-mahrusa
al-Zayyat, Murad. Secretary general, Engineers' Association

Personal Interviews, June–July 1997

Abu-l-'Ila, Abu-l-'Ila Madi. Founder, Wasat Party
Hussein, Ashraf. Researcher
Mubarak, Hisham. Director, Center for Human Rights Legal Aid

Personal Interviews, November 2000

'Abd al-Fattah, Nabil. Researcher, al-Ahram Center for Political and Strategic Studies
'Abd al-Raziq, Gasser. Director, Hisham Mubarak Law Center, Cairo
Abdalla, Ahmad. Director, al-Jil Center for Youth Studies
Abu-l-Futuh, 'Abd al-Mun'im. Secretary general, Medical Doctors' Association
Abu-l-'Ila, Abu-l-'Ila Madi. Founder, Wasat Party
Abu Sa'ada, Hafiz. Director, Egyptian Organization of Human Rights
al-Hawwari, Anwar. Researcher, al-Ahram Center for Political and Strategic Studies
Hilmi, Mustafa Kamal. President, Shura Council
al-'Iryan, 'Isam. Assistant secretary general, Medical Doctors' Association
Naggar, Sayyid. President, New Civic Forum
Qasim, Hisham. Publisher, *Cairo Times*
Rashwan, Diya'. Researcher, al-Ahram Center for Political and Strategic Studies
Sultan, 'Isam. General secretary, Association of Egypt for Culture and Dialogue

Personal Interviews, Spring 2001

Saadawi, Nawal. Founder, Arab Women's Solidarity Association

Index